WHEN THE CLOCK BROKE

WHEN THE CLOCK BROKE

CON MEN, CONSPIRACISTS, AND HOW AMERICA CRACKED UP IN THE EARLY 1990s

JOHN GANZ

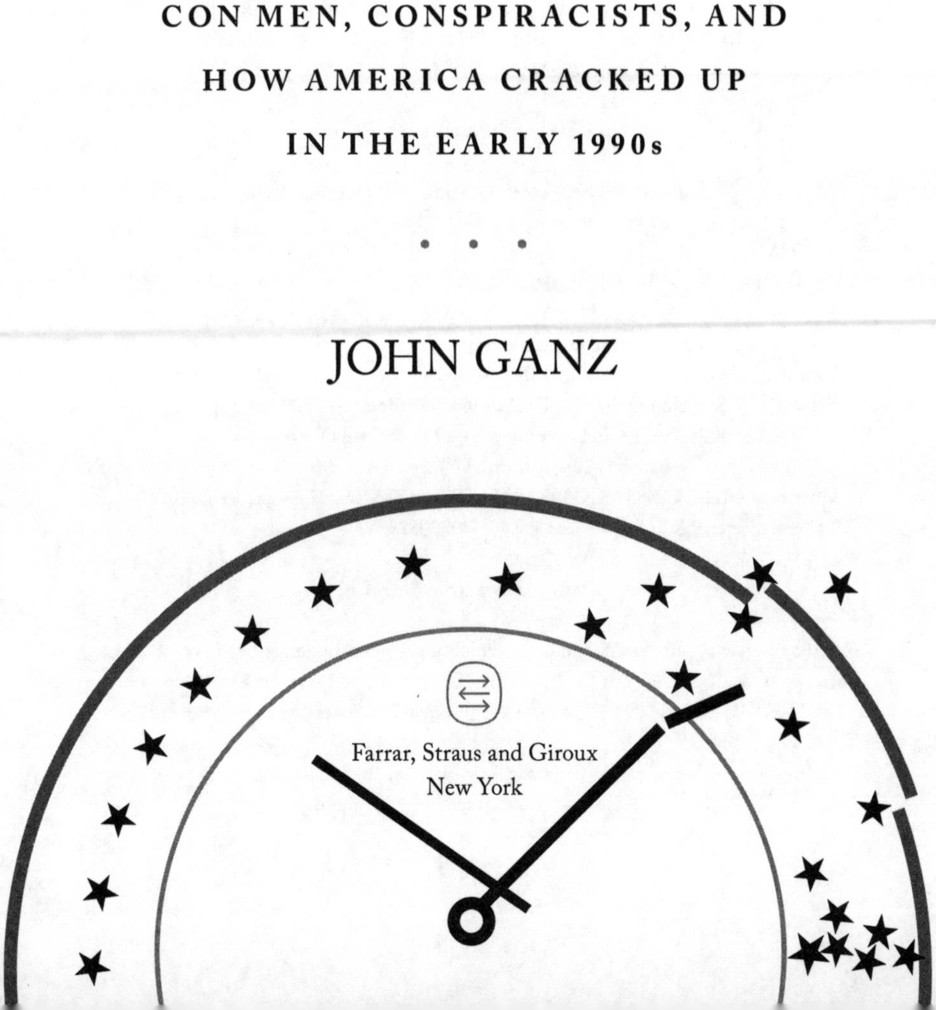

Farrar, Straus and Giroux
New York

Farrar, Straus and Giroux
120 Broadway, New York 10271

Printed in the United States of America
First edition, 2024

Grateful acknowledgment is made for permission
to reprint the following previously published material:
Excerpts from "Nationalism, Old and New," by Samuel Francis,
courtesy of *Chronicles: A Magazine of American Culture*, June 1, 1992.

Title-page clock based on illustration by Thomas Colligan.

Library of Congress Cataloging-in-Publication Data
Names: Ganz, John, 1985– author.
Title: When the clock broke : con men, conspiracists, and how America cracked up in the early 1990s / John Ganz.
Description: First edition. | New York : Farrar, Straus and Giroux, 2024. | Includes bibliographical references and index.
Identifiers: LCCN 2023051871 | ISBN 9780374605445 (hardcover)
Subjects: LCSH: United States—Politics and government—1989–1993. | United States—Politics and government—1993–2001. | Conservatism—United States—History—20th century. | Nineteen nineties.
Classification: LCC E839.5 .G308 2024 | DDC 320.52092273—dc23/eng/20240207
LC record available at https://lccn.loc.gov/2023051871

Designed by Patrice Sheridan

1 3 5 7 9 10 8 6 4 2

FOR GOTTFRIED BALLIN

CONTENTS

WHEN THE CLOCK BROKE

INTRODUCTION: THE END

History, as the cliché goes, is written by the winners, but this is a history of the losers: candidates who lost their elections, movements that bubbled up and fizzled out, protests that exploded and dissipated, writers who toiled at the margins of American life, figures who became briefly famous or infamous and then were forgotten. Some of the characters are still well remembered, but the substance of what they said, did, and meant is not. Their defeats are as important to the history of this country as the (temporary) victories of their opponents.

Just as socialism seemed to exit the world stage, the protagonists of this book envisioned another end. Sensing that America as they knew it was in peril, they hoped to recast American democracy around the "negative solidarity" of knowing who you hated or wanted to destroy: this system would be based on domination and exclusion, a restricted sense of community that jealously guarded its boundaries and policed its members, and the direction of a charismatic leader who would use his power to punish and persecute for the sake of restoring lost national greatness. In a period when some said that ideological struggle was irrelevant and that even history itself had ended, they looked for inspiration among the ideological ruins of earlier times: nationalism, populism, racism, antisemitism, and even fascism. In the words of one, they wanted to "break the clock" of progress—returning America to a previous dispensation while also creating an entirely new country of their own devising. And while they lost in the short term, they brought to the surface an intense anguish in American life, a politics of national despair that has returned with greater force.

This is also the history of a period whose significance hasn't been fully understood. The president of the United States at the time called it "weird." It's a time out of joint with the two eras of—at least superficial—prosperity and optimism that preceded and followed it—but it may feel more familiar today. It was an era where America felt itself to be losing out: losing its dominant place in the world, losing the basis of its security and wealth, and losing its sense of itself, as if a storm cloud rapidly gathered over the country and the national mood suddenly turned dour, gloomy, fearful, and angry. Americans were fed up. Leaders found once-loyal constituencies deaf to their appeals, the two-party system received its strongest challenge for nearly a hundred years, the country witnessed its worst single episode of public disorder since the Civil War, and oddballs, cranks, and even crooks captured the public imagination more than staid figures of reasonable authority. Paranoia was the new common sense. The country seemed to be seeking something new, a break with the exhausted possibilities of the past but also a restoration, a way to recover what had been lost. This episode of crisis was not unforeseeable or unprecedented: it was a conjuncture where chronic troubles briefly took on acute expression, but then appeared to go into remission or repose. A lightning flash revealed a fractious and fragmented nation; the thunderclap would not be heard for some time.

What added to the weirdness of the time is that it should have been a moment of triumph. At its start, America had won the Cold War. The Berlin Wall would soon fall. The Soviet Union was retreating worldwide and on the verge of collapse. Democracy and capitalism were apparently the only viable political and economic systems remaining. Freedom—both political and economic—had prevailed. This was the content of President Ronald Reagan's farewell message from the Oval Office in January 1989: "Countries across the globe are turning to free markets and free speech and turning away from the ideologies of the past. For them, the great rediscovery of the 1980's has been that, lo and behold, the moral way of government is the practical way of government: Democracy, the profoundly good, is also the profoundly productive." Reprising the rhetoric of his 1980 presidential campaign, Reagan spoke of America as a "shining city on the hill," borrowing John Winthrop's Puritan vision of early New England as a New Jerusalem that would provide an example to the world. "And how stands the city on this winter night? More prosperous, more secure, and happier than it was 8 years ago. But more than that: After 200 years, two centuries, she still stands strong and true on the granite ridge, and her glow has held steady no matter what storm. And she's still a beacon, still a magnet for all who must have freedom, for all the pilgrims from all the lost places who are hurtling through the darkness, toward home."

A cursory glance at one of America's cities might seem to confirm Reagan's vision: all the new glass and steel skyscrapers built during the commercial real estate boom of the 1980s would certainly glitter. But closer inspection of a tower might find it empty: the country would soon have 500 million square feet of vacant office space, the equivalent of two Manhattans. The bank or savings and loan that funded the office tower might have already collapsed, dragged down by bad real estate loans and investments in high-risk "junk bonds." Over the course of the following twelve months, more than five hundred banks would fail—the most ever in a single year. One might also find encampments of homeless people sheltering at the foot of the tower, with the "glow" on the glass facade provided by their campfires. Or it might be the reflection of police lights: over the next couple of years, the surrounding city would record unprecedented crime rates.

Reagan's farewell did have its notes of concern: namely a dearth of patriotic sentiment in popular culture. Although freedom was winning, it was also vulnerable and could be lost through inadequate communication of its blessings: "Our spirit is back, but we haven't reinstitutionalized it. We've got to do a better job of getting across that America is freedom—freedom of speech, freedom of religion, freedom of enterprise. And freedom is special and rare." Then Reagan made a small slip: "It's fragile; it needs *production*." In the actual text of the speech, that word was meant to be "protection." Despite Reagan's insistence on the economic "miracle" of the 1980s, the system of production upon which American freedom rested was looking very fragile, if not already fractured.

The restructuring of the American economy that took place in the 1980s, whether one called it "Reaganomics," "voodoo economics," "trickle-down economics," "supply-side economics," "financialization"—or, as it would come to be increasingly labeled, "neoliberalism"—provided a glitzy veneer of great wealth. The underlying reality was less pretty. With the power of organized labor all but broken and tight money policy in place to whip inflation, wages stagnated. At the same time, income from rents, dividends, capital gains, and interest exploded. The average income for 80 percent of American families declined between 1980 and 1989, while the top fifth of Americans saw an increase of nearly 50 percent. The income of the top 1 percent grew by almost 75 percent over the decade. The median net worth of a high-income family grew by 82 percent between 1984 and 1989, while the wealth of the lowest-income group dropped by 16 percent. While the rich got richer and the poor got poorer, the middle was being hollowed out: the proportion of Americans making between $18,000 and $55,000 a year shrank by 20 percent in the 1980s. Those who managed to enter the top decile did well, while many others entered the swelling ranks of the poor. Part of this hollowing of the middle class can be attributed to rapid deindustrialization and the loss of heavy manufacturing jobs, but economists would also identify the 1980s with an acceleration of "job polarization" and the elimination of middle-wage "routine" office and administrative jobs as well, the work of secretaries, bank tellers, bookkeepers, and filing clerks. The age of Fordism, with its need for a mass, routinized labor force, was rapidly drawing to a close. For most people in the middle, America was entering "an age of diminished expectations," as the economist Paul Krugman titled his 1990 book.

Even Reagan's supporters and surrogates had trouble denying that the policy regime of the previous decade—deregulation, tax cuts, high interest rates, and scaled-back social services—looked a lot like open class war waged on behalf of the rich. "If Marx had been scribbling away in the Library of Congress (our equivalent of the British Museum, where Marx scribbled), in January 1981, as Reaganites marched into Washington, he would have said: The class struggle is about to intensify. During the Reagan Terror, labor will lose ground to capital," wrote the conservative columnist George F. Will in a 1988 *Washington Post* op-ed. "In the Reagan years, a particular social stratum has gotten a lot. The people who get income from property have benefited . . ."

Commentators often spoke of a breach of the "social contract" between employees and employers. But the termination of the social contract meant not just class war, but also a war of all against all. Television told sensational stories about gang wars in the inner cities, but the state of nature prevailed in perhaps more subtle ways in the suburban office park as well. By the middle of the decade, "communitarian" social thinkers were already wringing their hands over a culture of atomized, grasping selfishness, of an "individualism grown cancerous." In his 1990 postmortem on the Reagan years, *The Politics of Rich and Poor*, the Republican strategist and former Nixon adviser Kevin Phillips characterized the economic and social conditions of the era as "Darwinian." For a putative boom time, there was an unusually high rate of business failure and bankruptcy. Reaganism preferred to devolve responsibilities to the state level: this contributed to a regional race to the bottom as states struggled among one another to attract capital with generous business incentives that strained their fiscal capacity.

Economists would describe the period as an eruption of "anarchic" or "fratricidal competition," where firms, once content to compete on a collegial, "fraternal" basis and count their profits, were coerced by market conditions to fight for their very existence, employing short-term "survivalist" strategies to remain profitable. Manufacturers struggled to keep up with inexpensive, high-quality imports from Japan, West Germany, and South Korea, brought in by the administration's free trade policies and the strong dollar. Of course, the foot soldiers suffered the most from this internecine war of capitalists: an employer's first move was usually to slash the workforce, close plants, and invest in labor-saving technology. But corporate managers also found themselves under intense pressure from activist shareholders demanding immediate returns. Rather than risk long-term investments in new plants or products, firms often preferred to get involved in financial chicanery—or simply swallow other companies whole and spit out the bones.

Mergers, acquisitions, and leveraged buyouts became the hot ticket, forming half of Wall Street profits by 1988. Corporate raiders and their financiers, like Michael Douglas's Gordon Gekko character in Oliver Stone's *Wall Street* (1987), became folk heroes or devils, depending on where one sat. Companies that fell victim to hostile takeovers were often stripped of assets or hobbled with debt that constrained productive investment. About half of the companies purchased during the buyout craze—which were supposed to be "restructured" for the sake of "efficiency"—would eventually just collapse. As the future Clinton adviser Robert Reich would note in 1989, a high-level manager's job became focused as much on avoiding or initiating predation as developing the company's potential: "Today's corporate executives spend an increasing portion of their days fending off takeovers, finding companies to acquire or responding to depositions in lawsuits instead of worrying about the quality of their products and how they can be distributed more efficiently."

The entire '80s economy ran on debt: borrowed money and borrowed time. Consumer, corporate, and government debt all exploded.

At the tail end of the decade, corporations struggled to get out from under their debts, banks and thrifts sagged and then sank under the weight of unserviced loans. Among ordinary people, personal bankruptcies and home foreclosures became a fact of life, hitting an all-time record during the coming recession. The military spending and tax cuts of the Reagan administration had racked up a $3 trillion national debt. And the credit granted by the public to the political establishment looked like it would be spent soon.

Just as the bubbles popped and the bills started to become due, President George H. W. Bush took office. The Gipper's vice president presented himself as the caretaker of the successes of the Reagan revolution. But he also proposed a revision, a period of national calming down and consolidation. Distrusted by those who called themselves conservative, he was one of the few genuine conservatives in the country: he desired maintaining the status quo above all. He rejected casting himself in a world-historic role as the master of great and tumultuous times. He did not put high stock in what he called "the vision thing." Both his rhetoric and his actions made this clear: his economic advisers were "Tory" moderates rather than free trade ideologues; he called for a "kinder, gentler" America, and "greater tolerance, an easy-goingness about each other's attitudes and way of life." But the call for kindness and gentleness rang hollow: Reaganites took the remark as an insult, and everyone else found it hard to buy after Bush had waged a notably nasty and negative campaign.

Bush did not aspire to the presidency out of a sense of political passion; his ambition was for a successful career befitting a person who was quite literally of the senatorial class: it was simply the last step in the *cursus honorum* of ascending offices. He had no interest in the permanent campaign of his predecessor, the "Great Communicator": Bush was the representative of a class bred to govern, not to lead. Its predominance was taken for granted. He had been happiest as leader of the nation's Super Secret Club for Privileged Boys, the Central Intelligence Agency, and he took with him the clichés and behavior of a bureaucrat: everything was a contingency, a particular case to be reacted to and then managed competently—"prudent" was one of his favorite words, as Dana Carvey's famous *Saturday Night Live* send-up of the president highlighted with glee. He possessed the ditziness of the high WASPs: a love for games, toys, and practical jokes; he spoke in non sequiturs and inside or private gags. It was difficult, even for him, to know what he really meant sometimes.

Bush was not an incompetent, a feebleminded product of aristocratic inbreeding, rather he was competent within small bounds and small groups: he was comfortable within the clubby confines of state offices and as president of a council of ministers rather than in the bully pulpit. He appeared to succeed in diplomacy and warfare, those true callings of patrician statesmen, but although he attempted to use those strengths to make up for a lack of domestic vision, and especially for his image as a "wimp," he still could not shape the meaning of events in any sort of convincing way. In late June 1990 he reneged on the famous pledge he'd made at the 1988 convention—"Read my lips: no new taxes"—as he negotiated a budget deal with Democrats. It was the prudent thing to do, and much of the GOP establishment supported him, but the rank and file would not.

When Saddam Hussein invaded Kuwait in August 1990, a shock in the price of oil pushed the slowing and fragile economy definitively into recession. The political stakes were clear to an administration that remembered the oil crisis of the 1970s. At first the rationale for moving troops into the Middle East was explicitly economic: Bush spoke of our reliance on Middle Eastern oil, and Secretary of State James Baker said of the Persian Gulf situation, "If you want to sum it up in one word, it's jobs. Because an economic recession worldwide, caused by the control of one nation, one dictator if you will, of the West's economic lifeline will result in the loss of jobs on the part of American citizens." The public seemed to largely accept this materialist, even cynical justification. But as war approached, the rationales and reasons started to shift. "It's not about oil," Bush said, instead speaking more of "aggression,"

Saddam's human rights abuses, and his weapons of mass destruction program. Then he started to compare Saddam Hussein to Hitler—no, he was even "worse than Hitler." It was as if Bush, a decorated hero of World War II, had a sense that the country needed something more, not just another filibuster against a tin-pot dictator, like his military expedition to Panama to get Noriega. It needed a cause, a larger purpose.

From a tactical perspective, the war was a smashing success: Saddam's army was crushed, he retreated from Kuwait, America rejoiced, and Bush's job approval soared to 87 percent. Having achieved his declared aims, the president was content to restore the *status quo ante*. Removing Saddam would not be prudent. But how could you leave Mr. Worse Than Hitler in place? The rationales and justifications didn't add up to a coherent picture. Anyway, a good enemy was the best friend you could have. Bush's nostalgia for the good old bad guys was so strong that even as a cold warrior, he couldn't bring himself to dance on the grave of the Soviet Union: he treated the USSR's collapse as an untoward event to be dealt with cautiously and carefully, preferring to deal with representatives of the old regime than with whoever might follow. He did speak boldly of a "New World Order"—with the United States acting in concert with the world's leading powers to protect borders and keep the peace—but even this bold-sounding vision was offered on behalf of stability. And the idea wasn't even Bush's: he cribbed it from his reformist Soviet counterpart, Mikhail Gorbachev.

The only people the "New World Order" seemed to make much of an impression on were conspiracy-minded members of Bush's own coalition, who saw in the phrase sinister adumbrations of a new totalitarian, "globalist" government. In 1991, the televangelist and Christian Coalition founder Pat Robertson, who had launched an unsuccessful primary challenge to Bush in 1988 before returning to the fold, published *The New World Order*, which became a bestseller. It was a mélange of conspiracy thinking that included the Illuminati, the Freemasons, the New Age movement, and the Trilateral Commission in a secret plot to control all the money and power in the world. Naturally, Jewish bankers in the form of the Rothschilds make an appearance as well.

The confused message and unclear meaning of the Gulf War only contributed to the rapid turn of the American people from jubilation to disillusionment. In the economic sphere, the war did not accomplish its putative goal either: the campaign in the Persian Gulf failed to stem the tide of recession. The war created only an ephemeral sense of national unity, a "mirage in the desert" as creative journalists would label it.

Economists struggled to pinpoint a single cause of the recession that took hold over the course of 1990: the drawing down in Cold War military spending, the debt hangover of the '80s and the consequent credit crunch, and tight monetary policy were all possible culprits and contributors. It happened, like bankruptcy, gradually, then suddenly: a slowing economy and then a sudden decline of consumer confidence and drop in aggregate spending, a loss of the country's "animal spirits." People were suddenly worried that they could no longer afford things. The peak rate of unemployment—7.8 percent—might look fairly mild on paper, but in some regions the devastation would approach Depression-era levels. The recovery would also be slow and incomplete: the recession of 1990–91 would be the first of the so-called "jobless recoveries" as it permanently eliminated many positions; employment wouldn't reach its prerecession level until 1996. The recession did not affect just blue-collar America, either: college-educated white-collar employees, middle managers, and even executives found themselves lining up for unemployment and public assistance, too.

Not surprisingly, the recession brought to the surface the growing sense of dissatisfaction. Over the course of 1990 and 1991, more than two-thirds of Americans told pollsters that America was on "the wrong track." A 1991 report prepared for the Kettering Foundation, *Citizens and Politics: The View from Main Street America*, showed a large portion of the public no longer viewing America as a democracy, but as "a behemoth system spiraling dangerously beyond their control." The respondents viewed the political system as dominated by lobbyists, special interest groups, political action committees, and a sensationalist media. A report for the Centel Public Accountability Project noted that "many citizens, even those who still vote, have concluded that they do not exercise real authority over the political system. Americans desperately want to believe that theirs is a government of, by, and for the people; deep down, however, very few think we have that today"; and it went on to register "a corrosive cynicism that threatens to undermine American politics."

Despair over the state of government could figure as apathy or anger: many voters simply dropped out of the electorate altogether. Others began to mobilize and vent their spleen at their representatives and even at the representative system as a whole. This divide had a class component: while the worst off usually just gave up on politics, it was the middling sort that got mad. "The average voter's increasing frustration with the domination by special interests of representative government . . . aroused sentiment for popular direct rule or plebiscitary government," Kevin Phillips observed. In the wake of the collapse and bailout of politically connected savings and loan associations, pollsters and political observers picked up a rising wave of generalized "anti-incumbency" sentiment. A coalition of grassroots organizations pushed for term limits for elected officials. In 1990, California, Oklahoma, and Colorado passed ballot initiatives to limit the terms of their state legislators. As a method of democratic control, term limits were contradictory: they appeared to discipline elected officials, but they were substantially *un*democratic, limiting voters' options. But it was a mode of political expression more than a real solution. "It's simple, it's quick, it's the guillotine," the vice president of Common Cause explained. Term limitation was a symbolic act, perhaps the indication of a larger national movement. "A spokesman for We The People . . . says the movement is part of a political tidal wave that synthesizes right and left in a populist and nationalist upsurge," wrote the *Washington Times* columnist Samuel Francis. "It's not term limits by themselves that promise to save entrapped Middle Americans but rather what term limits symbolize and what they could lead to: an enduring popular radicalism that would challenge both the direction in which the country seems to be moving as well as the power of the entrenched leadership that presides over the slow submersion of the vessel of state and its Middle American passengers."

A shelf of bestselling books told similar stories of despondency and frustration. Two *Philadelphia Inquirer* reporters, Donald Barlett and James Steele, published their nine-part series *America: What Went Wrong?* as a book, telling with newspapermen's bitter irony the story of disappearing manufacturing jobs, falling middle-class incomes, and rising health-care costs alongside the Babylonian spoils of junk bonds, leveraged buyouts, "corporate restructuring," and tax cuts for top earners. There was also *Who Will Tell the People: The Betrayal of American Democracy*, by the former *Washington Post* editor William Greider, which described a system so deteriorated it could no longer function, with all the channels of feedback between public and government totally corrupted: "At the highest levels of government, the power to decide things has gravitated from the many to the few, just as ordinary citizens suspect. Instead of popular will, the government now responds more often to narrow webs of power—the interests of major economic organizations and concentrated wealth and the influential elites surrounding them." The former Kennedy speechwriter Richard N. Goodwin penned *Promises to Keep: A Call for a New American Revolution*, decrying "the ascendance of money power" and the rise of special economic interests, an onset of the rule of "faction" that James Madison once warned about.

The threat of national fragmentation and factional warfare was reflected in the cultural sphere as well. In his book *Culture Wars: The Struggle to Define America*, the sociologist James Davison Hunter introduced the eponymous concept to the American public, describing a conflict between advocates of traditional and progressive values roiling every level of state and civil society. The biggest wave of immigration since the first decade of the twentieth century and the changing demographic face of America created a great deal of worry about what "multiculturalism" meant for national unity. The crucible or melting pot—incidentally an image that originated in the early-twentieth-century rise of American heavy industry—was no longer forging a single people. The sentiment expressed by Charles Krauthammer of *The Washington Post* would be echoed in dozens of op-eds: "Our great national achievement—fashioning a common citizenship and identity for a multi-ethnic, multi-lingual, multi-racial people—is now threatened by a process of relentless, deliberate Balkanization."

Concern about "multiculturalism" and its enforcement arm, "political correctness," migrated from the right leftward. Arthur M. Schlesinger Jr., the official court historian of the Kennedys and keeper of the sacred flame of the post–World War II liberal consensus, published *The Disuniting of America*, warning that it would mean "the decomposition of America" and even the "disintegration of the national community, apartheid, Balkanization, tribalization." The term "Balkanization" itself became a favored cliché, conjuring up the specter of ethnic civil wars now menacing the decommunizing East.

Freedom may have triumphed globally, but now it was apparently under threat on campus and in the classroom. Following the surprise success of the philippic *The Closing of the American Mind* (1987), by the University of Chicago professor Allan Bloom, with its warnings that liberal open-mindedness was tending not only toward relativism but toward nihilism, a spate of conservative epigones took aim at higher education: Charles J. Sykes's *Profscam: Professors and the Demise of Higher Education* (1988) and Roger Kimball's *Tenured Radicals: How Politics Has Corrupted Our Higher Education* (1990) and Dinesh D'Souza's *Illiberal Education: The Politics of Race and Class on Campus* (1991). The media took the bait and started sensational coverage of the "P.C. controversy" on college campuses. In the last week of December 1990, *Newsweek* stamped its cover with the words "THOUGHT POLICE—There's a 'Politically Correct' Way to Talk About Race, Sex, and Ideas. Is this the New Enlightenment—or the New McCarthyism?" With war just three weeks away, Saddam Hussein got only a little box at the top of the cover. Apparently the "New Hitler" wasn't as juicy a story as the incipient totalitarianism of literature professors. Both sides of the controversy claimed conspiracy: for the right, there was a concerted effort by left-wing academics to undermine the basis of Western civilization; for the left, the assault on higher ed was a carefully coordinated media campaign orchestrated and funded by a network of conservative think tanks and foundations.

A growing nihilism among the young wasn't just the hallucination of grouchy conservatives. In the late 1980s and early '90s two burgeoning popular music genres represented different sides of cultural despair: gangsta rap and grunge. They both bloomed on the West Coast, where the American frontier had long ago run out. And they both originated among working-class youths in centers of former defense production: Los Angeles and the Seattle metro area. Gangsta rap expressed despair in the form of anger and violent self-assertion, grunge as depression and crushing self-doubt. Both gambled that personal and subcultural authenticity could stand in for a wider society bereft of meaningful opportunity. Writing in the wake of the Rodney King riots, the African American public intellectual Cornel West, who was teaching philosophy at Princeton at the time, saw a virulent "nihilism in black America," reflected most potently in the popularity of gangsta rap, as a result of the "market-driven shattering of black civil society" that hollowed out old buffering institutions like churches, families, and schools and threw Black communities into a Hobbesian state of nature: "Black people have always been in America's wilderness in search of a promised land. Yet many black folk now reside in a jungle ruled by a cutthroat market morality devoid of any faith in deliverance or hope for freedom."

On close inspection, even the most triumphant interpretations of the moment were remarkably downbeat and pessimistic. Francis Fukuyama's 1989 essay "The End of History?"—published in *The National Interest* and later expanded into a 1992 book, *The End of History and the Last Man*—heralded "the total exhaustion of all viable systematic alternatives for Western liberalism" but concluded that the end of history would be a period of continued ethnic conflict as well as cultural fatigue and depletion: "The end of history will be a very sad time . . . The worldwide ideological struggle that called forth daring, courage, imagination, and idealism, will be replaced by economic calculation, the endless solving of technical problems, environmental concerns, and the satisfaction of sophisticated consumer demands. In the post-historical period there will be neither art nor philosophy, just the perpetual caretaking of the museum of human history." Not much of a future at all, really.

While Fukuyama and many others believed they were witnessing the ultimate victory of liberal democracy, others thought they were observing its death throes. The cultural critic and historian Christopher Lasch wrote, "Having defeated its totalitarian adversaries, liberalism is crumbling from within." For Lasch, liberalism was being undermined by its own faith in human progress, which was running into immovable limits: "The belated discovery that the earth's ecology will no longer sustain an indefinite expansion of productive forces deals the final blow to the belief in progress . . . The attempt to expand Western standards of living to the rest of the world would lead very quickly to the exhaustion of non-renewable resources, the irreversible pollution of the earth's atmosphere, drastic changes in its climate, and the destruction of the ecological system upon which the earth depends." He argued in his 1991 magnum opus, *The True and Only Heaven: Progress and Its Critics*, that the very notion of progress and optimism should be abandoned in favor of a more frugal and restrained model of human flourishing. Lasch would deny that this was a stance of despair: he proposed that a more modest ideal of "hope" should replace the unconstrained optimism of the progressive tradition, whose attempts to deny the reality of life's limitations were its own form of despair. As a replacement for liberalism and its infinitely expanding universe of spoiled consumers and bureaucrats, he sought inspiration in the lower-middle-class ethos of the American populist tradition, with its emphasis on the community-centered, "heroic" morality of small-scale producers—artisans, shopkeepers, and farmers.

Lasch called for a renewal of populism's "appreciation of the moral value of honest work, its respect for competence, its egalitarian opposition to entrenched privilege, its refusal to be impressed by the jargon of experts, its insistence on plain speech and on holding people accountable for their actions." He would say that populism "was not a panacea for all the ills that afflict the modern world," and he admitted that "it would be foolish to deny the characteristic features of populist movements at their worst—racism, anti-Semitism, nativism, and anti-intellectualism, all the other evils so often cited by liberal critics." However, Lasch attributed the reactionary turn in "petty-bourgeois movements" to an "increasingly defensive" posture in the face of "large-scale enterprise crowding out small producers." Since Lasch's history stressed the increasingly grim outlook for the American middle class and the proliferation of massive, alienating bureaucracies in both the public and private sector, it's not clear why the renewed populism he hoped for would avoid that same sort of defensiveness. Still, he believed that "at a time when other ideologies are greeted with apathy, populism has the capacity to generate real enthusiasm." The principal figures of this book would agree. Like Lasch, they wanted to recover a "submerged tradition" that was an alternative to Enlightenment liberalism, although the populism they envisioned and helped to create looked different from Lasch's idealized picture. And, as we shall see, they thought the enthusiasm populism could generate was because of, not despite, all those "other evils."

When Lasch wrote that the "old political ideologies have exhausted their capacity either to explain events or to inspire men and women to constructive action," he was expressing something nearly identical to the account of a "crisis of authority" or "crisis of hegemony" put forth by the Italian Marxist Antonio Gramsci: a period when "the great masses have become detached from their traditional ideologies and no longer believe what they used to believe previously." Writing in the 1920s, Gramsci maintained that such crises "were situations of conflict between representatives and represented," and that when the "ruling class has lost its consensus," the populace feels that the existing political and public institutions no longer provide a vision of national leadership, but merely dominate and coerce, serving their own narrow self-interest. In such a situation, both politics and the economy take on the aspect of a zero-sum squabble between competing factions and cliques. The sudden loss of faith and credit in the American system was the acute onset of just such a crisis of hegemony. Gramsci had written that "in every country the process is different, although the content is the same," with such upheavals occurring when "the ruling class has failed in some major political undertaking for which it has requested, or forcibly extracted, the consent of the broad masses (war, for example)." In this period, that failed political undertaking was the project of Reaganism: the reorganization of the economy for short-term gain and sharp upward redistribution and its unexpected and expensive victory in the Cold War. The electorate believed Reaganism's promise and sunny optimism, but it left the country battered productively and rudderless ideologically. Gramsci famously remarked that in the "interregnum" when "the old is dying and the new cannot be born . . . a great variety of morbid symptoms appear." Such an interregnum, he believed, would also provide an opening for "violent solutions, for the activities of unknown forces, represented by charismatic 'men of destiny.'"

As we will see, some of the most intense and visionary responses to the failure of the Reagan settlement came from within that camp's own ranks: true-believing conservative activists and intellectuals, as well as Sun Belt capitalists who had once been reliable Republican donors. For them, the 1980s represented a betrayal: they understood Ronald Reagan as the champion of the economic interests and cultural values of white Middle Americans, but now they seemed worse off than ever. So too had their own fortunes within the movement declined. Entering the decade with great expectations of career advancement and important titles, they found they were not the leading lights of the cause any longer: they had been overshadowed by more recent arrivals, immigrants to the movement and sometimes to America.

They wanted what they considered the historic core of American society to become a self-conscious movement, but they also despaired over the loss of that society's traditions, substance, and racial purity: only through the negative solidarity of opposing domestic enemies could it regain its coherence and meaning. Imbibing and interpreting the anger they saw around them, they made startlingly accurate predictions about the course of American politics—even as they worked to make those predictions come true.

Obviously, the figures in this book did not invent demagogy nor racist and xenophobic politics. These are fundamental features of American society from its inception, and all their manifestations cannot be catalogued here. The GOP's development and deployment of the "Southern Strategy" to win over Southern whites in the latter half of the twentieth century is well known and well researched, but a few incidents prior to the action of this book are worth emphasizing. During the presidential campaign of 1980, Ronald Reagan campaigned against "welfare queens." He also gave his "states' rights" speech at the Neshoba County, Mississippi, fair, not far from the spot where three civil rights workers had been murdered in 1964. Then there was the infamous Willie Horton ad of the 1988 Bush campaign, which stoked fears of Black criminality. While some on the right were content to use racism and domestic enmity cynically and opportunistically to whip up votes, the principal figures in this book brought it to the center of their political consciousness. They self-consciously placed themselves in a tradition that encompassed the prewar America Firsters, Strom Thurmond's Dixiecrats, Joe McCarthy's anti-communist witch hunt of the 1950s, and George Wallace's rabble-rousing campaigns of the 1960s and '70s. In a way, this book charts the transformation of the Southern Strategy from a regional to a national campaign.

Some might object that this book is focused too much on the morbid, macabre, or pathological: David Duke, the gang of "paleoconservative" malcontents, Patrick Buchanan, the billionaire-populism of Ross

Perot, survivalist cranks in the Rocky Mountains, the transformation of mob boss John Gotti into a folk hero. After all, right-wing and reactionary politics were not the only responses to the crisis of the early 1990s. It's important to note that there were other and, in the opinion of the author, more hopeful alternatives. Jesse Jackson's presidential campaigns of 1984 and 1988, centered around his vision of a multiracial working-class coalition, provided one of the earliest rejections of the Reagan consensus and tapped into currents of popular energy the Democratic establishment struggled to fight off. In 1990, Bernie Sanders won his first campaign for Congress as a democratic socialist. One of the first bellwethers of a populist wave was Democrat Harris Wofford's stunning victory—with a message of "middle-class populism" and a demand for universal health care—over the former Reagan and Bush attorney general Dick Thornburgh in the 1991 Pennsylvania Senate special election. That campaign would produce the famed political wizards Paul Begala and James Carville, who would be responsible for the economic focus of the late phase of the 1992 Bill Clinton campaign. In the Democratic primaries that year, Iowa senator Tom Harkin would take an early lead carrying the banner of prairie populism and keeping the faith of the New Deal. The former California governor Jerry Brown would have even more success transforming himself from a man who once pejoratively called universal health care "socialist" into an angry left populist, railing in alternative media against the Democrat-Republican duopoly. The obscene spectacle of masculine domination in the Clarence Thomas confirmation hearings of 1991 would trigger a feminist mobilization that would make 1992 "The Year of the Woman" for its record number of female senators and representatives elected. These are all important aspects of the period as well, and they arguably have taken on increased significance. But at the time, the established leadership of the Democratic Party was able to contain, co-opt, or absorb these forces. Benefiting from a wave of popular discontent, the Clinton administration opted to continue many of the Reaganite policies that contributed to the crisis in the first place: reducing or redirecting the welfare state, deregulating finance, and pursuing free trade agreements.

Of course, the most salient reason to focus on the right is the election in 2016 of Donald Trump, who represented the crystallization of elements that were still inchoate in the period of this book. In general, the politics of national despair described here have now taken hold of the Republican Party: it is dominated by figures and ideas that once would have been considered fringe. On the global scale, too, left populism seems to be abating while far-right movements are sustaining themselves and even gathering strength. The problem has not gone away, it's gotten worse. We still are working to answer why the loss of faith in the old order has registered as intensified anti-egalitarianism rather than a renewed egalitarianism, why perceptions of public corruption and criminality have led to the open embrace of corruption and criminality rather than its rejection, and why discontent with the distribution of wealth and power has fostered closer popular identification with certain types of capitalism and capitalists. I hope this book will contribute to untangling these threads or at least showing how the knots were tied.

American democracy is often spoken of as being in peril. This book by and large agrees with this thesis. Others point out that democracy in America never fully existed in the first place: for them, it has always been a nation enchained by great inequalities and ruled by an unrepresentative system designed largely to keep those chains in place. This book also agrees with that thesis. And so it begins in a part of the country where democratic rule was delayed, frustrated, reversed, and, when established, tenuous at best. When the demand for democracy did arise there, it often took an authoritarian form. Even as Bush and his foreign policy team were searching for their own little Hitler in the deserts of the Middle East, one was emerging in the swamps of the Deep South.

1

SWAMP CREATURE

On January 21, 1989, the day after George H. W. Bush's inauguration, David Duke, the former Grand Wizard of the Ku Klux Klan, a neo-Nazi, and the head of an organization called the National Association for the Advancement of White People, finished first in an open primary for Louisiana's eighty-first legislative district. Running as a Republican, he came out ahead of the state party's preferred candidate, John Treen, brother of David Treen, Louisiana's first Republican governor since Reconstruction. While a majority of the District 81 voters were still registered Democrats, they had overwhelmingly voted for Ronald Reagan and then George H. W. Bush—and were now up for grabs. Republican National Committee staff members went to Louisiana to bolster Treen's beleaguered campaign and work against Duke. "We will do anything to defeat this man," the Bush campaign manager and then RNC chief Lee Atwater declared to *The Wall Street Journal.* The former and current Republican presidents endorsed Duke's opponent and made advertisements on his behalf, to little avail: Duke would go on to win the runoff a month later and enter the state legislature. Over the next three years, Duke would aspire to higher and higher office. These subsequent campaigns, unsuccessful though they were, garnered Duke an ever-expanding platform for himself and his cause, bedeviled the establishment, and suggested deep structural failures in American society and its political system. But how did Duke, previously an abject failure in both personal and political life, come to defy the direction of his chosen party and represent the crack-up of an old order?

Perhaps Louisiana provided particularly fertile soil for the emergence of a candidate with a neo-Nazi past. Justice Brandeis may have famously called the states "the laboratories of democracy," but the alluvial plains and dense swampland of the Mississippi Delta were less like a lab than a hothouse or a petri dish of inchoate American fascism. Its history can read like a specimen list of authoritarian regimes: the colonial governorships of the absolutist monarchies of France and Spain ruling by fiat without consulting representative bodies, the regime of planters lording over monstrously brutal sugar plantations, the post-Reconstruction Bourbon oligarchy that took power in an 1877 coup d'etat carried out by a white militia, and shared power with a Tammany-style urban machine in New Orleans. When challenged by the possibility of a Populist Party revolt at the polls in 1896, the Bourbon oligarchy resorted to force and fraud to push it back. In 1898, the Bourbons promulgated a new state constitution, with the express purpose of limiting voting, effectively disenfranchising the state's entire Black population and a good deal of its whites, too, and instituting a one-party state. As a result of the French heritage, the legal system is literally Bonapartist. In private life, patriarchal domination was inscribed in the state's Napoleonic Civil Code, which made the man "head and master" of his household and gave him extensive legal authority over his wife. The progressive reformers, who made weak and abortive attempts to clean up corruption and improve the backward conditions, also distrusted democracy, preferring rule by enlightened business interests and professional experts. (John M. Parker, a "progressive" governor who defied the Klan, had once been involved in the lynching of eleven Italian laborers in New Orleans; he never expressed any regret for the act.)

Tyranny coexisted with a certain kind of anarchy. The state's experiments in antidemocratic rule sat atop a society that was exceptionally underdeveloped and poor as well as extraordinarily fractious and difficult to lead. "Multicultural" before the word existed, Louisiana was a dizzying welter of competing ethnic and regional interests: French South against Anglo North, Catholic against Protestant, white against Black, great sugar planter against small cotton farmer, country against city, immigrant against native, rich against poor, elitist against populist. W.E.B. Du Bois called the state's politics "a Chinese puzzle" and a "witch's cauldron of political chicanery." The cauldron simmered with a constant roil of corruption, lawlessness, and mob violence: in the countryside, slavery was enforced through brutal vigilantism; in the cities, crime was endemic, both in the form of organized gangs and constant random killings; the Reconstruction era witnessed a low-intensity continuation of the Civil War between irregular militias; from the period of 1889 to 1922, three Louisiana parishes led the nation in lynchings. Another former French colony sprang to the mind of one reporter who attempted to capture Louisiana's fractured, multiethnic political balancing act: it was "of an intensity and complexity . . . matched, in my experience, only in the republic of Lebanon."

In 1928, a new kind of experiment began. "There is no dictatorship in Louisiana," Huey P. Long said. "There is perfect democracy there, and when you have perfect democracy it is pretty hard to tell it from a dictatorship." After winning the governorship by campaigning in a populist mode against the Bourbon oligarchy's concentration of wealth and power, "The Kingfish" quickly coordinated the organs of the state to concentrate his own wealth and power. In office, Long marshaled the governor's vast powers of appointment to build an empire of patronage jobs, sweeping from office the allies of his political opponents and replacing them with his own people. No state office was too petty to serve as an opportunity for rewarding a friend or avenging an enemy, as well as that enemy's family and friends. With this apparatus in hand, along with his fine-honed talents of personal insult and threat, Huey set himself to pushing through an ambitious legislative agenda: free textbooks for schools, improved funding for state colleges, thousands of miles of paved roads and bridges, and natural gas pipelines into the cities.

Long's support came from smallholding white farmers and shopkeepers rather than the laboring masses, a fact that would influence who received relief under his regime. His populism made no provision for union protection, child labor laws (he said picking cotton was "fun" for kids), or unemployment insurance. He is famous for his patronage of Louisiana State University, but the football team band received more money than the law school and graduate school combined. Part of the Long legend is that he distinguished himself from other Southern populist demagogues by avoiding race-baiting, but the reality is much less flattering. Jim Crow was such a settled state of affairs in Louisiana that racist demagoguery just had fewer uses. He nixed old-age pensions on the grounds that too much money would go to Blacks. When he reached the United States Senate, he opposed federal anti-lynching legislation. During his governorship, Black voter registration actually declined while white registration rose after the abolition of the poll tax. It's true that the state's Black citizens did benefit from some of Long's program, but their status in Longite Louisiana is perhaps best summarized through his brother Earl's gimmick of tossing coins to children while campaigning: he said he would give out "a quarter to the white kids and a nickel to the niggers."

Venality was not Long's only tool: he availed himself of violence as well. Critics of his regime had to fear the threat of beatings and kidnappings. On two occasions he instituted martial law: once to ensure the outcome of an election in New Orleans and once to put down a revolt of laid-off oil company workers. Distrusting the "lying" press, he created an apparatus of propaganda, replete with radio addresses, sound trucks blaring slogans, and his own newspaper.

Huey was a traveling salesman by trade, and the public loved his buffoonish histrionics, cornpone demagoguery, and flamboyant dress. They cheered his vituperative attacks on his enemies and relished his intentional flouting of decorum. Long enjoyed the destruction and humiliation of his enemies, and his people shared in his enjoyment. The rural poor began to look upon Long with religious ardor, flocking in droves to catch sight of a man they compared to an angel or to Jesus himself.

For both his admirers and detractors, the regime Long set up brought to mind fascism. The Communist *Daily Worker* screeched HUEY LONG IS LOUISIANA'S HITLER. In his 1935 book *Forerunners of American Fascism*, the liberal journalist Raymond Gram Swing called him a "coming of Hitler or Mussolini of America." The homegrown fascist Lawrence Dennis concurred, seeing in Long "the nearest approach to a national fascist leader" in America, also writing, "I think Long's smarter than Hitler, but he needs a good brain trust . . . He needs a Goebbels." The furiously antisemitic fundamentalist preacher Gerald L. K. Smith apparently wanted to play that role. After giving encouragement to the efforts of the writer William Dudley Pelley to set up a fascist paramilitary movement with his Silver Shirts, Smith shifted his allegiance to Long, became his chief propagandist and organizer, and slavishly worshipped him, insinuating himself into his inner circle, wearing the man's old suits, and even allegedly sleeping at the foot of his bed. Even Arthur Schlesinger Jr.—who denied that Long could meaningfully be called "fascist" and wrote that "Huey Long resembled, not a Hitler or Mussolini, but a Latin American dictator, a Vargas or a Perón"—called Long's Louisiana "the nearest approach to a totalitarian state the American republic has ever seen."

Long's appeal was not limited to Louisiana. His election to the U.S. Senate in 1932 gave him a national platform. As the rest of the country approached the desperate conditions typical of Louisiana, Long launched his "Share Our Wealth" campaign as an alternative to Roosevelt's New Deal. He traveled from state to state and spoke, gathering large crowds, not just in the rural South, but in every region. Long, with the help of Smith, himself a wildly charismatic orator, encouraged his admirers at each stop to form Share Our Wealth club chapters. These were to be the seeds of a mass movement and the base of a third-party presidential campaign against FDR. Long's movement also attracted followers of Father Coughlin, the popular radio priest whose social gospel veered sharply toward antisemitism. Its unrealistic program of wealth redistribution would keep private ownership in place but would aid a disappearing *Mittelstand*: "Where is the middle class today? Where is the corner grocery man, about whom President Roosevelt speaks? He is gone or going. Where is the corner druggist? He is gone or going. Where is the banker of moderate means? He is vanishing. The middle class today cannot pay the debts they owe and come out alive. In other words, the middle class is no more." Long's assassination in 1935 dissipated whatever potential the Share Our Wealth movement had as a challenge to Roosevelt.

Long had a pronounced gift for reaching accommodations with moneyed interests even while publicly attacking their rule. Even as he assailed Standard Oil in the press and accused it of trying to depose and assassinate him, he negotiated a compromise with the company: he would rebate most of the tax the company paid if at least 80 percent of the oil at its Baton Rouge refinery was drilled in Louisiana. Many of Huey's close backers were independent oil producers who would benefit from such a deal. In fact, Long had formed his own company, the Win or Lose Oil Company, to sell and lease state land to oil drillers, an arrangement that would go on to provide hefty profits for descendants of Long and his cronies well into the twenty-first century. "Louisiana had known corruption before Huey Long, but it had never been so gross or so cynical," one historian writes. "And corruption had never been elevated into a theory for governing a state."

The fates of oil and populism in Louisiana are inextricably bound together. Black sludge bubbled up to the surface long before it was drawn out. Legend has it that Hernando de Soto, while exploring the lower Mississippi in 1541, was shown oil seeps by Indians and used the tar to caulk his ships; it was not the last time oil would be used to patch the gaps of an unsound vessel in Louisiana. Natural gas burning in the bayous gave rise to the Cajun folklore of *feux follets*, "fool's fires," known elsewhere as will-o'-the-wisps. These eerie glows were thought to be the souls of unbaptized babies or angry avenging spirits that would lure hapless travelers into the swamps never to be seen again. These lights are, in scientific fact, like all fossil fuels, the transmogrified product of death: energy derived from decomposing organic matter. By the early 1990s the legacy of oil had become literally poisonous: thousands of uncapped abandoned oil wells were leaking toxic and radioactive waste into the soil and water.

It was oil that brought the Dukes to Louisiana. David Hedger Duke, David's father, originally from Kansas, was an engineer for Royal Dutch Shell who relocated his family to New Orleans after being stationed for a time in the Netherlands. Duke's father was a deeply conservative Goldwater Republican and a harsh disciplinarian, and his mother was emotionally distant and an alcoholic—probably not such an uncommon childhood of the 1950s and '60s. Duke was a lonely, unliked child—peers called him "Puke Duke" and refused to play with him. He retreated into books. In 1964, at age fourteen, he got hold of the Citizens' Council newsletter and showed up at their office.

The Citizens' Councils were formed across the South in the 1950s to oppose school integration and voter registration. The Greater New Orleans Citizens' Council was founded by "Judge" Leander Perez, who had been one of Huey Long's principal lieutenants and vote-getters. (He was so effective at his job that he managed to deliver more votes to Long than there were registered voters in his parish.) Although his patron was assassinated and he was removed from the judicial bench for misconduct, Perez persevered. Dubbed the "Caesar of the Swampland" by the press, he established a dictatorship in Plaquemines and

St. Bernard parishes for more than fifty years, doling out patronage and pocketing the sulfur and oil wealth from the desperately poor lower Delta parishes. As the civil rights movement rose, he averred that efforts to desegregate the South were ignited by the Jews, who, he said, "were supposed to have been cremated at Buchenwald and Dachau but weren't, and Roosevelt allowed two million of them illegal entry into our country." In 1960 Perez whipped up the crowd at a large Citizens' Council rally in New Orleans, creating a mob that would go on to attack Blacks in the street with knives and clubs. He also built a concentration camp of sorts to intimidate the freedom riders who were coming down to register voters in Plaquemines Parish.

The young Duke was looking for a particular book available at the Citizens' Council office: Carleton Putnam's *Race and Reason: A Yankee View.* Putnam had been director of Delta Airlines but left his post to dedicate his life to writing a biography of Theodore Roosevelt. In 1958 he abandoned that project and threw himself into the civil rights battle, penning an open letter to President Eisenhower in opposition to school integration, which gained him an enthusiastic Southern following. In 1961 he expanded his arguments into a pseudoscientific treatise on Blacks' putative biological inferiority and the dangers of racial miscegenation, targeted at the legacy of the "equalitarian" cultural anthropology of Franz Boas. Duke may not have been merely indulging his own intellectual curiosity: the Louisiana Department of Education made *Race and Reason* required reading for "select high school and college students." In his own telling, Duke says he was taught liberal platitudes about integration in school and came to the "truth" only through his own research for a school assignment, but it seems much more likely that his encounter with *Race and Reason* was through the standard curriculum.

In any case, Duke began to hang out at the Citizens' Council office and make himself a nuisance to the staff, who took pity on him when they learned of his unhappy homelife. When he showed up with a copy of *Mein Kampf* and started spouting off antisemitic opinions, members of the council would later say that they were horrified and tried to dissuade him from going full Nazi, but this version of events strains credulity. Leander Perez was hardly quiet about his antisemitism, and Putnam's *Race and Reason* posited Franz Boas's Jewishness as the reason why he had adopted racial egalitarianism.

It does seem true, however, that Duke's devoted Nazism did not improve his social life. At Louisiana State University in Baton Rouge, he failed to win friends by playing records of speeches by the American Nazi Party leader George Lincoln Rockwell and showing pictures of corpses in concentration camps that he had in his dorm room, which was decorated with a Nazi flag, a picture of Adolf Hitler, and German World War II propaganda. It was at LSU where Duke began his political career, delivering tirades against the Jews in Free Speech Alley on campus, otherwise home to anti-war and other radical protesters in the late 1960s and early '70s. Photographs of Duke tramping around campus in his Nazi uniform from this time would prove to be an encumbrance when he later tried to clean up his image for mainstream politics.

Duke's entire career would be characterized by attempts to simultaneously gain mainstream recognition and respect and be the predominant leader of the fringe, subcultural world of the Klan and neo-Nazism. Until 1989, he would largely fail to accomplish either. In his bid to rebuild the Klan in the 1970s, he attempted its embourgeoisement. He enjoined his lieutenants to avoid saying "nigger" in public with the press present (an exhortation imperfectly heeded even by Duke himself) and to present themselves as a white civil rights organization. Duke preferred to appear in public in a coat and tie rather than the traditional white robes. He permitted women full membership. As was required for recruiting in southern Louisiana, Duke's Klan also dropped the organization's traditional anti-Catholicism.

But Duke's penchant for personal self-promotion alienated his lieutenants and supporters. During a failed state senate campaign, he fought with a deputy over a TV ad he wanted to air that showed him lifting weights in a tank top and short shorts; the dispute eventually led to the deputy's resignation. At a Klan leadership conference, Duke performed a similar stunt live: a curtain rose onstage revealing a shirtless Duke pumping iron before a crowd of aghast Klansmen.

Equally embarrassing were the pseudonymous books he wrote and attempted to sell. The first, *African Atto*, was a fake martial arts guide for Black Power militants, written by one "Mohammed X," that diagrammed various fighting moves to use against white opponents. When confronted about it, Duke claimed that it was designed to be sold through the mail and thereby identify potential enemies for the coming race war; later he tried to pass it off as "satire in the best tradition of Jonathan Swift." It seems most likely it was part of a misbegotten moneymaking scheme.

It's difficult to imagine any political purpose for Duke's other volume, *Finders Keepers*, a guide to sex and dating for the modern single woman. Written under the pseudonyms Dorothy Vanderbilt and James Konrad, the book advised ladies how to please their men, mostly with stuff cribbed from women's magazines, equal parts revolting and banal: "Sooner or later, if you truly want to drive your man wild in bed, you should bring him to climax by fellatio. He will love you for it. To him it's more than just a beautiful sensation, it's really an expression of caring and concern and pure loving intimacy on your part." Duke had apparently hoped the book would become a bestseller and solve his financial difficulties, but it was an utter flop and further alienated his lieutenants, who quickly figured out that he wrote it.

Finders Keepers is, in fact, deeply revealing about Duke, and not because it provides some secret key to an underlying sexual pathology that can explain his entire personality. The salient thing about the book is that, as one of his aides said, it was "too hard-core for the right wing and too soft-core for the perverts." This remark sums up the essence of the Duke phenomenon: he was caught between his desire for publicity and mainstream acceptance and his infatuation with the secretive underworld of extremism. The Klan's white sheets, mumbo jumbo titles, and rituals were intended to hide the supposedly respectable citizens in its ranks, at the same time providing a mystique and allure to its recruits and delivering ghastly terror to its victims. Electoral politics and public advocacy, with their inherent need for publicity, were in contradiction with the air of secrecy that gave the Klan both its appeal and effectiveness as a terrorist organization. This is why Duke began to receive scorn and mockery from the other, more radical Klan leaders, who never fully bought his tactical preference for politics and understood that real violence and menace, which made the Klan unacceptable in polite society, were at the heart of the entire thing.

Duke's paradoxical effort to be a public Klan leader was born from a narcissistic personality that couldn't be satisfied with the rulership of an "invisible empire" and therefore craved public recognition, at the same time still desiring the frisson of ghoulish power that flows from conspiracism, secret societies, and terrorist machinations. This amphibian nature helps to explain both his successes and his failures: he found purchase as the acceptable public face of unacceptable private hatreds and paranoias, but he was always too "soft-core" for the radical vanguard of his own movement even as he was too tainted with the reek of the racist netherworld to fully cross over into the mainstream.

One piece of advice Duke offered in *Finders Keepers* is notable for having a real echo in his personal life: its exhortation for women to engage in extramarital affairs. In reality, Duke's compulsive womanizing had begun to put a strain on his relationship with his fellow Klansmen. Duke's chief adjutant, Karl Hand, left in the late '70s partly owing to Duke's philandering ways. In 1991 Hand told *Spy* magazine, "He had no qualms about putting the make on anyone's wife or girlfriend, and the flak always came back to me, because I was his national organizer. He was portraying himself as a family man, with his wife and two kids, but at the same time, he was involved in these sexual escapades." Another Klansmen recalled, "We had to get David out. He was seducing all the wives."

As a result of these mishaps, Duke and his organization limped through the 1980s. His breakaway lieutenants formed their own Klans, which were monopolizing media attention and attracting more members through their willingness to use violence. Duke's plan to use the Klan as a vehicle for his political ambitions seemed to be coming to naught, and he made the decision to leave and form a new organization.

In 1979, he created the NAAWP, the National Association for the Advancement of White People, a group ostensibly focused on discrimination against whites. But efforts to class up his operation did not succeed. Friends report Duke going from table to table at a Sizzler steak house asking for donations for the NAAWP, paying the bill with what he could scrounge up, and then pocketing the rest. Meanwhile, he would have his daughters share a hamburger to save money. Duke had been accustomed to living off Klan money, and the racist books and cassette tapes sold through the NAAWP were not an adequate substitute; he used the dues and donations to buy and refurbish his home in the New Orleans suburb of Metairie. Ever eager to burnish his bourgeois image, he adorned the living room with a piano, which he could barely play.

Yet Duke did somehow manage to scrape together the money for plastic surgery. He went to Dr. Calvin Johnson, the top plastic surgeon in New Orleans, to get a nose reduction and chin implant. Then Duke underwent chemical peels to remove wrinkles around his eyes. Around the same time, while paying no income taxes because he claimed he did not meet the threshold, he was showing up in Las Vegas and playing craps for tens of thousands of dollars.

Duke doggedly ran for office, losing again and again. In 1988 he even ran for president on the ticket of the far-right Populist Party activist and Holocaust denier Willis Carto and received 0.5 percent of the vote—but he did not give up. In 1989 he decided to contest the special election for Louisiana House District 81, centered in Metairie. During the 1970s Duke had outlined his political strategy in the Klan organ *The Crusader*. Running for local office was the first step in the effort to topple Jewish domination: "Because of the Jews' basic alien nature, the weakest link in his power comes from a national level downward with only its weakest tentacles reaching down to the local community. Local politics, working upwards, is the soft underbelly of their empire."

There were reasons why District 81 might be a particularly soft target for Duke. First of all, the district, plumped by white flight from New Orleans, was 99.6 percent white, petrified by the specter of Black crime in the neighboring metropolis. Parish residents repeatedly elected the Chinese American sheriff Harry Lee, who ordered his department to stop Black youths in "rinky-dink cars" and proposed barricading the streets that led to New Orleans. In addition, the state's economic situation had significantly deteriorated during the Reagan years. Always marching to its own beat, Louisiana had economic cycles that were contrapuntal to those of the rest of the country. The state had never suffered through the malaise of the 1970s: high oil prices filled public coffers and kept property and income taxes virtually nonexistent. But while some of America experienced the 1980s as a delirious boom time, Louisiana faced double-digit unemployment, leading the nation. The low price of oil throughout the decade hobbled the state's relatively generous public spending, just as it had done in another rusting, multiethnic empire: the Soviet Union.

On top of the state's oil woes, Metairie was a victim of the broader stagnation of middle-income wages that the entire country experienced in the 1980s. In Jefferson Parish, income from wages had dropped by 6.5 percent from 1982 to 1987, but income from dividends, interest, and rent rose by 19 percent. The parish lost nearly 45 percent of its oil and gas jobs, nearly 30 percent of its construction jobs, and 17 percent of jobs in manufacturing. The burden of the Reagan '80s seemed to fall on the lower-middle-class and blue-collar denizens of Metairie's low brick bungalows while the benefits redounded to the genteel occupants of its pillared-and-porticoed houses near the country club, from whose precincts the Republican establishment ruled. Jefferson Parish was, in Duke's words, "a microcosm of white America."

With tax revenues tanking, the state government had to find a stopgap for the deficit. The governor, conservative Democrat Charles "Buddy" Roemer, represented the other tradition of Louisiana politics, aside from populism: "good government" or "reform." In theory and rhetoric, good government candidates opposed the corrupt excesses of the Longite populists. In practice and policy, their regimes were often crafted at the behest of the business interests in the state, represented through such think tanks as the Public Affairs Research Council (PAR) or the Louisiana Association of Business and Industry (LABI).

Under Roemer, Louisiana largely followed the wishes of LABI, favoring a program of austerity—except for business, of course. He kept social spending flat, cut unemployment benefits, and raised tuitions at state universities; he also limited the ability of workers to sue their employers. The budget cuts imperiled one of the bases of middle-class life in Louisiana that had been created by the populist patronage regime: plentiful jobs in the state's schools and bureaucracies. Last, in order to shelter business from the tax burden, Roemer proposed to cut the state's much-vaunted homestead exemption, which exempted houses valued under $75,000 from any property taxes. This notion was particularly galling to the mass of Jefferson Parish voters, who, with the help of a powerful family of tax assessors, had effectively never paid any taxes on their homes. The Democratic governor's reforms fractured Jefferson's Republican coalition, which had managed to keep lower- and upper-middle-class voters united with the promise of low taxes. Into the breach slipped Duke.

When Duke began to make public appearances in Metairie, he found a receptive audience. Patrons at a working-class dive bar stood and applauded when Duke came through the door with campaign flyers. His appeal was not limited to downtrodden blue-collar whites; it crossed over, more quietly perhaps, into the precincts of middle-class respectability. Now registered as a Republican, he was invited by the Jefferson Parish party to address their candidates' forum. Behind closed doors, he received a friendly welcome, with the state Republican Party chairman slapping him on the back and praising his presentation.

When he addressed the Jefferson Parish chapter of the Alliance for Good Government, he failed to get their official endorsement, but a member confessed to Jefferson's registrar of voters, "I think like he thinks, but I'm in the closet about it."

Duke freely admitted to his past Klan membership, which, as he pointed out, he shared with many respectable public figures like Robert Byrd, but he denied ever being a Nazi. When inconvenient photographs reemerged of him in a brownshirt's uniform on the LSU campus with a sign reading GAS THE CHICAGO 7, Duke claimed that such antics constituted a "teen-aged stunt" and "a satire" rather than "a defense of totalitarianism." Absurd defenses such as these aside, his platform was undeniably shot through with thinly veiled anti-Black racism: he denounced "welfare dependency," affirmative action, and minority "quotas." He put a eugenic spin on these issues, calling for a reduction in "the illegitimate welfare birthrate that is bankrupting us economically and is the source of much crime and social ills." Duke was offering a standard Reagan-era conservative attack on welfare and affirmative action, aside from his willingness to touch the burning racial core of the issues. At the same time, he was attuned to the lower-middle-class homeowners he lived among: he also offered a full-throated defense of the homestead tax exemption.

Duke had the advantage of facing a divided field: there were four other Republicans running. According to Louisiana's open primary rules, every candidate regardless of party ran on the same primary ballot, and then the top two faced each other in a runoff. The system was devised by the wily former Democratic governor Edwin Edwards to stymie the Republican Party, which was beginning to reorganize itself and attract white votes in post–civil rights Louisiana. The idea was that Republican candidates would be forced to split their votes into tiny fractions of the total, but in fact the rules helped Republicans by splitting liberal and conservative Democratic votes as well. Edwards become jokingly known the father of the Louisiana GOP.

John Treen, the brother of the former Republican governor David

Treen, was a particularly vulnerable opponent for Duke. Both Treens had been involved in the segregationist movement as members of the Citizens' Council and the States' Rights Party, a fact that made a principled rejection of Duke's racism awkward at best and made civil rights groups hesitant to assist Treen's campaign. As a fiscal conservative, Treen supported efforts to cut the homestead exemption, which immediately made him a hard sell in Jefferson Parish. He also represented the establishment. "When you saw Mr. Treen on television, he looked like he was around Metairie Country Club all the time," one voter told *The Times-Picayune*. "I really didn't think he had my best interest at heart." Treen, a businessman first and politician second, just wasn't up to the task: the burden of facing off against Duke and all the forces of darkness was not what he felt he had signed up for as a local pol. "I got into this damn thing thinking it was going to be some sleepy little ol' election, a state representative kind of race where nobody gives a damn who wins," he later complained.

In the first round of voting, Duke came in first with 33 percent of the vote; Treen came in second with 19 percent. New Orleans archbishop Philip Hannan issued a statement to his parish priests to read at services before the runoff: "The election will determine the convictions of the voters of the district about the basic dignity of persons, the recognition of human rights of every person, the equality of races made by Divine Providence." Presumably, this moral message would resonate with the voters of the predominantly Catholic district. "This bishop in New Orleans, I never did like him," Earline Pickett, the seventy-four-year-old wife of a retired oil engineer, told *The Washington Post*. "He likes colored people. He says we should love colored people. But they've been different from the beginning, and God must have had a reason for making them that way."

The intervention of the national GOP had very little effect either. A party that was run by Lee Atwater, mastermind of the Willie Horton ad and Reagan's Southern Strategy, was ill-equipped to repudiate Duke's politics of bigotry. Their meddling just allowed Duke to further burnish his outsider credentials. "It's like the establishment closing ranks to prevent an independent from coming through," Duke told *The Times-Picayune*, taking the stance of Longite populist defiance. "David Duke is a modern David versus the Goliaths of money, power, media, and political corruption," a pro-Duke flyer inveighed. Despite Reagan's popularity in the district, East Jefferson residents seemed to agree: a homemade sign appeared by the interstate, declaring: NO ONE TELLS DISTRICT 81 HOW TO VOTE! Duke yard signs were sprouting up all around Jefferson Parish, quickly outnumbering any other candidate's and stretching "as far as the eye could see."

In February, the runoff vote was held. Turnout was unusually high for a local election: 78 percent. Duke edged Treen by 227 votes, finishing with 8,459 votes to Treen's 8,232 and thus winning office as a state representative. "Even the president of the United States came out against us," Duke told the crowd thronging his victory party at the Metairie Lions Club, "but we beat them." Then Duke's supporters turned on Black and Jewish reporters covering the event, calling them "niggers" and chanting, "We missed one of you in the gas chambers." Scrambling to get out of the hall, one reporter was punched in the chest.

"If I had anything to say to people outside the state," the author Walker Percy told *The New York Times* when they came down to report on the District 81 race, "I'd tell 'em, 'Don't make the mistake of thinking David Duke is a unique phenomenon confined to Louisiana rednecks and yahoos. He's not. He's not just appealing to the old Klan constituency, he's appealing to the white middle class. And don't think that he or somebody like him won't appeal to the white middle class of Chicago or Queens.'"

The Republican National Committee voted to "censure" Duke, but the Louisiana state party ignored the resolution, despite the efforts of a Louisiana GOP activist named Beth Rickey to discredit him. She had followed Duke to a Populist Party convention in Chicago and recorded a secret speech where he told the crowd of skinheads and Klansmen,

"My victory in Louisiana was a victory for the white majority movement in this country." He concluded his speech: "Listen, the Republican Party of Louisiana is in our camp, ladies and gentlemen. I had to run within that process, because, well, that's where our people are." He had good cause to boast: even when Rickey brought the photographs to the attention of the state GOP chairman and the press carried pictures of Duke shaking hands with the chairman of the American Nazi Party, Louisiana Republicans did nothing. Nor did they act after Rickey and her team were able to purchase *The Turner Diaries*, *Mein Kampf*, and a dozen other Nazi books out of Duke's legislative office. The party was scared of Duke's voters, who had reacted angrily when the national GOP tried to act against him. There may have been other reasons for the lack of initiative. "I began to suspect that there was more agreement with Duke on the race issue than I had heretofore believed," Rickey later reflected. Duke thought so, too. "We not only agree on most of the issues," he told the Baton Rouge *Morning Advocate*, "we've come to the point of friendship. They've accepted me. The voters have accepted me. The legislature has accepted me."

He succeeded in continually getting mass media attention for himself. In November 1989 he appeared on ABC News's *Primetime Live* with Sam Donaldson and Diane Sawyer. The usually formidable Donaldson had trouble with the soapy Duke. Confronted with selling *Mein Kampf*, Duke said he was just a bookseller who sold all sorts of books. Donaldson read out some of Duke's writing, and Duke denied having written it or finessed it into a more respectable-sounding opinion. When pressed about writing that "Negros are lower on the evolutionary scale than Caucasians," Duke replied, "Well, I don't think I wrote that. I do believe that there is a difference between whites and blacks. I think that there is an IQ difference. But I think the way to determine a person's quality and qualifications is in the marketplace of ideas, through testing, for instance in universities, through applications for jobs." This opinion was gaining mainstream acceptance: in 1989 the solidly center-right establishment American Enterprise Institute think tank began funding the research of Charles Murray that would culminate in his cowritten book *The Bell Curve*, containing its own claims about race and IQ. Showing a newsletter Duke had distributed during his days as a blatant Nazi, which suggested partitioning the country into different ethnic enclaves, Donaldson pointed to part of a map that had Long Island set aside as a homeland for the Jews. The New York studio audience laughed; Duke's plastic face curled into an innocent-looking smile—he found his way out: "Sir, that map is tongue-in-cheek." Duke encouraged viewers to write him at his Baton Rouge office. The volume of mail that poured in shocked the statehouse staff; it was more than they had seen for any other legislator. (The other feature on *Primetime Live* that night was Donald Trump, ranting about Japanese investment in the U.S. economy, under the headline "Who Owns America?")

In 1990, at large, raucous rallies across the state, Duke parlayed his high profile into a U.S. Senate race against the uninspiring conservative Democrat J. Bennett Johnston. Duke won 43.5 percent of the vote to Johnston's 54 percent, winning all the same parishes that Long won back in 1928. Johnston's victory was due to the fact that he won nearly the entire Black vote. But Duke netted 59 percent of the white vote. Duke's election night party at a Lions Club outside New Orleans was practically a victory celebration. There was much to look forward to: next year the governor would be up for reelection.

"I will swing the pendulum back," Duke told the small crowd at the announcement for his candidacy at the Hilton in Baton Rouge. "I am a populist like Huey Long, ladies and gentlemen, but we need a Huey in Reverse. We need a populist for less government and more power to the people." Instead of Share Our Wealth, it would be Hoard Our Wealth: no more "welfare abuse," no more affirmative action, no more social programs for the "underclass," but "more prisons," an end to busing, and the death penalty for drug dealers. It would also be a liberation from the strictures of political correctness, a win for freedom of expression. "Don't you see?" Duke told his followers. "You'll be more free to say whatever you want to say, man or woman, if I'm elected."

As the 1991 election neared, Governor Roemer had good reason to feel confident about his chances. Early polling showed him comfortably ahead of his main opponents, David Duke and former governor Edwin Edwards. Roemer had defeated Edwards in 1987 with a pledge to clean up the government. Edwards was amiable, fun, but he could not be called clean. First elected in 1972, he had been the first candidate since Reconstruction to openly campaign for the Black vote and the first Cajun candidate; he fused Louisiana's downtrodden ethnic minorities into a powerful coalition with organized labor, delivering on the egalitarian side of Long's populism. The high oil revenues of the 1970s meant that Edwards could share the state's generous services to a broader section of the public than ever before. Still, he felt the pressure of business interests: although he was elected with labor support, he reluctantly signed a right-to-work law in order to attract industry.

While the good times rolled, that public tolerated Edward's excesses: the womanizing, the gambling, the smiling-winking-backslapping insider deals and corruption. These things were not vices so much as tradition. At least Edwards was not a hypocrite: he did not moralize, but flaunted his bad behavior as harmless mischief that was as enjoyable for the public as it was for him. His appetites appealed to a state still governed in many ways by a Code Napoléon spirit on questions of gender relations. "Two out of ten women will go to bed with you, but you've got to ask the other eight," he once said. When the Louisiana mob boss Carlos Marcello was caught on an FBI tape saying of a man he counted as his friend, "He's the strongest sonuvabitch governor [we] ever had. He fuck [*sic*] with women and plays dice, but won't drink. How ya like dat?" he was expressing widely held admiration.

Barred from seeking a third consecutive term by the state's constitution, Edwards stepped down in 1979 and then returned to office in 1983, when Louisianians tired of their brief flirtation with Reagan conservatism in the person of Dave Treen. "The only way I can lose this election is if I'm caught in bed with either a dead girl or a live boy," Edwards quipped to reporters. But he failed to bring back the good old days of the '70s: the state's fiscal straits were too dire, and he was forced to use the immense power of the governor to jam through budget cuts instead of expansive giveaways to an adoring populace. He was still a "*Laissez les bons temps rouler*" guy in the laissez-faire world of Reaganomics and austerity. He may have laissez-ed a little too bon of a temps. The revelation of massive Vegas gambling debts led to a racketeering indictment. Edwards avoided conviction, but voters were fed up with his antics and promises of reform. Restraint looked appealing.

Roemer, a graduate of Harvard Business School, appealed to the public with his combination of technocratic competence and anger at corruption. On assuming office in 1987, his popularity and the unusually broad powers of the Louisiana governor's office allowed him to run roughshod over a legislature run by populist Democrats. His administration was dubbed "the Roemer revolution." But then the revolution lost momentum. Roemer had never liked being governor: he was aloof, ill-suited for the glad-handing style of Louisiana politics. He stopped making public appearances, brooding alone in the governor's mansion instead, a condition made worse when his wife, on whom he had dumped all the governor's social responsibilities, left him. It turned out that eliminating corruption alone couldn't rescue the state's fiscal situation. When a referendum on Roemer's fiscal reform plan was defeated in 1989 by many of the same voters who had put in him office, he seemed almost to give up. The local journalist John Maginnis observed that the base of the Roemer revolution was divided between two constituencies: "He sold his good government, educated, middle-class base on improving education and cleaning up pollution. He had sold the hard-core, conservative anti-tax, 'aginner' votes on paring down government to essentials." Duke, who built his statewide political movement stumping against Roemer's fiscal reform, understood that these were actually two different groups, and that the latter didn't really want cuts in government that hurt *their* interests. "The very coalition that had sent Duke to the state house was now protesting the probusiness austerity policies of the Roemer administration," one political scientist observed.

Roemer still harbored some ambitions. In early 1991, encouraged by George H. W. Bush's chief of staff John Sununu, he switched his party affiliation to Republican. The national GOP was happy to bolster the ranks of the Louisiana party with non-Duke Republicans. Roemer thought it would undercut the chances of any Republican to the right of him and to the left of Duke. At the time, with Bush's popularity soaring as a result of the Persian Gulf War, any association with the president seemed attractive. A possible 1996 Republican presidential primary campaign may have also been on Roemer's mind. The Louisiana GOP, which had long pushed for Roemer to switch parties, was left out of the loop, having been given the cold shoulder by Roemer, who preferred to deal with the big, fancy names of the national party rather than the cigar-chomping, backroom dealers of the state party. They would not forget.

For his part, Edwin Edwards was well rested for his comeback. At age sixty-three, he was living with his latest girlfriend, a twenty-six-year-old blond LSU nursing student named Candy Picou. Publicly, Edwards said he was a new man: "I like to believe that I have matured, grown mentally and emotionally as I have chronologically. I believe I'm more serious than I was. These are serious times." Privately, he joked that the only thing he and David Duke had in common was that they were "both wizards under the sheets." After Edwards lost in 1987, the *Shreveport Journal* had remarked, "The only way Edwin Edwards can ever be reelected is to run against Adolf Hitler." Edwards comprehended his state intimately, both its virtues and, more important, its vices. Although he was running to Roemer's left, Edwards presented his campaign in strikingly conservative terms, as a "counter-revolution to restore what was taken from you." As the *Times-Picayune*'s Tyler Bridges put it, "Edwards knew that every so often Louisiana, like a boozer swearing off alcohol, elected a reform governor but four years later always replaced him with a populist. 'Let the good times roll,' after all, is the state's motto."

Before the good times could roll there were months of campaigning. Although the open primary system meant that anyone could run, the GOP held a caucus to give a candidate the nominal Republican nod. Roemer believed that the caucus should be called off, as he was a Republican incumbent. State Republican leaders had other plans. They allowed the caucuses to proceed and gave the nomination to Clyde Holloway, a rock-ribbed fundamentalist who was popular with the state's evangelicals and pro-life community. But Duke demanded to address the caucus. After attempting to forestall Duke's speech with parliamentary maneuvering, party leaders relented to the crowds, who were chanting, "Duke! Duke! Duke!" The leaders were shocked by the frenzy. "It's like we're attending a party convention in Germany in the 1930s and Hitler is coming to power," a longtime GOP operative confided.

Though Duke never successfully passed a bill as a legislator, he managed to score something of a victory in the 1991 legislative session. He had proposed a bill to offer mothers on welfare $100 a year to have a Norplant birth control device implanted in their arms. In committee, the measure was watered down to just provide information about birth control to mothers on welfare, which was already provided for by state health policy. There was very little ambiguity in what was meant by "welfare mothers." At a rally, Duke said, "The greatest problem facing this state is the rising welfare underclass," and the crowd yelled back, "The niggers!" Duke pretended not to hear. But when he trotted out similar lines at a Kiwanis or a VFW hall, he received polite applause.

"They just have those babies and go on welfare," a single, unemployed white mother from Garyville, Louisiana, told *The New York*

Times. She admitted that she also received welfare payments but said that "the blacks get more." While Bush had used the image of the convicted rapist Willie Horton to stir up fear of Black crime in the 1988 campaign, Duke dropped the pretext of criminality: a Duke campaign ad featured a single image of a Black mother holding a child. When Duke returned to the LSU campus, where he had once been mocked and derided for demonstrating in a storm trooper's uniform, he met a friendly crowd of clean-cut white students who also cheered the lines about the "massive welfare underclass." "Amen, I'm tired of spending my tax dollars on them!" yelled one young woman in a sorority shirt.

David Duke was an implausible tribune for the overburdened taxpayer. *The Times-Picayune* reported that he had not paid his modest Jefferson Parish property taxes for three years. But charges of hypocrisy could not damage Duke, who had a strange power to make voters alter their opinions to fit him. Roemer's staff and RNC consultants organized a focus group of white, blue-collar swing voters from Jefferson Parish. They were asked a series of questions about a hypothetical candidate who had dodged the draft, avoided taxes, had plastic surgery, and never held a job. The group reviled the imaginary pol. But when the same questions were asked naming Duke as the candidate, the group grew testy and defended him. Roemer's media consultant Raymond Strother noted, "When we described a hypothetical candidate in the same way, the people hated him. But when you told them that person was Duke, they made the same excuses. Basically, we found that the guy was bulletproof."

"Only dumb people pay taxes," one woman said. "Politicians and millionaires don't because they are smart. Duke must be smart."

Despite the evidence from his own campaign, Roemer simply could not imagine that Duke had mass appeal, and he believed the polls that showed him comfortably ahead. Although advisers repeatedly warned him to go on the offensive, he refused to air attack ads, and he spent the last Sunday before the election watching football. Edwards ran first with 33.7 percent, Duke second with 31.7 percent, and Roemer third with 26.5 percent; the official GOP candidate, Clyde Holloway, got just 5.34 percent. The incumbent governor had finished third and was now out of the race. Although Edwards was in the lead, he faced challenges in the runoff: Duke handily won white Democrats and once again swept all the parishes Huey Long had once won. "We have a new trend going on in America, much like what's happening in Eastern Europe," Duke told reporters gathered at the Quality Inn in New Orleans. "People are revolting against centralized, bigger government . . . One person described me as the Boris Yeltsin of American politics. I like that. I'm certainly opposed to the way the establishment has conducted and run our government both in Louisiana and the nation."

Edwards, who certainly did not lack for worldliness and even cynicism, was unsettled by the degree of rancor Duke could inspire. At a debate in front of the state convention of the American Association of Retired Persons, Edwards discovered how deep the Duke appeal went. Edwards promised improvements in services for seniors; the crowd wasn't interested, but they gnashed at Duke's red meat about the illegitimate birth rate and the welfare underclass. Edwards tried to appeal to facts: "A welfare mother only receives an extra $11 a week with each extra child she bears. Can you see a woman sitting around the kitchen table scheming to get pregnant to get another $11 a week?" The crowd shouted back, "Yes!" Edwards protested: "He's appealing to your base emotions. Who is going to be next? The disabled? The old? You better think about it." He was drowned out by boos. The Louisiana AARP endorsed Duke.

But Duke came under assault from all sides, as if the immune system of the state and the entire nation was activated against a pathogen. Money poured into the Edwards campaign coffers. Frightened about the possible shunning of the state in the case of a Duke victory, business interests fully aligned themselves with the Democratic candidate. Civil society groups focused on surfacing Duke's past statements on race and the Jews. The press grew more aggressive against him, running piece after piece about his Nazi and Klan activities. A new pro-Edwards bumper sticker began to appear on cars throughout out the state: VOTE FOR THE CROOK—IT'S IMPORTANT. Even Buddy Roemer gave a full-throated endorsement of his former foe. But the massive onslaught yielded ambiguous results. Some polls showed Edwards ahead at just 46 percent to 42; Duke was dominating the white vote with 58 percent. When pressed about Duke's past, voters responded that Edwards, too, had an unsavory past. "We know about Duke's past, we know about Louisiana's future, we know he doesn't care for Negroes, we know he won't get along with the Legislature and, just maybe, we like it!" one voter wrote to *The Times-Picayune.*

Again, Duke had no problem attracting media coverage, particularly on TV. "Broadcast is always better," Duke said. On TV he could avoid the two great enemies of demagogues: context and memory. If questioned too sharply, he could just play the victim. Here was this nice-looking, clean-cut guy being badgered by some snooty journalist. He always got his message across, one way or another: "I just think white people should have equal rights, too." Seems like they were always picking on the white guy in those days. Now what was so unreasonable sounding about that? He could also just flat-out lie. He told a weekend anchor on a network affiliate in New Orleans that he had polled 8 to 12 percent of the Black vote in Louisiana—he was not pressed on it. He was like one of the Nazi or KKK freaks they liked to book on the new *Jerry Springer Show*, but he had prime-time looks. With coiffed hair and plastic surgery, he looked like a guy on a Just for Men bottle. "Take it from someone who has spent most of his adult life working in this medium," Ted Koppel lectured sternly into the camera at the start of ABC's *Nightline*. "Television and Duke were made for each other." Then *Nightline* proceeded to give him thirty minutes of free airtime. Duke did *Larry King Live* and *The Phil Donahue Show* in '91. Phil Donahue and his audience yucked it up to Duke's jokes. Duke refused to go on *Larry King* if faced with anybody to challenge him, but the show still booked him. King did not bring up a single one of Duke's racist or antisemitic remarks. *The Times-Picayune* called his

Larry King appearance "a solid hour of largely uninterrupted propaganda and uncontradicted lies."

The national TV appearances caused contributions to trickle to Duke from around the country. He had already tapped into the fundraising base of the far right during his 1988 run on Willis Carto's Populist Party ticket. But now he was breaking through to people who would not necessarily move in the Holocaust denial and KKK subcultures. He started to get small envelopes of $5, $20, $40—many from the elderly. A retired schoolteacher in Pittsfield, Massachusetts, told *The Boston Globe*: "I like the fact that he thinks that everyone should get an even break—white or black or Jewish or anything else. I think we have had a lot of antiwhite racism." George Marcou of Baraboo, Wisconsin, a retired brewery engineer, told the *Chicago Tribune*, "I don't really think he is a racist. Either that or I'm blind. There are probably things we've all done that we're sorry for." And William J. Zauner of Brookfield, Wisconsin: "He's saying what a lot of people are thinking."

In their first debate together, the surprisingly slick David Duke wrong-footed the consummate professional Edwin Edwards. With the last debate on November 6, Edwards would make sure it would not happen again. He began smoothly, rattling off facts and figures about the state in his warm Cajun drawl, with a friendly, optimistic mien, a performance Duke could not match. Duke seemed a step behind the agile Edwards, but he mostly held his own for the first half hour as the topics kept on quotidian budget and fiscal issues. Then Duke started to get rattled. One of the panelists, Jeff Duhe, a political correspondent for Louisiana Public Broadcasting, asked, "Mr. Duke, you claim and appear to be a spokesman for the common man and his common ideals. Since high school, could you please describe the jobs you've had and the experience they've given you to run a nine-billion-dollar organization such as the state of Louisiana?" Duke fumbled with the answer, citing a long-ago teaching job in Laos, various small-business efforts, and political campaigns. "Are you saying you're a politician and you run for office as a job?" Duhe pressed. Duke became agitated and angry, citing the efficiency of his campaign. Edwards piled on: "Fella never had a job! He worked for nine weeks as an interpreter in Laos and then they fired him because he couldn't understand anybody. He has been in seven campaigns in eight years, he won one. Is that an efficient kind of campaign? Heaven help us if that's the kind of efficiency he's gonna bring to state government."

Then it was the turn of panelist Norman Robinson, a Black correspondent for WDSU-TV in New Orleans. "Mr. Duke, I have to tell you that I am a very concerned citizen. I am a journalist, but first and foremost I am a concerned citizen," Robinson began slowly, with deliberate passion. "And as a minority who has heard you say some very excoriating and diabolical things about minorities, about blacks, about Jews, about Hispanics, I am scared, sir . . . I have heard you say that Jews deserve to be in the ashbin of history, I've heard you say that horses contributed more to the building of America than blacks did. Given that kind of past, sir, given that kind of diabolical, evil, vile mentality, convince me, sir, and other minorities like me, to entrust their lives and the lives of their children to you." Duke tried to play down his record—as having been "too intolerant at times"—and he brought up Jesse Jackson: "I don't think you would ask that question of him, but Jesse Jackson admitted he spitted in white people's food when he worked in a restaurant as a young man." Robinson would not relent: "We are talking about political, economic genocide. We're not talking about intolerance . . . As a newfound Christian, a born-again, are you here willing now to apologize to the people, the minorities of this state, whom you have so dastardly insulted, sir?" Duke gave an impatient apology and tried to change the subject to reverse racism again. Robinson tried to get Duke to admit that there was racism against Black people. "Look, Mr. Robinson, I don't think you are really being fair with me." Robinson: "I don't think you are really being honest, sir." Duke sputtered, lost his temper, and never regained composure.

Edwin Edwards finished Duke off. "In Texas and in Iowa, the Klan people there have already announced that they comin' down here to help their friend Mr. Duke. If they come, I hope they behave themselves," Edwards began, sounding like he was already governor. "I met with the sheriffs today and told them to be on the lookout, if any of them intimidate anybody or interfere with the election process they are gonna be dealt with harshly. Let me say this, Mr. Duke has given us twenty years of hate and hurt. If he's really reformed, let him go back into the community to give us twenty years of healing and help, then let him come back and ask to be governor." After Edwards's sonorous closing statement, Duke pulled his microphone off and sulked off the stage while the cameras were still shooting.

On Election Day, November 16, 1991, Black voters turned out at a rate of 78 percent. Edwards won the New Orleans area handily, beating Duke in Jefferson Parish with 59 percent of the vote; even Duke's Metairie district went for Edwards, with 56 percent. The final outcome was a total blowout: Edwards 61, Duke 39. Still, Duke won 55 percent of the white vote statewide. Duke, who was revealed during the campaign to have made up the "Evangelical Bible Church" he'd said he attended, won 69 percent of white evangelical and fundamentalist voters. He had also taken 56 percent of Cajuns, who had once flocked to their champion Edwards. And Duke's most concentrated area of success was the northern rural hinterland from which Huey Long once rose.

Edwards addressed a jubilant crowd at New Orleans's Monteleone Hotel. "I ask the nation, the national press, I ask all those whose opinions we respect to write and say of us that Louisiana rejected the demagogue and renounced the irrational fear, the dark suspicion, the evil bigotry and the division and chose a future of hope and trust and love for all of God's children," the white-haired governor-elect roared triumphantly in the cadences of a time gone by. "Prophecy is reserved for those who are given that special gift, which I do not possess. But I say to all of America tonight, there will be other places and other times where there will be other challenges by other David Dukes. They too will be peddling bigotry and division as their elixir of false hope, they too will be riding piggyback on the frustration of citizens disaffected by government . . . We must address the causes of public disenchantment with government at every level . . . Tonight Louisiana defeated the darkness of hate, bigotry, and division, but where will the next challenge come from? Will it be in another campaign in Louisiana? Or in a campaign for governor in some other state? Or a campaign for president of the United States?"

Duke had already hinted at the possibility of another run for president. And in Washington, D.C., and elsewhere, others with ambitions of their own were intently watching events unfold in Louisiana. But perhaps the Duke phenomenon was peculiar to Louisiana. David Duke grew up as the forces of segregation there fought a bitter rearguard action; his first political education—from the books he was given in school to the first political organizations that welcomed him—was the product of that rearguard action, designed to train a new generation in that political tradition. The seeds of dictatorship and autocracy were sowed even before Huey Long's reign, when the reactionary Bourbon oligarchs effectively ended democracy in the state for a generation. They had wanted to preserve their economic predominance and, with it, the predominance of the white race, and in doing so, they scarred the state with indelible furrows of caste rule that divided the population long after plantations had become museums and macabre tourist attractions. When democratic demand did express itself from below, it came in the form of a personalistic, charismatic, and vindictive regime: a champion of the people who could punish and humble the arrogant old ruling classes. Huey Long's deft manipulations of the state's poor and disaffected attracted admirers and hangers-on—from would-be fascist chieftains to gangsters. He institutionalized a corrupt bargain that deepened the cynicism of the state's voters and politicians, furthering the state's paradoxical combination of populist anger with a kind of let-it-be tolerance.

Sometimes this tolerance took admirable forms, as in the cosmopolitan, worldly attitude associated with the diverse, multicultural, and sophisticated place that is New Orleans. But such tolerance can be more akin to cynicism and indifference, leading to an acceptance of nearly open criminality in politics. Then comes shame at overindulgence and a turn to renunciation, as if the sequence of Mardi Gras followed by Lent, which governs the state's festive calendar, also is reflected in its political *corsi* and *ricorsi*. The apparently contradictory forces of corruption and populist antiestablishment indignation become embodied in the same political figures, as if the state will accept only leaders who can represent all its indulgence and renunciation in their own persons—the reformers are rogues, and vice versa. The festival of vice and lightly worn hypocrisy gives the state's politics its color and warmth but also creates an atmosphere of moral confusion, where harmless roguishness and vicious hate are apt to become mixed up. In that way, it's a political culture that anticipates the spectacle of tabloid TV, with its own festival of clowns and charlatans whose open extravagance and buffoonishness can hide actual malice.

But David Duke did represent something new: not just the cycles of Louisiana politics or the return of the old ghosts of the Klan. In his rise, a more profound failure and disintegration of the white middle class becomes evident and, with it, new dangers. Duke, unlike previous demagogues like Long and Perez, was also a social misfit who found personal solace in crackpot theories of racial superiority and underground organization. His public life was defined by a kind of narcissism: he craved approval and acceptance by the crowd and also relished his ability to frighten and repulse the society that rejected him. The ideology of race, with its image of permanent hierarchies, provided for him a seemingly more concrete and permanent station in life than the vagaries of class mobility and aspiration, which are always vulnerable to the winds of fortune and failure. The bohemian and subcultural rejection of class respectability in favor of extremist views provided another spurious superiority: a kind of authenticity in the face of polite social hypocrisy. But Duke could never fully give up on his hopes for mainstream success: he always desired to be accepted socially, cultivating a "yuppie" image, changing his appearance to make himself more attractive, and even attempting to enter New Orleans high society with the help of a socialite girlfriend. There, he was once again shunned or kept around as a curiosity, tolerated briefly as another of the "colorful figures" of the Louisiana scene. In the face of unfriendly and alienating social reality, there was always an imaginary world of power and prestige to conjure up, where the existence of a secret Jewish conspiracy explained his lack of status. Unmoored by normal ties to profession or community, Duke's only identity became "White Man." He departed reality in favor of race. Others would follow.

When pressed by a reporter to describe himself, Huey Long once snapped, "Oh, hell, just say that I'm *sui generis* and leave it at that." It is certainly tempting to say the same of the state of Louisiana. Some historians even seem to treat it not as part of America at all, but as a "proverbial banana republic or forlorn outpost of an ancient, Mediterranean, cultural imperium," as one historian complains. But back in the 1930s Huey Long had appealed to millions of disaffected Americans outside the state. Now David Duke, with his Longism in reverse, also resonated across the country. In his concession speech, Duke had inadvertently landed on the reason: "The people of America love what's going on here. Louisiana has been at the bottom of the heap for so long. It's about time we are in first place in waking up this country." Louisiana was so backward it was forward, so peripheral it was central. The rest of the country got its recession in 1990; Louisiana had been struggling with the oil bust for much of the previous decade. While the country experienced anxiety over the coming of "multiculturalism" and the possible fracturing of the nation into a welter of competing interest groups, that had been Louisiana's long-existing reality. The baleful legacy of white supremacy was particularly potent and violent in the old stronghold of Bourbon rule. In fact, each feature of the crisis that appeared at the national level—racism, poverty, stark wealth disparity, environmental fallout, neglected infrastructure, a suddenly vanishing industrial base, systematic corruption, elite self-dealing, political cynicism, and the people's loss of faith in their representatives—had been known in Louisiana earlier and in more intense forms. And so too was the weakness of the political system and the inability of its leadership to respond to these conditions.

No political formula on offer could win lasting and broad consent. The voters attempted to bring back Edwards's good-time populism, but the conditions were absent for its return. Rather than being a fount of largesse again, Edwards ended up having to cut services. In hard times, his jovial corruption was less cute than infuriating. Voters turned to the "good government," pro-business austerity regime of Roemer but then quickly rejected its reforms. The GOP was a latecomer in state politics, even compared with the rest of the Solid South. The apparent growth of Republican electoral strength on the back of Reagan concealed institutional weakness: neither state nor national intervention could fend off a fringe candidate. They could use and fuel racial resentment and animus, but could not control it. Ultimately, fear defeated Duke, fear of the economic disaster of a Duke win or fear of a return to the dark age of Jim Crow. With the appearance of the barely veiled Nazism of David Duke and its vision of politics as race war, Louisiana had demonstrated the politics of national despair in its most virulent and disturbing manifestation.

For some watching, Duke's appearance was not so much frightening as hopeful news. "If the ideals that I stand for are addressed, then I will only be a footnote in history," Duke prophesied. "But if the deterioration of the white middle class continues, then I will be president." And if not him, then maybe another like him.

2

WINTER OF DISCONTENT

Is this the Republican Party of Abraham Lincoln or is this the Republican Party of David Duke?" The question, like most of those posed from the well of the Senate, was rhetorical. Howard Metzenbaum of Ohio, the chamber's angriest liberal, was trying to shame President George H. W. Bush into signing the Civil Rights Act of 1990. His Republican colleagues smarted a little from the blow. "We repudiated David Duke," replied Senator Orrin Hatch of Utah. "I think bringing David Duke in is hitting below the belt a bit."

A series of Supreme Court decisions in the late '80s had made it harder for women and minorities to sue and win discrimination cases; the 1990 act was supposed to remedy this as well as ban racial harassment on the job and allow juries to provide punitive damages for sexual harassment. It had passed both houses overwhelmingly. Eleven Senate Republicans joined the Democrats in support. But Bush, at the urging of his aides, vetoed the bill, saying it "would introduce the destructive force of quotas into our national employment system." Labeling the act a "quota bill" was part of the hard-right push ahead of the upcoming congressional election. An ad by North Carolina senator Jesse Helms attacking his Black opponent Harvey Gantt showed a pair of white hands angrily crumpling up a job rejection letter: "You needed that job. You were the best qualified, but they had to give it to a minority, because of a racial quota. Is that really fair? Harvey Gantt says it is. Gantt supports Ted Kennedy's racial quota law that makes the color of your skin more important than your qualifications." The putative plight of the white worker was not the only consideration. A coalition of business groups led by the Chamber of Commerce and the National Association of Manufacturers, a faithful old patron of the conservative movement, urged Bush to veto the bill: they did not want to be saddled with all the lawsuits.

The Senate voted on whether to override Bush's veto, coming up one vote short. Present for the vote was David Duke. Fresh off his Senate campaign, he lurked over the chamber from the front row of the visitor's gallery. His presence convinced one Republican, Rudy Boschwitz, a Jewish senator from Minnesota who had fled Hitler's Germany with his family, to change his vote: "I found his presence in the chamber repugnant and I knew that I could not allow abstract legal arguments about this bill to be used to advance the discrimination and intolerance that David Duke stands for."

"My election campaign and my position over the last few months is one of the key factors in bringing the president around to vetoing the legislation, and one of the reasons his veto wasn't overridden," Duke crowed to reporters gathered at the Capitol. Afterward he dropped by the offices of *The Washington Times* to meet its reporters and editors. The *Times* was founded by the Korean cult leader Reverend Sun Myung Moon in 1982 as a conservative counterweight to *The Washington Post*, but also as a beachhead for his Unification Church in D.C. Another investor was the government of apartheid South Africa, which funneled several million dollars to Moon's outfits for an interest in the paper.

Duke had reason to suspect that he might get a warm welcome at the *Times* office. Just before his Capitol stunt, the paper had published an unsigned editorial, "David Duke's Revolution." Responding to Duke's election to the state legislature, the editors wrote that his issues were a "symbol" of what voters thought was wrong with America: "What is wrong . . . is that squeaky minority and special-interest wheels get the taxpayers' grease from politicians who seek only the perpetuation of their own power and privileges and that the serious problems confronting American society—the economy, taxes, crime and moral and cultural dissolution—get nothing but promises, platitudes and rhetoric." "Still," they admitted, "it is highly likely that Mr. Duke, despite his disclaimers, today believes the same things he believed when he was Grand Wizard and wore a Nazi storm trooper's uniform. It tells us much that voters in Louisiana didn't seem to care and that they cast their lot with him anyway. That ought to send a message to the politicians and pundits who keep missing the point of the Duke phenomenon. If they have a shred of wisdom, they will not leave it to characters like David Duke to champion legitimate and necessary causes that many decent Americans support and to which serious leadership ought to respond effectively."

Among the *Times* staffers Duke met with that day was the deputy editorial page editor Samuel T. Francis. In a column with the headline RESPECTABLE RACISM? Francis gave his own impressions of the Duke visit: "The interview [Duke] gave suggests that he has not only managed to separate himself from Klan-like racism but also formulated a message new to American politics, a message that might be called 'respectable racism.'"

> Mr. Duke, at least in his own mind, has managed to invent a new kind of racism that may become a new political creed. The distinguishing feature of that creed might be expressed as the acceptance of race as a biological and social reality, as opposed to the denial of race that both conservatives and liberals have endorsed . . . old political divisions between government and individual, permissiveness and traditional morality or communism and capitalism

> don't drive Mr. Duke's thinking or his appeal. What sits behind his wheel is the division between the races, a division Mr. Duke believes is at least partly biological, and what that division means in culture and politics.

For Francis, the political cachet of racial politics was enticing, even indispensable, as Jesse Helms's narrow victory over Harvey Gantt suggested. "It's interesting that Mr. Helms, despite a close contest with a black opponent, avoided racial issues like affirmative action in his campaign until last week. That may be why his campaign was floundering while Mr. Duke's flourished," he mused. "Conventional conservative themes such as Mr. Helms emphasized in most of his campaign may not attract voters anymore the way Mr. Duke's new racial appeal does."

Francis knew Helms. Prior to working at the *Times*, he had been a senior aide to John Porter East, the junior senator from the Tarheel State. (When East was elected in 1980, people joked that Helms was now "the liberal senator from North Carolina.") In the runup to the vote on making Martin Luther King Day a national holiday, Helms had taken to the Senate floor and read aloud a paper proposing that "King may have had an explicit but clandestine relationship with the Communist Party or its agents to promote, through his own stature, not the civil rights of blacks or social justice and progress, but the totalitarian goals and ideology of Communism." The author was Samuel Francis. Democratic senator Daniel Patrick Moynihan threw Helms's speech on the ground and stomped on it, calling it a "packet of filth."

Identifying the thinkers who helped transform the party of Reagan into the party of Trump may be an intellectual parlor game, but if anyone deserves a prominent spot on the list, it is likely Sam Francis, whose writings and advocacy would prove startlingly prescient as well as influential. He was born Samuel Todd Francis in 1947 to a well-to-do Presbyterian family in Chattanooga, Tennessee. His middle name marked his descent from the family of Mary Todd Lincoln, something to be proud of, even for his unreconstructed Southern clan, since the Todds had been slaveholders and Mary Todd's brothers fought for the Confederacy. Young Sam attended an all-boys prep school and military academy in Chattanooga before going to Johns Hopkins for his undergraduate degree and moving on to the University of North Carolina at Chapel Hill to pursue graduate studies in history. His dissertation was on the foreign policy of Edward Hyde, First Earl of Clarendon, a commoner who rose by his wits to become Lord Chancellor to Charles II during the Restoration. Revulsion at the New Left and the campus radicalism of the late 1960s and early '70s pushed Francis toward conservative politics. At Chapel Hill, he befriended two other grad students with right-wing sympathies, Thomas Fleming and Clyde Wilson, forming a circle that the novelist Walker Percy later dubbed "the Tarheel conspiracy." Fleming and Wilson founded the *Southern Partisan Quarterly Review*, intended to be a kind of neo-Confederate version of *The New Yorker* for the South. After *SPQR* folded, Fleming would go on to edit the conservative magazine *Chronicles*, which prominently featured Francis's writing.

While still completing his PhD, Francis took a job at the newly founded Heritage Foundation think tank in Washington, D.C., which was designed to be a Brookings Institution for the pugnacious heartland social conservatives that called themselves "the New Right." Francis's portfolio at Heritage was counterterrorism, focusing particularly on Soviet support for European and third world radical groups. With Reagan's election in 1980, Francis contributed the "Intelligence Community" section in the Heritage Foundation's *Mandate for Leadership*, the think tank's policy blueprint for the incoming administration. He recommended expanding domestic surveillance and investigation of the American left, including Tom Hayden and Jane Fonda's political action committee, Campaign for Economic Democracy, and the D.C.-based progressive think tank Institute for Policy Studies.

When Senator John East was elected on Reagan's coattails, he asked Francis to become his foreign policy adviser. East was an intellectual in his own right; he had been a political science professor at East Carolina University, and he wrote articles on Saint Augustine and the distinguished and idiosyncratic conservative philosopher Eric Voegelin. The junior senator from North Carolina secured a seat on the newly formed Judiciary Subcommittee on Security and Terrorism. This committee quickly attempted to orchestrate its own little Red Scare, hearing testimony from a Belgian aristocrat and former *Newsweek* correspondent turned spy novelist named Arnaud de Borchgrave (later editor of *The Washington Times*), who testified that the Soviet Union was undermining the West through a campaign of "manipulation of the Western media," naming such publications as *The Village Voice*, *Mother Jones*, *SoHo News*, and *The Progressive* as dupes of KGB disinformation. He gave no specific examples of disinformation, but the Senate Republican Conference ensured that tapes of the interview were sent to 290 radio stations, accompanied by a letter on United States Senate letterhead.

His teeth stained by a pack-a-day Pall Mall habit, Francis was described by one writer as a "fearsome toad." The columnist Joseph Sobran, in an otherwise affectionate remembrance for his friend, called him "alarmingly well fed" and remarked that "he reminded one of the character in P. G. Wodehouse who 'looked as if he had been poured into his suit and forgot to say "When!"'" Francis did not marry and lived a fairly lonely life, according to those who knew him. Those who considered him a friend and even sought closer intimacy often found that he was distant and would not reciprocate in kind. But despite his relentless pessimism, he possessed a cynical joviality and curmudgeonly sort of charm that endeared him to fellow Washington right-wingers. At times he could even completely disguise his views. "I sat there with him and chitchatted for a good length of time, very affably and pleasantly," recalled Allegra Bennett, a Black *Washington Times* editorial writer who worked with Francis. "His racism was not like a David Duke kind of racism, at least not in the kind of experience with him I had."

Glowering behind his thick glasses, Francis also had a temper. When a church group came to lobby Senator East to support sanctions against apartheid South Africa in 1985, they met with Francis. "If I had my way, I'd stomp people like you into the earth," he exploded in a profanity-laden tirade. The mild-mannered East reprimanded him, but kept him on as an aide. Francis took a special interest in wars of national liberation in Africa: unqualified support for apartheid South Africa against Nelson Mandela's African National Congress and the frontline states was a consistent part of Francis's Cold War policy prescriptions.

The term "New Right" was arguably more of a branding exercise than the designation of a coherent movement or ideology: in the 1970s, the direct mail fundraising maven Richard Viguerie had used the term to try to unify the single-issue campaigns conservatives were running against taxes, busing, the Equal Rights Amendment, abortion rights, and returning the Panama Canal. According to Viguerie, it also described a grassroots conservative backlash to Gerald Ford's naming Nelson Rockefeller, the ultimate Eastern Establishment liberal Republican, as his vice president in 1974. While the conservative movement had taken pains to portray itself as genteel and sophisticated—witness the witty sparring matches the *National Review* founder William F. Buckley held with liberal interlocutors on his talk show—the New Right base was proudly of a less patrician caste: evangelical preachers, self-made political entrepreneurs from the Sunbelt, and irate local activists. Though Ronald Reagan had long been a hero to the right, at the start of the 1980 campaign he was too soft for them: they preferred the hard-right Phil Crane or the bombastic John Connally as candidates. Still, they came around, and their mobilization helped propel Reagan into office.

While long on energy, mobilization, and organizational density, the groups that came to be lumped together as the New Right lacked an overarching intellectual vision. With the extensive use of direct mail fundraising using sensational and melodramatic appeals, they also had more than a touch of hucksterism and snake oil salesmanship clinging to them. But now they were on the verge of power. Their arrival in D.C. meant that they needed to class up the operation, make it look more serious. Francis was asked to provide an essay for a 1982 book that would do just that: *The New Right Papers.*

Francis's contribution to *The New Right Papers* was titled "Message from MARs: The Social Politics of the New Right"; it provided a grand—grandiose even—political theory and strategy to make the Reagan Revolution permanent. According to Francis, the New Right, "despite the incoherence of its name and sometimes of its message . . . is the political expression of a profound social movement that reflects the dynamics of American society and promises to dominate not only politically, but also perhaps socially and culturally." Borrowing a term from *The Radical Center: Middle Americans and the Politics of Alienation* (1976) by the sociologist Donald Warren, Francis identified this social movement with the interests of "Middle American Radicals," or "MARs." Although they were often white members of the lower middle class or "skilled and semi-skilled blue-collar workers," these MARs are "less an objectively identifiable class than a subjectively distinguished temperament." That attitude involved a sharp feeling of being exploited by and condescended to by the rich and having to foot the bill for minorities: "a sense of resentment and exploitation, mainly economic but also broader, that is directed upwards as well as downwards, . . . distrust of decision-makers in state and economy as well as fear of the economically depressed," and "the frustration of aspirations, . . . an alienation of loyalties and . . . a suspicion of established institutions, authorities, and values." These were the people who had voted for George Wallace's insurgent presidential campaigns of 1968 and 1972, they were Nixon's "Silent Majority," and the Reagan Democrats.

Francis interpreted the rise of Reagan and the late '70s explosion of social conservative activism to be a sign that the MARs aspired "to become the dominant political class in the United States by displacing the current elite, dismantling its apparatus of power, and discarding its political ideology." According to Francis, the reigning elite, which had held "political power since the 1930s," were the class of managers and bureaucrats necessitated by the mass scale of modern industry, politics, and culture. This class had displaced the old bourgeois ownership class with the help of FDR and the New Deal. Their legitimating ideology was cosmopolitan liberalism, which reflected "the material and psychological interests of a privileged, power-holding, and power-seeking sector of American society" and discredited the old bourgeois values as "backward, repressive and exploitative . . . outmoded, absolutist, puritanical, superstitious, and not infrequently hypocritical." The redistributive social liberalism of the New Dealers also "cemented an alliance not only among the different sectors of the new elite, but also between the new elite as a whole and the proletariat of American society—against the remnants of the old elite and an exploited and excluded middle class."

The managerial class, once ruthless and determined, had grown decadent and weak, so the MARs, who believed in "the duty of work rather than the right of welfare; the value of loyalty to concrete persons, symbols and institutions rather than cosmopolitan dispersion of loyalties," could overthrow the liberal elites and provide the nation "a discipline, a code of self-sacrifice for something larger than themselves, and a new purpose that are beyond the reach of the jaded, self-indulgent, increasingly corrupt elite of the present day." Francis believed this overturning would lead to a "cultural renaissance," as well as a morally and productively rejuvenated United States.

But what made Francis stand out from his fellow New Rightists was his abandonment of the idea of "conservatism" altogether. "Viewed in this sociopolitical perspective," he wrote, "the New Right is not a conservative force but a radical or revolutionary one." While the New Right's "social and cultural values are indeed conservative and traditionalist . . . unlike almost any other conservative group in history, it finds itself not only out of power in a formal sense but also excluded from the informal centers of real power. Consequently, the political style, tactics, and organizational forms of the New Right should find a radical, antiestablishment approach better adapted to the achievement of its goals." Although it would pursue a policy of "localization, privatization and decentralization" to degrade the power centers of the "managerial apparatus," Francis thought the New Right could not share much of the Old Right's dedication to laissez-faire, free market ideology: "MAR-Sunbelt interests require a strong governmental role in maintaining economic privileges for the elderly and for organized labor (where it now exists)" and "will also require (or demand) subsidization of construction and perhaps of characteristic Sunbelt enterprises (energy, defense and aerospace industries, and agriculture)." The smaller producers of this coalition would also "require protection against cheap imports and access to the raw materials and resources of the Third World, and they are less committed to international stability than to the continued predominance of the United States." Francis also believed that the old conservative preference for Congress and the courts should be abandoned, and the right should instead pursue what he called a "Caesarist" embrace of executive power: "The New Right will favor a populist-based presidency able to cut through the present oligarchical establishment . . . whose values and interests are hostile to the traditional American ethos and which is a parasitical tumor on the body of Middle America."

Francis's image of a United States under the domination of a managerial-bureaucratic regime originally derived from his primary intellectual guide, James Burnham. Before becoming a founding editor of *National Review*, a consultant for the CIA, and the right's master theorist of assertive anti-communism, Burnham had been a philosophy professor, a man of the left, a Marxist, and member of the Trotskyist movement. In the late 1930s he broke with Trotsky over the Old Man's insistence that the Soviet Union under Stalin remained a "worker's state" albeit a "deformed" one; Burnham had a different interpretation, which he described in his 1941 book *The Managerial Revolution*: civilization would not pass from capitalism to socialism under workers' control; instead a new exploitative ruling elite, the managerial class, was taking the reins of power the world over through their superintendence of growing state bureaucracies and corporations—Nazi Germany, Stalin's Russia, and FDR's New Deal America all reflected different manifestations of this tendency. Totalitarianism, not democracy, was the rising tide of world governance. Burnham predicted that nations as such would no longer exist; instead the globe would split into three massive power blocs, which would fight continuously. These dour prophesies profoundly influenced George Orwell's vision of a totalitarian future in *1984*.

Burnham's thought was essentially a revision of Marxism: the history of all hitherto existing society was not a class struggle that gave birth to ever higher stages of productive development, but simply the struggle of self-interested groups for dominance. New elites periodically emerged and, using a combination of force and fraud, coerced the masses into supporting their political conquests. To develop this "science of power," Burnham drew from a group of thinkers he called "the Machiavellians": these included Niccolò himself, but also the so-called Italian elite theorists of the late nineteenth and early twentieth centuries—Pareto, Michels, and Mosca—and the French heterodox socialist Georges Sorel. As Francis wrote in his 1984 monograph *Power and History: The Political Thought of James Burnham*, "Burnham and the Machiavellians saw politics—and to a large extent the human condition—in terms of savage and incessant struggle for power at all levels of society, regardless of how this struggle might be disguised by language, symbolism, and institutional forms." Driven by what Burnham called the "limitless human appetite for power" and "irrational beliefs," "men seek to dominate each other or to escape domination by others." As for democracy, it was just "a special kind of disguised oligarchy based on commercial and industrial power and not fundamentally different from earlier kinds of elitism."

According to Francis, what was notable and singularly important about Burnham's thought was what he called its "modernism": "Burnham's ideas, unlike those of virtually any other major American conservative thinker in this century, were profoundly modernist and at the same time counter-revolutionary." While the traditionalist conservatives diagnosed the spiritual and political decline of the West as a result of man's turning away from transcendent and absolute sources of moral order, Burnham recognized only an ongoing expression of man's appetite for power. And while traditionalists, taking their cues from Aristotle, Aquinas, and Burke, believed that man was naturally sociable and tended toward consensus, so long as there was the faithful transmission of an ethical tradition, Burnham saw only conflict. This bedrock belief in the "irrational" and violent core of man and the primacy of conflict over consensus and sociability put Burnham in the modernist tradition that included Machiavelli, Hobbes, Marx, Nietzsche, and Freud, as well as "the later sociobiologists who write of 'the imperial animal' and 'instincts of dominance.'"

Still, Burnham thought that his pessimistic worldview implied essentially conservative conclusions. Although he was inclined to grand visions of civilizational decadence, decline, and downfall, writing that "liberalism is the ideology of Western suicide," Burnham's politics of despair involved a realist acceptance of limitations and a resignation to hard reality, not wild defiance or the pursuit of treasons, stratagems, and spoils. Instead of inevitable catastrophe, he believed that when properly harnessed, natural instincts for power could form a system of mutually reinforcing checks and balances among elites that would generate some form of public good out of the very conflict of interests—not unlike James Madison's conception in "Federalist No. 10." In practice, Burnham favored neither radicals nor revolutionaries, but establishment, conventional, and center-leaning political figures like Nelson

Rockefeller or the French president Charles de Gaulle. Francis, on the other hand, believed that a proper reading of Burnham's reactionary modernism provided the key to a "more enduring victory" than anything envisioned by the soft, bourgeois sentimentalists of the conservative movement, whom he'd come to call "beautiful losers."

As the decade wore on, Francis's hopes for the New Right and Reaganism faded. He began to doubt it was capable of destroying the oligarchical elite and removing the "parasitical tumors" from the body politic, and he began to gaze deeper into the abyss for signs of revolutionary stirring. In the middle of the 1980s, a neo-Nazi group known as The Order or The Silent Brotherhood went on a killing spree that culminated in the 1984 assassination of the Jewish talk radio host Alan Berg outside his home. In 1985 Francis wrote a piece for *Chronicles*, "Revolution on the Right: The End of Bourgeois Conservatism," that interpreted the phenomenon of extreme-right terror groups like The Order—together with abortion clinic bombings and Bernard Goetz's vigilante shooting of four Black men on the New York subway—with ambivalent interest, if not outright sympathy. "The new militants," Francis wrote, "unlike the mainstream right, reject the old bourgeois order and, unlike the militants of the left, equally reject what is superseding the bourgeois system, the managerial regime of salaried technocrats and bureaucrats who promote a humanist and cosmopolitan myth." Drawing on Georges Sorel's theory of myth as animator of political action, Francis believed these militants were "in the process of articulating something that has never existed in America: a national myth, rising above and overshadowing private interests, to which a revolutionary right can adhere and for which its adherents would gladly spill their own blood and that of others." At the time Francis wrote this, his boss Senator East still sat on the Subcommittee on Security and Terrorism.

Wheelchair-bound from polio and suffering from hypothyroidism, John East committed suicide in 1986. Francis quickly found work at *The Washington Times* and became the clearest-eyed, most pugnacious writer on the editorial page, winning two American Society of Newspaper Editors Distinguished Writing Awards in 1989 and 1990. But despite his secure position and the recognition of his talents, Francis was increasingly alienated from the Republican Party and the mainstream of the conservative movement. A young conservative scholar interested in Burnham who visited Francis in D.C. for lunch to discuss the managerial theory was taken aback by Francis's frank extremism. "With a chuckle Francis referred to himself as 'a fascist,' pronounced the Italian way, 'FAH-shist.' I assumed he was joking," Francis's naive interlocutor recalled. He was certainly not joking when the topic turned to immigration. When told that Mexican Americans were "assimilating and intermarrying at the same rate as European immigrants had in the past" so that they were "not a threat to the continuity of American culture, Francis glowered and said emphatically, 'They are not our race!'"

As the 1980s drew to a close, the entire conservative movement seemed foundering on the shoals of fuck-all-to-do. Listlessness and infighting began to set in. Francis was not alone on the right in thinking of the Reagan years as something of a failure. Abortion was still legal, and prayer in school wasn't. There was still a welfare state. Reagan had amnestied illegal immigrants. The Iran-Contra scandal seemed to be soaking up all the administration's energy. In 1987, *The American Spectator* had a forum on "The Coming Conservative Crack-Up." The *Spectator*'s editor, R. Emmet Tyrell, author of *The Liberal Crack-Up*, asked readers forlornly, "As the Administration loses steam, we ask: Was it foreordained? Will life sour still more for conservatives?" The reliably rebarbative Joe Sobran, senior editor at *National Review*, wrote, "Reagan gave conservatism a beachhead in Washington, but he didn't follow through . . . The libs have sold the Administration on the myth which Reagan's victories should have demolished: that Republicans thrive by adopting 'moderation.'"

The sudden end of the Cold War and the collapse of the Soviet Union made everything worse. Militant anti-communism had long provided the glue that bound the various factions of the right together and gave them common purpose. The loss of the USSR was so traumatic that the John Birch Society went into full-blown denial: they insisted that the breakup of the Soviet Union was a KGB ploy to get the West to drop its guard. Who was to be the main enemy now? The answer increasingly was one another. As if following Burnham's pattern of churning elite conflict, the right was rapidly descending into its own bitter factional warfare.

The first signs of the divide had actually appeared in the heady days of Reagan's arrival in Washington, when it was time to divide the spoils of patronage, in this case the chairmanship of the National Endowment for the Humanities. A modest position compared with Washington, D.C.'s, great offices of state, it has the attraction of a considerable trough of funds to be distributed through grants. By directing money to favored subjects, a scholar in that role could help shape America's self-conception and at the same time reward his allies. In the fall of 1981 the scholar in question looked like it was going to be M. E. "Mel" Bradford, a friend and mentor of Francis's. Bradford, a Faulkner scholar from the University of Dallas in the Southern Agrarian tradition, had the backing of Senators Jesse Helms, John East, Strom Thurmond, Dan Quayle, and Orrin Hatch. In his corner was Edward Feulner, the president of the Heritage Foundation. He also had the support of intellectual luminaries from William F. Buckley to Russell Kirk, the Old Right godfather and author of *The Conservative Mind*.

Bradford had been a Democrat and a supporter of the insurgent campaigns of segregationist George Wallace before switching to the GOP to support Reagan's primary challenge to Gerald Ford in 1976. While campaigning for Reagan, Bradford became personally acquainted with the new president, another point in favor of his accession. But if he had become a Republican, he was certainly not reconstructed. In a 1976 essay in *Modern Age* titled "The Heresy of

Equality," Bradford railed against Abraham Lincoln's taking Jefferson's claim in the Declaration of Independence that "All men are created equal" as literally meaning what it said. He said that Lincoln's view was a "misunderstanding of the Declaration" that had unleashed "an endless series of turmoils and revolutions, all dedicated to freshly discovered meanings of equality as a 'proposition.'" For Bradford, "all men are created equal" designated simply that the colonies were on an equal footing with England as a sovereign nation. He called the doctrine of political and social equality a "millenarian infection spread and almost institutionalized by Lincoln," which originated among the Yankees in New England, "that 'other Israel' surrounding Boston."

The administration's decision to nominate Bradford elicited strong opposition from a different and ascendant faction of the Reagan coalition: neoconservative intellectuals such as Irving Kristol, cofounder of *The Public Interest*, and Norman Podhoretz, the editor of *Commentary*. Behind closed doors, Bradford's neoconservative foes persuaded the Reagan administration that his views were not appropriate for a high federal official in the party of Lincoln and that he would likely face defeat in Senate confirmation hearings, at which they would publicly oppose the Texan. In November 1981, the nomination was withdrawn. Bradford believed that the heads of the big philanthropic trusts that funded the conservative movement applied similar pressure to get Edward Feulner, the chairman of the Heritage Foundation, to retract his support. The battle probably had as much to do with securing the patronage bag as with ideas about what the Declaration meant. In Bradford's stead, the neocons proposed William Bennett, director of the independent National Humanities Center and a protégé of Irving Kristol and his wife, the historian Gertrude Himmelfarb. Whatever the true motivation of the actors, the battle lines of the Civil War recapitulated themselves in this miniature bureaucratic reenactment. For Samuel Francis and a small but growing number of others, Bradford's martyrdom at the hands of unscrupulous, grasping Yankees became part of a new "Lost Cause" myth and the source of a bitter grudge.

Conflict simmered between the two factions throughout the 1980s. For a group that identified itself as the Old Right, and eventually "paleoconservatives," the newcomers were barely real conservatives in the first place. Many of the neocons were former liberals who had only recently fled the Democratic Party out of disgust for the New Left and fear of the Black Power movement. Now they were increasingly monopolizing jobs and grant money, and even arrogating themselves the position of intellectual leaders of the movement. At a 1986 meeting of the conservative Philadelphia Society, now under the control of the vindictive Mel Bradford, the historian Stephen Tonsor pungently expressed the paleo disdain for the interlopers: "It is splendid when the town whore gets religion and joins the church. Now and then she makes a good choir director, but when she begins to tell the minister what he ought to say in his Sunday sermons, matters have been carried too far." Especially, Tonsor didn't have to say, when this town whore was probably a Jew.

These tribes huddled around their magazines, from whose pages they launched their printed missiles. The capital of neoconland was Norman Podhoretz's *Commentary*; major outposts were R. Emmet Tyrell's *The American Spectator* and Irving Kristol's *The National Interest*. In the paleo imagination, the Podhoretzes and Kristols were like two great feudal clans that would shower fellowship money on loyal retainers. The prominence of these two Jewish families in the conservative movement fed darker fantasies, too. Hawkeyed for signs of antisemitism, even self-identified neoconservatives—who by no means were all Jewish—came to regard the epithet "neocon" as a code word for "Jew." The fact that it definitely sometimes did mean "Jew" in the minds of their opponents did not help assuage their paranoia.

The paleos, as they were the first to point out, were not so well-endowed as their rivals. They had neither riches nor title: the coterie originally had no name of its own. The term "paleoconservative" was offered by one of their leading intellectuals, Paul Gottfried, as a way of defining themselves against the neocons, so deeply did negativity penetrate the very heart of their self-conception. Their relative poverty fed an already considerable bitterness. Dr. Gottfried obsessively documented the neoconservative stranglehold on the "Four Sisters"—the John M. Olin Foundation, the Lynde and Harry Bradley Foundation, the Sarah Scaife Foundation, and the Smith Richardson Foundation—which provided the conservative movement with its needed infusions of cash. What the paleos did have was one little think tank, the Rockford Institute, located in the far northern reaches of Illinois. Rockford produced the magazine *Chronicles*, edited by Francis's friend Thomas Fleming—formerly *Chronicles of Culture*, which in the 1970s had more subscribers than Buckley's *National Review*. Also in the paleo archipelago were the anti-immigration–focused *The Social Contract* and the highbrow *Modern Age*, founded in the early 1950s by Russell Kirk. Though the paleos may have been poorer in funding, they did have one big bruiser in their corner: Pat Buchanan, by the dawn of the '90s probably America's most prominent conservative; a veteran of the Reagan and Nixon White Houses, he was a panelist on *The McLaughlin Group* and had his own nationally syndicated column and CNN show.

These factions maneuvered for control and influence over the central nervous system of the conservative movement—the Heritage Foundation, with its ever-growing coffers, and *National Review*, from which William F. Buckley wielded pontifical powers of excommunication. *National Review* had grown closer to the neoconservatives in the age of Reagan and Bush, but it still published prominent paleos.

Two different visions of America divided these sects, or, to be more precise, two different versions of Americana. The neoconservatives largely still upheld the liberal mythos of America as the land of Lincoln and FDR. Self-consciously the sons and grandsons of immigrants, they championed the America of Ellis Island and the Statue of Liberty. They viewed the accomplishments of the civil rights movement as a point of national pride, even if they had a limited notion of it and often worked against the consolidation of its gains. They mostly believed that some form of the welfare state should exist, although significantly pared back from Great Society excess. Some were realists about foreign policy, but many believed that the United States had an obligation to spread democracy around the world—even at the point of a bayonet. To the paleos, the neos were just more representatives of the liberal modernity that they despised. And the neoconservative migration to the right seemed a microcosmic repetition of the larger demographic changes to the country that the paleos decried. "The offensives of radicalism have driven vast hordes of liberals across the border into our territories. These refugees speak in our name, but the language they speak is the same one they always spoke," wrote Clyde Wilson, Francis's Tarheel conspiracy comrade. To Francis, the neocons were just "the right wing of the New Class" of managers and technocrats "engaged in an effort to moderate its collectivist and utopian dynamic with a strong dose of bourgeois liberalism." Francis and his peers had come so close to power, only to see it snatched away by these upstarts.

Pat Buchanan had a soft spot for the idyllic 1950s, but for the most part the whole postwar period was a scandal to the paleo mind. They traced their lineage to isolationist, prewar America Firsters. The New Deal, the Second World War, the civil rights movement, the Great Society, immigration, the New Left, the Vietnam War, opposition to the Vietnam War—all these things were deeply regrettable to the paleos and had changed American society almost beyond recognition. If the neocons held up mid-century New York as the height of U.S. civilization, the paleos wanted to go much further back: to the 1920s at least, and preferably back to the nineteenth century, to the world before Lincoln and the Civil War. While the neocons upheld statistical research and the social sciences, the paleo intellectuals were mostly humanists who detested "managerial" technocracy.

The paleo aesthetic was American Gothic: white-sided Presbyterian and Congregational churches in small towns; stern, industrious folk; farmers, homesteaders, and frontiersmen. Added to this was the myth of the gallant South and the Lost Cause. Many were Catholic traditionalists, but they praised the character-annealing rigors of the Protestant ethic. In the paleo junk shop of discarded historical forms, the dour Puritan Roundhead made a strange peace with the chivalrous Southern cavalier. Their imagination resembles nothing so much as the rainy-day transports of a boy who lines up all his toy soldiers from different periods in a grand alliance—here's a knight, there's a cowboy, here's Davy Crockett, there's a Special Forces commando. And for all its eclectic-yet-selective evocations of white civilizational virtue, the movement's sentimentalism and romance was also steeped in Spenglerian gloom: the writing of this cohort of paleo thinkers is shot through with a deep cynicism, even nihilism, and a hard-hearted notion of power that questions democracy itself.

The balance of the decade saw periodic skirmishes between paleos and neos. Many of these scraps had to do with reflexive neoconservative support of Israel and paleoconservative charges of "dual loyalty," and consequent neoconservative suspicion of paleoconservative antisemitism. "Not seldom it has seemed as if some eminent neo-conservatives mistook Tel Aviv for the capital of the United States—a position they will have difficulty in maintaining as matters drift," Russell Kirk said in a speech at the Heritage Foundation. Midge Decter, chair of the Committee for the Free World and the wife of Norman Podhoretz, labeled Kirk's remark "a bloody piece of anti-Semitism." The columns of the Catholic traditionalist Joseph Sobran, William F. Buckley's protégé and a senior editor at *National Review*, also generated neoconservative *tsuris*. Sobran had developed what neoconservatives felt was an obsessive focus on criticizing Israel. In a 1985 column defending Ronald Reagan's controversial visit to the Bitburg cemetery in Germany, where Waffen-SS soldiers were buried, Sobran spoke of the "Jewish lobby" ginning up the fracas and wrote that *The New York Times* "really ought to change its name to *Holocaust Update*." In 1986, in his nationally syndicated column, Sobran recommended the white supremacist magazine *Instauration* to his readers, saying that it "faces the harder facts about race" and was "often brilliant, covering a beat no one will touch and doing so with wide-ranging observation and bitter wit. It is openly hostile to blacks, Jews, and Mexican and Oriental immigrants . . . It assumes a world of Hobbesian conflict at the racial level: every race against every race." (Sobran was returning a compliment—in 1985, *Instauration* wrote that Sobran, almost alone among conservatives, "has repeatedly defended white racial pride and solidarity.") In another syndicated column he wrote, "If Christians were sometimes hostile to Jews, that worked two ways. Some rabbinical authorities held that it was permissible to cheat and even kill Gentiles. Although the great theologian Moses Maimonides insisted it was as wrong to kill a Gentile as a Jew, it seems strange that this should even have been a matter of controversy." Midge Decter and Norman Podhoretz protested to Buckley. In 1985 he asked Sobran to stop writing about Israel, and while defending him from the charge of outright antisemitism, he acknowledged that one might "reasonably conclude that those columns were written by a writer inclined to anti-Semitism," and he distanced himself from "what we view as the obstinate tendentiousness of Joe Sobran's recent columns." For the time being, the neocons seemed satisfied.

Efforts to broker peace between the factions would not last. A new skirmish would involve Richard John Neuhaus, a Lutheran pastor and future Catholic priest who had been a civil rights activist and opponent of the Vietnam War before turning toward neoconservatism. Neuhaus had received a New York–based fellowship from the paleo-aligned Rockford Institute, publisher of *Chronicles*, and came to question his benefactor. In 1989 Neuhaus wrote a memo to Allan Carlson, the president of Rockford, complaining that *Chronicles* was edging into nativism and antisemitism with its "running polemic against those whom the reader is invited to view as rootless, deracinated, and cosmopolitan elites." The pastor had also overheard *Chronicles*'s editor Fleming make an "insensitive remark" about people with AIDS; Neuhaus said to him, "How can you say that, when we all have so many close friends who have been struck down by this terrible disease?" "Close friends?"

retorted Fleming. "I don't know anyone who has AIDS. I don't know anyone who knows anyone who has AIDS." After Carlson received Neuhaus's missive, five members of Rockford flew in from Illinois and put the Reverend Neuhaus out on the street: they raided his office and dumped his boxes and garbage bags full of his personal effects on Madison Avenue. The debacle even made the front page of *The New York Times*: MAGAZINE DISPUTE REFLECTS U.S. RIGHT.

But it was in the run-up to the Gulf War that the split appeared to be made fully irreparable. In August 1990 Saddam Hussein, the dictator of Iraq, invaded neighboring Kuwait, annexing the country. The United States rapidly deployed troops to Saudi Arabia in what was called a "defensive" action to prevent a possible Iraqi invasion of the kingdom. The Soviet Union under Mikhail Gorbachev showed no desire to defy the United States, and President Bush spoke of a "New World Order" where the superpowers would cooperate to uphold global security. That same August, panelists on *The McLaughlin Group* debated possible military intervention to remove Saddam Hussein from Kuwait; Pat Buchanan uttered the words that launched a thousand op-eds: "There are only two groups that are beating the drums for war in the Middle East—the Israeli Defense Ministry and its amen corner in the United States." "Those are fighting woooords," McLaughlin squawked. Indeed, they were. Buchanan named four Jews in favor of action against Saddam Hussein—A. M. Rosenthal, Richard Perle, Henry Kissinger, and Charles Krauthammer. As Bill Buckley pointed out later, he could've named Alexander Haig, George Will, Frank Gaffney Jr., or James Jackson Kilpatrick, but didn't. On another episode of *McLaughlin*, Buchanan called Congress "Israel-occupied territory," coming perilously close to the "Zionist Occupied Government" canard spoken of by neo-Nazis. The insinuations were off base: far from being an Israel lover, H. W. Bush represented an old tradition of WASP pro-Arabism. Although the neocons certainly joined the chorus for war, his foreign policy team was driven not by neoconservative pro-democracy idealists, but by a brutally realist conception of national power; they explicitly wanted to secure access to Kuwait and Saudi Arabia's oil supply. And, as would later be uncovered, the real backroom lobbying effort in favor of the war was done (in some cases illegally) by agents of the Kuwaiti monarchy, not the Jewish state. On top of that, the prospect of war was not just relished by Israel's "amen corner," but by much of the American public.

The New York Times's venerable Abe Rosenthal, executive editor emeritus, let loose in his column. Accusing Buchanan of antisemitism—"blood libel," even—he brought up the whole litany of offenses of Good Old Pat. Patrick J. had indeed been at it for years: while still at the White House, he defended the good name of John Demjanjuk, the retired Ukrainian American autoworker accused by U.S. prosecutors of being a concentration camp guard who'd gassed hundreds of thousands at Treblinka, even going so far as questioning whether gassings on that scale were possible. When the United States apologized to France for sheltering the Gestapo chief Klaus Barbie, Buchanan wrote, "To what end, all this wallowing in the atrocities of a dead regime?" He had encouraged Reagan to lay a wreath during his Bitburg cemetery visit so as not to be seen as "succumbing to the pressure of the Jews." When Cardinal John O'Connor apologized for Catholic antisemitism, Buchanan wrote, "If U.S. Jewry takes the clucking appeasement of the Catholic cardinalate as indicative of our submission, it is mistaken."

Rosenthal merely alluded to all these episodes rather than quoting Buchanan in detail. The column was widely seen as long on emotion and short on evidence; old Abe's harpoon had missed its mark. Even liberals rose to defend Pat. It probably did not help that the neoconservatives had developed such a hair-trigger response to accusations of antisemitism that their charges no longer shocked.

From his column at the New York *Daily News*, William F. Buckley tried to arbitrate a peace. Calling both columnists his friends, he said that Rosenthal was known for his "footloose emotional gyrations" and had "gone ballistic," while Buchanan was probably just "attracted to mischievous generalizations." Buckley attempted to turn the matter into a condescending parable of ethnic tolerance. "The Buchanans need to understand the nature of sensibilities in an age that coexisted with Auschwitz. And the Rosenthals need to understand that clumsy forensic manners are less than a genocidal offense." Buckley failed to calm things down. Buchanan fired back that he was being smeared, and the arrows flew.

Opposition to war in the Persian Gulf brought Joe Sobran, Sam Francis, and Pat Buchanan together. All three of them had once been Cold War hawks. Francis had even once hoped that the United States would adopt a more bellicose stance toward noncommunist Third World dictators if they defied America. Now they responded to Bush's war by rejecting "globalism," "utopian internationalism," and "the diminution of our national sovereignty and independence and . . . absorption into some other, non-American entity" represented by the intervention in the Gulf, according to Francis. They started to meet at the Hunan Lion in McLean, Virginia. In his cups, Sobran, a former English professor, would regale his cronies by acting out scenes from Laurence Olivier's version of *Richard III*—no doubt to the bewilderment of their fellow patrons. One can't imagine that he skipped the famous "Winter of our discontent" soliloquy: "To entertain these fair well-spoken days, I am determined to prove a villain."

The trio would repeat this dinner date every month for a decade. Their columns began to echo each other. Buchanan: "If communism was the god that failed the Lost Generation, democracy, as ideal form of government, panacea for mankind's ills, hope of the world, may prove the Golden Calf of this generation." Sobran: "Now that democracy has overthrown communism, we can turn to the problem of how to overthrow democracy." Francis: "Serious conservatives ought to ponder . . . whether the failure of the Reagan experiment means that conventional conservative policies can be implemented in a mass democracy." And Francis and Sobran urged their friend, who had flirted with the idea in 1988, to run for president.

3

CHAOS AND OLD NIGHT

By the fall of 1991, Operation Desert Storm was a quickly fading memory. The country experienced the war—which involved no draft and was only a month and a half long—on television. And unlike with Vietnam, there were no gory images of wounded soldiers being medevacked from the rice paddies; the footage of missiles being guided neatly to their targets gave the audience mostly just the rocket's red glare and bombs bursting in air. In the national consciousness, Saddam Hussein's ouster from Kuwait had the staying power of a made-for-TV movie.

Now America was in the midst of economic contraction. At first the Bush administration tried to deny that there even was a recession, and then they declared it was over months before it had peaked. From his Gulf War high of 89 percent, Bush's approval rating sank below 50 percent.

How had all of this happened? The country's '80s-era growth had been fueled by debt. Driven by a wave of deregulation in the early part of the decade, lenders had aggressively sought out new markets. Wall

Street created new instruments for financing massive corporate takeovers, issuing "speculative grade" bonds—or junk bonds—as miracle funds. Real estate was booming; banks freely lent to developers who couldn't borrow fast enough. By the mid-'80s, some banks had 50 to 60 percent of their portfolios tied up in commercial real estate. As the FDIC put it in their postmortem, "Prices soared, construction skyrocketed and banks seemed prosperous." Then everything went south.

First, the thrifts started to collapse. Thrifts, or savings and loans, had once been modest financial institutions that helped middle-income people deposit their savings and get a mortgage. Think of Jimmy Stewart's Bailey Brothers Building and Loan in *It's a Wonderful Life*. Thrifts had existed since the nineteenth century, but the industry grew as a result of the New Deal regulatory regime created in response to the Great Depression. The thinking was that they would provide low-cost loans to working people, encourage homeownership and housing construction, and be generally more community-focused and less profit-oriented than banks. Many S&Ls had a mutual ownership structure, meaning that their depositors were also their owners, an arrangement thought by thrift boosters to encourage responsible citizenship. Bound by law to serve their locality, they could not lend beyond a certain geographic limit. They were tightly supervised by the federal government to exclusively encourage homeownership and saving—and to prevent management from self-dealing—and thus were prevented from making speculative loans. They were also protected from competition and had a comfortable niche in mortgage lending. All in all, they formed part of the patchwork of federal programs and consumer finance that served as a substitute for a welfare state. When the Fed jacked interest rates up in the late 1970s and '80s to combat inflation, thrifts began to have to pay out more to savers than they were taking in through mortgages, which created an unsustainable situation. They struggled and began to fail, so the Reagan administration, with broad bipartisan and financial industry support, deregulated them. One major change was altering the mutual structure, so that a single person could own a thrift. Only federal regulators, now much less strict, would know what they were doing. At the same time as deregulating their lending practices, the federal government fully guaranteed thrift deposits, increasing their managements' appetite for risk. The Federal Savings and Loan Insurance Corporation (FSLIC) guaranteed even more deposits than the more well-known FDIC.

The S&Ls got into speculative schemes like leveraged buyouts, junk bonds, and commercial real estate and appeared to make a fantastic turnaround. The magic of the market seemed to work on the old, dowdy thrifts; new ones mushroomed up all over the country. The S&L business suddenly attracted the elite of the elite, including the offspring of big-name politicians, such as New York governor Mario Cuomo's son Andrew and Vice President George H. W. Bush's son Neil. The promise of easy cash and loose regulation also attracted organized crime members, who were just as eager to get their hands on the free-flowing, federally guaranteed bucks. The competitive structure of the market itself was "crimogenic"; unscrupulous and risky business practices became de rigueur, the only way to maximize profits or, as time wore on, to hide losses. Under the surface, thrifts had billions of dollars in bad loans on their books; some had been totally looted by their management; many were insolvent, "zombie" institutions, but cover-ups and regulatory forbearance allowed them to keep going for years. At the end of the '80s they began to die by the thousands, creating the largest mass failure of financial institutions since the Depression. By some measures, close to half of failed thrifts showed signs of criminal activity by their management. The collapses overwhelmed their deposit insurance and emptied the coffers of the FSLIC: taxpayers would have to pick up the check; since their deposits were federally guaranteed, taxpayers bailed them out. The widespread fraud, as well as the deep involvement of politicians and the politically connected, created an air of corruption that enraged the public, which was already put off by having to pay for all this. Five United States senators came under scrutiny for helping the thrift owner Charles Keating avoid an investigation by federal regulators in exchange for campaign support and gifts. But the retrospective remarks of a former member of Reagan's Commission on Housing could well apply to the entire economy: "What happened to create the disgusting and expensive spectacle of a diseased industry was that the government, confronted with a difficult problem, found a false solution that made the problem worse."

Then Iraq's invasion of Kuwait in 1990 sent a shock through the system: oil prices soared, and the bottom fell out of the already stalling real estate market. A credit crunch set in; unemployment rose. Fearing the stagflation of the '70s, the Fed kept high interest rates in place. Foreclosures and bankruptcies started to pile up. Banks, which had also gotten in on the commercial real estate bubble, began to collapse by the hundreds.

There were two great symbols of the '80s debt craze: junk-bond wizard Michael Milken and Donald Trump. By November 1991, Milken was in jail for financial fraud for unloading worthless junk bonds on naive or corrupt S&L managers and Trump was going bankrupt, defaulting on his payments for his Taj Mahal Casino in Atlantic City. Trump appeared before the House Budget Subcommittee on Urgent Fiscal Issues and told Congress, "I truly feel that this country right now is in a depression. It's not a recession. People are kidding themselves if they think it's a recession." Characteristic hyperbole no doubt, but from where Trump sat, it could certainly look that way. Employment fell by 10 percent in New York between 1990 and 1992, with real estate jobs particularly hard hit.

Polls were looking worse and worse for Bush—70 percent disapproved of the way he was handling the economy. The time was approaching for Buchanan to make his move. While covering a David Duke rally in Evangeline, Louisiana, for TV, Buchanan was mobbed by Duke supporters who urged him to run.

In an October 23 column, after David Duke pulled past Buddy

Roemer in the primary, Buchanan laid out the strategy the Republicans should use to co-opt the insurgent. "The way to deal with Mr. Duke is the way the GOP dealt with the far more formidable challenge of George Wallace. Take a hard look at Duke's portfolio of winning issues and expropriate those not in conflict with GOP principles." Buchanan continued: "In the hard times in Louisiana, Mr. Duke's message comes across as Middle Class, meritocratic, populist, and nationalist." He urged Bush "to take a hard look at illegal immigration, tell the U.S. Border Patrol to hire some of those vets being mustered out after Desert Storm, veto the Democrats' 'quota bill,' and issue an executive order rooting out any and all reverse discrimination in the U.S. government, beginning with the FBI."

Two days after Buchanan's column came out, the White House and the Democratic leadership in the Senate agreed on a compromise version of the Civil Rights Act. In his next week's column, Pat was apoplectic: "Using the totemic term 'fairness,' neo-socialists have effected an immense transfer of wealth from producers to a parasitic government. Elected by small business and Middle America, this administration has betrayed both. It is today the willing accomplice of Big Government, providing liberalism with political cover as it gradually extends its vast dominion." On the phone with his sister Angela "Bay" Buchanan, Pat made up his mind. "He kept going on and on about neoconservatives," Bay later told Pat's biographer. "I couldn't see how any of it matters, but he was obsessed."

"It's a go," Bay told *The Washington Times* in mid-November; the paper put the announcement on page A1. "His platform in many ways is expected to parallel that of Louisiana state Rep. David Duke, a former Ku Klux Klan wizard, who is in a surprisingly close race for governor of his state," the article noted. The White House tried to act blasé. "Oh, the bug bites everyone once in a while," the president joked. Said White House press secretary Marlin Fitzwater, "We had a Buchanan once."

Behind the scenes, they were trying furiously to get reporters to connect Buchanan to Duke and antisemitism. "I find it astonishing," Buchanan hit back, "that these White House mites who had complained just two weeks ago that people were calling George Bush the father of David Duke are now calling me his brother. I certainly reject everything I have read about what David Duke said and did in the past." In the meantime, Duke lost his shot at governor.

Before Buchanan could officially announce his candidacy, Duke announced his on December 5 at the National Press Club in New York. Forsaking the Populist Party, he said that this time he would run as a Republican. An ACT UP activist shouted from the crowd, "Nazi, Nazi, you're a goddamn Nazi." Rabbi Avi Weiss of Riverdale jumped on stage with a sign that said DAVID DUKE: NAZI FOR THE '90S. They were ejected. In his remarks, Duke presented himself as the conservative alternative to Bush, saying that he had put his youthful "intolerance" behind him. Then he said that the United States should tell Japan, "You no buy our rice, we no buy your cars." He said he would contest the GOP primary in every state except New Hampshire, where the first primary was coming up on February 18, 1992.

It was in the sullen North that Buchanan wanted to make his stand. New England was particularly hard hit by the recession: the real estate bubble burst there before it hit the rest of the country. One *Boston Globe* columnist called New Hampshire "the Willy Loman of our states: small, pushed-around, insignificant in the long run, crowded to the edge and the back row when anyone talks about the Big Picture." And as for Willy, the glory days were past, and what was left was hollow and humiliating. Sanguine developers had built too much retail space in Nashua; now the empty shopping centers and stores glutted the market.

By the end of 1991, unemployment in the Granite State was above the national average, and bankruptcies were up by 86 percent since the previous year—they had grown by 538 percent since 1985. The FDIC had to bail out five of New Hampshire's biggest banks, and twelve more failed outright: some 25 percent of all New Hampshire banking assets were on the books of the banks that collapsed. There were larger forces at work, too: globalization was winding down a textile industry that had grown up with the Industrial Revolution, and the end of the Cold War was killing defense jobs. Pease Air Force Base closed, the Portsmouth Naval Shipyard laid off 700 workers and threatened to lay off 1,800 more, and Sanders of Nashua, which built the radar jammers that allowed the air force to rule the skies over Iraq, laid off 1,200 workers, more than a third of its workforce. New Hampshire was set to lose more than 20,000 jobs for the third year in a row. Former white-collar professionals found themselves forced into doing manual municipal labor to pay off loans from local welfare officials.

"I was in Nashua yesterday at a job-training center," a reporter who covered New Hampshire for *The Boston Globe* told a colleague. "To see these 50- and 60-year-old engineers who've been laid off. By now, they've run through everything—their savings, what they could borrow on the house, their IRAs. And no one will hire them. What are they supposed to do? Spend the next 10 years on the dole? When they used to be 70-thousand-dollar-a-year engineers? Or are they supposed to compete with 18-year-olds for service jobs?"

In the mid-1980s, Sharon and Wendell Rouse of Troy, New Hampshire, had bought a house and a camper and started a construction business with easy-flowing credit. Sharon, a bird lover, bought nearly a hundred exotic birds and edited a popular newsletter on bird keeping. By 1990 the Rouses were $195,854 in debt, had lost their house, and declared bankruptcy. They were supporting two children on less than $7,700 a year, most of it from food stamps, workers' comp, and temporary jobs, and they were struggling to find a place to live. The town gave them a $40 food voucher; in return Wendell had to put in hours at the Troy recycling plant. An army veteran, he'd been swept with patriotic fervor during the Persian Gulf War, flew a large

American flag in his front yard, and tried to reenlist; he was too old. "I'm proud to be American," Rouse said. There wasn't much else to feel proud about. "You learn to be humble," Sharon told the *Globe*. "And someday you hope you'll get out of it."

At his home in the tony D.C. suburb of McLean, Virginia, Pat Buchanan plotted his northern campaign with the who's who of the righty set. The direct mail mavens who had ginned up the populist groundswell for Reagan, such as the Heritage Foundation founder Paul Weyrich and Richard Viguerie, rubbed shoulders with enthusiastic College Republicans. Bay Buchanan would manage the campaign, and its central committee would be called the America First Committee. As the crowd at Buchanan's confab died down, Sam Francis took Pat aside. "I told him privately that he would be better off without all the hangers-on, direct-mail artists, fund-raising whiz kids, marketing and PR czars, and the rest of the crew that today constitutes the backbone of all that remains of the famous 'Conservative Movement.'"

"These people are defunct," Francis remembered telling Buchanan. "You don't need them, and you're better off without them. Go to New Hampshire and call yourself a patriot, a nationalist, an America Firster, but don't even use the word 'conservative.' It doesn't mean anything anymore."

It would be difficult, impossible really, for Buchanan to drop the label "conservative." Buckley was his hero, and reading the early *National Review* had been almost a spiritual experience for the young Catholic. "My first reaction was not unlike that of John Keats 'On First Looking into Chapman's Homer,'" Buchanan wrote in his memoir, *Right from the Beginning*. "There was nothing within the pages of Bill Buckley's blue-bordered magazine with which I disagreed . . . What *National Review* did was take the word *conservatism*, then a synonym for stuffy orthodoxy, Republican stand-pat-ism and economic self-interest, and convert it into the snapping pennant of a fighting faith." Buchanan had been educated by Jesuits, "the Pope's Marines," for whom anti-communism was practically a sacrament.

As a young man, he certainly put the fighting into "fighting faith." Toughness, pugilism, aggression, and bellicosity were the cardinal virtues in the Buchanan household in Washington, D.C. His father, an accountant, hero-worshipped Joe McCarthy, General Douglas MacArthur, and Generalissimo Francisco Franco. Pat was one of nine children. Buchanan and Bros. became a firm of roving hooligans, graduating from terrorizing neighborhood children and crashing house parties to more serious affrays. "Pop," a strict disciplinarian who would avail himself of the belt, did not punish his boys for fighting; if they came home bruised and bloodied, he was just curious to know if they had acquitted themselves well. Buchanan boasts that he and his brothers beat a man so severely they had to "hold him up," presumably to finish up his working over. Later, sitting in the police station, Buchanan caught sight of the man, who, on his telling, had been the aggressor: "His appearance made it all worthwhile. His face was almost unrecognizable and he had a thick bandage covering a wound on the back of his head. Which had, we were told, been opened up by some sharp instrument, perhaps a beer can."

The Buchanan horde also possessed a tribal consciousness, which their Jewish neighbors, the Bernsteins, would feel the brunt of. When Harry Bernstein drove over to complain about the Buchanan boys playing football in the yard at midnight, the boys nearly tipped over his car, with cries of "Get the Jews!" Harry called the cops. Later that night, beer bottles rained down on the Bernstein house. Harry's daughter Karen told Buchanan's biographer, "They didn't like the Jews. There's no question about it . . . They would call us 'Dirty Jew.'"

At not quite thirty years old, Buchanan left his job as an editorial writer for the *St. Louis Globe-Democrat* to work for the Nixon campaign. Then he followed Nixon into the White House, serving as speechwriter and the conservative movement's virtual attaché. Most conservatives of the Buckleyite ilk distrusted Nixon: to them, he was a moderate, an opportunist. Buchanan even called him "the least ideological statesman I ever encountered." But he formed a filial bond with Nixon, referring to him as "the Old Man." Nixon may have been pragmatic, but to Buchanan he also *represented* something: Middle America, the forgotten man, the hopes and aspirations of the "silent majority"—a phrase Buchanan coined. The Watergate crisis was an attempt by the establishment to reverse the will of the true American people, but it was also a missed chance to act decisively, to make a countercoup on behalf of the people. He called it "the lost opportunity to move against the political forces frustrating the expressed national will." The lesson was that a more ideologically reliable statesman was needed: "To effect a political counterrevolution in the capital . . . there is no substitute for a principled and dedicated Man of the Right in the Oval Office." In 1985, he at last got a chance to serve a Man of the Right when he became communications director under Reagan. He interpreted the Iran-Contra scandal as another attempt by the establishment to do in a Republican president à la Watergate. For real righties like Pat, the Reagan Revolution had stalled out. Although he admired and honored the man as he had Nixon, Buchanan envisioned an expansive frontier beyond Gipperism: "The greatest vacuum in American politics," he said, "is to the right of Ronald Reagan."

Buchanan delivered his announcement speech on December 10, 1991, at the State House in Concord, New Hampshire. The room was thronged with reporters and Pat's backers. In an unusually highbrow stump speech, Buchanan seemed to attack Francis Fukuyama as much as Bush. He declared that victory in the Cold War had "not brought with it an end to history," declaiming that "beyond these shores, a new world is being born for which our government is unprepared, and we are unprepared. The dynamic force shaping that world is nationalism." He called for "a new nationalism" that would put "America first"—meaning, he said, that "our Western heritage is going to be handed down to future generations, not dumped onto some land fill called multi-culturalism." It also meant that in "in every negotiation, be it arms control or trade, the American side seeks advantage and victory for the United States."

The appearance of "nationalism" in the "Far East" was a cause for concern: "The rising economic power of Japan has filed a claim to displace the United States as the dominant power of the 21st Century." Buchanan warned against the lumping of "ancient states" into international organizations like the European Community: "A Conservative prime minister is today being pressed to lead the Mother of Parliaments into yielding up to bureaucrats in Brussels what generations of British soldiers fought to preserve. We Americans must not let that happen here. We must not trade in our sovereignty for a cushioned seat at the head table of anyone's New World Order."

Buchanan raised the image of a Washington, D.C., invaded by the establishment, calling for a Reconquista: "The people of this country need to recapture our capital city from an occupying army of lobbyists, and registered agents of foreign powers hired to look out for everybody and everything except the national interest of the United States." He painted Bush as "a man of graciousness, honor, and integrity" but also as a clueless has-been: "He is yesterday and we are tomorrow. He is a globalist and we are nationalists. He believes in some Pax Universalis; we believe in the Old Republic. He would put American's wealth and power at the service of some vague New World Order; we will put America first. So, to take my party back and take our country back, I am today declaring my candidacy for the Republican nomination for the President of the United States."

As at Duke's announcement, the spirit of conflict roiled the crowd. An ACT UP activist started to shout, "Fight back! Fight AIDS!" Buchanan's special events coordinator and a supporter tackled the man and dragged him outside. From the podium, Buchanan told his followers, "Be gentle with him." A man in the crowd yelled, "I have AIDS and I don't hold those beliefs at all." Buchanan: "When I came up to New Hampshire, I had a sense of nostalgia for 1968 and my friend here made it sorta complete. The demonstrators are still here." While the protester lay on the ground outside, Buchanan's state campaign chief stood over him and said, "Every time you come here, this is what you are going to get. Tell your friends."

Buchanan had an uphill fight. Polls showed him in the 20s in New Hampshire; he would have to get about 35–40 percent of the vote to qualify even as a viable protest candidate. Just about the same time Pat gave his announcement speech, a special issue of *National Review* was reaching subscribers. Almost all of it was dedicated to a long essay by William F. Buckley titled "In Search of Anti-Semitism"; Joe Sobran and Pat Buchanan were the main subjects, along with Gore Vidal and *The Dartmouth Review*. Five years after his first rebuke of Joe Sobran, with his characteristic opaqueness and logic-chopping, Buckley hemmed and hawed his way through the evidence and finally concluded, "I find it impossible to defend Pat Buchanan against the charge that what he did and said during the period under examination amounted to anti-Semitism, whatever it was that drove him to say and do it: most probably, an iconoclastic temperament." Buckley called the linkage some made between Buchanan and Duke "morally irresponsible." Once again, Pat's liberal friends rose to defend him. "As a Jew, I never felt any hostility from Buchanan on that score, never heard him make a disparaging remark about Jews, never noticed any difference in the way he treats Jews and non-Jews," wrote Michael Kinsley of *The New Republic*, Pat's opposite number on CNN's *Crossfire*.

Hitting the shows the day after his announcement, Buchanan flipped the script on Duke. He told NBC's *Today*, "David Duke, I think, has been reading a lot of my past columns and if he keeps it up and keeps stealing my themes, I think we're going to go down to Louisiana and sue him for intellectual property theft." (This is the man who wrote a column calling for Republicans to "expropriate" Duke.) Duke was playing in a different league now: if he was pretty good at TV, Buchanan was an absolute master. He knew how to dominate panels, deal with interviewers; he gave reporters total access, and he went to every campaign stop mic'ed up so they'd get everything. He knew how to show a softer side to the cameras. At a campaign event at a mall in Manchester, Buchanan sat down next to a man in fatigues who was unemployed and apparently homeless, telling the man that if the cameras intimidated him, he could send them away. The man said they did. But Buchanan didn't send them away; he asked the man about being unemployed, asked if he was on welfare, which the man claimed not to be. Pat wished him good luck and a merry Christmas and moved on, cameras in tow. A few weeks later he called for the chronically homeless to be jailed.

Buchanan sailed into Duke's wind and stole it completely. Duke's effort was falling apart—he was not a disciplined campaigner. He pulled out of Maryland for lack of funds. Stumping in Florida in December, he made a spectacle out of himself—and not in a good way. At a West Palm Beach club, the *New York Post* caught him downing Sex on the Beaches and dancing on the bar with a "Teutonic temptress, a gorgeous blonde with close-cropped hair and a German accent, outfitted in a clinging black dress." But Duke was described by an onlooker as a "terrible dancer." He and the Teutonic temptress collapsed to the floor "in a heap of gyrating flesh." And he could no longer fill a hall. Delivering his speeches in a "detached monotone," he would make "irrelevant jokes" and "burst into giggles."

Duke was even losing the interest of his core supporters among the nuttiest of the nuts. Willis Carto's *The Spotlight* began enthusiastically editorializing in favor of Buchanan as a Duke without the baggage. As the founder of the "Institute for Historical Review," Carto was the architect of organized Holocaust denial in the United States. Buchanan had been carefully managing a relationship with *The Spotlight* and Carto's Liberty Lobby and Populist Party for some time. The publication began to syndicate Buchanan's column briefly in 1990, but when this was pointed out to him, he asked them to stop. He claimed ignorance that they had bought the column in the first place. But this episode didn't prevent him from meeting with members of the Populist Party's executive committee in early 1991. Now people who once were part of Duke's contributor base were sending their money to Buchanan instead.

Without the baggage of a Klan and Nazi past, Buchanan could indulge freely in rhetoric that Duke could only dance around. At an event for Dartmouth students, Buchanan said that Jack Kemp, Bush's secretary of housing and urban development who advocated policies to help inner cities, had "gone native." A student pressed him on whether he had said in a column that AIDS was "God's retribution." Buchanan denied divine insight. He didn't mention that what the column actually said was that AIDS was "nature's retribution." Another student was curious about a 1971 White House memo from Buchanan that had come to light; it had brought Richard Herrnstein's work on race and hereditary intelligence to Nixon's attention, stating to the president, "Every study we have shows blacks 15 IQ points below whites on average" and that Herrnstein's work might form "an intellectual basis" for reappraising government programs. Buchanan told the students he had submitted the memo so the study could be debunked by Irving Kristol or Daniel Patrick Moynihan.

Like Duke, President Bush was also making missteps on the campaign trail. The Andover- and Yale-educated Connecticut WASP had maybe the worst common touch of any American president since John Quincy Adams. In an effort to relate to the people, Bush made a sojourn to a JCPenney to buy socks. It was widely mocked in the media. At a National Grocers Association convention in Florida, Bush was shown a new supermarket scanner that could read damaged barcodes and had a built-in scale to weigh produce. He politely listened to the manufacturer's pitch and tried out the scanner. "I just took a tour through the exhibits here," he told the grocers. "Amazed by some of the technology." Andrew Rosenthal, son of Abe, wrote it up in *The New York Times* under the headline BUSH ENCOUNTERS THE SUPERMARKET, AMAZED, and presented the story as if Bush had never seen a checkout scanner. The media went wild with the story, though it wasn't really true: Bush was just reacting to the salesman's pitch for this special new scanner. (So agreeable was Bush that he even got the word "amazing" from the salesman himself.) The White House press secretary Marlin Fitzwater tried to correct the record, but it was too late. It probably didn't help that Fitzwater told the media that the last time he saw Bush at a supermarket was in Kennebunkport, Maine.

Instead of going to New Hampshire, Bush at first sent his malapropic VP, Dan Quayle. Buchanan hit him for that, too. Bush traveled to Japan with the chiefs of the "Big Three" automakers instead. Even though his plan was to carry a tough message, it cemented the impression that he cared more about foreign policy than about what was going on at home. Buchanan, visiting a gun factory in New Hampshire, jabbed a finger at a paunchy worker. "You vote for me, my friend, and there won't be all those foreign trips. Japan, China, Korea and Germany—we've been supporting them for so long and they're putting nothing back." Intending to run on Bush's betrayal of his "no new taxes" pledge, Buchanan found that trade was a bigger concern to the down-beaten and unemployed, so he shifted emphasis. While at a state dinner in Japan, Bush fell ill and collapsed into the lap of the Japanese prime minister, where he vomited.

Buchanan's TV ads seemed deliberately tailor-made to target the MARs, the Middle American Radicals that the sociologist Donald Warren had described as the backbone of the Wallace movement in the 1970s and that Francis had turned into his revolutionary subject in the 1980s. In one ad, a couple sit together in the living room; the wife goes on at length about Bush's betrayal of ordinary folk, looking at her husband for continued support for her missive; the mustachioed man interjects, angry, quick, and with the last word, "Mr. Bush said, 'I know how you're suffering.' You're not suffering! By going to JCPenneys and buying socks? That makes you know that I'm suffering?"

The dynamic mirrored Warren's ethnographic observations of the MARs: "The wife usually took the initiative in inviting the interviewer into the home, getting seated, and also usually was the most anxious to answer the questions. The male maintained his dominance by the fact that his wife showed deference to him whenever he did wish to speak. However, his answers were almost always short and to the point, whereas the wives often went on at considerable length and with considerable articulateness."

When Bush finally felt forced to come to New Hampshire, things did not go smoothly. Nervous about the trip, he took a sleeping pill the night before, and the effects may have lingered into the next day. At a town hall in Exeter, he read directly off a note card meant to remind him of the day's themes. It read "Message: I care." In Dover, he told a group of insurance workers, "Remember Lincoln, going to his knees in times of trial and the Civil War and all that stuff . . . And we are blessed. So don't feel sorry for—don't cry for me Argentina," inexplicably referencing the hit Andrew Lloyd Webber musical *Evita*. Environmentalists and logging companies were clashing over the shrinking habitat of the northern spotted owl; Bush attempted to split the difference, saying that his paramount concern was the loggers' jobs, but, "Yes, we want to see that little furry-feathery guy protected and all of that." When pressed about extended unemployment benefits: "If a frog had wings, he wouldn't hit his tail on the ground—too hypothetical." Less hypothetical to the unemployed workers perhaps. "This ain't the easiest job in the world," he told another crowd. "Listen, here's the final word. Vote for me. Don't vote for them. Vote for me, O.K.?" At one event he trotted out Arnold Schwarzenegger: "Send a message to Pat Buchanan—Hasta la vista, baby!" Buchanan was steadily gaining ground.

As the new year rolled by, the politics of racial resentment Buchanan and Duke catered to were beginning to worry the Democrats, too. The journalists Thomas and Mary Edsall published their book *Chain Reaction*, cautioning liberals that their "censorious set of prohibitions against discussion of family structure among the black poor, absent fathers, crime, lack of labor-force participation, welfare dependency, illegitimacy, and other contentious race-freighted issues" was fueling the right-wing backlash. Massachusetts congressman Barney Frank wrote an op-ed in the January 13, 1992, *New York Times* headlined RACE AND

CRIME: LET'S TALK SENSE: "Race and crime together show the 'notsaposta' syndrome at its worst. Liberals are notsaposta take note publicly of the fact that young black males commit crimes in a significantly higher proportion than any other major demographic group."

In the middle of campaigning, Buchanan went back to D.C. From January 17 to 19, the paleocon John Randolph Club was holding its second annual meeting at the Renaissance Hotel near Dulles Airport, (incidentally the same hotel where the Iran-Contra middlemen met with CIA agents). Named for an early Virginian congressman and planter who famously said "I love liberty; I hate equality," the society was formed in 1990 by members of the Rockford Institute and the Ludwig von Mises Institute to seal an alliance between the paleoconservatives and a group of dissatisfied right-wing libertarians who had started to call themselves "paleolibertarians." (At one meeting of the club, David Duke had even shown up—attendees later claimed to ignore him.) Although on paper they should have had considerable differences on the issues of free trade, open borders, and even the existence of the nation-state, the two groups found an amicable modus vivendi. For instance, the paleolibertarians came around to supporting immigration restrictions, on the basis that continued immigration would likely expand the welfare state. Everyone expected Sam Francis—who generally hated libertarians—and the leader of the paleolibertarians, the economist Murray N. Rothbard, to clash; they got on swimmingly. Pat Buchanan was to deliver his "New Nationalism" speech as the keynote address for the club's meeting, but another speaker stole the show: the president of the club, Murray Rothbard.

Rothbard grew up as the child of Russian Jewish immigrants in a heavily communist Bronx milieu in the 1930s. While many friends, relatives, and neighbors were members of the Communist Party, Rothbard's father, David, a chemical engineer, adopted what his son considered to be "devotion to the Basic American way: minimal government, belief in and respect for free enterprise and private property, and a determination to rise by one's own merits and not via government privilege or handout." As Rothbard's biographer Justin Raimondo writes, this was part of a desire to become real Americans: "The Rothbard family's determined effort to integrate themselves in American life meant political as well as cultural assimilation." The son followed suit, taking his father's side in the frequent kitchen table arguments with communist aunts and uncles. At one, in the throes of the Spanish Civil War, the precocious young Rothbard shocked the dinner table by asking, "What's wrong with Franco anyway?"

Rothbard's recollections of his boyhood read like an America First Committee version of Woody Allen's *Radio Days*: he fondly recalls Depression-era New York as an idyll—full of cafeterias filled with lovable eccentrics, Dixieland jazz in the clubs and auditoriums, W. C. Fields and the Marx Brothers in the picture houses—but instead of the funny papers, the young Rothbard preferred the yellow journalism of *The New York Sun*, the Hearst press, and Robert R. McCormick's *Chicago Tribune*, with broadcasts by the America First Committee founder John T. Flynn blaring on the radio instead of a serial. Later, Rothbard would defend Charles Lindbergh and the other Firsters from charges of antisemitism, saying that what hostility to Jews there was among the America Firsters was provoked by Jews themselves.

The brainy Rothbard was bullied in Bronx public school, so his parents put him in the private Birch Wathen Lenox School on the Upper East Side. He thrived academically, but he resented the Park Avenue–bred limousine liberals among his peers and set up shop as class contrarian and sole right-leaning voice: "I soon became established as the school conservative, arguing strongly in the eighth grade against Roosevelt's introduction of the capital-gains tax in 1938 and later against Mayor Fiorello La Guardia's left-wing policy of coddling criminals." He was admitted to Columbia University at sixteen. While his classmates were all Popular Front liberals and leftists, exploring Marx, Trotsky, and John Dewey, Rothbard dove into H. L. Mencken and Albert Jay Nock. As a grad student at Columbia in 1948, he horrified fellow students by helping to found a Students for Thurmond group to show support for the anti–civil rights stance of the Dixiecrat presidential candidate, Senator Strom Thurmond. Rothbard found solace in the seminars of the Austrian economist Ludwig von Mises, who advocated the virtues of an unbridled free market. After Columbia, he found work at the William Volker Fund, organized by the businessman and former America First Committee member Harold W. Luhnow, where he became a prolific writer of strategy memos for the right. Inspired by Senator Joseph McCarthy's Red-hunting, he began to articulate a populist strategy to make an "electric, shortcut appeal, direct to the masses," writing a memo titled "In Defense of Demagogues."

But Rothbard's faithfulness to Old Right isolationism made him an oddball amidst the Cold War hawks at *National Review*. Buckley mocked Rothbard publicly for his eccentric ultra-libertarian views, such as the idea that federal lighthouses should be privatized. In exile from the mainstream, he attempted to pursue "ideological entrepreneurship" to seek out new allies, a policy that brought the bow-tied Rothbard into coalition with part of the New Left, who shared his anti-war and anti-statist bent. His Upper West Side living room became a salon for offbeat politics, bringing together Maoists from the Progressive Labor Party with Old Right anti-communists such as Colonel Eddie Rickenbacker, the World War I fighter ace and head of Eastern Air Lines.

Rothbard's political philosophy ultimately did not jibe with the New Left; he believed they ignored "the iron law of oligarchy" that governed political affairs, and that their egalitarianism was a revolt "against the ontological structure of reality itself." Human beings were innately, biologically unequal, and the workings of the market would reveal the elect of the race. But the existence of the state disrupted the natural workings of the free market: it was a parasitic organism that fed off the honest toil of the real producers. Where Karl Marx saw the two great classes facing each other as the bourgeoisie and the proletariat, Rothbard, drawing from the thought of the political theorist of slave power, Senator John C. Calhoun—"the Marx of the master class"—believed that the class struggle was between taxpayers and tax consumers.

After Rothbard's New Left dalliance, he met Charles Koch, the heir to Koch Industries. Koch was so impressed he gave Rothbard the funding to help form a new libertarian organization, which became known as the Cato Institute. He outlined his vision for Cato in the 1977 memo "Toward a Strategy for Libertarian Social Change." The resolute anti-communist advised the libertarian movement to adopt the strategic plan of Lenin's Bolsheviks to carry out their revolution: they should keep the ultimate goal of abolishing the State always in mind, while pursuing practical, intermediate projects as well; "purity of principle, combined with entrepreneurial flexibility of tactics," he advised. Two other twentieth-century figures were also given as instructive examples: Mussolini and Hitler. He notes with particular interest Mussolini's use of "myths" and emotionally stirring propaganda to rouse the masses, as well as Hitler's adoption of a clear distinction between "good guys and bad guys." When the memo leaked, *National Review* expressed horror at the invocation of Lenin. In any case, Rothbard's vision of the Cato Institute as the nucleus of a libertarian mass movement would never come to be. His obstreperousness and unwillingness to compromise on his ideals led to his purge from his own foundation. He joined up with the more radical Ludwig von Mises Institute in 1982, founded by Llewellyn Rockwell, who had previously served as chief of staff for the Texas congressman Ron Paul.

At the John Randolph Club meeting, Rothbard called the occasion "a triple celebration": "First, we celebrate the death and disintegration in 1991 of one of the most monstrous despotisms of all time, the Union of Soviet Socialist Republics." Second, he was celebrating his "return home to the Right-wing, after 35 years in the political wilderness." And third, after his long exile from meaningful politics, they were celebrating the newfound political relevance of the paleo alliance: "We have suddenly vaulted from the periphery to a central role in the

American Right." According to Rothbard, the Old Right, as it existed from 1933 to approximately 1955, had sprung back into existence. This "original Right" was a partnership of individualist libertarians and traditionalist conservatives, which he once called a "coalition of fury and despair against the enormous acceleration of Big Government brought by the New Deal." Like Moloch—"the fiercest Spirit / That fought in Heav'n; now fiercer by despair"—addressing pandemonium in *Paradise Lost*, Rothbard called for open war against the "Menshevik" establishment of neocons and liberals that defined the terms of debate.

Ranging over the entire history of postwar America and the supposed dilution of the right wing into loyal opposition of the liberal project, he mocked William F. Buckley's antisemitism essay as a "Christmas encyclical" and accused the *National Review* editor of having "purged the conservative movement of the genuine Right." He called Buckley "the Mikhail Gorbachev of the conservative movement," a leader who had lost his sway. He asked the crowd, "How long are we going to keep being suckers? How long will we keep playing our appointed roles in the scenario of the Left? When are we going to stop playing their game, and start throwing over the table?" He urged them to stop calling themselves "conservatives . . . gentle souls who want to conserve what Left-liberals have accomplished" and instead embrace the mantle of the "radical right" or "radical reactionaries." He told them to reject the liberal "psychobabble" that labeled them "paranoid," "resentful," or possessing "status anxiety": "Yes, the status anxious, paranoid, deeply resentful, radical Right is back, and this time we're not going to succumb to the smears and the excommunications."

Summoning the ghost of Joe McCarthy, Rothbard declaimed, "The proper strategy for the Right-wing must be what we can call 'right-wing populism,' exciting, dynamic, tough, and confrontational, rousing, and inspiring" leadership "that could short-circuit the media elites, and reach and rouse the masses directly . . . In short, we need the leadership of Patrick J. Buchanan." While many conservative intellectuals had perhaps agreed with McCarthy's anti-communist goals but decried his demagogic means, Rothbard thought it was precisely his means that were worth emulating: using television, McCarthy had been able to get around the traditional media, talk directly to the masses, and menace the ruling elite.

Then Rothbard reached his furious coda. He recalled how he was once told that his libertarian ideas were outdated and that socialism or communism was inevitable. "'You can't turn back the clock!' they chanted, 'you can't turn back the clock.' But the clock of the once-mighty Soviet Union, the clock of Marxism-Leninism, a creed that once mastered half the world, is not only turned back, but lies dead and broken forever." The task of the paleo movement was now to "finish the job," to end the "soft Marxism" of liberalism that still dominated America:

> With the inspiration of the death of the Soviet Union before us, we now know that it can be done. With Pat Buchanan as our leader, we shall break the clock of social democracy. We shall break the clock of the Great Society. We shall break the clock of the welfare state. We shall break the clock of the New Deal . . . We shall repeal the twentieth century.

The place went wild. "Up to Murray's speech it had been a pleasant, almost scholarly atmosphere," an attendee recalled. "Murray's speech changed the tone. At the conclusion, the crowd leapt to their feet, cheering wildly, ready to storm the capital. I have never seen anything like it. Some even had tears in their eyes."

Rothbard's vision was heavily freighted with personal grievance: he wanted to stick it to the conservative establishment that had cast him out and humiliated him. He relished being both a pariah and a parvenu: for his extreme ideas he was marginalized in mainstream society and in the conservative movement, but now he found himself among the elite of what he called "*the original Right*," those who had dubbed themselves the most American Americans. He was exceptional: a child of immigrants accepted among the nativists, a Jew accepted by the antisemites. He could embody the spirit of malcontent among this crowd of malcontents even as he craved their sense of entitlement to power and prestige. The present was a foreign country, but a real America was still out there, and the paleocons were its vanguard. Even if the crowd knew that Buchanan's revolt was unlikely to uproot Roosevelt's America, it provided a mythic narrative of national redemption.

In a lecture given a month earlier at the Heritage Foundation, Russell Kirk, American conservatism's most eminent sage, had quoted T. S. Eliot's injunction to "redeem the time." In Rothbard's vision, the time could not be redeemed: the clock had to be broken. "Nothing less than a counter-revolution" was required, and to do it necessitated not a "conservative, but a *radical* Right." In *The Politics of Prudence*, Kirk defined "the conservative person" as "simply one who finds the permanent things more pleasing than Chaos and Old Night." Rothbard often returned to the image of "Chaos and Old Night" from the pandemonium scene in Milton's *Paradise Lost*, but he did not find it unpleasing. His speech reveled in chaos and darkness. He told his crowd not to be afraid to frighten. His proposal for a right-wing populist strategy was precisely the rejection of the politics of prudence, the genteel politics of respectability, in favor of rage, resentments, menaces, and affronts. While Kirk had counseled his flock to reject "the doctrines of despair," Rothbard encouraged them to embrace the power of despair.

As Buchanan rose in the polls in New Hampshire, Buckley and the *National Review* softened their interdict. Three weeks before Election Day, *National Review* ran a cover story on "Bush's Goofy Politics." The editor's note in the February 17 issue called for "tactical support" of Buchanan's protest candidacy. The night of the primary, February 18, 1992, exit polls showed Buchanan and Bush neck and neck. By the time Buchanan took the stage after 10 p.m., it looked like he still had around 40 percent of the vote. It felt as good as a victory. "Tonight, what began as a little rebellion has emerged and grown into a full-fledged middle-American revolution," he told the crowd. "We are going to take our party back from those who have walked away and forgotten about us." (When the night was over, he had 37 percent of the vote; he was short of the 42 percent Eugene McCarthy had captured to sink LBJ's candidacy in 1968; Trump would win 35 percent in 2016.)

Buchanan did not do well with women. Men went for Buchanan 53 to 43, while women preferred Bush by 51 to 35. First of all, there were the policies: total opposition to abortion, the ERA, and affirmative action. Then there was Buchanan's way of expressing himself—the women in an otherwise receptive crowd booed and hissed when he referred to the Bush administration as the "the geisha girls of the New World Order." Women also did not like the way Buchanan behaved around his wife, Shelley. A caller into C-SPAN told Bay Buchanan that she "admired Pat," but watching the New Hampshire primary, she'd noticed "that he always walks off in front of her," and that she "felt sorry for her because she's always pushed into the background." When exit polls showed women favoring Bush, the president's campaign launched a massive phone banking effort to get more women voters to the polls. But more than half of the people who showed up to vote on primary day were men. Buchanan also played up his bully-boy image, making a number of roguish asides to reporters who asked about his youth. To the frustrated and wounded American manhood of New Hampshire, Buchanan had an undeniable appeal. Even if they realized that the textile mills weren't coming back, Buchanan gave their despair shape and direction.

In the February issue of *Chronicles*, Sam Francis's monthly column was headlined THE EDUCATION OF DAVID DUKE. Francis mused, "It's possible that future historians will look back on the Louisiana gubernatorial election of 1991 as a turning point in American history." Copping to the fact that liberals were "dead right" about their belief that "David Duke represents the logical culmination of the conservative resurgence of Ronald Reagan," Francis identified what he thought was the true essence of the Reagan revolution:

> Reagan conservatism, in its innermost meaning, had little to do with supply-side economics and spreading democracy. It had to do with the awakening of a people who face political, cultural, and economic dispossession, who are slowly beginning to glimpse the fact of dispossession and what [it] will mean for them and their descendants, and who also are starting to think about reversing the processes and powers responsible for [it].

According to Francis, the old conservative issues of limited government and free markets were losing their appeal to voters. "They are essentially bourgeois issues and mirror the social and moral codes of the small, independent businessman, his family, and his community," Francis explained. "Once upon a time, such entrepreneurs were the dominant core of American culture and politics, but they are so no longer, and with their demise, the appeal of their ideology has withered." And for Francis, the constant emphasis on Duke's Nazi and Klan background did not result in his loss, but actually contained part of the key to his appeal:

> There was a subtext to what Mr. Duke explicitly and formally said in his speeches and his campaign literature, and the subtext, communicated by the continued depiction of Mr. Duke in Nazi uniform and Klan hood by his enemies, is that the historic core of American civilization is under attack. Quotas, affirmative action, race norming, civil rights legislation, multiculturalism in schools and universities, welfare, busing, and unrestricted immigration from Third World countries are all symbols of that attack and of the racial, cultural, and political dispossession they promise to inflict upon the white post-bourgeois middle classes.

Francis called the middle class "post-bourgeois" because, as a rule, it no longer possessed the kind of property that made it economically independent: massive corporations and government bureaucracies had swallowed up small businesses and farms. This white middle class was now entering a final phase of "proletarianization," which could only be reversed with its political and cultural awakening. Not only was its economic independence stripped away by the rise of corporate society, so too was its "Anglo-Saxon" and "Victorian" culture of sobriety and discipline. As "new immigrants rose socially and economically, especially through the mass entertainment industry they helped create, they displaced the Victorian ethic with their own anti-bourgeois patterns of living." As a result of all this, the "new nationalism" would not "dwell on limiting the size of government but rather on the issue of who and what controls the government"; its purveyors should seek to seize the state and combat the elites who had effected the middle class's "dispossession." Of course, if this white middle class no longer possessed a distinct cultural ethic and lacked a shared economic basis, it was unclear what identity it still possessed other than being white.

For their part, Buchanan's supporters in New Hampshire made similar noises about the hollowing out of the American middle. "There is no middle class anymore. There are the people who have and the people who don't," Ken Golomb, listening to Buchanan in the rain outside of an unemployment office, told a reporter. "It's us vs. them, and he, Bush, is one of them. I'm waiting for one of us to step forward." Golomb, a forty-five-year-old Vietnam vet who lost his job doing deliveries for Venture Golf and Battery, had two children and one on the way.

In the crowd outside the unemployment office, a local coffin maker held a homemade sign with his ideal ticket: PAT BUCHANAN FOR PRESIDENT, RUSH LIMBAUGH FOR VICE PRESIDENT. Limbaugh had become the most listened-to radio talk show host in the country. With the help of the political consultant Roger Ailes, he was about to get a nationally syndicated TV show in the fall of '92. And he was starting to signal friendliness to Buchanan, framing it in terms of disciplining the wayward Bush: "Look, if we want to win this, there needs to be a conservative debate, a conservative element to this campaign." On CBS News, Limbaugh called Buchanan "a great American," adding, "I hope he's able to hold George Bush's feet to a more conservative fire. I think what he's going to be looking at is 1996." Limbaugh knew that many of his listeners were already all-in for Pat.

Limbaugh still cleaved to the establishment line. Speaking after Buchanan at the Conservative Political Victory Fund dinner in Manchester, New Hampshire, on February 8, Limbaugh said that the recession was "not the end of the world," and that it would be ended by unleashing the forces of free enterprise. At the end of his speech he addressed the chippy campaigning that had taken place at what was supposed to be a celebration of Reagan's birthday: "There's been some stridency in the room tonight, obviously some partisan politics, when the occasion was really geared for a salute to President Reagan. It was predictable that this would happen tonight, and it's fine and it is healthy. But I would like to say to the people of America watching, and I would like to also say to those of you in this room that regardless of the outcome of our contest, the simple fact is that we believe in the same things and we will be united in the pursuit of those things." The message was clear in its vagueness: a stance of armed neutrality. Directly after New Hampshire, Buchanan went south to campaign in Georgia, the next primary state. At a rally in Atlanta, he told a cheering crowd, "Rush Limbaugh does a terrific job on radio. I'll tell you this: he is really the voice of Middle America. And I say, I've only given away one job, and Rush Limbaugh's gonna be director of communications in Pat Buchanan's White House!"

4

THE VOICE OF AMERICA

The "voice of Middle America" was truly the product of heartland conservatism. Rush Hudson Limbaugh III was born in 1951 in Cape Girardeau, Missouri, a small city on the banks of the Mississippi one hundred miles south of St. Louis. Its Main Street of two-story red-brick storefronts and green awnings looked like a Norman Rockwell painting. Rush's grandfather, Rush Senior, was born and raised on a nearby farm and became a town lawyer. In early 1931 he was elected to the Missouri State House, serving one term, and he became chairman of the Cape Girardeau County Republican Committee. As a young man, he had been a progressive, but he became a conservative believer in limited government, recoiling at the coming of a New Deal, whose bureaucracies he felt were detrimental to the self-reliant character of the American people. (He was not, however, an America Firster: in a community with its fair share of isolationists, he addressed the local chamber of commerce on the necessity for America's involvement in Europe's war.) During the Eisenhower administration he was made a special legal ambassador to India. One of Rush's biographers called him a "pillar of the community"; another, one of the "wise elders of Missouri." He was certainly one of the city fathers: president of the Rotary Club, a trustee of the local hospital, on the board of the Salvation Army, a Boy Scout leader, and vice president of the State Historical Society of Missouri. In 1992, at age 102, Rush Senior retired from his legal practice. His sons had followed in his footsteps, entering the legal profession. Stephen N. Limbaugh was made a district court judge by the Reagan administration. Like his father, Rush Junior headed the Cape Girardeau GOP and was deeply involved in such civic organizations as the American Legion and the Veterans of Foreign Wars, and he taught Sunday school at the Methodist church.

As one biographer put it, "The Limbaughs were one of the most highly regarded families in town, with plenty of money to command substantial social clout," but young Rush Limbaugh III—Rusty, as he was known—struggled to convert his family's social capital into personal popularity. He was a lonely kid, with the football team failing to convert him into a social success. "I played to be popular," he told one biographer. "It didn't work." He was particularly handicapped in the social department by his lack of aplomb with the opposite sex. He was heavy and awkward with girls and could not acquire the girlfriend that would have allowed him to move into the popular set.

"He was introverted and shy. He lacked confidence," recalled one of his few friends. "He once hid himself in the backseat of a car so that he could steal a peek when a friend was with a date upfront—and thereby learn how to do it himself." When his chance came, it went spectacularly badly: in a game of spin the bottle, he landed on one of the "prettiest girls in high school," but she wouldn't kiss him. An "unauthorized" biographer dramatized the catastrophe: "She looked at him and gasped. Couldn't do it. Not with *him*. And everyone in the room witnessed his humiliation. It was a wound he would nurse forever after."

In love with the radio, Rusty would sit alone in the basement with a tape recorder working on his DJ act. At sixteen, he got an early shot on a small local radio station, owned partly by his father. Dubbing himself "Rusty Sharpe," he cribbed his on-air schtick from Midwest radio stars like Chicago's Larry Lujack—famous for his dry, exasperated mockery of his listeners' letters on the air—and Harry Caray, the famous Chicago Cubs broadcaster. Limbaugh's show was a big hit with his classmates, who didn't know it was Rush coming through their sets. A square with a flattop, he liked being the guy playing the records more than he liked the records. "I never really listened to the lyrics," he later recalled. "Rock to me was never anything special. It's all about rebellion and blue jeans. I have never owned a pair of blue jeans." His radio debut was in the summer of 1967. (One rock and roll song did catch his imagination, though: he played "Under My Thumb" by the Rolling Stones so much at one later job that he got fired for it.)

But success on the air didn't make him a hero to his classmates. "I wanted to be popular," Limbaugh told *Vanity Fair* in 1992. "I have no problem admitting this. And I thought: Here I am, playing the music these people like; they can call me and make requests; I can be a source of happiness, a source of satisfaction—that will make me popular. It didn't. All it did was make people think that I walked the halls of high school as a stuck-up snob."

The difference between his real-life impression on others and his persona on the air would follow him into fame and fortune. "The truth is, he becomes a different person when he's on [the air]," reflected his younger brother David. "I didn't even know he had a passion for politics. I didn't know he had a sense of humor, either. I was always the clown, and he was quiet. He was shy, but radio has allowed him to come out of his shell. Why does a person who's ordinarily quiet become comfortable when he's talking to 11 million people, unless it's that they're invisible? But he changes when the mic goes off."

Rusty's other refuge from pariahdom was politics. "The Republican Party is like a microcosm of those of us who are conservatives," Limbaugh told his then-massive audience in 1992. "Every day we are inundated by what is supposedly natural, what is supposedly normal, what is supposedly in the majority, by virtue of what the dominant media culture shows, and most often it's not us. Most often, what we believe in is made fun of, lampooned, impugned, and put down. Then, we don't want to feel that way. We want to feel as much a part of the mainstream as anybody else." Rush Limbaugh III's conception of the Republican Party was no longer quite the GOP of Rush Limbaugh Jr. or Sr., the natural home of a moderately successful, staid Midwestern bourgeoisie. Instead of the party of the prosperous and secure, Limbaugh viewed it as the haven of the alienated and angry.

But there was a long road to eleven million listeners on 450 stations. Rusty's father wanted him to go into the law like the other Limbaughs. Rusty told his father he was dropping out of college to go become a DJ in Pittsburgh, and he received a stern lecture. His father predicted a life of failure, a drop in his social standing, a loss of friends, and the inability to find a "decent woman" to marry. At first it looked like father might have known best. After being fired from two jobs in Pittsburgh, he returned home and lived with his parents before finding another job in Kansas City. He was fired from that one, too. Feeling himself "a moderate failure," and under pressure, he temporarily gave up on the radio, taking a job with the Kansas City Royals, selling ticket packages. Offered another shot on the radio, within a year he was fired again. Then he was offered a talk show on KFBK in Sacramento. He was to replace the outrageous Morton Downey Jr., who had been taken off the air after a racist joke involving a "Chinaman." Limbaugh would not blow this opportunity: the show was a success, leading to his WABC New York show and national syndication.

But there were other setbacks on his road to fame and fortune: not one, but two of his marriages failed. The first to a secretary at a radio station, the second to an usher at the Kansas City Royals stadium.

In this regard, Rush Limbaugh was hardly exceptional. Between 1972 and 1989, America split up. The rate of divorce in the United States, which had slowly climbed since the founding and only briefly dipped during the 1950s, suddenly exploded with the widespread adoption of no-fault ruptures in the 1970s. Nearly half of all marriages had split up by the beginning of the last decade of the twentieth century. The national anxiety over broken marriages and broken homes didn't abate, but only seemed to intensify. Celebrity divorces splashed across tabloid covers; TV talk shows featured couples on the verge of a split alongside marriage experts and psychologists to bring them back from the brink; the comedian Eddie Murphy dedicated a significant portion of his smash-hit 1987 stand-up special, *Raw*, to the perils of alimony: "They'll get half your money, your house, your car, alimony, child support, and your children. You will be on the cover of the *Enquirer* like this" (Murphy mugs the likeness of a mouth-agape, distraught sucker). "So be careful!"

There was talk of a "divorce revolution" that had taken place in the 1970s and early '80s, and now, in the wake of that revolution, there were second thoughts and even hopes for a Thermidor. Dreams of a return to the old dispensation were hardly confined to the religious right. In 1992, the *Chicago Tribune*'s moderately libertarian columnist Steve Chapman called for "rolling back the divorce revolution" in order to "impose some healthy costs on irresponsible behavior." In the cultural ferment, the causes of the no-fault turn were forgotten.

The right liked to blame the rise of feminism for the new regime of divorce, but the trend toward no-fault laws in the states predated the women's movement. In any case, the new laws were not really proposed to institute gender parity as much as to put an end to the often needlessly painful and difficult courtroom dramas required by "at-fault" divorces: even couples who mutually wanted to part had to contrive situations where one party could be implicated in misbehavior to the law's satisfaction. Courts often winkingly colluded in these charades. Whatever its consequences, no-fault was as much about making a concession to reality and reforming institutionalized dishonesty as about signaling a great ideological change in society. Still, conservatives imagined a grand historical narrative of decline and destruction: according to *National Review*, no-fault divorce was the drawn-out consequence of the Protestant Reformation and "the domestic equivalent of a political revolution," sharing with historical revolutionaries "a common willingness to scrap a civilization . . . and start again."

Revolution or not, there was a certain degree of tumult: no-fault was meant to end the charade of adversarial divorces, but it created real conflicts, countless desperate struggles over assets and custody. With the acceptance of divorce, society seemed to have taken a more mercenary and more cutthroat turn—marriage, it seemed, was now a business partnership, liable to be dissolved, usually at the expense of one partner. It was once customary for the woman to initiate divorce, and the gentlemanly thing to do was for the man to pretend adultery or some other misbehavior to save the lady from possible disgrace. Even if they didn't need to prove it in court, now men and women could equally claim that they were the aggrieved party. Men organized themselves as fathers and demanded recognition of their own set of rights around custody and child support.

Feminists, though they hadn't authored the no-fault laws, largely welcomed them. By the middle of the '80s, however, some expressed concerns about the consequences of divorce for women. *The Divorce Revolution: The Unintended Social and Economic Consequences for Women and Children in America* (1986), by the sociologist Lenore J. Weitzman, found that after a divorce, there was a 73 percent drop in women's standard of living, while men saw a 42 percent rise in their standard of living. Weitzman's goal, based on the "inequalities that marriage itself creates," was a more equitable arrangement for dividing property at the time of divorce, as women, especially those who had been housewives and mothers, were unlikely to have the same work experience and skills as the husband. *The Illusion of Equality: The Rhetoric and Reality of Divorce Reform* (1981), by law professor Martha Albertson Fineman, made similar critiques of the no-fault regime's material consequences for women. But such authors' arguments about the just division of property and compensation for women's labor were often put aside; instead, they were seized upon as proof that divorce just wasn't working out and women would be better off staying married.

There was a national interest in "working it out." The late 1980s and early '90s injunction to "work on marriages" and the consequent campaign of self-improvement and self-help may have slowed the rate of divorce, but the burden fell mostly on women. Men were excused. Often literally. The trend in ladies' magazines and female-focused daytime talk shows was toward forgiveness of infidelity and the cultivation of efforts to maintain the sexual interest of the husband. Despite the urge to stick together, there was also recognition of irreconcilable differences. Men and women had different spheres, even different planets. John Gray's *Men Are from Mars, Women Are from Venus*, 1992's runaway bestselling guide to relationships that eventually became the bestselling nonfiction work of the decade, gave men the prerogative of "retreating into their cave" to deal with the stress of relationships.

Autonomy might be the desire, but anomie and atomization were the fear. The nation was undergoing an "epidemic of loneliness." "Loneliness is one of the unshaped political problems of our times. It is the curse of American life. You find it everywhere, from New England to California," declared the presidential historian Theodore White. Sometimes the loneliness conversation went directly to divorce. "When I grew up in a small city in the Midwest, hardly anyone was getting divorced. Indeed, society put a stigma on divorce that undoubtedly caused many unhappy marriages to continue when divorce might have been a better solution," wrote Godfrey Sperling Jr. of *The Christian Science Monitor*. "No one can prove that there was more marital happiness in those days, but there wasn't all this divorce and separation—and accompanying loneliness—either."

Other factors were recognized as well. The author Louise Bernikow traveled across the United States and interviewed three hundred people to write *Alone in America: The Search for Companionship*. Speaking to *U.S. News and World Report* in 1986, she painted a grievous picture of the country, a nation of loners, desiring connections but unable to find them. "Loneliness permeates the culture. Look at the ads. New York Telephone says: 'Don't be lonely, pick up the phone.' AT&T's recent ad campaign urged people to 'reach out and touch someone.'" Bernikow identified "large social, economic changes behind the spread of loneliness: the decline of the social movements of the 1960s, the ease of divorce, the end of lifetime employment with one company and the rise of mergers and acquisitions and layoffs." A decline in values and the new economic principles of the '80s boom seemed to be equally to blame: "American life has become privatized. People are wrapped up in selfish, individual pursuits of material goods. We're not often encouraged to value people."

Convenience-providing tech was part of the story, too, Bernikow thought: "The television, the computer, the bank-teller machine allow us to do without others what we used to have to do with them. There are great numbers of people who have VCR's, stay home and watch a movie on TV instead of being, in a sense, forced to go to a movie theater where they would be around others. All the advances in our life may not cause isolation, but they have made it more possible to live that way." The slow, painful death of industrial America provided a particularly acute case study: "Of all the places I visited, the area south of Pittsburgh was where people seemed most lonely. The steel mills were the connecting point in their lives, and they lost that. Many retreated into horrendous isolation. They stayed home, watched TV, drank beer and beat their wives. Family life fell apart under the stress." Women didn't need to marry for "economic reasons" anymore, but there was now a sense of alienation between the sexes: "Today, many men don't really know how to deal with women and vice versa."

Fears of more literal dismemberments followed the rending of American family life. A police investigator on the case of Jeffrey Dahmer, the serial killer captured in 1991 after he'd murdered, mutilated, and partially eaten some seventeen people, attributed his pattern of luring gay men and boys back to his house, killing them, and chopping them up to "an intense fear of loneliness that goes back to his parents' divorce." This fear of abandonment "surfaced each time one of the men wanted to leave his apartment." Psychologists who were consulted by the Associated Press for the story said that the theory, largely a paraphrase of Dahmer's own explanation, sounded plausible to them. Children of divorce were often presented in the media as fragile, even potentially damaged for life—now they might even grow up to be serial killers.

In order to escape the pain of being alone, Americans turned to talk. Intellectuals explained the mushrooming of talk radio and TV talk shows in the 1980s and '90s as a consequence of the loneliness epidemic. "For one thing, in a world where front-porch, front-stoop conversation is disappearing people yearn to connect," wrote Mike Hoyt, the associate editor of the *Columbia Journalism Review*, in 1992. The novelist David Foster Wallace landed on a similar formulation in a 1993 essay on the relation between fiction and television: "Lonely people, home, alone, still crave sights and scenes. Hence, television." Peter Laufer, a former talk radio host who had become convinced that "talk radio is the latest example of the degeneration of American popular culture" and authored an exposé of the industry, believed that "callers to talk shows are seeking companionship. They are lonely, stuck at home, or stuck in traffic. They feel disenfranchised from society and desire an opportunity to be heard; they are convinced they have something to say."

Others blamed the media itself for the breakdown of family ties. Barry Levinson's 1990 film *Avalon*, a saga about an immigrant Jewish American family's assimilation, pointedly used TV watching as a leitmotif in a tale of alienation and isolation, with lively, warm family dinners giving way to a gaping, silent brood eating frozen dinners in front of the tube. But tuning in was mostly understood to be compensatory rather than corrosive. "I hear a lot of chatter in America," opined Richard Rodriguez, PBS *NewsHour*'s resident essayist. "People are talking all day on television. We've just continued the discussion. We're stuck somewhere between *Oprah* and *Geraldo*. Americans are talking about being gay, about, you know, having one leg, about being divorced, but it seems to me that a lot of that talk comes out of this extraordinary loneliness in America."

Talk can be divided into two spheres corresponding to media: daytime TV talk and talk radio. In turn, these spheres loosely encompassed differences in politics and gender. Daytime TV talk shows, hosted by a relatively diverse cast of characters such as Phil Donahue, Geraldo Rivera, Oprah Winfrey, and Sally Jessy Raphael, were targeted mostly toward women, dealt with "women's issues," and were mostly liberal in their sensibility. Although such shows were often sensationalistic and exploitative in their own right, even the most debased ones, like *The Jerry Springer Show*, famous for its fistfights, unruly audience, and profanity, put on the pretense of dealing sensitively or therapeutically with people's issues: Jerry closed each show with his "Final Thought," an earnest moral reflection on the themes raised by the guests, and the admonition to "take care of yourselves and each other."

Talk radio was dominated mostly by white male stars, like Don Imus, Howard Stern, Morton Downey Jr., and Rush Limbaugh, who all, to various degrees, reveled in being crass, cynical, sarcastic, rambunctious, and vicious. Women, minorities, and gays, who could all expect a sympathetic if condescending hearing on daytime TV, would come in for particularly brutal treatment on the radio. The characteristic expression of the daytime TV host was a concerned furrowing of the brow; for the radio host, an incredulous sneer. Sincerity, a tone that conveyed openness and a desire for honest exchange, even when it was actually a bit oily and disingenuous, was the characteristic mode of talk TV; authenticity, the appearance of no-holds-barred self-expression, more often than not a carefully cultivated schtick, was the quality affected by radio shock jocks.

Still, it would be a mistake to think that TV talk was a land of gentle understanding. Guests who might have explosive confrontations were deliberately put together. In 1988, Roy Innis, the head of CORE, shoved Al Sharpton to the ground during a taping of the notoriously rowdy *Morton Downey Jr. Show*. That same year, Innis attempted to strangle the KKK chieftain Tom Metzger on *Geraldo*, leading to a brawl. Geraldo Rivera dutifully made a show asking if television had gone "too far," prompting Harold Rosenberg of the *Los Angeles Times* to crack that the question was "about as sincere as Adolf Eichmann questioning the excesses of genocide." For their part, Innis and Metzger took the show on the road, appearing together on *A.M. Los Angeles*.

The hosts of the talk radio shows, when they were not explicit political conservatives, usually evinced a kind of libertarian petulance, particularly bridling at suggestions that they tone down or "censor" their more outrageous material. Even the timing of the broadcasts and the nature of the media themselves seemed designed to address men and women in their traditional roles: a housewife could relax at home with daytime TV; the man on his commute to or from work could get worked up with a shock jock. (By 1990, some two-thirds of radio listeners tuned in outside their homes, in their car or at work; the image of a family gathered round the radio set for one of FDR's fireside chats was long gone.)

The public was represented in two different ways on the shows as well: the daytime talk show had a live studio audience, a kind of assembly that combined the roles of jury and chorus and was asked by the host to weigh in on the bad attitudes and misdeeds of the guests. Talk radio had callers, disembodied voices who confronted or affirmed the host one at a time. Originally, talk radio callers were limited to the locality of the originating station, but with the adoption of national syndication, satellite uplink, and toll-free numbers it seemed like the entire nation could weigh in. The shows presented two different models of the republic: on TV, a town square packed with a small but vocal and engaged public; on the radio, a far-flung empire peopled with autonomous, equal citizens, each with a sense of his own right to be heard and redressed. Women were from Athens; men were from Rome.

But the vast majority of viewers and listeners were never to be part of the *agora* of studio audience, guests, or callers. Whatever sense of community or inclusion they got was by proxy, a phenomenon that was postulated very early in the era of mass broadcasting. Observing the rise of TV talk shows in the 1950s, psychologists invented the term "parasocial relationship" to describe the fantasy of intimacy and friendship that could develop between the audience at home and the host's persona. This coinage was tinged with clinical concern: people were thought to be compensating for real loneliness with a simulacrum of companionship. The shows apparently had a cathartic or purgative effect for the lost souls of splintering America. In 1992, *Time* magazine spoke to a "frequent caller" of the *Howard Stern Show* who said that "an ugly divorce had left him almost suicidal: 'It was such a release from the tension. It probably saved my life.'" He wasn't alone: Donald Trump became a regular caller to the Stern show around the time of his highly publicized divorce from Ivana, even using an interview on Stern's short-lived cable show to get back at his ex; Stern took the shots at Ivana's character, and Trump gamely assented to Stern's takes.

Not everyone responded with a feeling of warmth or gratitude for their ersatz buddies on the radio; the rise of the shock jocks in the mid-'80s was greeted by considerable listener anger and disgust. But a prurient desire for outrage, insult, and affray was understood to be part of the appeal. One of the first major notices of the shock jock phenomenon in the press was a 1984 *Time* magazine feature, "Audiences Love to Hate Them." Steve Kane, the king of "drive time" Miami ratings, told the magazine, "I judge my success by the amount of hate mail I get." Apparently the forty-five-year-old Kane could turn "parasocial interactions" into real ones: a favorite topic was his "recent separation from his third wife, a 21-year-old woman whom he met when she called his show a few years ago to console him on the loss of his girlfriend."

But the stakes could be considerably more serious than hate mail and adoring, prospective wives. The occasion for the *Time* interest in radio trends was the 1984 assassination of the Denver late-night shock jock Alan Berg. One of the few liberal voices in talk radio, Berg was no less obstreperous than his right-wing counterparts. Favorite topics for Berg included oral sex, the hypocrisies of the Christian religion, white fears of Black people, and white women's lust for Black men. Over time, Berg mellowed, his show became less hostile and more constructive and community-focused: he tried to connect the unemployed with jobs, hosted a group therapy session, and badgered bosses for raises on behalf of shy workers. He would still explode at callers who expressed bigoted views, particularly neo-Nazis and Klansmen who called in to challenge and threaten him. The threats were not idle. In June 1984 Berg was gunned down by automatic weapons in an ambush outside his home by members of The Order, the white nationalist terror group inspired by William Pierce's novel *The Turner Diaries*. (The Order was one of the groups Samuel Francis wrote about in 1985 that signaled the awakening of a new radical right energy.) Some hosts were frightened, toning down their antics after Berg's death, but the nationally syndicated New York–based Don Imus quipped that Berg's "act couldn't have been very successful or interesting" as he was doing it out in Denver. Solidarity was apparently in short supply among radio hosts.

Not all responses were so callous. Berg's murder and the prospect of real violence surrounding the microphone provoked an anguished and searching response in some members of the American intelligentsia. The actor and monologist Eric Bogosian wrote a one-man play, *Talk Radio*, based partially on Alan Berg; it was made into a 1988 feature film of the same name, directed by Oliver Stone. Bogosian plays Barry Champlain, a Jewish American talk show host, an amalgamation of Morton Downey Jr., Alan Berg, and Howard Stern. Champlain is on the verge of a national syndication deal and trying to reunite with his ex-wife, whom he'd lost through the monstrous growth of his ego as he achieved radio success and his consequent infidelity. Champlain bullies and humiliates his alienated, lonely, and often downright disturbed late-night callers, who react with a mixture of chiding affection, worshipful reverence, and outright hate. Overwhelmed by the pressures of the job, he breaks down and delivers a final, furious monologue, a combination confession and indictment. "I'm a hypocrite," Champlain tearfully admits. "I denounce the system as I embrace it. I want money and power and prestige. I want ratings and success. And I don't give a damn about you, or the world. That's the truth. For this I could say I'm sorry but I won't. Why should I? I mean who the hell are you anyway, you audience." He goes on to tell us who they are: "[a] bunch of yellow-bellied, spineless, bigoted, quivering, drunken, insomniac, paranoid, disgusting, perverted, voyeuristic, little obscene phone callers. That's what you are!" The rage is misconstrued by the audience; the callers respond as if this is still part of his schtick. The tragedy is complete: sincere communication is forever out of reach, and our hell is permanent. Champlain is gunned down shortly thereafter; love and honesty are never to be his.

It was the question of sincerity that preoccupied Bogosian's conscience, even more than the politics of a liberal Jewish host gunned down by a Nazi death squad. "Barry Champlain is entertaining, but does he mean what he says?" Bogosian asked in a *New York Times* op-ed. "When one of today's fiercer talk-show hosts says that homosexuals in prison who have contracted AIDS deserve to die, is that his idea of entertainment? When another talk-show host insults a black caller on the air . . . are they joking? How many people listening agree? Are these honestly held opinions or is this acting? Often I think stars of the mass media don't know themselves when they are being sincere or playing a part. When playing a part works so well, excites the audience so much, why drop it?" America's character was imperiled just as it seemed to find its freest expression.

Bogosian was correct in at least one crucial respect: the market rewarded the brash personas of the shock jocks whether it was an act or not. And the market, or at least corporate power, had been unleashed. The FCC, created by the Communications Act of 1934, was part of the New Deal "alphabet soup" of bureaucratic agencies. A key provision of its charter was to regulate the airwaves—a limited resource—"in the public interest." In 1978, Jimmy Carter's FCC, which declared that the New Deal–era regulation had grown "ossified" and wanted to encourage free market competition, eliminated the rules that forced stations to devote a certain amount of their broadcasting time to news or public affairs. With the election of Ronald Reagan and the ascension of Mark S. Fowler, the former radio DJ turned media attorney, to the FCC chair, the agency went into an all-out drive for "free market" deregulation. Fowler, who called the commission "the last of the New Deal dinosaurs" and told stories about stations being terrified of FCC inspections, was even more of a market ideologue than the president: "The theory is 'free the businessman; let the businessman react in the marketplace; let the consumer, in other words, be sovereign.'" Fowler preferred to call deregulation "unregulation": he wanted a totally unregulated marketplace, with the FCC reduced to the role of an "electronic traffic cop."

Fowler's FCC began to slash and burn the dense forest of regulations. In 1982 the commission ended the three-year anti-trafficking rule, which had required buyers of radio stations to hold the stations for at least three years before selling them. In 1985 the FCC expanded the number of stations a single company could own on a given band from seven to twelve. In 1992 the number expanded again to eighteen. A brisk market for mergers and acquisitions followed, with about 10 percent of stations trading every year in the late '80s. These deals, often highly leveraged affairs financed by astronomical debt, could be fantastically lucrative. In 1987 Sconnix Broadcasting bought eight stations from John Blair and Company for $160 million and then sold just one of them to Infinity Broadcasting for $82 million. The price tags were determined by ratings and ad sales. Using syndication and satellite distribution, a single entity could pipe the same shows to its subsidiaries, saving on production costs. In addition, the widespread employment of mini shock jocks in both talk and music formats helped the stations capture the key eighteen-to-thirty-five-year-old male demographic during the crucial morning drive time. For every superstar like Stern or Imus, there were dozens of local epigones.

From the beginning of Fowler's reign at the FCC, a particular target was the so-called Fairness Doctrine. Since 1949 the commission had stipulated that licensees had to devote time to the discussion of controversial issues and had to give reasonable opportunity for opposing viewpoints to be heard on those issues. A related regulation was the personal attack rule, which said that if an individual's character was attacked on the air, that person must be given airtime to respond within one week of the original broadcast. In the 1970s, most of the FCC's decisions not to renew licenses revolved around adherence to the Fairness Doctrine. In 1985 Fowler's FCC released a report saying that the Fairness Doctrine had a chilling effect on First Amendment rights and that the scarcity of certain opinions had been a nonissue since the birth of cable TV. In 1987, under Fowler's successor Dennis R. Patrick, the commission voted 4–0 to no longer enforce the doctrine. Congress tried to codify it into law, but the legislation was vetoed by President Reagan. Bush would veto a similar attempt. Stations broadcasting nonstop opinion no longer had to worry about running afoul of any regulations. In 1988 Rush Limbaugh got his first national syndication deal. Between 1987 and 1992, the number of stations running all-talk or talk-news format grew from 238 to 850.

Although stations didn't fear revoked licenses as much anymore, the Reagan-era FCC couldn't abandon all its regulatory responsibilities. It still had its mandate to punish indecency and obscenity on the air, and the presence of the religious right in the Reagan coalition meant that there was significant pressure to flex that muscle. The National Federation for Decency, founded by the United Methodist minister Donald Wildmon, began to picket the FCC's offices in 1986, calling for a crackdown on indecent TV and radio. Fowler, although he said he was "sympathetic" to the protesters, issued a circumspect bureaucratic reply: "In view of the fact that a critical legal element in assessing material alleged to be 'obscene' is whether it violates 'local community standards,' it is more appropriate that such allegations be referred to local prosecutors, including U.S. attorneys, for potential adjudication. If a local jury makes a finding of 'obscenity' against an FCC licensee, it will then take appropriate action, including a possible stripping of the license."

The question of "indecency" was even more ambiguous than "obscenity." A Supreme Court decision in 1978 upheld an FCC finding that George Carlin's "Seven Dirty Words" routine aired on WBAI-FM in New York had been "indecent." The majority opinion stated that indecency was to be defined as "language or material that depicts or describes, in terms patently offensive as measured by contemporary community standards for the broadcast medium, sexual or excretory activities or organs." The FCC stuck to merely going after instances of the "seven dirty words," but the tapes of the *Howard Stern Show* being sent in by groups like the National Federation for Decency and individual listeners didn't have actual four-letter words, just broadly lewd content such as Stern threatening to sodomize the ventriloquist Shari Lewis's puppet Lamb Chop. Other offensive content didn't fit "indecency" as it related to "sexual or excretory activities." "From March of 1986 to April of 1987, I counted 79 complaints against Howard Stern," Roger Holberg of the FCC Complaints and Investigations Division told the *Los Angeles Times*. "But they weren't all for indecency. There were quite a few for racial slurs."

Mary V. Keeley, a forty-eight-year-old homemaker from Philadelphia, was horrified to discover her fifteen-year-old son tuning in to one of Stern's many prolix discourses on lesbianism—"I mean, to go around, porking other girls with vibrating rubber products, and they want the whole world to come to a stand-still"—and began to send complaints to the commission. With Fowler replaced by Dennis R. Patrick, the FCC cracked down in 1987 with a broader interpretation of the indecency rules. Along with Stern's show, the FCC targeted KPFK-FM in Los Angeles, a public radio station run by the left-leaning nonprofit Pacifica Foundation, for airing *Jerker*, a radio play about the AIDS epidemic that included descriptions of gay sex. The FCC stated that the play was not just indecent but even possibly obscene, and it referred the case to the Justice Department.

The fines imposed on the *Howard Stern Show* and its corporate parent Infinity Broadcasting were practically nothing compared with the ad revenue the show generated. Infinity also had an army of lawyers to dispute and delay the rulings. With each run-in with the FCC, Stern went on doing the show as before, ranting about being "censored" and unleashing invective on the commissioners. "Nobody wants to see anybody get AIDS . . . unless they sit on the FCC," he quipped. When Patrick's successor was revealed to have prostate cancer, Stern said, "I pray for his death." Stern also complained about double standards: "When these kids come home from school . . . You know what's on—Donahue, Oprah. My daughter was sitting, I caught her the other day, they were doing a transsexual show; it was so graphic I can't begin to tell you." For its part, KPFK-FM, not having Infinity's resources and unsure of where it could run afoul of the still-undefined indecency standards, began to pull programming, including an on-air reading of Alice Walker's Pulitzer Prize–winning novel *The Color Purple.*

Along with titillating content, and the prospect of new friends or enemies, talk radio was also where you could pick up a personality or, at least, a persona. In the 1990 coming-of-age movie *Pump Up the Volume*, Christian Slater plays a shy, friendless nerd, a virginal outcast during the day at his suburban high school, but at night he becomes "Hard Harry" a.k.a. "Happy Harry Hard-On," the caustic, libidinous, angry—but very authentic—host of a pirate radio show obsessively taped by his unsuspecting classmates. This Dr. Jekyll and Mr. Hyde conceit applied to Limbaugh of course, but not only to him.

Howard Stern came from a modest middle-class background in Long Island. The early part of his childhood he spent in Roosevelt, New York, a haven for the Black middle class. Stern recalled being bullied and feeling out of place. "Being Jewish is a real pain in the ass sometimes. I was totally out of my culture. I wanted to be black in the worst way then." Stern later told Geraldo that being at an all-Black school made him worry about his insubstantial penis size, but since he'd left Roosevelt somewhere around junior high, this is probably as much Stern's nebbish shtick as an admission of real neurosis. By the time he went to high school, the Sterns had moved to the Polish Catholic and WASP community of Rockville Centre. The alienation only got worse. Howard had the sense that non-Jewish girls would not date Jewish boys. "I became a total introvert."

Lanky and tall at six feet plus, he didn't make much of an impression on his peers or teachers; one teacher even recalled him as "a personality-less character." With a pretty meager social life, Stern stayed glued to the radio, imbibing the New York stations that made it out to Nassau County. One favorite was Bob Grant, a rebarbative talk show host who bounced from station to station; Grant would shout "GET OFF MY PHONE" at callers, called for the sterilization of any women with two illegitimate children supported by welfare, and labeled Blacks "mutants" and "savages." David Duke was a repeat guest on the show. (Limbaugh was also a big fan. At an event honoring Grant in 1991, he said, "Bob, you are a man who has paved the way for others to come along and do it. I am grateful to you.") One time, Stern impressed his friends and got a big laugh: improvising a spiel into the mic of a friend's tape recorder, Howard declaimed, "I am Stern, master of the universe!"

The hosts often seemed to be making up for lost adolescence. Limbaugh would begin his broadcast by lamely flirting with his newsreader. During a C-SPAN simulcast of his show in 1990, he can be heard saying to a studio staffer, "Hi, Denise, wearing your black pantyhose again today?" The twice-divorced Limbaugh had been giving it to feminists, whom he dubbed "feminazis," since before his ascension to fame. A caller mocked the idea in a news report that women were a "husband away from poverty": "Does this mean that men are a woman away from wealth?" Then Rush read out an advertisement for a new "investment vehicle" called "Collateralized Mortgage Obligations."

Other show hijinks included putting a condom on the microphone to mock "safe sex" initiatives, playing "My Boy Lollipop" for sections on the openly gay Massachusetts congressman Barney Frank, and "caller abortions," where he played vacuuming noises and screams to get an annoying caller off the line. Even for the self-declared pro-life Limbaugh, the gag was too good to give up. One bit he had to give up was the AIDS report, where Limbaugh played "Kiss Him Goodbye," "I Know I'll Never Love This Way Again," and "Looking for Love in All the Wrong Places." ACT UP activists interrupted his appearance on *The Pat Sajak Show*, and Limbaugh later said he regretted the act.

Limbaugh had various accounts of himself. Sometimes he presented himself as an entertainer and businessman first; other times he was a political satirist who would "demonstrate absurdity by being absurd." In his 1992 book *The Way Things Ought to Be*, he insisted that he presented his views with "the utmost sincerity and responsibility," but then only because he realized "the increasing importance of his views in acquiring and holding an audience." Sometimes he reveled in being called "the most dangerous man in America," then called himself a "lovable little fuzzball." Signing off on his Friday program, he would tell his listeners to enjoy their weekend and not to worry about the news; he'd tell them what to think about it next week. Then he said that was a joke and he was parodying the liberal media's propaganda, while he encouraged his listeners to "think for themselves." Joke or not, one favorite reply some of his callers had to Limbaugh's harangues was "ditto," and they started to call themselves "dittoheads." Dittoheads would gather during their lunch hours in "Rush Rooms," special areas in bars and restaurants where patrons could listen to the show together. They also paid premiums to see Limbaugh at concert halls and arenas and to go on cruises with him.

In 1987, *Talk Radio and the American Dream*, by the political scientist Murray Levin, analyzed hundreds of hours of call-in shows from the late 1970s and determined that talk radio was an outlet for "proletarian despair" and a "channel for the vast underground of discontent that lies below the calm surface of American life." But by the '90s, whether the listeners were despairing or reveling, the audience was no longer strictly proletarian and the discontent was no longer below the surface. Limbaugh's listeners were mostly white, skewing higher income than the general population. The well-fed host continued the Reaganite cult of prosperity, extolling wealth and the wealthy, even taking callers with cell phones first because they were most likely to be rich. The sense of despair, whether expressed as hostility or resignation, had become generalized.

With the formation of loyal communities, talk radio was also beginning to flex political muscle. In 1989, twenty talk radio hosts organized a nationwide protest against a proposed congressional pay raise, urging their listeners to mail tea bags to their representatives to remind them of the Boston Tea Party. That same year, in Boston, the first annual conference of the National Association of Radio Talk Show Hosts triggered fears among the big networks and newspapers of a syndicate or even a "conspiracy" of "hometown demagogues." The conference organizer, Jerry Williams, a self-declared "populist," repeatedly inserted himself and his listeners into the state's budget debates, triggering complaints of "government by talk show." In 1990, talk show hosts helped organize a "Taxpayer Action Day," with rallies in 241 of the 435 districts. Even nonpolitical hosts like Geraldo declared, "There's a populist aspect to what I do."

Howard Stern, whose show combined the tones of a high school lunch table and a gangster's hideout, could not resist trying to play political kingmaker on occasion. In an April 1992 episode, Stern and his cronies, between faking orgasms, roasting critics, making fun of "Elephant Boy"—a recurring character with a speech impediment—and assessing the hotness of celebrity wives, took time to bash the left-populist Democratic presidential candidate Jerry Brown, who had used radio and cable talk show appearances to great effect as part of his outsider campaign. Stern had actually backed Brown in New Hampshire and put him on the show, but now, gaining momentum with polling leads for the New York and Wisconsin primaries, the California governor was apparently hesitant to return the embrace. Even worse, for Stern, was Brown's floating Jesse Jackson as a running mate: Howard called him a "jerk" who "can't speak the English language" and went on: "Screw Jerry Brown with that Jesse Jackson idea. And he's not kidding, he'd make Jesse Jackson his vice-president, so he's out, we don't want him! He's gone! If he calls, tell him I don't want him on the air, let him go screw himself." Addressing his African American cohost Robin Quivers, Howard declaimed, "We got power, Robin! People listen to our opinion! H. Ross Perot for president!" Brown lost both Wisconsin and New York to Bill Clinton.

Other politicians were learning to use the talk show format more deftly. Pat Buchanan became a national figure partly through his appearances on the syndicated TV panel show *The McLaughlin Group* and CNN's *Capital Gang* and *Crossfire*. John McLaughlin, a former Jesuit priest, had created a confrontational, wild political discussion show where topics were squawked out in staccato by the eccentric host and panelists had to quickly give capsule answers. It often degenerated into shouting, with sedate, middle-of-the-road liberals from *The New Republic* given the business by experienced right-wing knife fighters like Buchanan and Robert Novak. Often McLaughlin would interrupt his panelists and just shout, "WRONG!" The show was a virtual mouthpiece of the Reagan administration: McLaughlin's wife was Reagan's secretary of labor, and Buchanan moved from his gig as a panelist to the White House Office of Communications and then back again. *The McLaughlin Group*, with vaudeville antics, had brought the zaniness of the radio call-in show to the Washington establishment set.

When Don Imus, shock jock on WFAN, was razzing the rising Democratic candidate Bill Clinton as a redneck during the primary campaign and calling him "Bubba," the Arkansas governor met the challenge with aplomb. Going on Imus's show on April 2, 1992, days before the New York primary, he gently grabbed the bull by the horns and came off as charming, telling the host, "I'm disappointed you didn't call me 'Bubba.' It's an honorable term where I come from. It's just Southern for mensch." And he wittily parried Imus's next thrust. Imus: "At least you haven't been accused of having any sort of relationship with unattractive women. I mean what if Roseanne Arnold were calling Ted Koppel, saying, 'Yeah, I been sleeping with Governor Clinton'? I mean that would be a problem." Clinton: "Listen, if she did that, I'd file a palimony suit against her. She's got the number-one TV show in the country, and I could finance the rest of this presidential campaign."

Clinton had emerged as the clear front-runner in the Democratic primary race after his decisive Super Tuesday win, but he was still dogged by the "character issue" after *The Star* tabloid claimed that he'd had a twelve-year affair with the nightclub singer Gennifer Flowers. For their part, the Clintons portrayed their marriage as one of those that had "problems" they had worked on. During a taping of *Donahue*, the silver-haired host harangued Clinton about his alleged affairs for nearly half an hour. The Arkansas governor was able to turn the tables on Donahue: "I'm not going to answer any more of these questions. I've answered them until I'm blue in the face. You are responsible for the cynicism in this country. You don't want to talk about the real issues." The audience burst into applause. He had won them over. When it was time to open things up to audience questions, Clinton got an assist. Twenty-five-year old Melissa Roth, a registered Republican, laid into Phil: "I think, really, given the pathetic state of most of the United States at this point—Medicare, education, everything else—I can't believe you spent half an hour of air time attacking this man's character." The audience cheered.

Buchanan was brilliant on TV, his challenge to Bush impressive, but it would take a "people's billionaire," a populist tycoon, to fully exploit the paradoxical insider-outsider potential of the talk show. In 1991 H. Ross Perot had become a regular guest on *Larry King Live* on CNN. (He was also a crowd favorite on *Donahue*.) Larry King, who had turned a successful radio call-in show into a cable sensation, followed the opposite strategy of the shock jocks. Instead of putting his personality and opinions front and center, he was almost a blank slate, barely even preparing for his interviews. The folksy, highly opinionated, and short-of-stature Perot found the perfect pedestal on King's show, holding forth in his motormouthed Texas twang on the Persian Gulf War (against), the Iran-Contra conspirator Oliver North (against his taking the Fifth in the investigation), and how best to distribute jobs (veterans first). King had asked Perot in 1991 if he planned on running; Perot demurred. In the meantime, private citizens had organized to draft Perot as a candidate for '92. One of those citizens was Jack Gargan, a semiretired financial planner from Florida who founded the group THRO—Throw the Hypocritical Rascals Out—in response to the savings and loan scandal and the congressional pay raise, two favorite issues of the talk radio sphere. Gargan's THRO organized rallies for Perot, and the diminutive magnate took notice of the group, addressing one of its meetings in November '91, with thousands in attendance. A group in the crowd chanted "Run Ross Run!" Still, Perot did not commit. In late February, Gargan got a call from Perot telling him to watch *Larry King Live* on February 20.

King's first question: "Are you going to run?" H. Ross Perot: "No." Larry said, "Give me something Ross Perot would do if he were king?" Perot refused to issue an edict, and said he just had "one wish" for the country: a strong family unit in every home. Like Julius Caesar refusing the crown offered by the consul Antony, Perot declined twice. But not the third time. After taking some calls, King pushed Perot again: "Is there any scenario in which you would run for President? Can you give me a scenario in which you'd say, 'OK, I'm in'?" Perot replied, "Number one, I don't want to." Then he said, "I'm not asking to be drafted. I'm saying to all these nice people that have written me if you're dead-serious then I want to see some sweat." The dealer also induced some action. King: "Are you saying groups all across America—all across America—can now, in New York, Illinois, California, start forming independent groups to get you on the ballot as an independent, and you would then—If this occurred in 50 states with enough people, you'd throw in the hat?" Perot: "I am not encouraging people to do this—but the push has to come from them. So, as Lech Walesa said, 'Words are plentiful, but deeds are precious.' And this is my way of saying, 'Will you get in the ring? Will you put the gloves on? And do you care enough about this country to stay the course?'"

In a few weeks after this brilliant piece of theater, Perot would come to be synonymous with revolt. Everyone seemed to want to come along. "Talk media is to the dominant media institutions what Ross Perot is to the dominant political institutions," Rush Limbaugh told *Broadcasting* magazine. "It is the portion of the media that the people trust the most."

5

LITTLE CAESAR

Ross Perot would later claim that his performance on *Larry King Live* was totally spontaneous, that he had given an "impulsive answer" on the show. But two weeks prior to his Larry King appearance, he had appeared on WLAC talk radio in Nashville and made the same offer to run—if citizens put him on the ballot in all fifty states. The local paper picked it up, but no one else seemed to notice. Perot had been giving obvious signs that he was itching to run for years. If only he could be "persuaded." In November 1991 he gave a speech to Jack Gargan's anti-incumbent THRO—Throw the Hypocritical Rascals Out—group at a Holiday Inn near Tampa International Airport. "Read the new book on George Washington," Perot extolled the crowd. "And your mind will immediately go to all these Democrats who say, 'I don't think I want to run this time.' Washington didn't want to run, but he ran because his nation needed him." Gargan clearly understood his cue; at the end of the speech, he joined Perot onstage and said, "Do you feel the same way I do? This is the guy who ought to be the next President of the United States! I know what he's gonna say, and Ross, before you say another word, may I paraphrase something I heard less than hour ago, George Washington didn't wanna run, but he did it because he loved his country." Perot did his best to look sheepish and honored.

"We have let our country go from a country of deeds, to a country of words and images," Perot had said. And as much as he decried this, he knew all about public relations and image-making, and was a beneficiary of the media's cooperation. *U.S. News and World Report* called him "the Davy Crockett of our time, an honest to goodness folk-hero." They were getting the idea from an earlier *Texas Monthly* piece from 1974, which the writer began in an only slightly less celebratory fashion: "I see Ross Perot as a throwback, a distinct cousin to two types of 19th century mythical American heroes. In his deeds, Perot is as gargantuan—as wonderful and awful and ridiculous—as Davy Crockett. In his idealisms, Perot would fashion himself, and the rest of us, after one of the proper and patriotic boy heroes dreamed up by the Rev. Horatio Alger." David Remnick at *The Washington Post* offered that "Ross Perot may be one of the last real Texans." Perot seemed perfectly aware of his created image, if not entirely where it came from. When NBC's Maria Shriver referred to him as a "living legend," he retorted, "I'm not a living legend, I'm just a myth." Sometimes he was a little more mordant and called himself "P. T. Barnum without the elephants."

Perot surrounded himself in mythology. His Dallas office was a shrine to Americana. Among the decor: Frederic Remington's famous *The Bronco Buster*, a bronze sculpture of a cowboy astride a bucking horse; Archibald Willard's oil painting *The Spirit of '76* (also known as *Yankee Doodle*) hanging over the desk; several Norman Rockwells, including *Homecoming Marine*, depicting the titular character showing a group his souvenir Imperial Japanese flag. And then there was Rockwell's *Breaking Home Ties*, showing an eager young lad in a new suit, about to depart for college, sitting on the running board of the family car next to his tired-out old dad, who is clothed in rancher's gear; a loyal collie plaintively nuzzles into the boy's lap. "That's my life," Perot would say to visiting journalists, pointing to *Breaking Home Ties*.

Recalling his idyllic youth in Depression-era Texarkana, Perot said, "I had the finest parents any could have, just too good to be true."

Ross's father, known as "Big Ross," although also diminutive like his son, was a successful cotton broker on the Texas side of Texarkana. Ross's mother, Lulu May Ray, was a devout Methodist who brought the family up in pious discipline. It was Lulu May Ray who set up Norman Rockwell as a religious icon for the young Ross: she tacked a Rockwell print of a praying Boy Scout above his bed. "It was part of my mother's continuing effort to keep me straight," he told *The Washington Post*. "Rockwell painted what I strived to be."

He credited his father's frugality with their family's weathering the Depression. Going into any kind of debt was a painful moral failing; Big Ross was sure to pay off the loan he had to take to buy the family's brick bungalow. (When Perot made his fortune, he bought back the house, which had been sold and painted white. In order to restore the original look, he had the entire building taken apart and rebuilt with the same bricks, turned around to reveal their unpainted side. The house sat empty but immaculate, watched over by a caretaker who lived above the garage. Perot also bought and restored a favorite boyhood movie theater.)

Throughout the Depression, Perot's parents managed to send him and his sister to an experimental private elementary school that emphasized both a kind of artsy, creative expression curriculum and rigorous Bible instruction. From a young age Perot demonstrated constant industriousness and thrift, the "worldly asceticism" that Max Weber associated with the Protestant sects. At age seven, young Ross found his calling of selling things: Christmas cards, bridles and saddles, seeds, and *The Saturday Evening Post*, featuring illustrations by none other than Norman Rockwell. But his most cherished occupation from his youth was delivering newspapers. "Dad's paper route," his daughter Nancy later recalled. "It was like a childhood myth, a fairy tale."

In Perot's telling of the tale, he was the first person to deliver newspapers to the poor Black neighborhoods in segregated Texarkana, and he did so on his pony so as to escape any sudden danger. When an otherwise fawning biographer cast doubt on the horseback deliveries and suggested that a bicycle was more likely, Perot sent the author and his editor a large map that diagrammed the route, along with testimonials from his sister and childhood acquaintances, as well as letters of retraction the author and editor could sign.

When not engaged in commercial activity, the young Perot was busy scouting. He graduated quickly from the Cub to the Boy to the Eagle Scouts. His well-thumbed Scout handbook, hatchet, and beaded belt are preserved under glass at the Ross Perot Scout Center in Texarkana. An indifferent student at school, he was on the debate team and generally well-liked, although an increasingly evident ego and a tendency to boss and order others sometimes grated his peers. His short stature, big ears, and broken nose, which he said was the product of breaking horses, made him a little shy with girls.

Perot wanted to join the U.S. Navy officer corps, but without political support, an appointment to the academy was difficult to obtain. Instead he enrolled at Texarkana Junior College, where he rushed around campus getting involved in every extracurricular activity he could, reviving the school newspaper, getting elected school president, and giving a presentation to the college deans that encouraged the college to buy more real estate and expand. To other students, he came off as overbearing, too intense, a bit of a try-hard. A professor recalled that Perot was "a leader, very mature, and had a fine personality," but "he was likely involved in too many projects outside of school."

After two years at junior college, Perot finally got his commission to the Naval Academy in Annapolis, having been appointed by retiring Texas senator W. Lee "Pappy" O'Daniel. Perot immediately took to the discipline of the academy and excelled as a midshipman despite his average grades. He received high evaluations from his fellow cadets and commanding officers, got himself elected student vice president and then president, headed the school's honor committee, and rewrote the honor code. He threatened to resign as class president when one midshipman wasn't properly punished because of his important family connections. During his time at Annapolis, Perot went on a blind date with Margot Birmingham, a coed at Goucher College who was from an old Pennsylvania family. According to Perot, it was love at first sight. The future Mrs. Perot told her friends, "Well, he's clean."

At age twenty-three, Perot got his first active duty assignment aboard the destroyer USS *Sigourney*. This was during the Korean War, but Perot's ship never got near combat. Still, the anxiety of possible fighting was enough to drive the men into religious services given by the ship's Protestant chaplain. "I preached to standing-room-only audiences on the fantail of that destroyer," Perot recalled. "I thought I was Billy Graham." When the war ended mid-cruise, the churchgoing population suddenly dropped off. But Perot's moral probity made him the natural choice for shore patrol officer, tasked with rounding up wayward sailors on leave.

Having to chase after drunken sailors in brothels or bail them out of jail disgusted him. As the ship's prosecutor for courts-martial, he got convictions in the nineteen cases he tried, but he felt uneasy with his commanding officer, who had a lax attitude toward the men, allowing them to gamble and shoot the ship's antiaircraft guns at cans they threw overboard. Perot also claimed that the captain pressured him to grant access to the ship's store of liquor and its recreation funds so he could redecorate his cabin. Perot wanted out early. His father started to lobby their congressman, Wright Patman. Perot then tried to submit a letter of resignation to his commanding officer. "I have found the Navy to be a fairly Godless organization (with the exception of the Naval Academy), according to my personal beliefs," wrote the twenty-four-year-old. "I do not enjoy the prospect of continuing to stand on the quarterdeck as Officer of the Deck in foreign ports, being subjected to drunken tales of moral emptiness, passing out penicillin pills, and seeing promiscuity on the part of married men." Big Ross even took the letter to Senator Lyndon B. Johnson.

The navy did not look favorably on Perot's suit. The admiral in charge of the destroyer fleet denied Perot's request for a discharge, also noting that he was "emotionally maladjusted for a regular Navy career." For the remainder of his four-year active duty service he was assigned to the USS *Leyte*, an aircraft carrier, where he seems to have readjusted to life in the service. Shortly before his stint ended, an IBM executive invited on board by the secretary of the navy observed Perot commanding an exercise and was impressed. He offered the young officer an interview.

In the mid-1950s, IBM was hardly less regimented than the U.S. Navy. Every employee was required to wear a dark suit with a white shirt and a "sincere" tie. The company swelled during World War II and was now an integral part of the Cold War, providing the massive computers the military needed for its vast fleets of planes, missiles, and ships. The company also provided for its employees. This was the age of what the economist Hyman Minsky called "managerial-welfare capitalism" or "paternalistic capitalism": the corporate behemoth and state leviathan moved harmoniously together; the average man sheltered under them. IBM culture was "cradle to the grave": it offered lifelong employment and such benefits as free membership in the company's own country club and golf courses around the country. As at the Naval Academy, Perot excelled in the high-discipline, buttoned-up world of IBM, surpassing his quotas as a salesman and rankling his coworkers. But his ideas for expanding IBM into services and software were ignored by management. Self-starting Perot was running up against "the bureaucracy" again at IBM.

Then transcendental inspiration struck. According to the story Perot told, he was waiting for a haircut (close-cropped, of course) and reading *Reader's Digest*. He noticed a quotation from Thoreau's *Walden*: "The mass of men lead lives of quiet desperation." Perot was called to his purpose. "At that moment," Perot later claimed, "I got the idea for EDS." He said he got the name itself while at services at Highland Park Presbyterian Church in Dallas, scribbling ideas down on the back of a pledge envelope: "Electronic . . . Data . . . Systems. Electronic Data

Systems. EDS." The Spirit of Capitalism had come down and moved the Protestant ethicist.

Perot organized Electronic Data Systems on an almost paramilitary basis. He preferred to hire veterans. "EDS attracts people who would like to be on the SWAT team," a former employee would say. A hiring questionnaire probed into prospective employees' private lives and attitudes. Lie detector tests were used. He copied the IBM uniform: white shirts, dark suits, conservative ties. (No pants allowed for the few female employees.) No facial hair allowed. Alcohol was forbidden at company meals. Adultery was grounds for dismissal. Discussing salaries was grounds for dismissal. You could be fired if your wife misbehaved, too. Unions were out of the question. Perot expected long hours and backbreaking work. Early employees said they practically lived at the office.

The culture was not just military, it was imperial. When EDS finally got its own massive, gated campus in North Dallas, a carved stone eagle soared over the lobby. Sculpted eagles could be found throughout EDS's offices. To Perot it was a symbol of patriotism and individualism. "Eagles don't flock," he liked to say. But the emphasis at Electronic Data Systems was on unit cohesion, teamwork, company loyalty. Later, Perot was highly flattered when a group of Japanese executives called EDS "the most Japanese" American company they had visited. "There's a sign over the gate at Toyota City and it says 'Every worker is a brother,'" Perot told *The Washington Post*. "That's EDS." In return for loyalty, Perot provided. Employees told stories about Perot showing up at hospitals when workers or their family members had emergencies, footing the bill for private jets to specialists, expensive treatments, and long-term care.

For all the high-concept corporate culture, the discipline, the austerity, the frugality, the long hours, and the commando squad atmosphere of the start-up, EDS was barely getting by. The initial concept was straightforward: the company brokered between companies that owned massive IBM computers but didn't need them all the time, and those that needed computers but couldn't afford them: in essence, computer owners would sell spare time to other companies. (Remember: computers took up rooms, even entire floors.) Then EDS came up with a "facilities management" model, getting contracts to run companies' computer systems for them for a fixed price. EDS netted the potato chip giant Frito-Lay as a customer. In 1964, after two years of operation, the company posted just over a 1 percent profit on $400,000 in revenues: $4,100. The number of companies that needed massive computing power and were willing to pay a lot for it was relatively small. Perot had to moonlight at the Texas Blue Cross and Blue Shield office that shared the same building as EDS. The year 1965 would turn out better.

On July 30, 1965, as part of his Great Society expansion of the welfare state, Texas's own President Lyndon B. Johnson signed two amendments to the Social Security Act of 1935. Title XVIII, which provided medical insurance for the aged, became known as Medicare, and Title XIX, enabling states to support health care for those who needed or were near needing public assistance, which became known as Medicaid. Suddenly some fifty million Americans were entitled to government-supported health benefits. This would become a massive feat of administration, requiring computers and people to run those computers.

And there was Perot and EDS ready to help. Or ready to help themselves. Medicare and Medicaid provided federal matching funds for the states, each of which was responsible for administering its own health system with the help of the nonprofit Blue Cross and Blue Shield associations—"the Blues," as they were known. Instead of one giant customer, there were fifty giant customers. Surely this potential windfall would provoke sharp competition among firms wanting to get in on the action. Well, Perot had a way around that. He still worked at Texas Blue Shield; he had an inside track. In 1966, Texas Blue Shield signed a deal with EDS to obtain computer processing time for Medicare claims. The people at the Social Security Administration, not informed at the time, were alarmed when they learned the details a year later: there was no competitive bidding and no record of any contract negotiations. There was no provision for the government to inspect EDS's books to ensure that no profiteering was going on.

The SSA scrambled a team to go down to Texas to lecture Texas Blue Cross on conflict of interest issues and to check out EDS's books. Perot said he would show the books to the auditors, and then, when they arrived, he decided they couldn't see them. SSA told Texas Blue Shield that they'd have to let them preview their next contract with EDS and told Perot that he'd have to open his books if there was a contract. In 1968 Texas Blue Shield re-signed with EDS. Once again, there was no audit, no bidding, no contract sent back to D.C. for review. When the bureaucrats finally got to review the contract, they were horrified. Government analysts estimated that the cost of processing each claim was $0.36 and that a fair profit for a provider would be $0.55, a 50 percent gross margin. EDS charged $1.06 per claim, a 200 percent margin. EDS also appeared to be double-counting claims.

The new contract had another clause: a quarter of a million dollars for the development of a software program to process claims. The SSA insisted that this program belonged to the American people, as they paid for it. Perot felt otherwise. He had good reason for holding things close to the vest: EDS was selling the program state by state at a considerable profit. In 1971, a congressional investigation into EDS business practices revealed that between 1966 and 1971 the federal government paid EDS $36 million. In 1971 alone, $20.2 million of the $23.2 million paid to Medicare subcontractors went to EDS. The company's profits went from an emaciated 1 percent to a chubby 40 percent. During this time EDS also lost most of its corporate clients. Perot, the champion of thrift and rugged pioneer virtues, was dependent on the welfare state.

From this point on, the line between capitalism and politics grew ever blurrier for Perot. He was certainly a capitalist, but not much of a free marketeer: when he ran for president, he would bemoan the antagonistic relationship between business and government; he thought they should work hand in hand. "The United States is the largest and most complex business enterprise in the history of mankind," he liked to say. But if the USA was a kind of business, EDS was also a political entity, even its own kind of government. Not only did EDS rely on the state for its business prospects, it was increasingly an adjunct of the state, a privatized section of the bureaucracy. Perot had to cultivate political ties—friendly politicians who could help him get the contracts and smooth things over. But EDS was also a state within—or at least beside—the state. It supplied its own model of the state and society: regimented, cooperative, militarized, hardworking, efficient, with an inspired, paternal leader at the helm. EDS even began to develop its own foreign policy and security apparatus. In the coming cultural foment of the 1960s, it provided an alternative vision of the nation: technology would advance, productivity and efficiency increase, but conservative values would remain in place. As far as EDS and Perot were concerned, the 1950s never had to end.

At the same time it was reaping benefits from the Great Society, EDS had less time for the Civil Rights Act or the sudden explosion of self-expression. EDS landed its biggest Medicare and Medicaid contract of all with Blue Shield of California, with the blessing of a Reagan gubernatorial administration otherwise obsessed with welfare abuse. As part of the deal, EDS would take over data processing for the entire California Blue Shield system. EDS teams alighted like commandos on unsuspecting Blue Shield offices—or, as some complained, like "storm troopers." The company toughened its dress code for California: no "mod looks," miniskirts, flat shoes, long hair, colored eye shadow, or "gaudy jewelry." The questionnaire for employees asked about their church attendance, their level of indebtedness, and how often they paid their bills. Workers who didn't comply were out—immediately.

Another thing that was forbidden by the EDS dress code: Afro hairstyles popular in the late 1960s. Black programmers and analysts were made to feel particularly unwelcome. Half the Black employees were fired outright. There were suspicions of a systematic purge of Blacks through dismissals and demotions. Flimsy pretexts were used to get rid of Black workers, as when Hardy Green, a Black operations analyst, was fired for insubordination because he wanted to keep some old manuals near his desk for reference. "We were considered undesirable, because we didn't fit the EDS image," Green said. "The EDS image was a white image, as white as the shirts we had to wear." Green also said that he heard EDS managers from Texas call Black men "boys." (Green, however, told a 1992 *Newsday* investigation into then-candidate Perot that he didn't consider the boss himself to be personally racist and was considering voting for him for president.) EDS lost several Unemployment Insurance Appeals Board hearings, but it wasn't until 1983 that the Labor Department demanded that EDS institute an affirmative action plan.

Electronic Data Systems's new windfall brought Wall Street calling. There was a bull market for tech stocks in the late '60s. EDS was still a relatively modest enterprise, with earnings of $7.7 million for 1968, which came out to 14 cents a share. Ken Langone of R. W. Pressprich and Co. offered to underwrite the public offering of EDS at $16.50 a share, around 118 times earnings. The prospectus for investors didn't mention the company's reliance on Medicaid or Medicare or that federal auditors were sniffing around, even refusing to reimburse some claims. Perot placed only 650,000 of the 11.5 million outstanding shares on the market: they climbed to $38 on opening day and reached $160 by the next year.

Perot was a billionaire. At least as far as the New York Stock Exchange was concerned. But now EDS had to keep growing in order to justify its massively inflated value on the market. And with most of the state Medicare and Medicaid processing market already dominated by EDS, there were only a few customers who could afford the multimillion-dollar contracts the company needed to keep its growth rate going. At the same time, Perot had to contend with an increasingly restive and unhappy Social Security Administration breathing down his neck. He needed new connections. Then, in 1968, the chairman of PepsiCo, a former client, invited him to meet the Republican presidential candidate Richard Nixon to discuss how computers could benefit modern political campaigns.

Perot lent the Nixon campaign seven "volunteers" from EDS. When Nixon won, they went to the inauguration. Soon enough, Perot started to lend staff members to the White House for special projects. Perot's self-made, folksy image—and the fact that he was not part of the hated Eastern Establishment—fit in well in the ideological firmament of the Nixon administration; he became a frequent caller and visitor to the White House and was subsequently made a board member of the Richard Nixon Foundation. Perot suggested grand schemes to help Nixon, such as buying ABC or *The Washington Post* in order to soften their coverage. He came up with a plan to counter campus protests with a pro-war student organization that he would personally fund. Most of the notions he cooked were up infeasible, but the White House did have at least one project where they needed his help.

By 1969, the war in Vietnam was not going well and the anti-war movement had attained a level of popular legitimacy. The Nixon administration came up with a public relations campaign to reverse the tide and rally support for the war. Internally called "Go Public," the plan would focus media attention on the plight of prisoners of war and missing in action servicemen. Most of them were airmen: handsome, dashing young officers from privileged backgrounds, some of whom had been captured during the earliest phases of American involvement in Indochina and were being held under appalling conditions in North Vietnam, often undergoing torture. They left behind young, sympathetic, and often photogenic wives who were deeply concerned for their well-being.

The administration—Perot claims it was Henry Kissinger himself, but it was probably Chief of Staff H. R. Haldeman—contacted Perot to help bring attention to the POWs, in concert with a November speech on Vietnam to be given by President Nixon. Perot formed an organization—United We Stand America—and worked with Madison Avenue firms to create newspaper advertisements. The full-page ads, printed in papers across the country, showed a photo of a family at prayer, with the caption "Bring our Daddy home, safe and sound" and the message "THE MAJORITY SPEAKS—RELEASE THE PRISONERS." At the bottom of the ad was a coupon that could be clipped out and a request for donations on behalf of the prisoners. A television special funded by Perot also included an appeal for donations. Perot claimed that he received three million responses within two weeks of the campaign. It's not clear what happened to the money. But the names and addresses of millions of potentially sympathetic Americans now sat safely in EDS's hoard of data.

The POW issue fired Perot's imagination, and he found another calling: as a propagandist. On his own initiative, he flew a jumbo jet full of Christmas dinners and gifts to Laos and demanded that the North Vietnamese allow him to deliver them to the prisoners. He held United We Stand rallies. He built bamboo cages containing life-size wax figures of POWs, cockroaches, and rats, to be displayed at the Capitol.

In apparent gratitude for his help on Vietnam, favors were returned: the Social Security Administration dropped its inquiries into EDS business practices, and without executive branch cooperation, the congressional investigations went nowhere; Perot got new, large contracts with the Department of Health, Education, and Welfare (HEW), and the White House lobbied on Perot's behalf for EDS to become the sole data processor for the entire Social Security Administration. But for the most part, Perot didn't deliver on his promises to the Nixon administration: $50 million for campaign ads never turned up, nor did $10 million for a think tank, nor did he contribute any money to the Nixon Foundation, despite being on the board. Perot did get the other top executives of EDS to give to the Nixon campaign, even if he personally did not. But his PR offensives arguably redounded more to the benefit of H. Ross Perot than of Richard M. Nixon.

Despite an increasingly tense relationship with the White House, Perot did do one clear favor for Nixon. In 1971, the hallowed Wall Street brokerage firm F. I. Dupont, Glore Forgan and Co. was on the verge of collapse following involvement in a pension fund fraud debacle. Some $15 million in securities owed to clients had mysteriously disappeared from Dupont's records. If Dupont, the second-largest brokerage house, failed, the administration feared it would bring all of Wall Street down with it. With the help of the president of the New York Stock Exchange, Nixon aides talked Perot into infusing blue-blooded old Dupont with fresh Sunbelt capital. Perot was interested. He'd had previous contracts with Dupont, and Wall Street was one of the only places other than the federal government that could potentially afford the huge deals that EDS needed to keep its stock price afloat. But his effort was a spectacular failure: an initial investment of $10 million eventually became one of $100 million as Perot kept having to pour in money. Wall Street brokers did not want to cooperate with EDS-style military regimentation and could just leave their firm with their client lists if they wanted to. EDS stock declined from $162 a share in 1970 to $11 a share in 1974. Perot was not quite ruined, but he was certainly reduced. Dupont dissolved for good.

The Nixon administration was no longer inclined to do Perot any favors. When he barged into the office of the secretary of HEW to demand Medicare contracts, the new secretary, Caspar Weinberger, stonewalled him. Perot stormed out. "This is a very unpleasant man," Weinberger would later recall. The Nixon administration was fed up. Perot, claiming there were still prisoners being held in Laos, announced to the press that he had set up a private spy network in Indochina to get information on POWs. Then he upstaged the Nixon administration's celebration for returning POWs with his own events: a lavish party in San Francisco replete with appearances by John Wayne, Clint Eastwood, Red Skelton, and the Andrews Sisters. Among the attendees: John S. McCain III and the eighty-five Green Berets who had performed a daring helicopter raid on the Sơn Tây prison camp. (The camp was empty. Senator J. W. Fulbright charged that the Defense Department knew the prisoners were gone and had launched the raid for public relations purposes. The Green Beret commander said that the mission was "a complete success with the exception that no prisoners were rescued.") Perot threw another celebration for POWs a few months later at the Cotton Bowl in Dallas. He said he had skipped the San Francisco bash so the focus could be on the POWs, but in Dallas he couldn't keep away. Spotlights found him in the bleachers, where he stood up to receive his triumph from the adoring crowd.

Despite Perot's moment in the lights, EDS's fortunes were flagging. The company again lost many of its corporate clients. IBM had caught up in the facilities management game and was competing for data processing contracts. EDS lost Medicare contracts in Massachusetts, New York, and California. A Government Accountability Office audit into EDS revealed huge backlogs in claims processing, substandard work, and improper accounting practices. In some cases, EDS had even destroyed claims to get rid of the backlogs. At the same time, the company was getting advance notice of competitors' bids, giving it an unfair advantage. The government slapped fines on the firm and set up a special unit to monitor its activities.

A latent paranoid streak in Perot grew more accentuated: he hired private investigators to check out employees, competitors, daughters' boyfriends. He moved EDS headquarters to a walled compound patrolled by armed guards. Employees were physically searched and given polygraphs. Perot became convinced that the North Vietnamese had contracted the Black Panthers to assassinate him. He later claimed that would-be assassins had scaled his walls but had been chased off by his guard dogs. He traveled with bodyguards and bought a specially designed bulletproof car with special emplacements for firing submachine guns. When Texas governor Bill Clements appointed Perot to a special commission on narcotics, Perot demanded permission to build a helipad on his property to avoid ambushes by the cartels. His neighbors successfully resisted that one.

With EDS running out of profits in the United States, Perot looked abroad, to the periphery of America's imperial dominion. In 1976 EDS landed a $41 million contract with the Iranian Ministry of Health and Social Welfare. In order to get the contract, EDS had to arrange for payments to the various charitable "foundations" of the shah and his relatives. One Iranian official flatly demanded a bribe, which came in the form of free computer services for the queen. High officials in Iran were certainly better at securing their favors from Perot and EDS than the Nixon White House had been. EDS's business with the Iranian state grew to around $90 million in value. But the political protection available in Iran was neither stable nor long-lasting.

In 1978, unrest gripped Iran. The Ministry of Health and Social Welfare stopped making its monthly payments to EDS. Troops fired on a protest in Tehran and killed scores of demonstrators; the shah declared martial law, but the country descended further into chaos. In a last-ditch effort to try to appease the opposition to his regime, the shah also made an effort to clean up corruption. The minister of health and social welfare and several members of his staff were arrested. One of them was on the EDS payroll. Perot began to pull his people out of Iran, leaving a small staff to try to get the Iranian government to resume its payments. Late in the year, a special prosecutor arrested two EDS executives in Tehran as part of a corruption investigation. They were held on $12.6 million bail.

Perot immediately began to pressure the State Department, all the way up to Secretary Cyrus Vance, demanding that the situation of EDS employees be given top priority and irritating the U.S. embassy staff, who started to believe that the corruption allegations might be legitimate. With the U.S. government unable to secure the release of his men quickly enough, Perot got in touch with Colonel Arthur D. "Bull" Simons, the leader of the raiders on the Sơn Tây prisoner of war camp. Simons organized a small team of EDS employees who had military experience to storm the Iranian Ministry of Justice and free the prisoners. The team managed to slip into Iran, only to find that the prisoners had been moved to a more secure jail. The State Department begged them not to attempt the raid, saying it would endanger other Americans remaining in the country whether it succeeded or failed. They cast around for another solution, such as bribing an official. Events outstripped their efforts: the shah fled the country; Ayatollah Khomeini returned; revolutionary mobs descended on Tehran's prisons; and the EDS employees walked out of their cells and into the Hyatt, where they met Simons and his team, who drove them across the Turkish border.

Perot wanted to immortalize the story in a bestselling book and tasked a team with finding an appropriate author. At first he hired Robin Moore, who wrote the novel *The Green Berets*, which the John Wayne movie was based on. But Moore asked too many questions, and he was fired. Perot's wife was reading a novel by the thriller writer Ken Follett, and Perot instructed his staff to get in touch. At first he didn't like the looks of the fellow on the back cover: "He looks like a faggot to me." (Insufficient masculinity was a recurring anxiety for Perot. He would often disdain others as "sissies" or "limp-wristed"; recruiters were instructed to be on the lookout for weak handshakes, as they might indicate a homosexual, and when running for president in 1992, he made negative news for himself by saying he wouldn't put any homosexuals in his cabinet.)

In Follett's version of events—presented in the 1983 *New York Times* bestselling novel *On Wings of Eagles*—the mob that facilitated the EDS prisoners' escape was egged on by an EDS trainee, a young man named Rashid. Other prisoners there at the time cast doubt on that story. The 1986 NBC television miniseries *On Wings of Eagles*, starring Richard Crenna as Perot and Burt Lancaster as Bull Simons, depicted a firefight between the revolutionaries armed by Rashid and the prison guards, as well as Simons blowing up an Iranian base on their way out of country. None of that happened. Nor was Perot waiting for the team as they crossed the Turkish border. In classic vigilante-culture style, the miniseries depicted the U.S. government bureaucrats as weak and feckless, unable to protect or free their own people at the embassy, but Ross Perot came across as a man of action who cared for his own. A country-and-western song recorded during the U.S. embassy hostage crisis that followed praised Perot: "There ain't no real-life heroes / Throughout this wretched realm / Where are you now when we need you, Ross Perot?" Letters of support from the public poured into Perot's office. He wondered aloud if he should run for president. "No. King," an employee joked.

The spectacle of helpless American hostages and a government that was apparently unwilling or unable to do anything for them reopened the never-quite-healed wounds of Vietnam. "Now that the public preoccupation with the Iranian hostage crisis is ending, Americans ought to be reminded 113 of their countrymen known to have been prisoners of war in Vietnam and 1,037 other servicemen listed as missing in action have never been accounted for by Hanoi," the *New Castle News* in Pennsylvania opined after the Iranian government released the embassy hostages in 1981. "Isn't it ironic that the Administration and practically everybody are so enthusiastically backing (as indeed they should) the release of the 50 hostages in Iran while ignoring the plight of the families of the MIA (Missing in Action) who are suffering the extreme agony of uncertainty," wrote the father of an MIA serviceman in an op-ed in the *Los Angeles Times*. "The National League of Families of American Prisoners and Missing in Southeast Asia has obtained sufficient evidence to prove that American prisoners (alive) are being held in Southeast Asia." There was nothing approaching sufficient evidence. A House select committee investigation during the Ford administration declared that there were no living prisoners of war still in captivity in Indochina, infuriating POW/MIA activists and fueling their suspicions that the government was deliberately keeping a lid on the terrible secret of the missing men.

The idea that there were abandoned Americans still alive in Southeast Asia synthesized the pro-war and anti-war imagination: paranoia and distrust of government born of revelations about the intelligence agencies, Watergate, and the secret wars in Laos and Cambodia mingled with the sense that the country was stabbed in the back by cowardly and deceitful bureaucrats and liberal elites. The myth gave hope to the families of the 2,500 men still "unaccounted for"—a category that included those believed by the military to be dead—that their fathers and sons might still be alive. And it gave hope to the nation that its honor could be restored through the rescue—or the resurrection, really—of the lost men. What began as a public relations blitz had transformed into a veritable national cult.

Perot positioned himself as a messianic figure in this nationalist cult of the undead. Here was a man who could overcome the traitors who had left America's warriors behind, rescue the captives, and redeem the nation's sense of loss and humiliation. If the government was unwilling or unable to act, a patriotic private individual would. Perot's Persian foray attracted the attention of General Eugene F. Tighe, the director of the Defense Intelligence Agency, who approached Perot and put him in touch with James "Bo" Gritz, a retired former Green Beret and Vietnam vet. The idea was that Perot would fund an expedition to Laos, led by Gritz, in order to locate MIAs. Perot was not interested in recovering remains that would remove men from the "unaccounted for" list and perhaps permit some family to finally grieve. "I don't care about bones. I wouldn't pay one cent for a bone," he reportedly told Gritz. That stipulation was more important than Perot knew: after one of his expeditions, Gritz would deposit "remains" with the U.S. embassy in Bangkok that turned out to be chicken bones.

Gritz's raids would prove to be farcical. During one 1982 assay, he crossed into Laos only to be ambushed by an indigenous militia that killed two of his men and captured another. On his retreat, Gritz ran into Pathet Lao forces who chased him back to the border. Gritz apparently had to abandon all his gear and strip down to his underwear to cross the river into Thailand, where he was arrested by Thai authorities, prompting a flurry of embarrassed U.S. diplomatic cables. Both Perot and the U.S. government would downplay and deny their connections with Gritz. "If I and my people don't do it, I don't know anyone in Washington who will. It takes action, and both Teddy Roosevelt and John Wayne are dead," Gritz wrote in the "Intelligence Summary and Situation Report" of one his operations.

The growing confusion between reality and Hollywood was to be a hallmark of the arriving Reagan era. Along with Perot, Gritz counted among his other backers Clint Eastwood and William Shatner, the latter of whom paid Gritz for the movie rights to his life story. Eastwood was to be Gritz's connection to the White House. During a meeting at the president's Rancho de Cielo in Santa Barbara, Reagan reportedly told Eastwood that if Gritz located a single prisoner, he would "launch World War III to get the rest out."

Ronald Reagan was a longtime supporter of the POW/MIA movement. In 1954 he had starred in *Prisoner of War*, playing a soldier who voluntarily gets himself captured to investigate reports of torture in a North Korean POW camp. He called it "the only experience that I had that was at all in keeping with what you have gone through" to a group of former POWs. Reagan publicly wore a commemorative bracelet engraved with the name of a missing man, and he kept five more displayed in a study adjoining the Oval Office. (H. Ross Perot was the honorary first recipient of such a bracelet back in the 1970s.) And Reagan was absolutely convinced of the existence of live prisoners, obsessing over the issue in consultations with his national security advisers. The president declared the MIA issue to be "the highest national priority of his administration." Not long after his inauguration, he authorized a mercenary incursion into Laos based on a satellite photo that showed shadows that analysts believed were "too long" to be cast by Asians. The raids revealed nothing, but a Pentagon official told *The Washington Post* that they were "helpful to the Reagan administration's effort to convince prisoner of war families that it is determined to pursue every avenue to rescue any Americans still held captive in Southeast Asia."

For reasons both ideological and practical, the Reagan administration displayed a liking for the kind of privatization of foreign policy pioneered by Perot. Government was, after all, the problem. But also, if something failed or was an embarrassment—or was illegal or even unconstitutional—the private nature of the capers gave the administration a work-around and "plausible deniability." In 1981 Reagan named Perot to his Foreign Intelligence Advisory Board, where he quickly became a conduit for questionable information and dubious schemes. But perhaps more important to the administration, Perot was also a possible source of cash. Private money raised on behalf of POW/MIAs ended up being funneled by the National Security Council to anti-communist guerrillas in Laos. A National Security Council staffer, Lieutenant Colonel Oliver North, working with a covert Pentagon unit called the Intelligence Support Activity (ISA), began to hit Perot up for ransom money to free the American hostages taken by Hezbollah in Lebanon and General James Dozier, who'd been kidnapped by the Red Brigades in Italy. In neither case did Perot's money end up securing the release of the prisoners, but he came up with it happily. Perot also claimed that the government wanted him to organize a rescue attempt for Dozier. (The same secret DOD group—ISA—was also responsible for providing support for Bo Gritz's Southeast Asian activities.)

North also approached Perot about providing a "donation" to the Contras, the brutal anti-communist rebels in Nicaragua that Congress had explicitly forbidden the United States from funding. North had at one time been considering resigning from the Marine Corps and taking a job at Electronic Data Systems, but apparently he was convinced to stay in the service after a patriotic pep talk from Perot. "So, Iran-Contra is all Perot's fault," North would later half joke. When the scandal broke in the press and the Reagan administration's illegal effort to fund the Contras via proceeds from the sale of arms to Iran became widely known, Perot leapt to defend North's integrity. But according to North, behind the scenes Perot was attempting to suborn his testimony, offering to take care of his legal fees and family if he cleared the president. (The congressional Iran-Contra report reveals at least one conversation between Perot and White House chief of staff Donald Regan concerning North's testimony.) When North's allegations against Perot aired with the publication of his memoirs in 1991, Perot called North a liar and said that he'd only been encouraging North to "tell the truth." He went on *Larry King Live* and played part of a tape-recording to vindicate his version of events. Perot also later claimed that the administration had approached him with the Iran-Contra scheme and he'd refused to participate.

"I have one mission in life," Perot declaimed, "and that's to get to the bottom of the POW-MIA situation." But there seemed to be no bottom. The boundary between fantasy and reality had deteriorated. Inspired partly by the exploits of Gritz and other self-appointed rescuers, Hollywood took to the POW/MIA issue: there was *Uncommon Valor* (1983) starring Gene Hackman, *Missing in Action* (1984) with Chuck Norris, and, of course, Sylvester Stallone in *Rambo: First Blood Part II* (1985). All these films feature a nation governed by shadowy cabals of bureaucrats and politicians involved in the nonstop betrayal of the missing fighting men. A hero is required in order to take action and cut through the dark jungles of bureaucracy. The movies soon reentered reality. In 1985 the chairman of the Subcommittee on Asian and Pacific Affairs, New York Democratic congressman Stephen Solarz, was greeted with boos and chants of "Rambo! Rambo!" when he addressed the National League of Families convention. CBS's *60 Minutes* aired a segment called "Dead or Alive?," which presented the idea that a government conspiracy to cover up the existence of live POWs was a credible notion worthy of serious investigation. When asked by chairman Solarz if he had evidence of living POWs, Gritz replied, "I have the same evidence, sir, that might be presented by a clergyman to convince you that God exists." The cult became a religion.

The Stallone movies provided the White House name for the most radical—and most dubious—section of MIA activists: the "Rambo set" or "Rambo faction." It was this "Rambo set" that had Perot's ear, and often his wallet. There wasn't much else to occupy his time. General Motors bought Electronic Data Systems in 1984, part of the '80s fad of mergers and acquisitions. The idea was that EDS could help modernize the creaky giant of American industry. Perot didn't have much to offer in the way of concrete information, just repeated public criticism of GM's executives in the press. In order to get a greater share of pay and power for EDS executives, he even plotted shutting down GM's entire computer system. In 1986, General Motors CEO Roger Smith decided to buy out Perot's remaining shares in GM, essentially paying him $750 million, almost twice the value of GM's stock on the market, to go away. (Perot initially objected, saying it was "morally wrong" and that he couldn't take the money while GM was closing plants and laying off workers. He eventually took the money.) Forbidden by the terms of the deal from starting a new business for two years, Perot threw himself into the POW issue.

The Reagan administration appeared desperate for ways to occupy Perot. He resigned from the President's Intelligence Advisory Board out of impatience. The administration offered him a role on a special commission headed by former DIA director Tighe on the POW/MIA issue. He turned it down, but showed up at the congressional hearings anyway and gave impromptu testimony, hinting that he knew people with secret knowledge, but then he became evasive when asked for their names so they could be subpoenaed. Tighe accused the administration of inaction and said that he was more convinced than ever of the existence of living prisoners.

There was now talk of legislation to form a "Perot Commission." It was opposed by the administration and the National League of Families. A Vietnam veteran staged a hunger strike in a bamboo cage at the Vietnam Memorial to try to force the Reagan administration to answer questions about missing POWs. Three women snuck past Secret Service agents to plant a black POW/MIA flag on the White House lawn. Gritz showed Perot a videotape of a Burmese opium lord named Kuhn Sa, who claimed that Richard Armitage, the assistant secretary of defense for POW/MIA affairs, was involved in a drug trafficking operation that was using the POWs as slave labor. (Armitage had revealed that Gritz's "remains" were chicken bones.) Perot began to shop wild rumors and accusations about Armitage around D.C. By 1991, a *Wall Street Journal* poll revealed that 69 percent of the U.S. population believed that there were live POWs left behind in Vietnam and that the government wasn't doing enough to get them out. Things were getting out of control.

Instead of shutting Perot out, the Reagan administration at first tried to bring him closer. There was the matter of the $2.5 million pledge by Perot for the Reagan Library. But perhaps there was also the recognition that Perot was becoming a political force of his own. "We didn't want this man mad," Deputy Chief of Staff James Cannon frankly admitted. Vice President Bush tried to humor Perot. He called him for help in verifying a story told by two former Green Berets who claimed to have seen a tape showing about forty POWs chained together, digging for gold somewhere in Southeast Asia. The tape was almost certainly falsified, if it ever existed: it was held by a shady British businessman in Singapore who had been arrested for fraud. Perot paid the defrauded party to drop the complaint. The tape never materialized, and the U.S. government balked at reimbursing Perot. Perot was convinced the tape actually existed, and he blamed Bush for bungling the operation.

Bush decided that the way to make Perot's suspicions go away was to give him complete access to the classified DIA intelligence on POW/MIAs. But having access to the files only inflamed Perot's paranoia: he believed he was being followed by government agents, and he took to shifting hotel rooms and driving around in a beat-up old Volkswagen to lose his "tails." The attacks against Richard Armitage increased in intensity, with Perot calling up the vice president to demand his firing. Daniel Sheehan, a public interest lawyer turned conspiracist who ran the left-wing Christic Institute, approached Perot with more tales of CIA drug trafficking—not to mention the possible involvement of

Bush's sons in Iran-Contra. Perot went to Bush with the allegations as "one father to another." Bush thanked Perot for the tip but replied that his sons were "straight arrows." Perot finally got fed up and called Bush, telling him he was canceling his pledge to the Reagan Library and severing his ties with the administration. He left for Vietnam the next day.

Although they had encouraged Perot's private initiatives in the past, the Reagan administration was in fits about his solo flight to Vietnam. "It would have been disastrous if the Vietnamese had perceived Perot as an official representative," recalled Richard Childress, a staff member on Reagan's National Security Council. "He tried to take over the negotiations by portraying himself as close to the president and vice-president. He was running his own foreign policy." Ever the businessman, Perot was convinced that the Vietnamese were holding on to the POWs as bargaining chips and that they wanted money and deals. He was willing to pony up. He returned from Vietnam with the idea that he would pay $1 million per prisoner or buy the entirety of Cam Ranh Bay. The administration had had enough. Perot was ushered into a perfunctory meeting with Reagan, where, surrounded by aides and reading from index cards, the president emphasized the need for a single foreign policy. If the message was unclear, Reagan read one of the cards twice. A couple months after Perot's Vietnam jaunt, the army canceled a $63 million contract with Electronic Data Systems, citing a "technical error." In point of fact, a congressional audit from that year concluded that EDS had been "improperly favored" over lower bidders. (EDS had been bought by GM at this point, but Perot was still its top executive and, incidentally, the largest individual shareholder in GM.)

For their part, the Vietnamese must have been puzzled about what Perot was after. They did not interpret his intentions as fully humanitarian: one of his employees returned from Vietnam with a signed letter of intent from the foreign minister that read in part, "The Socialist Republic of Viet Nam will appoint Mr. Ross Perot and/or his companies as an agent of Viet Nam in the procurement of capital investment and establishment of joint venture companies . . . in the following areas: Electronics, Oil and gas, Metallurgy, Food/agriculture, Transportation, Real estate development." (In 1992, Perot would tell the Senate Select Committee on POW/MIA Affairs, "I have had no business conversations with the Vietnamese, have no interest in business conversations with the Vietnamese.")

Back in the States, the Dallas Press Club threw a homecoming celebration for Perot. A thousand guests sat at tables decorated with boxes marked SECRET and toy soldiers firing machine guns. A hotel clerk dressed as a POW/MIA was chained to an hors d'oeuvres table. "I'm here honoring H. Ross Perot," he told *The Washington Post*'s David Remnick. "If I were real, he'd set me free, I guess. That's what they tell me." Uniformed soldiers escorted Perot to a throne onstage set up to look like a "dark dungeon cell." An "angry-looking banner" written in Arabic letters formed the backdrop. "Run, Ross! Run for president!" a woman shouted from the floor. After a gentle roasting from local celebrities, the *Post* reported, "the band pumps out 'Hail to the Chief,' a gigantic American flag unfurls above the stage and Perot rises from his throne." In 1988 Perot was permitted to start his own company again. Perot Systems' first customer: the United States Postal Service. There was no competitive bidding. As one biographer would put it, "His was a triumph of the system."

The day after Perot's February '92 appearance on *Larry King Live*, the switchboard at Perot's Dallas headquarters was overwhelmed. A toll-free number was set up: a million callers phoned in. Perot continued to hit TV. After an appearance on the *Donahue* show, MCI reported eighteen thousand calls into Perot's number in a thirty-second period, causing the system to jam. Volunteers answered his call to get him on the ballot, fanning out across the country to collect signatures for petitions. As his running mate, Perot picked Admiral James Stockdale, a decorated Vietnam vet and former POW, whose wife, Sybil Stockdale, had founded the National League of Families. Stockdale was on the board of the Rockford Institute and a contributor to *Chronicles* magazine. "Perot's nomination of paleo-con Admiral Stockdale as his interim veep is most interesting; Stockdale was not only a heroic POW of Communists in Asia, he also testified early about the fraudulence of the Gulf of Tonkin incident that enabled LBJ to escalate the war in Vietnam. Which of the other two major candidates are anywhere near this good?" Murray Rothbard excitedly declaimed. As for Perot's intimate connections to the welfare state, Rothbard, the anarcho-capitalist, said, "So what? Are we all supposed to be fiercely opposed to all government contracts? Actually, Perot was only carrying out the famed libertarian Robert Poole concept of privatizing by contracting out government!"

But what was Perot's platform? The size of the deficit was one big gripe, the incompetence and immobility of D.C. another, but Perot was otherwise happy to be free of specifics. One idea floated: removing Congress's ability to raise taxes—of course one of its core constitutional powers. Perot bemoaned what he called the "adversarial relationship between government and business." Another proposal on an April appearance on *Larry King*, televised electronic town halls, led the journalist Sidney Blumenthal to grumble from the pages of *The New Republic*, "Thus the Madisonian system would be replaced by the *Geraldo* system; checks and balances by applause meter."

Few were much paying attention to *The New Republic*, however. Nor to the newspapers that started to do their jobs and report out Perot's past, poking holes in his "outsider" facade. "I just thought someone like Ross Perot to be honest," the Perot volunteer Larry McCallum—a forty-one-year-old former contractor turned landlord and amateur stock trader—told *The Seattle Times*. "Maybe he'd help us try to regain the country." A poll revealed that only 5 percent knew a lot about Perot, but 75 percent of the country thought he had "strong leadership qualities" and "could get things done." The coverage on CNN and other TV stations marveled over and over at the Perot "phenomenon." Whenever TV reporters tried to get a little sharper with him, pressing him on specifics, the networks were inundated with complaints from viewers and calls into Perot's phone banks. "If I want one hundred volunteers more, all I need is to go on some national show with adversarial people . . . When people are rude or arrogant or condescending, the switchboard just goes nuts for three days," Perot told *Time.*

A lot of Perot's volunteers were previously not involved in politics, but felt called to enter now. Some had long histories of civic and political engagement, but felt disgusted with the two-party system. Many were unemployed and had time on their hands to volunteer. A majority identified as "conservative" or "Republican," but they also supported national health insurance. Despite his opposition to the Gulf War, he was popular among veterans. The black POW/MIA flag was a frequent sight in the crowd at his rallies. (His opposition to the war was not exactly pacifist: he thought that Saddam should instead have been taken out by commandos, and he later complained that the invasion had left the regime in place.) "This is the silent majority coming out in force," one Fort Worth volunteer opined. "They feel like they are part of something—they are not sure what, but something." It was also an insurrection or a revolution: "We're staging a bloodless coup against the government." Another source of support was from small businessmen and entrepreneurs. To them, Perot was not even really a politician, he was just a problem solver, and together they were going to clean up the country. The people who showed up to sign Perot petitions were a diverse cross section of America: a couple of guys in a pickup truck with Confederate flag stickers declared Perot "the greatest American to run for president since George Wallace." A few minutes later they were followed by a man with shoulder-length hair and sandals, wearing a SAVE THE WHALES T-shirt. One demographic quality united them, though: they were almost all white; Perot was garnering very little minority support.

He was also attracting a new constituency: they were being called "techies," "computer freaks," and "nerds." Subscribers to electronic bulletin boards and the new dial-up "InterNet" services Prodigy and CompuServe were particularly enthusiastic for Perot. They used these services to distribute information and coordinate volunteer activity. Writing on the rage for technology among Perot supporters, a reporter noted that "one of the problems with computer-based electronic democracy is that it's too fragmented." One Perot volunteer provided a solution: he created a gateway that linked hundreds of disparate Perot discussion boards into a single network. Perot's campaign was itself high-tech: he used satellite links to address rallies in multiple cities at once. Campaign HQ in Dallas was filled with rows of fax machines and phone banks, constantly abuzz. "It doesn't look like a campaign office. It looks like someone is preparing for a NASA launch," one visitor observed.

Perot had one foot in the future and one in the past. He was a double throwback: on the one hand, there was all the mythological Americana, the cowboy and Western imagery, the Texas accent, the folksy idioms, the Norman Rockwells. He was also a throwback to another, more recent past, a past in contradiction with the America of self-reliance and rugged individualism but increasingly the source of its own nostalgia: the postwar regime of industrial prosperity, economic security, and corporate paternalism. On TV Jay Leno made fun of Perot's unfashionable haircut, but he missed the point. With his "wash-and-wear" cut, "not quite a flattop, not quite a crew cut, just long enough for a slight part," done by the same Dallas barber for twenty years, Perot skipped over the cultural discontents of the 1960s and '70s, representing an eternal Middle America. But as a technologist, he also showed a path to the future: a technocratic solution to the problem of politics, a vision of government not based on bickering, on corrupt petty politicians who represent only their own interests, but one that directly represented the people through electronic media, and one that would be administered according to the principles of an efficient and profitable business enterprise. He was the America that should have been and perhaps now could be. He could fix it.

Volunteers swarmed the parking lot on the Texas Rangers' opening night; George W. Bush was an owner of the team. After the game, he told his dad to take Perot seriously. By May, Perot was on the ballot in twenty states. "I don't plan to spend a lot of time on 'Phil Donahue' shows . . . I'm President. I try to conduct myself with a reasonable degree of dignity, seriousness," H. W. Bush told *The Dallas Morning News*. By June, Perot was leading Bush and Clinton in three-way polls by double digits. Rush Limbaugh was invited to stay at the White House that month; the president carried his bags to the Lincoln Bedroom.

6

RAGE

"Voter rage." That's what it was being called. The term appeared not long after the emergence of "road rage," the phrase coined to describe the irrational explosions motorists were having against one another on America's highways. "It is like a monster in a cave, and no one is sure how big or how dangerous it is. Politicians everywhere are startled by its rumblings and the fire it emits," wrote Mary McGrory in her syndicated column. "So far, there's only one, single, overriding message emerging from Election '92 in the United States: Americans are angry," the *Toronto Star* reported from Washington with an air of amused distance.

Uprising was in the air. "They're going to have a revolution in this country one day," warned Jerry Clifton, vice president of the aptly numbered UAW Local 1776—the local for the shuttered Willow Run plant in Ypsilanti, Michigan. "People have pride. They want jobs." Eggheads agreed. The Harvard University political scientist Tom Ferguson compared the atmosphere to the revolutionary wave of the nineteenth century: "To say Americans are angry is an understatement. The only comparison I can make is to Europe in 1848."

The results were in on the experiment of unchained market forces. The front page of the March 5, 1992, *New York Times* had a piece, replete with pie charts and graphs, announcing THE 1980S: A GOOD TIME FOR THE VERY RICH. It had turned out that "the richest 1 percent of American families appear to have reaped most of the gains from the prosperity of the last decade and a half." The average income of families in the top percent gained 77 percent. The rest didn't do as well. "At the same time, the typical American family—smack in the middle, or at the median, of the income distribution—saw its income edge up by only 4 percent, to $36,000. And the bottom 40 percent of families had actual decline in income." The conservative columnist George Will, no great critic of Reaganomics, had to concede that the picture was stark, with families working twice as hard to stay in the same place: "The wages of average workers are below 1979 levels, but family incomes have been maintained by wives going to work." Depression-era scenes could be witnessed across the country. Nine thousand workers camped out outside the new Sheraton Hotel in Chicago, each hoping for one of five hundred jobs. One of them, Bobby Vaughn, whose construction business went under with the housing bust, got a job as a janitor to feed his two kids—the position paid $200 a week, a quarter of what he had made before. The country appeared to be moving backward. "Inequality has increased back to where it was before the New Deal," the economist Paul Krugman told the *Times*. "But maybe the New Deal only drove the rich underground."

The "monster" of voter rage also had a new scandal to chew on. The previous year, a General Accounting Office report revealed that members of the House of Representatives had regularly overdrawn their House checking accounts without incurring penalties, writing "bad checks." In effect, they were getting interest-free loans from the House's internal clearinghouse. Almost two-thirds of congressmen had overdrawn at least one check, but there were egregious cases where members would've bounced hundreds of checks had it not been for the arrangement. Some turned the shady perk into an opportunity for outright fraud. Congress had had a Democratic majority for nearly four decades, and most of the violators were Democrats. Sixteen Democrats but only three Republicans were on the list of the worst offenders. A group of ambitious junior Republicans led by the minority whip, a Georgia representative named Newt Gingrich, led the offensive against their entrenched colleagues.

"This is about systemic, institutional corruption, not personality," Gingrich told the press. "To ask the Democratic leadership to clean things up would be like asking the old Soviet bureaucracy under Brezhnev to reform itself. It ain't going to happen." The battalions of talk radio, with Rush Limbaugh at their head, followed. Under pressure, the House voted to release the names of all the overdrafters. Newt Gingrich, who said he had engaged in the practice "a handful of times," turned out to have overdrawn his account on twenty-two occasions, totaling some $26,000. The Whip was quieter in subsequent House debates on the issue. But the bomb throwing did its job, despite some collateral damage: the voters were getting even angrier. (So angry, in fact, that they almost threw Gingrich out in a July primary; his opponent's main issue was the twenty-two bad checks.)

"With a whoop and a holler, politicians have suddenly discovered that there's a wild animal called the American middle class prowling around the voting booths, and officeholders are pounding down the stairs to make sure the rough beast does no damage once it gets inside the house," wrote Samuel Francis in *Chronicles* with a note of grim satisfaction. "Almost every issue that has emerged in national politics in the last year—term limits and taxes, housing and health care, racial quotas and rascals in government—centers around the cultural identity and material interests of the middle class, and the nation's incumbent oligarchs well understand that all the growling about such matters is rather like the roaring of lions in the jungle night. It's when the roaring stops and the hunt begins that they better start worrying."

"None of the above" was an increasing response from the voting public. Across the country, polls showed discontent with all options on the table in the primaries. Voters listlessly moved around, failing to quickly coalesce around the initial front-runner and apparent choice of the party brass—Arkansas governor Bill Clinton, recently declared "The Anointed" and the "most electable candidate" by *The New Republic*'s Sidney Blumenthal. Maybe former Massachusetts senator Paul Tsongas's *A Call to Economic Arms*, as his campaign booklet was rousingly titled, would be the answer. But far from populism, his program to make America "the pre-eminent manufacturing nation on earth again" called for a "marriage" with "corporate America" in a business-friendly program that combined industrial policy with austerity and anti-labor measures.

Tsongas, a cancer survivor, compared what the country would have to undergo to his own treatment. Describing his ordeal, he recalled, "The next ten months contained no happy talk. Monthly sessions of intravenous chemotherapy were followed by target radiation . . . I know that my hard-nosed, no-margin-for-error doctors saved my life. But I also know that I resented their tough approach during that period . . . Avoidance of hard truths makes the inevitable dealing with them all the more difficult. And what is true for individuals is also true for nations." Grim enough for the times perhaps, but the message of "I had cancer and so should you" was going to be a tough sell. Less sublimated forms of anger were catchier, even if less plausible. Former California governor Jerry Brown was now piquing voter interest. Once nicknamed "Moonbeam" for his hippie-dippie ways by Mike Royko, Chicago's voice of the ethnic white working class, Brown returned from Japan, where he had been studying Zen Buddhism, suddenly reincarnated as an epithet-slinging populist, stumping in a UAW jacket. After the fizzle of Iowa senator Tom Harkin, Brown became the default voice of labor. "He's the only one speaking for us," said one member of UAW local 1776.

Bush, too, tried awkwardly to get in on the revolutionary spirit.

Appearing at Philadelphia's Congress Hall, the site of the first House and Senate, he demanded reforms in the way Congress did business, calling himself the leader of "the forces of change" and saying that because of "one-party control, one party's lack of supervision, lack of new blood, lack of change there isn't the competition to make these institutions in the Congress more efficient." He called for term limits, the banning of political action committees for unions and corporations (but not for ideological groups), and an end for special privileges for Congress. But the White House's own special privileges were coming into focus, as well: the House demanded that the Bush administration stop balking on disclosures of what they spent on travel on Air Force One and other federal aircraft. The Democratic chairman of the House Post Office and Civil Service Subcommittee estimated that the White House spent close to $130 million a year on travel.

There would be no victory lap for Bush. In August 1991 the Soviet old guard put Mikhail Gorbachev under house arrest, but their attempted coup collapsed, prompting Gorbachev's resignation and the USSR's sudden collapse. Yet no one seemed to care much when Bush and the Russian president Boris Yeltsin jointly declared a formal end to the Cold War at a Camp David summit, proclaiming an era of "friendship and partnership." Foreign policy was supposed to be a strong suit for the president. Richard Nixon, now considered a sagelike elder statesman, privately circulated a memo to journalists and policymakers titled "How to Lose the Cold War," battering the administration's halfhearted and stingy support for democracy in the post-Soviet states. "The West has failed so far to seize the moment to shape the history of the next half-century," Nixon wrote. "If Yeltsin fails, the prospects for the next 50 years will turn grim. The Russian people will not turn back to Communism. But a new, more dangerous despotism based on extremist Russian nationalism will take power . . . If a new despotism prevails, everything gained in the great peaceful revolution of 1991 will be lost. War could break out in the former Soviet Union as the new despots use force to restore the 'historical borders' of Russia."

The prediction of war had already come true, but it wasn't Russia making its historic claims. Two of the new states in the Caucasus, Armenia and Azerbaijan, were already fighting over a disputed enclave. Grim reports of massacres filtered out of the mountains. Across the Black Sea and another range of mountains, in another former Communist federation, masked Serb militias were cutting off the roads around a city called Sarajevo, the new capital of Bosnia and Herzegovina. In the west of Europe, Jean-Marie Le Pen's National Front, postmodern heirs of Vichy and the anti-Dreyfusards, made gains in regional elections at the expense of Mitterrand's governing Socialists. The tide of ugly nationalism was coming in fast.

Campaigning in the states of the old Confederacy, which were less affected by the recession than New England was, Pat Buchanan was leaning heavily into another abiding myth. In Georgia, with cameras in tow, he gazed up admiringly at Stone Mountain, the massive bas-relief monument to Robert E. Lee, Stonewall Jackson, and Jefferson Davis. He told gathered supporters there that the Voting Rights Act was "an act of regional discrimination against the South." In the midst of a dramatic downpour, he stopped to lay flowers at the grave of his great-grandfather William Martin Buchanan, a Confederate soldier who he claimed had owned a plantation. He said that another great-grandfather "died on the way to Vicksburg" during what he was calling "the war of northern aggression." He vowed to avenge his forebear's capture by General Sherman by winning in Georgia. "I'll tell you my friends, this time we're going to settle accounts for our ancestors with those Yankees up in Washington," he repeated to crowds across the South, referring to the city where he was born and raised.

The message certainly got through to one constituency. "In one sense, Pat Buchanan can be viewed as a clean Duke," the white-supremacist *Instauration* editorialized. Tom Metzger, the head of the White Aryan Resistance and a rival Klan leader to David Duke, said, "It's time that we divide the truly sensitive Republicans, sensitive on the race issue, from the phonies. We are more interested in what Buchanan's doing than what Duke's doing. I think if he is truly honest, he could really be laying the foundation for something big." For his part, Duke seemed to have lost interest. He spoke to empty halls, appeared distracted, and would start to laugh inexplicably. When a reporter asked if he was involved with anyone romantically, he replied, "It is a female, I can tell you that much. These days you have to ask," prompting a fit of giggling. He liked the line so much, he repeated it on a religious talk show. Still, some supporters felt he was being dealt with unfairly. "A lot of Republicans distance themselves from their own past by jumping on the bandwagon and beating up on David Duke. Duke's been made a scapegoat for a lot of Republican guilt," complained his South Carolina campaign manager, a chiropractor by profession. "Wasn't it George Bush that put out the Willie Horton ad? There's a certain amount of hypocrisy out there."

Not only friendly voices got the vibe. In his syndicated column, the neoconservative heavy Charles Krauthammer dropped the f-bomb. "The Washington pundits have worked themselves into a tizzy over whether some of Pat Buchanan's TV colleagues have been too soft on Buchanan's anti-Semitism," Krauthammer wrote. "But the real problem with Buchanan is not that his instincts are anti-Semitic but that they are, in various and distinct ways, fascistic . . . With communism defeated, Buchanan emerges, like a woolly mammoth frozen in Siberian ice, as a preserved specimen of 1930s isolationism and nativism." Reprising Abe Rosenthal, Krauthammer blasted Buchanan's comments defending the accused concentration camp guard John Demjanjuk and casting doubt on the Treblinka gas chambers: "What ultimately and irrevocably discredited fascism was the Holocaust, the fact that the denouement of the fascist idea produced the supreme act of human barbarism. Buchanan, child of the pre-war right, confronts this unpleasant fact simply: He wishes the Holocaust would go away. Ergo, he finds himself, perhaps even despite himself, moved to debunk Treblinka, demean survivors (as given to 'group fantasies of martyrdom and heroics') and defend those who were part of the genocide machine."

The media started to notice the far-right shift from Duke to Buchanan and report on the endorsements. "It's the worst kind of guilt by association to tar Buchanan's campaign with accusations we're getting support from people we don't know, don't want and haven't had any contact with," objected Jerry Woodruff, Buchanan's spokesman. As it happened, the association was often very close. An AP reporter overheard Buchanan's New Jersey volunteer coordinator, Joe D'Alessio, compare interracial marriage to the crossbreeding of animals. D'Alessio was forced to resign, but no one at the time reported that D'Alessio was also the state chairman of Willis Carto's Populist Party. Nor did the media catch that Boyd Cathey, Buchanan's North Carolina chairman, was a member of the ultra-traditionalist Society of Saint Pius X, a senior editor at *Southern Partisan*, and on the board of the Institute for Historical Review, the center for organized Holocaust denial founded by Carto.

Buchanan was starting to collect "scalps," as he put it. He stumped hard against the National Endowment for the Arts, a target for the religious right because the NEA had provided funding for art that had queer themes. In particular, cultural conservatives were apoplectic about *Tongues Untied*, a documentary about Black gay men that received some indirect NEA funding and was aired on PBS, where it was very popular. The public curiosity was galling. "So 'Tongues Untied', the tasteless, foul-mouthed film on black homosexuals garnered WPBA-Channel 30 its highest audience ratings since the acclaimed series 'The Civil War,'" sputtered Dick Williams in *The Atlanta Journal-Constitution*. "The Civil War comparison is as it should be, for 'Tongues Untied' is about war—the cultural war being fought across the country. It reveals a popular division almost as deep as the War Between the States." Shortly before Buchanan's Georgia sojourn, he told the Conservative Political Action Conference that the Bush administration was "subsidizing both filthy and blasphemous art." The next day, Bush asked John Frohnmayer, the head of the NEA, to submit his resignation.

That didn't stop the Buchanan campaign from airing a new ad in Georgia attacking Bush and the NEA, using clips of shirtless and leather-clad men from *Tongues Untied.* "The Bush administration has invested our tax dollars in pornographic and blasphemous art too shocking to show," a voice-over intoned. "This so-called art has glorified homosexuality, exploited children, and perverted the image of Jesus Christ. Even after good people protested, Bush continued to fund this kind of art." On the stump in Dixie, Buchanan told supporters he would "padlock and fumigate" the National Endowment for the Arts. The Bush campaign complained about the "demagoguery" of the Georgia ad, but it had given Buchanan the initiative. The president also told the *Journal-Constitution* that going back on his "Read my lips: no new taxes" pledge was the biggest mistake of his presidency. *Newsweek* asked, "Is Buchanan Running the Country?"—"It isn't true, as the critics claim, that George Bush stands for nothing: he seems to stand for whatever Patrick Buchanan wants him to."

Despite the fact that Georgia's economy was in much better shape than that of New Hampshire, Buchanan nearly repeated his total, getting just a little under 36 percent of the vote to Bush's 64 percent. But the Buchanan wave was cresting. On Super Tuesday a week later, he couldn't match the success he'd had in New Hampshire or Georgia. In many Deep South states, Duke was still on the ballot, and while Buchanan crushed him, the two split the protest vote. In Mississippi, Duke managed 11 percent to Buchanan's 17, but in Louisiana, remarkably, Buchanan kept him in the single digits—he came short of 9 percent. Buchanan claimed credit for "having buried Mr. Duke in some bayou in Louisiana," but he became infuriated when the RNC chairman Rich Bond called him "David Duke in a coat and tie." (The crack didn't make much sense: David Duke was David Duke in a coat and tie.) Buchanan still struggled with women voters, who were proving to be particularly loyal to George Bush and the First Lady, Barbara. Buchanan tried to soften his "bullyboy" image, having childhood friends downplay the stories of fights and beatings, to little avail. The press pointed out that his wife, Shelley, seemed to do little more than smile and wave. When she told reporters that she preferred to be called "Ms." rather than "Mrs.," her husband was visibly shocked.

Perot's nascent candidacy was also soaking up protest energy and voter rage. "Some folks I've talked to profess to find Perot a little frightening. But what ought to scare them is the alienation and frustration, the wrecking impulse, that he's tapping," wrote John Shelton Reed in his *Chronicles* column dedicated to Southern issues. "All things considered . . . voting for Ross Perot is a pretty harmless way for that to surface." Just as Buchanan had sailed into Duke's wind, now Perot sailed into Buchanan's.

In any case, Buchanan was starting to flap in the breeze. The next plan was to target Michigan, where the aged conservative grandee Russell Kirk was the largely honorary campaign chief. General Motors had just announced more plant closures—most famously, it would shut down the Willow Run plant in Ypsilanti where the B-24 Liberator was built during World War II, destroying four thousand jobs. It would also close plants in Flint and Saginaw, costing another six thousand jobs. Buchanan's team believed that his message of protectionism and tough talk about Japanese imports would resonate with the shell-shocked autoworkers. "Mr. Bush's campaign is virtually a wholly owned subsidiary of Japan Inc.," Buchanan declared at a press conference in Michigan. "He has got too many advisers around him or close to him who have interests or linkages to foreign interests and are arguing for these interests, rather than objectively for what is best for the United States." This was a tamer version of the message he had delivered in New Hampshire, where he said that the "big Republican tent" was being replaced with "the big Republican pagoda."

Buchanan wanted to go to one of the closed General Motors plants to set a dramatic scene of American decline. But United Autoworkers Local 1776 refused to let him have his photo op and locked him out. Bush had run an ad in Michigan saying that Buchanan drove a Mercedes-Benz. Buchanan admitted that he did drive the German car and that he considered the three Cadillacs he had owned over the past two decades "to be of poor quality." The workers inside the union hall heckled him as he stood out in the snow and shouted back, "Come out and talk to me." In its dreary Alamo, American organized labor made a last stand against the phony patriotics of America First populism.

Buchanan got a warmer welcome from Chicago's white ethnic communities. Visiting the Ukrainian Cultural Center, he reaffirmed his belief in the innocence of the accused concentration camp guard John Demjanjuk, receiving cheers. The Lithuanian and Croatian communities, whose ancestral countries' fledgling national aspirations Buchanan had promoted in his columns, were similarly friendly. At an Irish pub he visited, the patrons were "cheering their heads off." It wasn't enough. His heart wasn't in it anymore. On Election Day in Dearborn, Michigan, he asked a woman leaving the polls, "Are you a voter? We need a voter. We're just coming here to do what we call a photo op." He decided to scrap the rest of the day's events. Buchanan got only about a quarter of the votes in both states.

He had good reason to pin his hopes on "Japan bashing," as it had come to be called. Trotted out by politicians since the early '80s, Japan's responsibility for America's economic decline had become a major theme of the year's campaign. "The Cold War is over—Japan won," Paul Tsongas told the United Auto Workers convention, as he switched from blaming his rivals for Japan bashing to calling for a boycott of Japanese products. Nebraska senator Bob Kerrey ran an ad in New Hampshire showing him walking out on an ice hockey rink and saying, "I'll tell Japan if we can't sell in their market, they can't sell in ours. And if they don't get the message, they'll find that this president can play a little defense too." "Fight back, America!" went the closing voice-over. Then the seventy-nine-year-old conservative speaker of the lower house of Japan's parliament, Yoshio Sakurauchi, told a group of supporters that U.S. workers were "lazy," "wanted to be paid without working," and "cannot even read."

When the news of Sakurauchi's comments reached the USA, it

inflamed an already irritable nation in the midst of political campaigns. To make matters worse, the Japanese government and Toyota Motor Corporation appeared to be backing away from the informal pledge to buy more American cars and auto parts, which they had made during Bush's Tokyo trip. In protest, a group of autoworkers smashed a Japanese car with sledgehammers. South Carolina Democratic senator Fritz Hollings told a group of workers, "You should draw a mushroom cloud and put underneath it, 'Made in America by lazy and illiterate Americans and tested in Japan.'" Michigan Democratic senator Don Riegle echoed the sentiment, saying, "Mr. Sakurauchi's attitude in slandering American workers was the same view the Japanese held the day its warplanes struck Pearl Harbor. Their arrogance was gone by 1945, when they learned the full measure of America's capabilities." Missouri's Democratic representative Dick Gephardt used the remarks to push for his bill to restrict Japanese car and truck imports if the trade deficit between the nations was not reduced to zero.

Fear of possible Japanese hegemony had already reached pandemic proportions in the United States. A *Business Week* survey in 1989 showed that Americans were more concerned about the power of their ally across the Pacific than about the Soviet Union. By the end of 1991, a *New York Times*/CBS Poll found that half of all Americans believed that Japan would claim the title of "No. 1 economic power in the world" in the twenty-first century. Half of Americans had a negative view of Japan. "I am delighted to see the wave of pro-American, anti-Japanese sentiment sweeping our nation. My only regret is that it is coming much too late," wrote one "M. F. Swango" to the *Houston Chronicle*. "As a veteran of World War II in the Pacific, four campaigns and occupation duty in Japan, I know first hand the ruthless and merciless bent of the Japanese mind. They bow and speak in polite terms, but they give no quarter."

In January '92 the popular novelist Michael Crichton published *Rising Sun*, a murder mystery whose villains are Japanese businessmen buying up American property and putting their hands on young blond

American women. It shot quickly to the top of the bestseller lists. The detective protagonist in the novel counsels other characters to "Remember Pearl Harbor," and a senator contemplates the prospect of "dropping another bomb." If the message was too subtle, Crichton helpfully included an afterword that included references to several nonfiction books warning of Japan's encroaching influence. Among Crichton's source materials were *Agents of Influence* (1990) by Pat Choate, *Trading Places* (1988) by Clyde Prestowitz Jr., and *The Enigma of Japanese Power* (1989) by Karel van Wolferen. All these books combined factual information and analysis with sensationalism, borderline-crackpot theories, hints of racism, and paranoia. Japan was characterized as not really a democracy at all, but a Borg-like hive mind that interlaced industrial cartels, the media, and politicians and had no center of responsibility or power. They were part of a growing genre of books on the "Japan Problem," with dozens of entries, such as William Dietrich's *In the Shadow of the Rising Sun* (1991), which claimed that Japan "threatens our way of life and ultimately our freedoms as much as past dangers from Nazi Germany and the Soviet Union," and *The Coming War with Japan* (1991), which imagined an actual shooting war between the transpacific rivals. This was not the sole province of middle-brow airport fare and potboilers: James Fallows of *The Atlantic Monthly* modeled his 1989 "Containing Japan" article on George Kennan's 1947 warning on the Soviet Union, and *The Rise and Fall of the Great Powers* (1987) by the Yale historian Paul Kennedy predicted that Japan would grow "much more powerful" and be the "leading or second nation" in the coming years.

Japan bashing appeared to be having disturbing effects. The U.S. Commission on Civil Rights report "Civil Rights Issues Facing Asian Americans in the 1990s" connected Japan-bashing rhetoric to a wave of hate crimes against Asian Americans, many of whom were not even of Japanese descent. In Boston and Philadelphia, northeasterly centers of souring white ethnic pride, Asians were more likely than any other group to be the victims of hate crimes. In 1989, a man with an AK-47 massacred five young students at a school in Stockton, California, all children of refugees from Southeast Asia. Coworkers had heard him complaining that immigrants were taking American jobs. At a party in Coral Springs, Florida, a nineteen-year-old Vietnamese American named Luyen Phan Nguyen was beaten to death by other teenagers who shouted racial slurs. A cross was burned outside an Asian restaurant in the L.A. suburb of Lakewood. A Japanese businessman in Ventura was found stabbed to death in his garage two weeks after he had an altercation with two men who harassed him over American job losses. A group of Japanese American Girl Scouts selling cookies in Los Angeles were called "Japs" and told "I only buy from American girls," triggering anxiety in their parents and grandparents, who had lived through internment during World War II. Dr. John Hara, a St. Louis dentist who had been interned with his parents, told the *Post-Dispatch*, "Sometimes I wish we could stamp our forehead with a mark that says, 'Made in the USA.'"

The fiftieth anniversary of Pearl Harbor at the end of 1991 put the community particularly on edge, a feeling not soothed by the press's insistence on comparing the current economic tensions with the conditions during the war. A Japanese couple in San Francisco had a Molotov cocktail thrown at them. The Japanese American activist Kyle Kajihiro wrote an op-ed in *The Oregonian* that brought attention to the absence of coverage of another fiftieth anniversary. February 19, 1992, marked the date of Roosevelt's Executive Order that interned Japanese Americans in camps: "Given the current reactionary political climate of this country, it is not surprising that many of the mainstream media readily took part in the Japan-bashing on the 50th anniversary of Pearl Harbor while devoting relatively little attention to this other observance."

Politicians were noticing that these fears cut across ethnic differences and created a possible new constituency of Asian Americans. By the perverse logic of politics, at the same time as they became targets, Asian Americans became politically valuable. Campaigning in heavily

Vietnamese American Orange County, California, in March, Vice President Dan Quayle told a crowd at a Little Saigon mall, "America is your home but not everyone seems to acknowledge that. I bring this message from your president. 'You belong here. This is your home.'" He decried the heated rhetoric between Japanese and U.S. leaders, saying that it incited violence against "innocent Asian-Americans." In April, the *Seattle Post-Intelligencer* reported that Democrats feared Republican encroachment in the Asian American vote and were making their own outreach efforts. "The Democrats potentially run the risk of losing the current generation of immigrants as well as losing out on their children and grandchildren," warned Los Angeles city councilman Michael Woo, a candidate aspiring to replace Mayor Tom Bradley. "It's already happening," said Bob Matsui, a Democratic congressman from California who, in 1991, became the first Asian American appointed to a national party post. "We're much better when it comes to civil rights or the issue of hate crimes. But those issues don't really seem to appeal to them (new immigrants)." Still, going into the convention season, Asian American Democrats worked to temper the party's Japan bashing.

While critics of Japan saw foreign lobbyists everywhere, they were often working for industrial interests of their own, albeit ones closer to home. In 1991, Pat Buchanan contributed the foreword to a volume called *America Asleep: The Free Trade Syndrome and the Global Economic Challenge*, which included essays by Samuel Francis, the billionaire Boone Pickens, and even the liberal John Judis of *The New Republic*. "Ex-officials . . . from Cabinet officers to White House staffers, have gone geisha for the economic Empire of the Rising Sun," wrote Buchanan. "Suspicion of Japan is not only related to race . . . but to a sense that Tokyo's trade policy is a bastard child of Hirohito's imperial policy of 1941. It is related to a sense that Japan's invasions of U.S. markets have been plotted at the highest level in Tokyo with the same thoroughness that Admiral [Isoroku] Yamamoto plotted Pearl Harbor, that Japan's objective is to go 'the economic road' to acquire the hegemony in Asia and the world her army and navy were unable to win half a century ago."

The book was published by the United States Business and Industrial Council, a group founded in 1933 by small and medium manufacturers to lobby against the New Deal, labor unions, and minimum wage laws. Since the mid-1980s, the organization's controlling force was Roger Milliken, one of the richest men in America. Milliken had previously poured the profits of his mills into *National Review* and the Heritage Foundation and had become one of the conservative movement's leading industrial patrons, called "Daddy Warbucks" by Republican pols.

Now besieged by importers and frustrated with the Heritage Foundation's staunchly free trade stance, he cut his money off from the mainstream institutions and moved it into protectionist efforts, including the Economic Strategy Institute, run by Clyde Prestowitz, author of *Trading Places*. In 1985 Milliken went to the White House to convince communications director Pat Buchanan to get President Reagan to sign a textile protection act that had made its way through Congress. "No way, I told Mr. Milliken," Buchanan later reflected. "I'm the biggest free-trader in the building, except for the fellow down the hall, who was Ronald Reagan." The president vetoed the bill, and Buchanan wrote the signing statement. In the next few years, Buchanan wrote that "he had seen the light" and "enlisted in Roger's crusade." In late 1991 Milliken's chief lobbyist, Jock Nash, was among the attendees at what *The Washington Times* called "a secret meeting with conservative leaders," where Buchanan revealed his "strategy to bloody President Bush."

As a consummate White House insider, Buchanan might have known that "Japan's invasions of U.S. markets" were actually "plotted" at the "highest level" in Washington as much as in Tokyo. In 1983, Lee Morgan, the chairman of Caterpillar Tractor, paid a call to top officials at the White House, the Treasury Department, and the Council of Economic Advisers. Speaking as a representative of the Business Roundtable lobby and of his own firm, which was now struggling to compete with the Japanese manufacturer Komatsu, he delivered a report prepared for Caterpillar by two economists. The study argued that the strength of the dollar and the weakness of the yen had created the trade imbalance between the two countries—and that it could be rectified by liberalizing Japanese financial markets, which would cause capital to flow into Japan and thereby strengthen that nation's currency. The idea got an enthusiastic hearing in the Reagan administration, providing a win-win whereby they could help American business without compromising on their dedication to free market ideology. The administration pressured the Japanese to open up both inflow and outflow in their capital markets, and the Japanese agreed. On the same trip, Reagan addressed the Japanese Diet, where he joked, "Sometimes I wonder if we shouldn't further our friendship by my sending our Congress here and you coming over and occupying our Capitol Building for a while." But Caterpillar's plan was based on dubious economic logic even in theory. Japan was the nation with excess savings to invest, not the United States. Instead of foreign capital flowing into Japan, Japanese capital flowed into the United States.

U.S. Treasury bonds, with their more than 11 percent yield as a result of Fed chair Volcker's hawkish anti-inflationary measures, became a particular favorite for Japanese investors. The sudden influx of billions in foreign capital came at an opportune time for the U.S. government, then engaging in furious military spending as part of Reagan's re-intensification of the Cold War. Japan might not have won the Cold War, as Paul Tsongas claimed, but Japanese pensioners paid for it. Japanese investors quickly turned from Treasuries to real assets, investing in industrial capital and real estate. Japanese buyers were so thrilled with the returns possible in the United States—so much better than those available at home—that they often paid as much as 30 percent above market rates for commercial real estate to obliging U.S. sellers in a market already frenzied by S&L deregulation and junk bonds. Between 1987 and 1991, Japanese investors poured more than $62 billion into U.S. real estate, with a special preference for such blue-chip behemoths as Rockefeller Center in New York and the ARCO Plaza in downtown Los Angeles, prompting public backlash at the prospect of these great obelisks of American capitalism being owned by foreigners.

After Sakurauchi's intemperate remarks, a "Buy American" campaign gained steam across the country. In Los Angeles, the county transportation commission canceled a $122 million deal with the Sumitomo Corporation to build a commuter rail line. Fay Vincent, the commissioner of baseball, announced an interdict on foreign ownership of Major League Baseball teams after Nintendo made an offer for the Seattle Mariners. (It would later be reversed.) The town of Greece, New York, canceled its contract for a $40,000 Komatsu excavator, which was $15,000 less expensive than the equivalent "American-made" John Deere model. Never mind that since 1988, John Deere excavators were built by a joint venture called Deere-Hitachi Construction. Meanwhile, Komatsu had opened plants in Chattanooga, Tennessee, and Peoria, Illinois—Caterpillar, which had boosted the dubious financial liberalization scheme to best its competitors, found its archrival now across town.

Even though the wages offered at Caterpillar's plants were considered among the best in the country, workers could no longer support a family on a single income. In response to a November strike by the UAW, Caterpillar shuttered two plants in East Peoria and Aurora and threatened to hire replacement workers. In April, Bill Clinton, eager to build up cred with a distrustful labor movement, visited the picketing workers in Peoria to declare his opposition to the hiring of permanent replacements. To keep costs down, the company had been outsourcing to foreign as well as "union-free" plants in the South. In 1991 they decided to use a Japanese company to make engines for their earthmovers, even though Caterpillar's plants were operating at between 60 and 70 percent capacity. Between 1979 and 1992 Caterpillar halved its American workers and closed six union plants. Caterpillar stayed competitive not through international financial wizardry, but by squeezing its workforce. The new CEO, Donald Fites, managed to put this in humanitarian terms. "There is a narrowing of the gap between the average American's income and that of the Mexicans," he said in an interview with *The New York Times*. "As a human being, I think what is going on is positive. I don't think it is realistic for 250 million Americans to control so much of the world's G.N.P."

But even as the cultural fear of Japan intensified, there were signs that the boom in Japan was cooling off: the stock market there had lost nearly half its value in two years. "From 1988 to the end of 1990, Japanese investors put about $52 billion into the United States, snapping up everything from tire makers and real estate to new factories," *The New York Times* reported in March. "In the first nine months of last year, that figure plummeted to $2.3 billion. The Japanese made a net investment of $30.7 billion in United States Government securities in 1988, the peak year; they are now net sellers of government securities." Meanwhile, the above-market prices Japanese buyers had been willing to pay for American real estate turned out to be disastrous as the U.S. commercial real estate bubble popped. The financier Minoru Isutani put the Pebble Beach golf resort on the market at a loss of nearly $350 million. In 1991 Japanese investment in U.S. properties fell by 61 percent. In Los Angeles, where Japanese investors owned 45 percent of prime downtown commercial real estate, building values fell by 20 to 30 percent.

The sudden retreat of Japanese capital pulled the bottom out of a struggling Southern California economy. The end of the Cold War brought a sudden cut in Department of Defense orders from the aerospace industry, the region's major manufacturing sector. Between the end of 1990 and 1994, 40 percent of defense-related manufacturing jobs disappeared. So did about a quarter of all manufacturing and construction jobs. Los Angeles County as a whole lost nearly half a million jobs—and the region had 27 percent of all job losses during the early '90s recession. Even before the recession hit, the situation in Los Angeles was growing dire. In 1989 the UCLA research group on the Los Angeles economy released a report entitled "The Widening Divide," which reported that "inequality and poverty in Los Angeles are greater than two decades ago." The income disparities and poverty seen across the country had set in earlier in Los Angeles and were starker. The plant closures of the late 1970s and early '80s had already torn out most of the unionized manufacturing jobs that once supported the Black and Mexican American working class. The middle class was disappearing: "The overall result of this growth in both high-wage and low-wage jobs has been a disturbing decline in the middle range of the wage distribution, especially for men," the research group found. In L.A., the wage stagnation that beset the entire nation fell almost exclusively on the city's Blacks and Latinos, with incomes actually declining in latter case. Boom times still attracted immigrants from Central America and Mexico, who found work in low-wage jobs like light manufacturing and construction, but the poverty rate among Latinos had already been growing "alarmingly" before the recession. Now there were growing encampments of homeless migrants on the sides of Crown Hill and the bed of the Los Angeles River. Three days before Christmas 1991, the *Los Angeles Times* reported in THOUSANDS OF NEEDY GATHER FOR GIVEAWAY ON SKID ROW, twenty thousand men, women, and children lined up for the promise of a chicken, a dozen corn tortillas, three toys, and one blanket. "I don't have any chance for Christmas food but in this line," thirty-year-old Rosario Hernandez told the paper. In the same issue was RECESSION PUTS CHARITIES IN TWIN BIND OF NEED, FUNDS—all of a sudden, when they were most needed, charities found that their supply of money had dried up. Local observers found the situation so grim as to suggest apocalypse. "In Los Angeles there are too many signs of approaching helter-skelter: everywhere in the inner city, even in the forgotten poor-white boondocks with their zombie populations of speed freaks, gangs are multiplying at a terrific rate, cops are becoming more arrogant and trigger-happy, and a whole generation is being shunted toward some impossible Armageddon," wrote the historian Mike Davis in *City of Quartz*, his 1990 dystopian portrait of L.A.

The first seal of Revelation was now opened: on March 6, 1992, the trial of four police officers—charged with the brutal beating of the Black motorist Rodney G. King a year earlier—opened in Simi Valley with the replaying of an amateur videotape of the assault.

7

THE THIN BLUE LINE

The Gulf War was over. America was triumphant. Now it was time to turn to another war, one the country seemed to be losing: the war on crime. On March 5, 1991, a week after the cease-fire and the day Iraq revoked its annexation of Kuwait, President Bush addressed Attorney General Dick Thornburgh's Crime Summit at the Sheraton Washington, which brought together cops, judges, and prosecutors from across the country. The president called it an "unprecedented council of war." He went on: "My message to you today is drawn from the lessons of America's great World War II admiral, William F. "Bull" Halsey. 'Carry the battle to the enemy,' he said. 'Lay your ship alongside his.' And on the eve of the battle of Santa Cruz, in which his ships were outnumbered more than 2 to 1, Halsey sent his task force commanders a three-word dispatch: 'Attack—repeat—attack.' . . . The kind of moral force and national will that freed Kuwait City from abuse can free America's cities from crime." And, he added, every war needed heroes: "Just look at the all-American heroes here today . . . people like L.A. police chief Daryl Gates."

As it so happened, Chief Gates was not even in the room—he was already on his way back to Los Angeles. A few hours after Bush's remarks, CNN started showing the Rodney King video.

"MAR. 03 1991" read the time stamp on the grainy footage. George Holliday, a plumber, had taken the nine-minute clip from his balcony in Lake View Terrace on his new camcorder, which he said he had "instinctively" grabbed when he heard a commotion. It was the first minute and nineteen seconds of the tape that showed a Black motorist named Rodney King being swarmed and beaten by four LAPD officers—Theodore Briseño, Stacey Koon, Laurence Powell, and Thomas Wind—while dozens more stood nearby. At first King is prone, and he suddenly gets up in what looks like an effort to escape or the response to a shock. He later said he was scared for his life. The officers claimed that King was attempting to charge them. Then the cops start to beat and kick him—fifty-six times in all as he lay flat or tried to crawl away. The wires of a taser are visible. An overhead LAPD helicopter obscures almost all the sound, but the metal baton blows were so hard that a clear clink on the pavement from one of the strikes across King's legs can be made out on the video. Emergency room physicians later reported that King's fillings had been knocked out by the blows. One of King's eye sockets was shattered; his cheekbone was fractured, his leg broken; there were burns where the stun gun had been used; he had a concussion and nerve damage in his face. The negligence suit that King would file alleged "11 skull fractures, permanent brain damage, broken bones and teeth, kidney damage, and emotional and physical trauma." King, a twenty-five-year-old part-time groundskeeper at Dodger Stadium, had been chased by a California Highway Patrol car before he stopped in Lake View Terrace in the San Fernando Valley. He had been drinking with his two friends in the car and was worried that since he was on parole for a second-degree robbery charge, he would return to prison. The passengers in the car, Bryant Allen and Freddie Helms, were ordered to lie prone and not look up. One of the officers drew a gun on them. They could hear King's screams, and when

Helms tried to raise his head out of the dirt, he was kicked in the side and hit in the head with a baton, drawing blood. Allen said he was kicked several times as well.

For years, Black and Hispanic Angelenos said that this sort of thing happened all the time. But now it was caught on tape. There could be no denying it. Tom Bradley, the former police lieutenant who had become Los Angeles's first Black mayor in 1973, declared himself "shocked and outraged" by the tape. Local prosecutors and the FBI opened investigations into the beating. President Bush declared himself "sickened" and directed Attorney General Thornburgh to determine whether any federal crimes had been committed. Chief Gates, who had campaigned for Bush in '88, was no longer Bush's "all-American hero," he was just "in many ways, an exemplary police chief." Gates was accustomed to taking fire from the ACLU and Jesse Jackson, but now the conservative columnist George Will called for the chief's resignation on ABC's *This Week with David Brinkley*.

How would Gates respond? In his thirteen years as chief, he'd handled even the mildest criticism of his person and his officers with no-holds-barred counterattacks. A representative sampling of Gates's public statements would have to include the time when he said that the reason Latinos were not being promoted in the LAPD was because they were "lazy," or when he remarked that so many Blacks were dying from police choke holds because their "veins and arteries do not open up as fast as they do on normal people," or when he told the Senate Judiciary Committee that "casual drug users ought to be taken out and shot" (Gates's own son had a drug problem and was convicted of robbing a Huntington Beach drugstore—Gates disowned him), or when he drew the ire of the city's Central American community by referring to a suspect in a police shooting as an "El Salvadoran drunk—a drunk that doesn't belong here." Now Gates sounded relatively conciliatory. He said the tape made him "physically ill" and called for prosecutions of the officers involved. But he also cautioned that "one incident doesn't indict an entire department. I would hope the public on this one case not make a judgment on the Los Angeles Police Department," and he later called the beating an "aberration." Gates even went so far as to offer an apology to King. He couldn't resist adding that he was doing so "in spite of the fact that he's on parole and a convicted robber," adding more fuel to the public outrage. Still, opponents noticed a change in Gates. "He was not the blustery, argumentative, you know, swaggering Chief Gates," Melanie Lomax, a Gates critic on the civilian Police Commission told the *Los Angeles Times*. "He appeared more conciliatory and somewhat worried." Other members of the commission agreed, noting that he was "surprisingly cooperative"—"he was a very different man."

The kinder, gentler Gates wouldn't last long. Calls for resignation mounted. During a public hearing of the Police Commission, Gates had to sit, quietly, with eyes downcast, and listen to protesters denounce him and call for his firing. It wasn't just activists. The *Los Angeles Times* gingerly suggested that it might be time for the chief to go. Bradley and the L.A. City Council were working on a proposal to strip the police chief of his civil service protections and make it easier to force him out of his job. Gates said he would not resign. He taped a video for his "troops": "It'd be easy for me to pack up and go away. But I didn't put 42 years into this job to see it blow up in smoke. I'm not going to resign. I'm going to be here to make sure that what I say is done." He said that the morale of the department was at stake. The brass and all the police unions and associations were backing him. "We are gratified that Chief Gates is not going to submit to the lynch-mob mentality by resigning," Lorne Kramer of the Police Command Officers Association told the press in a news conference staged in front of the police academy. At the Los Angeles County Professional Peace Officers Association "LAPD Day" luncheon, Gates held up the department's human relations handbook and ripped into the civil libertarians, saying that they had "violated every precept of human relations that we set forth" . . . Objectivity? Objectivity! Do you see any objectivity at all? . . . Courtesy! Anything courteous about them? Compassion!

Have they shown one ounce of compassion? . . . Prejudice! They are so prejudiced against police. They hate us and clearly they hate me. I know that, and I don't blame them for hating me, but I blame them for hating you." They gave him an extended standing ovation.

This was the constituency that mattered, anyway. "You know, in so many situations, I could be a good guy," Gates told the *Los Angeles Times*. "(But) my police officers would say, 'Oh, man, the chief is selling us out.' I could be a *great* guy. I could be very popular. But that's not the way you develop confidence and respect from your personnel." So the tough-guy stuff was a performance for his men. Another way to put it was that Gates was two-faced. "My own experiences with Gates have revealed the two personas," a lawyer who once chaired the mayor's committee on finance and the budget wrote to the *Times*. "In private meetings, I found him to be courteous, understanding and sincerely interested in trying to resolve problems. Public sessions were another matter . . . I was shaken by his attitude. He was aggressive and abrasive, so much so that he ended up alienating many of his supporters on the budget committee I chaired." Still, this was understandable politics: "To earn the respect of the street officer, Gates had to project the 'tough cop' image. While this image has cost him dearly among some constituencies—including the mayor—it was and is necessary to maintain the morale of the police force."

At a city council meeting, the old Gates was back and baring his teeth. He reminded the members that he had responded to their personal requests for police services in their districts. "If you don't speak out on the Los Angeles Police Department at this crucial moment then this department won't be the kind of department this city deserves," Gates said. There was more than a hint of menace in his words. Councilman Michael Woo asked, "Did you mean that as a threat . . . that if I or other members of the council are going to be critical of you, you will withhold support services?" Gates exploded. "That's the most insulting thing I've ever heard on this council floor and I've been here longer than you've been alive. That's an insulting question. We're a professional organization. I'm talking about morale. My officers work and they work hard. Don't insult me or the police officers of this city."

"A professional organization." The chief, the unquestionable authority, standing up to the petty little politicians and telling them off. Shouting down the city council for the impertinence to question *him*. Telling them what they should do. Telling them where they could stick it. That was what the LAPD was supposed to be and what its chief was supposed to do. The cops were supposed to be above the politicians. That's how the old chief William H. Parker wanted it. Gates learned it all from Parker, his mentor, his idol, his father.

Parker was born in the Old West: the place was Lead, South Dakota, in 1905. His grandfather had been a lawman in neighboring Deadwood. In the 1920s, the Parkers, like many others from the Plains states and the Midwest, moved to the new frontier town, Los Angeles. Young Bill worked as an usher and a cabbie, going to law school at night. Then he joined the police, working the night shift. When he finished law school, the LAPD seemed like a better career bet than being a lawyer. The LAPD of the 1920s and '30s was corrupt and brutal. The cops took payouts, shook people down, and if those people didn't pay up or if the cops just didn't like the looks of them or got some lip, they beat the shit out of them. Parker was a straight shooter, though. He didn't go along with the program of petty graft and relaxed attitudes toward vice. When he was manning the desk at the precinct, he told the cops under his watch to take their perps somewhere else to get beaten. He didn't want to see it. He got a reputation as a martinet, a disciplinarian, a tight-ass, dour and severe. It slowed his rise but couldn't stop it: his performance and test results spoke for themselves.

Even while Parker disdained laxity and corruption among his fellow officers, he worked to protect and insulate them from the outside world. As a representative of the Fire and Police Protective League, the city's police union, Parker proposed a sweeping amendment to the city charter. Police officers would now only be judged and disciplined by their own. The chief would be granted "a substantial property right" in his role and could only be removed by the part-time Police Commission for "good and sufficient cause shown upon a finding of 'guilty' of the specific charge or charges." Removal was designed to be practically impossible: a mayor trying to get rid of the chief would have to fight through the nearly impenetrable trench works of rights to judicial appeal at city, state, and federal levels, a process that could take years. To a public tired of stories of corruption, it all sounded like good government reform, and when the amendment was put to a referendum in 1937, they passed it. Parker had made the LAPD the chief's private, unaccountable fiefdom. "With the approval of the electorate, a weird balkanization had taken place," writes Joe Domanick, historian of the LAPD. "A quasi-military organization had declared itself independent of the rest of city government and placed itself outside of the control of the police commission, City Hall, or any other public officials, outside of the democratic system of checks and balances."

With his independent kingdom established, now there was just the matter of Parker's ascent to the throne. During the war, he had been part of the military occupation authorities in charge of "denazifying" police forces in Frankfurt and Munich. When he returned, he had the vision of turning the LAPD into an elite, professional unit. The model was the Marine Corps. Elevated to chief in 1950, he effectively ended the notorious corruption of Hollywood cops. Parker applied rigorous modern bureaucratic methods of statistical analysis, organization, administration, and training. He oversaw investment in cutting-edge communications and surveillance equipment. He expanded the intelligence squad. Its ostensible purpose was to keep track of organized crime figures, but it soon began to compile files on activists and elected officials, including details of their personal lives. On more than one occasion Parker used his precious dossiers to derail political opponents.

The LAPD became a "mobile army of occupation" armed with a doctrine of "proactive policing." "If someone looked out of place in a neighborhood, we had a little chat with him. If a description of a thief could be obtained, we stopped everyone fitting that description, even if it meant angering dozens of innocent citizens," Daryl Gates would write in his memoirs. But the city that boosters called "the Great White Spot" was changing. The war had brought in hundreds of thousands of Black workers from the South to man the defense plants. Parker made sure that they were kept in line. "We were a mercenary army unofficially empowered to arrest anyone at any time for any cause," recalled an officer who worked in the 1950s and '60s. "Black people could not venture north of Beverly or much west of La Brea after dark without a strongly documented purpose." In 1989 the *Los Angeles Sentinel* reported that an unmarked LAPD car was discovered parked in South Central with the national emblem of apartheid South Africa on its grille.

Although Parker had insulated the department from political control, he understood the necessity of public relations, and he worked hard at producing propaganda for his department. He believed that the LAPD had to be *sold*. "There must be created a desire and a demand on the part of the community for the quality of police service that is offered. In this respect, law enforcement does not differ greatly from private industry," Parker explained in a lecture on the police and PR given to a group of California chiefs. "The real problem is not that of doing a good job; it is not even that of telling the public that it is being done. The most important and most difficult task is the securing of a market for professional police work—a public that will demand it, pay the cost of it, and stand behind it." The LAPD's Public Information Division planted favorable newspaper stories in the press, published its own magazine, and closely cooperated with the creators of the popular TV series *Dragnet*, down to reviewing each one of its scripts. (The future creator of *Star Trek*, Gene Roddenberry, worked in the PID and was Parker's speechwriter for a time. He based Mr. Spock, the coldly rationalistic science officer, on Parker.) They arranged for the chief to address as many civic organizations as possible, sometimes giving two speeches a day, on a permanent campaign. A particular effort was made to lecture business groups, which Parker took to be his primary constituency. The Public Information Division also put the chief directly on his own TV show, *The Thin Blue Line*, where he could answer the public's questions.

That phrase—"the thin blue line"—was Parker's invention and the core of his philosophy of policing. On the one side were the forces of disorder, on the other was the public; in between them stood the police: "Between the law-abiding elements of society and the criminals that prey upon them stands a thin blue line of defense—your police officer." Civilization itself was under threat by internal enemies. "Egypt, Babylon, Greece, and Rome rose, then fell, as strength gave way to weakness, alertness gave way to complacency, and virtue gave way to corruption," Parker explained to the National Automatic Merchandising Association in 1952 in a speech titled "Invasion from Within." "It is interesting, and perhaps productive, to recall that the high walls of these civilizations were never toppled by barbarians from without. But the walls crumbled into rubble and the enemy poured through when BARBARIANISM within rotted the moral supporting timbers. Today America faces the kind of attack which destroyed these brave civilizations of the past. We face a three-pronged threat, a simultaneous assault in three dimensions: the armed might of Soviet Russia, the Communist Fifth Column within our borders, and organized crime." The police were at war with what Parker called "human parasites," which had to be "eliminated" lest they would "substitute the holy designation of our city with another name of Spanish derivation, Los Diabolos, the city of the devils."

Although the public was to be protected from the forces of chaos, it could not be trusted. "The American people possess a greater degree of sympathy for the 'under-dog' than any other peoples on earth. Thus, when police measures are applied against an individual, we are inclined to extend sympathy to that individual and are therefore prone to overlook the deeds of the individual that made police action necessary." Hence, the constant need for public relations. "The police must help them understand," Parker said. But any criticism of the police from the outside degraded the "morale" of the cops who were standing on the thin blue line and put the critic on the other side of it along with the other "parasites."

Although the police were on the front lines of maintaining the "patterns of order" on which the "entire social structure" depended, their role was strictly limited: "We are not healers of social ills. Our job is to apply emergency treatment to society's surface wounds; we deal with effects, not cause." He dismantled the youth programs and social outreach services of the LAPD. That wasn't the cops' job. To the devout, conservative Catholic in Parker, humanity was intrinsically fallen and depraved. In an article for *Police Chief* magazine, he wrote, "It is the premise of some eminent theologians that man is inherently corrupt. If such is the case, there is an inherent tendency on the part of humankind to engage in improper courses of behavior that will include activities that have come to be labeled as criminal." He spoke of the "melancholy" and "despair" implicit in this view. If humanity could not be improved, at least there was the nightstick. "Lacking the ability to remedy human imperfection, we must learn to live with it. The only way to safely live with it is to control it. Control, not correction, is the key."

In Parker's opinion, any tool to maintain control and order was justified, including racial profiling. "At the present time, race, color, and creed are useful statistical and tactical devices . . . If persons of Mexican, Negro, or Anglo-Saxon ancestry, for some reason, contribute heavily to other forms of crime, police deployment must take that into account. From an ethnological point-of-view, Negro, Mexican, and Anglo-Saxon are unscientific breakdowns; they are a fiction. From a police point-of-view, they are useful fictions and should be used as long as they remain useful." Of course, the useful fiction of race did not apply to diversifying the police: there they must be a strictly color-blind meritocracy: "Another problem which plagues the police administrator is organized group pressure to promote officers and make command assignments on the basis of race, color, or creed. Before a recent Los Angeles election, I encountered tremendous pressure to replace an Anglo-Saxon commander of a detective division with another commander belonging to a certain minority group. I refused to engage in racial discrimination against the Anglo-Saxon commander."

Parker bragged that his policy of "enforced order" had solved the problem of "community relations." Despite Los Angeles growing and becoming more diverse, and having "intolerant citizens" and "incidents of conflict," "those factors have not been permitted to accumulate into mass disorder." That was 1955. A decade later it would be a different story.

The Watts riots of 1965 were triggered by rumors that police had manhandled and slapped a pregnant Black woman during a traffic stop. The atmosphere was already angry: there was endemic unemployment in the city; a referendum had overturned the Rumford Fair Housing Act that was supposed to end residential segregation; and a month earlier an LAPD officer had pulled over and raped a twenty-two-year-old Black woman. The officer was quietly removed from his job, but he never faced criminal charges.

The commission established to investigate the riots, led by the businessman and former CIA director John McCone, largely exculpated law enforcement, even though the supposedly elite and über-professional LAPD had altogether failed to control the riots, retreated, and required help from the National Guard. Criticisms of Chief Parker were dismissed. "Many Negroes feel that [Parker] carries a deep hatred of the Negro community," the report reads. "However, Chief Parker's statements to us and collateral evidence such as his record of fairness to Negro officers are inconsistent with his having such an attitude." (The LAPD was in effect segregated until 1964; future Mayor Bradley would recall not being allowed to ride in a car with a white partner.) Parker's statements to the commission evidently did not include his characterizing the rioters as "monkeys in a zoo." Nor did they include

Parker's remarks aired on television: "It is estimated that by 1970, forty-five percent of the metropolitan area of Los Angeles will be Negro. If you want any protection for your home . . . you're going to have to get in and support a strong police department. If you don't, come 1970, God help you." Parker's testimony to the commission did include his belief that "the police of this country, in my opinion, are the most downtrodden, oppressed, dislocated minority in America."

The McCone Commission was mostly concerned for the preservation of "police authority," the "thin thread" without which "chaos might easily spread"; it concluded that, "while we must examine carefully the claim of police brutality and must see that justice is done to all groups within our society, we must, at the same time, be sure that law enforcement agencies, upon which so much depends, are not rendered impotent." The McCone Commission specifically ruled out more civilian control: "The Commission feels that a civilian review board, authorized to investigate, and perhaps to decide, complaints, but with no other law enforcement responsibilities, would endanger the effectiveness of law enforcement, which would be intolerable at a time when crime is on the increase throughout the country." According to the leadership of the LAPD, these review boards were part of the fifth column, a "national conspiracy" to "emasculate law enforcement" that "did not displease the Communist Party."

Parker resented having to answer to anybody about anything. He railed at the city council. He particularly bridled at the reasonable yet persistent questioning by councilmember Tom Bradley. Parker had once sent out the "polished, articulate" Sergeant Bradley to do liaison work with the Black community, until the chief heard through his intelligence squad that Bradley was criticizing the LAPD to "dissident groups." "Bradley, he fumed, was an absolute traitor to the department," Daryl Gates would write in his memoirs. Thereafter, Bradley was banished to a graveyard shift and could not rise above lieutenant. With advancement in the LAPD closed off, he turned to law and then politics. Now this ungrateful son of the department, Black no less, the man Parker had wanted to make a public face of the force, this man had betrayed Parker and dared to question him. "I think you are trying to pin this on the police," Parker snarled at Bradley. "I'll go to my grave thinking this was your intention." That would happen sooner rather than later: within a year, Parker dropped dead of a heart attack.

Parker might be dead, but his legacy was intact. The city might change, become more Black, Asian, Jewish, and Latino, but the LAPD would not. "Anglo" conservatives might no longer hold all the power in city hall or on the council, but the LAPD became the de facto center of white power in L.A. One political scientist called it "a sort of government-in-exile for conservative Los Angeles." Ensconced in the Parker Center, its downtown modernist keep, the LAPD was more of a state within a state than a government in exile. When Bradley was elected mayor in 1973 and his commissioners tried eventually to press the police administration, they discovered a deeply secretive, as Joe Domanick wrote, "byzantine" organization with a "monolithic resistance to and suspicion of the rest of the world" whose officers were "masters" at avoiding basic oversight. The LAPD was an "exclusive, inbred club, with . . . little cross-fertilization, and few new ideas."

The LAPD's leadership reproduced itself not through inbreeding, but through grooming. Daryl F. Gates did well at the police academy, but he was working in traffic control when he was selected to be Bill Parker's driver. Parker loved him for his looks: a high school football player, Gates was suntanned, blue-eyed, and in perfect shape, conforming to the military image of the LAPD. Perhaps most important, he was just about the same height as Parker, sticking to a rule that his chauffeurs couldn't be taller than he was. Parker would often make Gates stand up during his speeches to display his comely appearance. "This," Parker would say, showing off his young driver to the crowd, "is a *policeman* . . . Look at him!"

Gates was friendly, soft-spoken, and well-liked, but was internally brimming with wounded pride, anger, and ambition fueled by his family's descent into poverty during the Depression and his Irish dad's turn to alcoholism. Gates did not want to be Parker's driver, a "toady" as he put it; in fact, he'd barely wanted to become a cop at all—but he quickly grew to worship Parker, saying that he was "totally smitten" with the older man. "He didn't have any children, and I think he saw in me an opportunity to mold somebody," Gates later recalled. "He knew I had tremendous respect for him and that I hung on every word." As they drove around Los Angeles, Parker would discourse on his philosophy and opinions from the back seat. He also taught contempt for the city's elected officials. In his memoirs, Gates recalled an episode where he and Parker were late picking up the mayor, Fletcher Bowron, for the Rose Bowl. The infuriated mayor, "short and on the chunky side . . . called 'Old Chubby Cheeks' by reporters at city hall," struck a comical note to Chief Parker; he started to giggle uncontrollably during the car ride. Gates followed suit. "Don't you realize," seethed Bowron, "I'm the mayor of this city?"

This surrogate dad still had some of the sins of the old father. Parker—nicknamed "Whiskey Bill" behind his back—sometimes was so drunk that Gates had to help him as he stumbled out of the car or walked back to his house, becoming "a paternal image in more ways than I would have liked." But Daryl never did leave daddy's side, progressing from driver to adjutant to lieutenant in charge of the intelligence division, the keeper of Parker's precious files.

Gates was made chief almost by default. Twelve years after Parker's death, and three commissioners later, Mayor Bradley appointed him in 1978. "At least with Gates, you knew what you were getting—a straight conservative," said Stephen Reinhardt, one of Bradley's new liberal advisers and member of the police commission. "He was a police bureaucrat, someone who totally reflected the status quo, a Bill Parker product. But I felt he was clearly the best of the lot. In the end, we simply had no other choice." Gates reinforced discipline. The shagginess of the 1960s and '70s would not be allowed to infiltrate the department. "Our standards of appearance were eroding. Hair began to grow long, sideburns were forever inching downward and officers kept testing us every single day," Gates would later write. But he would "categorically refuse to let officers look like flower children. It was about control, the image of control: The neatness of the uniform, the way an officer wears his or her hair, having clean fingernails and shiny shoes and badge—these immediately convey the impression of a person who is in control of himself or herself."

In power, Gates quickly ended the nascent community policing efforts of his predecessors and returned the LAPD to Parker's paramilitary vision. In response to Watts and Black radicalism, he had fostered the SWAT team—the acronym stood for Special Weapons and Tactics. Gates had initially wanted it to be the "Special Weapons Attack Team"—and made it the model of his operation, removing officers from patrol and placing them in "highly trained, technically sophisticated, specialized units that had little day-to-day contact with the community." According to Domanick, these special forces formed Gates's political base: "The department's macho men . . . the hard-driving troops in Metro, the men of SWAT, the old-time detectives . . . —more than the city council, the businesses, and the homeowner's associations—were his true constituency." He admired them and craved their approval. He went to lengths to flatter them: Gates claimed that his SWAT team would be able to rescue the hostages in Iran if the Carter administration could not. Bradley managed to stand up to the more preposterous demands of the militarized LAPD—"he asked for everything from a tank to a submarine to an airplane and I took those out of the budget"—but the deafening sound of LAPD helicopters, their blinding searchlights and blaring directives from the loudspeakers were a constant feature of life in Los Angeles.

So too were killings by police. The LAPD killed the greatest number of civilians, adjusted for its size, of any American force. One out of every three people shot by the LAPD were unarmed. In 1979, the shooting of a thirty-nine-year-old Black woman named Eula Love, a recent widow with small children who was undergoing a mental breakdown, caused a brief political and press firestorm. Otherwise, these "officer-involved shootings," as they were known in LAPD PR speak, were brushed under the table with thin justifications and barely any media interest.

The 1980s brought crime, crack, and gangs to the city. Preoccupied with the fiscal issues and fixated on development deals, Bradley and the city council were off the LAPD's back. The crack wave of the mid- to late 1980s and the lurid stories about South Central's colors-wearing Bloods and Crips gangs seemed to confirm Parker's old adage that the police were the "thin blue line" against total social collapse. Pressed by the overwhelming presence of crime in their neighborhoods, even the LAPD's critics in the Black community had to accede once again to some degree of police hegemony. The *Los Angeles Sentinel*, the city's largest Black-owned newspaper, was known for its intensely critical coverage of the LAPD, but its tone now marked a certain amount of resignation, if not despair. In an editorial asking if the battle against drug dealers had just been lost, the paper opined, "We can defeat the drug dealers, but we cannot do it alone. It will take a concerted effort on the part of committed people in our neighborhoods. Every resource we have at our command will have to be brought into play and we will have to hold hands with Chief Daryl Gates and Sheriff Sherman Block." In the same editorial, the paper supported County Supervisor Kenneth Hahn's proposal to use the National Guard to fight the war on drugs. (Hahn, a crusading liberal who built a loyal constituency in the Black community through his association with the civil rights movement, became a law-and-order-focused Gates ally in the 1980s.) After Gates's 1990 comments about shooting casual drug users, the *Sentinel*'s op-ed page prevaricated, with columnist Stanley G. Robertson writing, "As one who has not always agreed with the public comments of Los Angeles Police Chief, Daryl Gates, I think the negative public reaction to his comments that 'casual drug users should be shot' is one of the reasons why we will never ever defeat the drug problem in this country . . . Chief Gates has said he did not mean his comments to be taken 'literally,' as I didn't when I first heard them. But unless we are really ready to play 'hard ball' with a number of the social ills which are running our society, such as drugs, then we'll never rid ourselves of them."

In this permissive political environment, Gates and the LAPD ran wild. Even as Ross Perot was calling for society to "declare civil war and the drug dealer is the enemy" and "start to deal with the problem in straight military terms," the LAPD was already implementing that sort of program. "This is Vietnam here," declared the head of the District Attorney's Hardcore Drug Unit. "It's like having the Marine Corps invade an area that is still having little pockets of resistance," Gates proffered. "We've got to wipe them out." But as in Vietnam, efforts that looked spectacular could be impotent or counterproductive. Gates's Operation Hammer, an effort to round up gang members, resulted in the arrest of tens of thousands of young Black men, with only sixty felony arrests and thirty-two actual charges being filed. Even in a public environment friendly to the police, Gates's excesses re-inflamed criticism. An August 1988 raid by dozens of officers on an apartment complex on Dalton Avenue and Thirty-Ninth Street found six ounces of marijuana and resulted in no charges. It did result in the arrest and beating of dozens of residents. "The police smashed furniture, punched holes in walls, destroyed family photos, ripped down cabinet doors, slashed sofas, shattered mirrors, hammered toilets to porcelain shards, doused clothing with bleach and emptied refrigerators. Some officers left their own graffiti: 'LAPD Rules.'" The police even ripped an outside stairwell away from a building. The Red Cross had to provide disaster relief for some displaced residents. At the station house, those arrested were forced to whistle the theme of *The Andy Griffith Show* while being beaten with metal flashlights. The LAPD ended up having to pay $4 million in damages to the residents, and several officers were disciplined. But when Mayor Bradley submitted a letter asking for a full investigation into the incident, Gates shot back, with characteristic diplomacy, that it was a "dumb letter."

Against his inclination and his judgment of the political terrain,

Bradley was being forced into taking more vigorous action. After the Rodney King beating, a poll showed Gates's support eroding, but only 31 percent of Angelenos supported his resignation. On April 1, Bradley set up a commission to examine the LAPD, chaired by attorney Warren Christopher, who had been deputy attorney general under Lyndon Johnson and a vice chairman of the McCone Commission on the Watts riots. A full-page ad in the *Times* featured a flag-draped casket with the caption "In the line of duty"; the rest of the copy read, "Where was this outcry for the cops killed protecting you? People will not even remember who they are, even though they died for you. There were no community leaders or ACLU attorneys demanding that officers be provided more protection or concerned about why it happened." It was signed by seventeen enforcement organizations, including the LAPD officers' union. The same day, Bradley publicly called for Gates's resignation. Gates refused. The Police Commission placed Gates on indefinite paid leave for the duration of the investigation into the department. "This whole action of the board defames me," Gates told the commission. "And I would like the record to show that I hold each and every one of you personally responsible for any defamation [or] any harm that this brings me."

The LAPD's traditional constituency in the San Fernando Valley middle class reacted to the news with alarm: the president of the Pacoima-area homeowners' association called the decision "shocking." Bud Brown, the president of the Foothill Advisory Boosters Association, a group of Valley business owners who "contribute money, equipment and services to help police activities," declared, "We are extremely disappointed. The department needs strong leadership and that's what Daryl Gates provided. I worry about the repercussions." Brown noticed an uptick in interest in his group since the beginning of the Rodney King scandal. "Businesses want to express their support for the Police Department," Brown told the *Times*. "The incident was horrible—everybody agrees with that. But it's an isolated incident. The whole department should not be painted with the same brush." On the far side of the Hollywood Hills and civil society, Jesse Jackson led a demonstration of several thousand in front of the Parker Center, calling for a boycott of the upcoming Super Bowl to be held in Los Angeles. Mayor Bradley pointedly objected to any talk of boycotts.

The day after Gates's suspension, the city council voted 10–3 to order the city attorney to settle Gates's lawsuit with the city and reinstate him. The liberal members worried about their "law and order" credentials right before an election. Probably just as decisive was the reaction of the business community. Richard Riordan, a Bradley supporter and founding partner in the private equity firm Riordan, Lewis and Haden, told the *Los Angeles Times* that the business sector was "rallying around Gates" and that the mayor had to "back off." The *Times* later revealed that the chief had done his own lobbying among "conservative elements in the business community." For his part, Gates appeared to be having a good time. He was welcomed by a "thunderous" ten-minute standing ovation by a crowd of nine hundred at the Sportsmen's Lodge ballroom in Studio City. Among the crowd were the uniformed commanders of the LAPD and former mayor Sam Yorty, Bradley's conservative predecessor. Also present was George Holliday, the man who had filmed the Rodney King tape. The ostensible purpose of the event was for a group called Citizens in Support of the Police Chief to present Holliday with a plaque commending him as an ideal citizen for bringing his tape to the public's attention. "If it wasn't for the helicopter, the lighting would have been horrible," Gates quipped to the crowd. The irony was a little deeper than Gates probably realized: the LAPD's electronic goodies were now conspiring in his downfall.

Meanwhile, another, even ghastlier video appeared in the news. This time it was security camera footage from the Empire Liquor Market in South Central. The tape depicted fifteen-year-old Latasha Harlins briefly scuffling with the shopkeeper, fifty-one-year-old Soon Ja Du, turning to leave the store, and being shot in the back of the head by Du. The altercation was over a bottle of orange juice: Du claimed that Harlins was attempting to steal it by placing it in her backpack, and that she snatched at Harlins when she came to the counter, pulling on her sweater and bag. Harlins responded by hitting Du, who then threw a stool at her, but missed. Du then drew a .38-caliber revolver from a holster. Harlins picked up the orange juice, placed it on the counter, and turned to leave. Du's shot killed her instantly. She had $2 in her hand when she died. "There was no attempt at shoplifting. There was no robbery. There was no crime at all," according to the responding police commander. Du was arrested on suspicion of murder. But in the strange, euphemistic argot of the LAPD, the incident was described as a "business dispute." The joint statement of Black and Korean American community leaders that met immediately after the killing was similarly odd in its phrasing: "This senseless loss of a young girl's life reflects the worst type of violence perpetuated upon a consumer by a merchant."

The careful, stilted talk of "business disputes" and "consumer" and "merchant" pointed indirectly to the growing tension between Black patrons and the Korean markets that dotted underserved and underdeveloped neighborhoods. Under Bradley, the city's Community Redevelopment Agency largely neglected South Central development in favor of more impressive glass-and-steel banking towers downtown. The one shopping center the CRA helped rebuild in a minority area was at the foot of Baldwin Hills, an affluent Black neighborhood in Bradley's old district. Big national chains shunned the blighted neighborhoods. Black residents generally did not have enough capital or access to credit to start their own businesses, and if they did, they generally moved westward, out of South Central. After the Watts riots, many of the Jewish storekeepers left too. Many of them were simply at retirement age, and their upwardly mobile children were not interested in continuing the family business. Into the gap came a new wave of Korean immigrants. They'd arrived with small amounts of capital that could go toward buying and starting grocery stores, and they could rely on tight-knit community resources for credit rather than the financial system. Unlike the older Jewish businesses that often hired Black clerks, the viability of Korean businesses came from the unpaid labor of close family members, who often worked long hours.

The two communities increasingly faced each other as deeply alien rivals. By the early 1980s the *Los Angeles Sentinel* reported on a pervading sense of a "takeover," a "problem" or crisis of "Asian" convenience stores. Black customers particularly complained about the sudden dismissals of the few Black workers they did hire as well as rude or abusive treatment and accusations of theft, and they expressed frustration that the Black community was being denied the requisite loans to buy these sorts of businesses for themselves. Black business owners perceived Korean arrivals as deliberately setting out to drive them out of business by undercutting their prices. Religious leaders decried the sale of liquor on Sundays, drug paraphernalia, and pornography in communities they felt were already straining under the burden of vice. For their part, the shopkeepers complained about aggressive behavior and rudeness as well as rampant shoplifting and more serious offenses like shootings, armed robberies, and arsons. (Rodney King's own robbery conviction came from a rather pathetic 1989 attempt to hold up a Korean shopkeeper with a tire iron for $200. The merchant, Tae Suck Baik, said that he grabbed King's jacket and began whipping him with a metal rod he kept near the cash register, at which point King dropped his own weapon and attempted to flee, chased by the enraged owner, who continued to rain blows on him. Baik later expressed regret for turning the incident violent and said that he felt sorry for King.)

Despite intercommunal tensions, Los Angeles hadn't witnessed the organized boycotts of Korean stores that had taken place in Black neighborhoods in other cities. A few months after the killing of Latasha Harlins, however, a man named Lee Arthur Mitchell was shot and killed after attempting to hold up a Korean shopkeeper; it turned out he was unarmed. In the aftermath, community groups organized a boycott of John's Liquors, the site of the Mitchell shooting. The store was also the target of an attempted firebombing. Eventually the Korean American Grocers Organization and the boycotting community groups, brought together by Mayor Bradley, reached an agreement to end the boycott, putting together guidelines for merchants and encouraging a more courteous treatment of patrons and a plan for Korean markets to hire one hundred employees from the communities they were in, a pitiful number that could not possibly hope to alleviate economic distress.

Even if entirely Black owned and Black staffed, the small convenience stores could not hope to be a replacement for the loss of industry. In July, during the boycott, General Motors announced that it was going to close its Van Nuys assembly plant, the last major auto factory in the Los Angeles region, eliminating 2,600 unionized jobs. The structural roots of the intra-ethnic conflict were ignored, and the solution to the problem now depended on the very limited resources of the communities themselves. It did very little to relieve grievances, which got a national airing with the release of Ice Cube's sophomore album *Death Certificate*, featuring the song "Black Korea." The lyrics, interspersed with lines from Spike Lee's *Do the Right Thing*, were direct: "So don't follow me up and down your market / Or your little chop suey ass'll be a target / Of a nationwide boycott." Ice Cube imagined other remedies as well: "So pay respect to the Black fist / Or we'll burn your store right down to a crisp." The only nationwide boycotting forthcoming was one carried out by Korean grocers' associations, who organized some three thousand stores to stop carrying St. Ides, a malt liquor brand that employed Ice Cube as a TV and radio pitchman. With their distribution network in serious jeopardy, St. Ides's producer, the Mackenzie River Corporation, quickly brought the rapper and the Korean grocers' groups together to discuss the issue, and Ice Cube adopted a more conciliatory tone.

Locked in stalemate, Gates and Bradley publicly declared a "truce," brokered by John Ferraro, the city council president, an event that fully revealed the extent to which the two men led rival political power centers.

Gates announced that he would resign if the Christopher Commission found he had been "derelict" in his duties, perhaps expecting the same sort of gentle treatment that the McCone Commission had given to his mentor, Chief Parker. In the meantime, Gates started to move against his enemies, demoting subordinates who cooperated with the commission. Reporters covering the Rodney King case and the proceedings at city hall alleged that they were being harassed by the LAPD. Then there were more sinister suggestions: the police union had been visiting city council members at their homes, and the chief had secret files on council members to guarantee their cooperation. "The only files I have are in my head," Gates responded with a smile when pressed by council members on the "secret files" issue. "As you know, I'm writing a book." On another occasion, Gates said that he "knows people very, very well."

Then, in July, the Christopher Commission's report dropped. The commission found a pattern of excessive force "aggravated by racism" and tolerated by supervisors, who regularly took no disciplinary action against "problem" officers. The LAPD was almost totally unaccountable. "Although the City Charter assigns the Police Commission ultimate control over Department policies, its authority over the Department and the Chief of Police is illusory," the report read. "Real power and authority reside in the Chief." The panel recommended an overhaul of the Police Commission that would make it able to exert real control over the department. As for Chief Gates in particular, the panel tried to deliver its news diplomatically, praising his record of public service and gently asking for him to step down. "Chief Gates has already served 13 years as Chief of Police, three years longer than the maximum of two five-year terms that we have recommended for any future Chief . . . We believe that commencement of a transition in that office is now appropriate." But a little below this, there was stronger criticism, albeit it avoided naming names: "If the leaders are careless in their comments or equivocal in their commitments, some rank-and-file officers may find encouragement for their misconduct."

As for the rank and file, the commission's review of the squad cars' computer messages from 1989 to 1991 was damning. "Sounds like monkey slapping time"; "I would love to drive down Slauson with a flame thrower . . . we would have a barbeque"; ""That last load went to a family of illegals living in the brush along side the pas frwy . . . I thought the woman was going to cry . . . so I hit her with my baton"; "Did you really break his arm—Along with other misc parts"; "I almost got me a Mexican last night but he dropped the dam gun to quick"; "If you encounter these negroes shoot first and ask questions later." The commission noted that the same messages were available to the LAPD and had virtually never resulted in disciplinary action. In fact, they were often sent by supervisors. On a radio talk show, Gates suggested that some of the messages were "black humor" exchanged in many cases by minority officers themselves. He reiterated that he would retire on his own schedule.

With the delivery of the report, the city council suddenly regained its courage—or at least its political cover. Gates now also lost the backing of the business class, including the Chamber of Commerce and Richard Riordan, who told the *Los Angeles Times* that he would now be "willing to urge Gates to agree to a timetable for retirement." A majority of the council voted to implement the Christopher Commission's reform recommendations, and they endorsed Gates's resignation. The amendments to the city charter recommended by the commission would have to be voted on by the public as a ballot initiative, slated for June 1992.

In response, Gates first told city council members that he'd retire at the end of 1991. Then he agreed to retire in April 1992, but he went on to hedge, prevaricate, and give conflicting dates. He seemed to want to link his retirement to the referendum on the police reforms, hinting that he might remain if they failed. "I think it's something for everyone to think about, myself included, and I'm thinking about that," Gates told reporters. "I said April because I thought the election was going to be held [by then] . . . Now I'm waiting for the City Council to urge me to stay until the election is held, if they want to do that."

Despite Gates's dance, there was a sense that the era of police domination was over. The evidence—in the form of the King tape and the Christopher Commission—was just too overwhelming. In the trial of the four cops in the Rodney King case, when the Second District Court of Appeal granted a change of venue to Simi Valley in Ventura County, the prosecutor, Terry L. White, barely objected, even though Simi Valley was 79.9 percent "Anglo" and only 1.5 percent Black. It was also "Copland": the chosen bedroom community of many LAPD officers. The jury did not include a single Black juror and only one Hispanic and one Asian. Surely the video evidence would be enough.

Justice was apparently still difficult to get, even in Los Angeles County. In November, Soon Ja Du was convicted of voluntary manslaughter in the Latasha Harlins case—murder charges were ruled out—but the superior court judge, Joyce A. Karlin, suspended her sentence, ordering community service, probation, and a $500 fine. "Did Mrs. Du react inappropriately? Absolutely," Karlin said. "But was that reaction understandable? I think it was." Suspended sentences for violent crimes in Los Angeles were exceedingly rare, for homicides almost unheard of—but still an exception was made. A local elected official warned of a "time bomb." An editorial in *The Orange County Register* hectored about the lack of "values" taught to Latasha Harlins: "Was it too much to dare think that a 15-year-old girl should have a shred of respect for an adult? If Latasha Harlins had been taught even the forbidden Golden Rule, maybe this accident wouldn't have escalated into the tragedy." Harlins's mother had herself been murdered when Latasha was nine years old. The author totally reimagined the event at the store—"every time I saw the rerun, I expected Latasha to come back yet once more to beat Du"—and ignored that it was Du who initially attacked Harlins. Five days later, the news reported that a Glendale man was sentenced to jail time—for animal cruelty after harming his dog.

Still, everyone in Los Angeles and the rest of the country seemed to think a guilty verdict for the four officers in the King case was inevitable. The video evidence would surely make it impossible to acquit. Terry White concluded his case by showing the jury the video again: "Now who are you going to believe, the defendants or your own eyes?" While Gates had declared the beating an aberration, the defense brought in a SWAT veteran who testified that the use of force was perfectly in keeping with LAPD policy. Gates declined to testify for the prosecution: "In the back of my mind, I dreaded the worst possible designation by police officers anywhere, the chief's a wimp." The defense brought up Parker's "thin blue line" again and again: on one side, there were nice people like the Ventura County jurors, on the other there were "the likes of Rodney King." "This unpleasant incident is what we have police for," one of the defense attorneys told the jury. "The circumstances here were consistent with the job the man was hired to do. He was part of the line between society and chaos."

On April 29, 1992, the jury announced it had a verdict. On ten of the eleven charges, the jury found the defendants not guilty. On the eleventh charge it was deadlocked. Police boosters were ready to declare victory. "This will be a big plus for the vote 'no' on the Charter Amendment F campaign," the head of an anti-reform group predicted. "It will instill in people the belief that maybe Chief Gates was right all along. Maybe our Police Department is better than we realized." (Of course, Gates ostensibly believed that the officers should have been prosecuted.)

What Chief Gates knew was that the LAPD was as much about image as anything. Officers had to look tough, they had to look imposing, they had to look professional to represent the idea of an elite praetorian guard for society. This was part of their marketing to the public, as Parker had put it. The beating of Rodney King was its own kind of propaganda, in keeping with the LAPD's image, a propaganda of the deed: this was a message, a statement that this is what will happen to you. It was a message delivered many times before, but it was not meant to be seen by the entirety of the public, that stuff was just to be known about by certain communities.

Outside the Simi Valley courtroom, Black and white spectators began to argue and scuffle. "I would like to see all the brothers in South Central L.A. get together, get out in the street, and start dealing with what the real problem is," a man told a TV news crew. "And who is the real problem? White people. You got all the economic power. You selling the country to the Japanese. We been here 436 years and don't get nothing."

The great conflagration required many little sparks to smolder before it could sweep the city. At the intersection of Florence and Normandie, television cameras recorded sporadic violence from 4:00 p.m., an hour after the verdict was announced. An hour later, taunted and being pelted with bottles, the LAPD—the macho, militarized, proactive, professional LAPD—withdrew from the area and would not return in force for days. The violence steadily gathered intensity.

By 6:00 p.m., a mob at Florence and Normandie began to stone motorists and drag them from their cars and beat them. At around 6:30 p.m., Reginald Denny, a truck driver hauling a load of sand to a nearby cement plant, drove through the intersection and came under attack. He was hauled from the cab of his truck and severely beaten. The assault was broadcast live on TV by an overhead news helicopter. With the police absent, Denny's rescue fell to locals, including an unemployed aerospace engineer who first saw the attack on television and rushed to the intersection to intervene.

At around the same time, a crowd outside the Parker Center began to surge forward and threaten to storm the building. Chief Gates had already left for the evening, telling Police Commissioner Stanley Sheinbaum that he "had something to do." That "something" was a fundraiser in Brentwood for the campaign against Charter Amendment F. The attempts to storm and vandalize the Parker Center "riveted the attention of Police commanders," in the words of the official report on the disturbances, "although their focus should have been on South Bureau where the first incidents of arson were beginning to occur." Only at 6:45 p.m. did the LAPD declare a "Tactical Alert," not entering an "emergency mobilization" until 8:00 p.m., and this required several more hours to be put into effect. In the meantime, the city began to burn.

According to the Webster Commission report, so named because the commission was chaired by the former FBI and CIA director William H. Webster, the riot in the first four hours after the verdict was localized and containable. "Our analysis of events shows . . . that as late as 7:00 p.m., outbreaks of violence were largely confined to part of the 77th Street and Southwest Areas . . . It was within the next hour after 7:00 p.m. that the fires started and the violence began to spread. Thus, any chance the Command Staff had to contain the disturbance at the onset ended around 7:00 p.m. on the first night. After that, the violence steadily worked its way north and west."

The Webster report made a point of Gates's "curious absence" on the first night and noted that the "mystifying decision of the Chief of Police to absent himself during the early stages of the disturbance compounded all of the Department's command and control problems." Then there was the matter of his Brentwood jaunt. "Chief Gates himself cannot justify his decision to take a leisurely car ride to a Brentwood political event at this critical time. Nor can he explain his two-hour helicopter ride after he finally returned from the far side of the City." All this while usually ubiquitous LAPD reconnaissance helicopters suddenly disappeared from the sky. The report also cited an incident prior to April 29 where a deputy chief brought up the need for a riot plan in a meeting and "was roundly chewed out" by Gates. "During the entire crisis, the Chief of Police appears never actively to have taken command of the Department and its response, preferring to leave that critical responsibility in the hands of less experienced subordinates." Gates, once so concerned with total control over his department, adopted a laissez-faire attitude. Even as late as 11:00 p.m. on that first night, Gates resisted Bradley's call for the National Guard, informing the governor that he wasn't sure the police needed the assistance. When the guard members were finally called up, it took them a long time to mobilize owing to a shortage of ammunition; they arrived on the streets only the next day.

Police across the city reported being overwhelmed and outnumbered, but witnesses reported the police sitting by in their squad cars and even "cynically enjoying the spectacle of a city on fire." The Webster report would note that while the police "responded effectively to troublesome situations" in other parts of town, such as mostly white Westwood Village at the foot of Beverly Hills, they "could not keep up with the violence that erupted in the seven most active police Areas." Looting spread from South Central to the desperately impoverished Central American neighborhoods south of downtown. At the end of the six days of rioting, the tally showed that 51 percent of those arrested were Latino, which may have been an undercount, as many rioters were handed directly over to immigration authorities for deportation rather than being processed through the courts.

Korean merchants disproportionately bore the brunt of the looting and arson. Some 2,300 Korean-owned stores in South Central and Koreatown were sacked, and of the $785 million in property damage, $350 million of it fell on Korean businesses. When you add other Asian ethnicities, perhaps mistaken for Koreans or swept up in the general anti-Asian sentiment, well over half of all the destruction fell on Asian-owned businesses. Korean shopkeepers later accused the LAPD and the city of abandoning them and focusing on protecting Anglo neighborhoods instead. In Koreatown, the residents took matters into their own hands, arming themselves and standing guard in front of shopping centers and stores, even organizing informal militias led by military veterans. Perched on rooftops to espy and deter intruders, the armed Koreans made striking television images. They also engaged in pitched gun battles with would-be looters, with one of these claiming the life of the eighteen-year-old college freshman Edward Song Lee. The May 4 edition of *The Korea Times*, a Los Angeles–based newspaper serving the immigrant community, carried on its cover an article titled

ICE CUBE THE PEACEMAKER, detailing the rapper's meetings with and letters of apology to the Korean merchants' associations.

Several news reports made reference to *Blade Runner*, Ridley Scott's dystopian portrayal of a decaying city beset by ethnic hordes. Another comparison was to Lebanon, whose multi-sectarian civil war was not long over. In the coming weeks, newspaper readers would have to squint at captions to see if the images of urban destruction were from Los Angeles or Sarajevo. It was being called the worst civil disorder since the New York Draft Riots during the Civil War. Sixty-three people had been killed, 2,383 were injured, 12,000 arrested. George Bush invoked the Insurrection Act, but the marines arrived only after the worst violence had mostly subsided.

For Samuel Francis, the rioting confirmed the soundness of the Rodney King verdict: "The flabby fastidiousness of our leaders at every level about the rights of Rodney King illustrates exactly why the jurors were correct in acquitting the four horsemen of the local police force. In a country where no one in government cares about their basic duty of enforcing civil order, where the leaders' only concern is massaging the resentments of minorities, somebody has to take nightstick in hand."

But now it was the slow response and even timidity of the usually badass LAPD that was coming in for public criticism. Why did the police retreat from the early hot spots? Why didn't they respond to the fire department's requests for protection? Why did the LAPD abandon Koreatown? On talk radio, Gates tried to blame the criticism of the cops for their failures. "I know police officers on the streets are scared to death to use any kind of force," Gates charged, "because they think they're going to be second-guessed."

As the upheaval ebbed, the media duly raised the specter of Watts and Nixon's 1968 victory; boosts for Bush in the polls were predicted. But if Gates was hoping to ride a wave of support for law and order as Chief Parker and Mayor Yorty had, he was to be disappointed. Two weeks after the riot, Gates's disapproval rating reached 81 percent. Bradley's support also was collapsing; the two giants of city politics were dragging each other down. Support for Proposition F, which would restore civilian control of the LAPD, only grew.

In the aftermath of the riots, gun sales skyrocketed in California and around the country. In March, *The New York Times* reported that New England gunmakers, one of America's oldest domestic manufacturing industries, were struggling through the recession and a backlash against gun violence. But guns weren't in short supply or out of demand: it's just that people preferred deadlier and cheaper options than the finely tooled bolt-action rifles, revolvers, and shotguns of American lore. Gun consumers now preferred assault rifles, foreign semiautomatics, and inexpensive handguns sold by newer firms for as little as $60 a pop. The National Rifle Association found itself politically weakened and skittish about the public revulsion to gun violence, even joining gun control advocates in Sacramento to support a bill that would punish parents if their children got hold of their guns and hurt themselves or others. After the riots, they launched a new ad campaign, with a glossy four-page color insert in gun magazines declaring, "The fantasy of gun control smoldered in the reality of the streets."

On June 2, it was time to vote for Proposition F. Once-reliable police allies, like the Valley Industry and Commerce Association, supported the measure. So did the downtown-based oil behemoth ARCO. The predicted law-and-order backlash didn't materialize—at least not yet. Proposition F passed by a two-to-one margin. Even three predominantly white San Fernando Valley districts voted for it.

Gates had more one trump card to play. Hoping to enable the promotion of several subordinates, he told city officials that he might stay until July 15, which would disrupt the appointment of his successor, Willie Williams, the former police commissioner of Philadelphia. "I said I was going to retire at the end of June and my feeling is now, 'Screw you, I'll retire when I want to retire.'" The city government erupted, with the mayor, the police commissioner, and city council members issuing angry statements, calling once again for his removal. "How many times have we been promised that he'd finally leave?" Bradley asked. "I think the people have had enough of Daryl Gates' jerking them around." Gates told the *Los Angeles Times*, "I suppose everybody will just have to wait and see until I retire. After 43 years, people ought to give me a little grace to retire when I wanted." He added: "Vengeance is taking place. Vengeance."

A few days later Gates gave up the game. "I will admit that that was a threat, a bluff, but that's the only thing a lame duck has," he said. "The Los Angeles Police Department is now in the hands of crummy little politicians who are now manipulating the promotional process." He was off to his new job—as a talk radio host. There was one problem: audiences found him too nice, too levelheaded, too patient for the job. Callers were disappointed that he wouldn't bark at them. "I'd like to fight with you, but you don't provoke me, Chief," said one caller. "I guess it's too late to give you some career advice, but I don't think you should have given up the day job. I really don't think you have the transferable skills."

"One of my hopes with this show is to let people know Daryl Gates is not necessarily the guy whose image was built by the media, particularly the *Los Angeles Times*," Gates replied. "If you talk to almost anybody who knows me, the first thing they say is, 'He's a nice guy.'"

8

KEEPING AMERICA AMERICAN

But who would reap the political harvest of the riots? Pat Buchanan, with his campaign effectively over, saw an opportunity to make one last yank on the chain of white fear. He rushed to Los Angeles to stand in front of National Guard soldiers and talk tough: "There was one way to stop this riot, it wasn't with a new model cities program announced from Washington, it was with superior force dealing with hooligans, criminals, and thugs." He also brandished a photocopied flyer given to him by the LAPD, supposedly the product of the new truce between the Bloods and the Crips, publicly announcing plans for the gangs to join forces and shoot cops.

Buchanan made a sojourn in the desert, to visit the U.S.-Mexico border. "I am calling attention to a national disgrace," he told reporters and a couple dozen rather puzzled migrants who gathered to see what was going on and to sell sodas to the dusty, thirsty throng. He spoke of "the failure of the national government of the United States to protect the borders of the United States from an illegal invasion that involves at least a million aliens a year. As a consequence of that, we have social problems and economic problems. And drug problems." But a darker presence lurked nearby, ready to upstage Buchanan's photo op: the former California Klan grand dragon and founder of the White Aryan Resistance, Tom Metzger, and a group of his followers. Previously, Metzger had written supportively of Pat, called him a "sensitive Republican" on the "race issue." Now he was more confrontational. "Where's the great white hope?" he bellowed for the cameras that were filming his own cable access show. Buchanan's advisers tried in vain to keep Metzger away from the press conference, but he heckled from the sidelines. "Pat," he yelled, drawing the cameras to himself, "what are we gonna do about all those rich Republicans making millions off the wetbacks in the Imperial Valley?" Buchanan told reporters, "I don't have anything to do with him," saying that if Metzger contributed money to his campaign, it would be returned. The jibes forced Buchanan to retreat without a satisfactory photo op. Metzger was left to stand in front of the cameras and offer his own solution to the immigration problem: National Guard troops on the border with orders to "shoot to kill."

A June cover of *National Review* featured Lady Liberty putting up a hand to say "Stop"—TIRED? POOR? HUDDLED? TEMPEST TOSSED? TRY AUSTRALIA. The featured story on "rethinking immigration" by Peter Brimelow, an expat from Great Britain, fretted over the sheer number of immigrants from the "Third World" and called for the revision of the hallowed "nation of immigrants" mentality. "The current wave of immigration, and America's shifting ethnic balance, is simply the result of public policy. A change in public policy opened the Third World floodgates since 1965. Public policy could even restore the status quo ante 1965, which would slowly shift the ethnic balance back." Brimelow favored a 1920s-style immigration regime. "While the national-origins quotas were being legislated, President Calvin Coolidge put it unflinchingly: 'America must be kept American.' Everyone knew what he meant."

A day after Buchanan's desert foray, back in the safer environs of Leisure World in Seal Beach, an Orange County senior citizens' community, Buchanan called for a wall. "If I were President, I would have the [Army] Corps of Engineers build a double-barrier fence that would keep out 95% of the illegal traffic. I think it can be done." But he was realistic about the presidency: it was out of reach. The point now was political pressure. "If I get a third of the vote in the Republican primary in California, Mr. Bush would be building that fence in July and August." (As it happened, he would get 20 percent of the vote.)

The current of discontent no longer flowed through Buchanan's campaign. Even a new barn burner that Pat was testing out for his base didn't help rechannel it. "As America's imperial troops guard frontiers all over the world, our own frontiers are open, and the barbarian is inside the gates. And you do not deal with the Vandals and Visigoths who are pillaging your cities by expanding the Head Start and food stamp programs." The solution: reconquest. "Here were 19-year-old boys ready to lay down their lives to stop a mob from molesting innocent people they did not even know. And as they took back the streets of Los Angeles, block by block, so we must take back our cities, and take back our culture and take back our country."

Though still blowing blasts of war, Buchanan was already defeated. "Perot is the story," Buchanan had to admit. "The Buchanan people are going to Perot." But everyone's people were going to Perot, it seemed. A California poll showed 37 percent for Perot, 31 percent for Bush, and 25 percent for Clinton in a three-way race.

If Buchanan had a message that just wasn't getting through anymore, Bush couldn't settle on one. He responded to the riots in fits and starts, talking tough and then trying to show "compassion" and the idea of a helping hand, if not the actual hand itself. Right after the Rodney King verdict, Bush, preoccupied with a state dinner, told reporters, "The court system has worked. What's needed now is calm and respect for the law. Let the appeals process take place." There are, of course, no appeals for failed prosecutions. Bush didn't take Jesse Jackson's phone call, because, as Jackson put it, "he was eating spaghetti and so forth."

After the riots exploded, Bush's televised address made no allowances for a social crisis in the inner city: "What we saw last night and the night before in Los Angeles is not about civil rights. It's not about the great cause of equality that all Americans must uphold. It's not a message of protest. It's been the brutality of a mob, pure and simple."

But in the next few days Bush turned to his housing secretary, Jack Kemp, to show a different side. Kemp had focused intensely on finding conservative anti-poverty solutions for America's cities. He was largely alone in his effort. Pat Buchanan once again said that he had "gone native." In the White House, he was ignored, sidelined as a Cassandra and, perhaps most important, as a potential political rival to the president. In 1990 Kemp told the Domestic Policy Council that it was "past time for the Administration to aggressively highlight a new comprehensive anti-poverty agenda" and warned that the problems in the cities had reached "a moment of critical mass." Bush's aides decided that Kemp's efforts would just give poverty "greater visibility." Now he was back in the inner circle, giving interviews to the newspapers, trotted out on TV talk shows, and brought along for the ride to Los Angeles, walking right next to the president as he surveyed the devastation. And Bush emphasized Kemp's chosen programs to deal with the urban crisis: job training, urban enterprise zones, tenant ownership of public housing, school vouchers, and welfare "reform."

On the House floor, the always-outrageous James Traficant, of Youngstown, Ohio, famous for successfully defending himself against a federal RICO case, mocked the proposed remedies: "There are 15 million American workers working for peanuts, below the poverty level. But maybe they will be lucky and, with some of the training money, they may be trained as a jelly-roller or as a corncob pipe assembler or, if they are lucky, they may get a high-technology training program as a pantyhose crotch closer. If you think it is a joke, check the Department of Labor's Manual of New Jobs. The bottom line, Mr. Speaker, is most of the good manufacturing jobs have already gone to Mexico and our young people cannot get a job in America, even at levels below the poverty line. I think that says a lot about why American cities are in danger of all blowing up in flames."

Whatever sincerity Kemp lent to the administration's newfound interest in poverty, his presence couldn't prevent the president from having one of his moments of preppy ditziness. Visiting the hospital bedside of a wounded firefighter, Bush managed to bring up his vacation home in Kennebunkport: "I'm sorry Barbara's not here. She's out repairing what's left of our house. Damned storm knocked down four or five walls. She says it's coming along." In the midst of the smoldering, gutted frames of Los Angeles, the reference to those pesky repairs on the family compound in a genteel corner of the Northeast reached a height of bad taste only the well-born can hope to attain.

Being a little out of touch was one thing, but now the discourse surrounding the riots was about to spill out of the bounds of reality. On the prime-time CBS sitcom *Murphy Brown*, the eponymous character, a successful journalist played by Candice Bergen, a tough-talking, sharp-witted career woman, was going to have a baby in the new season—as a single mother. Speaking in San Francisco ahead of the primaries, Vice President Quayle began by recalling how he'd explained the riots to his hosts on a recent rip to Japan. "But the question that I tried to answer in Japan is one that needs answering here: What happened? Why? And most importantly, how can we prevent it in the future?" The problem was cultural. "In a nutshell, I believe the lawless social anarchy which we saw is directly related to the breakdown of the family structure, personal responsibility, and social order in too many areas of our society. For the poor, the situation is compounded by a welfare ethos that impedes individual efforts to move ahead in society and hampers their ability to take advantage of the opportunities America offers." Single parenthood was a main villain. "Bearing babies irresponsibly is simply wrong. Failing to support children one has fathered is wrong and we must be unequivocal about this." Then, the line that launched a thousand op-eds and late-night jokes: "It doesn't help matters when primetime TV has Murphy Brown—a character who supposedly epitomizes today's intelligent, highly paid, professional woman—mocking the importance of fathers, by bearing a child alone, and calling it just another 'lifestyle choice.'"

An entire ideology lurked behind this comment. Whether he knew it or not, Quayle was referencing the "new class"—a pet idea of Quayle's neoconservative handlers. Essentially, the notion was that the bureaucracy, academia, the media, and the professions had been captured by a liberal class who opposed "traditional values" and propagandized for their own "permissive" standards. One of the main architects of the theory was Irving Kristol, godfather of neoconservatism and actual father of William Kristol, one of Quayle's closest advisers. "New-class theory enabled the right to attack 'elites' without attacking big business," the cultural critic Christopher Lasch had tersely put it a year earlier in his book *The True and Only Heaven*. And now it provided a path to fight culture wars while avoiding racial provocations: "single mother" need not mean a poor Black woman. Perhaps it was really the fault of the liberals, anyway: they were selling "permissive lifestyles" to people who couldn't afford them.

Whether or not the "new class" had the subversive role the neocons gave them, they could not resist the flattery of being attacked, if even by fictional proxy. DAN QUAYLE BLASTS "MURPHY BROWN" AS MOTHER OF L.A. RIOTS, one headline screamed, overstating the case a bit. The front page of *The New York Times* featured a vignette of Murphy Brown holding her "baby," flanked by quotes from Quayle and Marlin Fitzwater. The Bush camp wasn't all on the same page about Brown. Fitzwater hedged. "We are certainly concerned about family values and the breakup of the American family, and again our concern is with the television networks and the production people who need to be aware of the ramifications of their programming." But then he quickly said that he was "not comfortable getting involved in criticism" of the show, saying it exemplified "pro-life values," as Brown was "having the baby." Fitzwater added a sweaty joke about Bergen's comeliness. "I'll meet with Candice Bergen any time, any place to discuss this." In a joint press conference with Prime Minister Brian Mulroney of Canada to discuss a proposed trade pact called NAFTA, Bush lost patience with all the reporters' questions about *Murphy Brown*. "I don't know that much about the show," he snapped. "I've told you, I don't want any more questions about it."

Ross Perot, flanked by a crowd of a thousand, was at the Kentucky state capitol filing the ballot petitions that his volunteers had gathered. He needed five thousand registered voters' signatures to get on the ballot; his volunteers took down forty thousand. "Only in America would that be a front-page story," he said of the Brown affair. "Only in America would somebody who's an incumbent just keep reacting to that. So, it must have been a very slow day in Washington. I just thought it was goofy."

Not everyone thought it was goofy. "This is not a trivial issue," the University of Maryland political science professor William Galston told the papers. "The American people believe, for good reason, that the American family is in trouble . . . If national Democrats sneer at this discussion and cede this terrain to the Republican Party, the result will be another richly deserved election disaster." Galston, shaken by his experience as an adviser to the disastrous Mondale run against Ronald Reagan, was now advising the Clinton campaign. He helped shape the policy agenda and political strategy of the Democratic Leadership Council (DLC), the club of rightward leaners and pushers in the Democratic Party that Bill Clinton had chaired prior to his run. Part of a circle of scholars calling themselves "communitarians," Dr. Galston and his fellows believed that American society was being corroded by excessive individualism, equally manifested in Reagan-era filthy lucre and the liberal "rights industry" that protected lifestyle autonomy above all. Instead, the communitarians believed that America should institute—or reinstitute—a sense of shared values and mutual obligations. In practice, this meant rejecting the "liberal fundamentalism" of the Democratic Party that supposedly created a "culture of entitlement."

Clinton kicked off his campaign by calling for a "New Covenant, a solemn agreement between the people and their government," invoking that most ancient and hoary myth of America, the founding before the founding—the Mayflower Compact, where the Puritans decided to "Covenant and Combine [themselves] together into a civil Body Politick." Galston, who helped out with Clinton's speeches, said that the ark of the New Covenant "embodies many core principles of communitarianism . . . including the idea that if you get something from the community, you owe something to the community." Responsibility. Responsibility was the answer. In one speech, Clinton mentioned "responsibility" twenty-eight times.

Clinton's resurrection of the Puritan past did not come solely from the influence of the communitarians in the DLC. Barely any major Clinton speech went by without him mentioning a remarkable figure: his old teacher at the Georgetown School of Foreign Service. "Over 25 years ago, my classmates and I all took a class in Western civilization, taught by a legendary professor named Carroll Quigley," Clinton recalled during one of his three New Covenant speeches at his alma mater. "He taught, at the end of the course, that the defining idea of Western civilization in general and our country in particular is what he called future preference—the idea that the future can be better than the present, and that each of us has a personal, moral responsibility to make it so." Or, as Fleetwood Mac put it in the Clinton campaign's chosen song, "Don't—stop—thinking—about—tomorrow."

As Quigley wrote in his mammoth thirteen-hundred-page tome *Tragedy and Hope*, the notion of "future preference" was secularized Puritanism: "Future preference came out of the Christian outlook of the West and especially from the Puritan tradition, which was prepared to accept almost any kind of sacrifice and self-discipline in the temporal world for the sake of future salvation. The process of secularization of Western society since the seventeenth century shifted that future benefit from eternity to this temporal world but did not otherwise disturb the pattern of future preference and self-discipline." But Quigley also saw a dark side of the Puritan ethic—a belief in the positive power of evil, that the devil "is a force, or being, of positive malevolence, and man, by himself, is incapable of any good and is, accordingly, not free. He can be saved by God's grace alone, and he can get through this temporal world only by being subjected to a regime of total despotism"; this implied "the basic struggles of this world were irreconcilable and must be fought to a finish."

Quigley believed that the emergence of the flower children and the 1960s counterculture was a sign that an older Christian ethic of "love and charity" was "basically reconcilable" with what he called the pluralistic, Western ideal of "diverse interests." But he didn't quite like the teenyboppers, the hippies or proto-hippies: they seemed to him woefully undisciplined, sentimental, and mercurial. After several generations of artistic and cultural assaults on bourgeois respectability, the younger generation had shed the Puritan exoskeleton of middle-class life without a suitable alternative. Worse still, they were regressing to a more primitive condition of mankind. "In many ways this new culture is like that of African tribes: its tastes in music and the dance, its emphasis on sex play, its increasingly scanty clothing, its emphasis on group solidarity, the high value it puts on interpersonal relations (especially talking and social drinking), its almost total rejection of future preference and its constant efforts to free itself from the tyranny of time . . . This Africanization of American society is gradually spreading with the passing years to higher age levels in our culture and is having profound and damaging effects on the transfer of middle-class values to the rising generation."

This praise of the Protestant work ethic came from an Irish Catholic. Quigley grew up in Boston, his family eking out lace-curtain respectability on the edge of "the Irish ghetto." He described himself as a "marginal person" growing up between different ethnic and communal worlds: "On the edge of the Irish community with the Yankee community intellectually and then with the Jewish community socially. My mother admired the Yankees, you see, and this would have us say, well, 'What is it we don't like about the Irish?' They're noisy, bigoted, and they drink a lot." Quigley vaguely referred to an intermarriage with the Kennedy clan generations back that was brought about by both families' participation in the bootlegging trade. Like the Kennedys, Quigley worked his way into the bosom of WASPdom: attending Boston Latin and Harvard University, where he received his bachelor's, master's, and doctoral degrees. Father James Walsh asked him to come teach at Georgetown, and his lectures became a cult favorite with students, particularly for his histrionics. Quigley thought that Plato's *Republic* was a "fascist tract," and he concluded his lectures on it by ripping out pages and tossing them out the window of the lecture hall, yelling "Sieg Heil!"

Quigley, whose Boston accent sounded a little like that of Bill Clinton's hero JFK, made an impression on the young man from Hope, Arkansas. After Quigley told his freshman class that history's great men slept no more than five hours a night and instead took naps throughout the day, Clinton went back to his dorm room and set his alarm for a twenty-five-minute nap. He also began to sleep five hours a night. Clinton got a B from Quigley, an impressive showing, as the demanding professor routinely handed out Ds.

Befitting an educator at a Jesuit institution, Quigley emphasized the role of elite cliques that dominated policy, to the point that he attracted attention—and briefly praise—from conspiracy theorists. When he published *Tragedy and Hope* in 1966, Professor Quigley was nonplussed to find out that some of its most enthusiastic readers were members of the John Birch Society. One passage in particular drew them, where Quigley said that "the radical Right fairy tale, which is now an accepted folk myth in many groups in America, pictured the recent history of the United States, in regard to domestic and in foreign affairs, as a well-organized plot by extreme Left-wing elements, operating from the White House itself and controlling all the chief avenues of publicity in the United States, to destroy the American way of life." This had, "like all fables, . . . a modicum of truth. There does exist, and has existed for a generation, an international Anglophile network that operates, to some extent, in the way the radical Right believes the Communists act." This was taken by Birchers to be confirmation of their fears. The eminently establishmentarian Quigley was partly amused, partly horrified by his embrace by the fringe. "You see," Quigley told *The Washington Post Magazine*, "originally the John Birch periodical had me as a great guy for revealing everything. But then they became absolutely sour and now they denounce me as a member of the Establishment. I'm just baffled by the whole thing." When *Tragedy and Hope* went out of print, bootlegged copies could be found at gun shows and conspiracist gatherings.

For young Bill Clinton, the talented and favored son of a modest background, Quigley illustrated a world not of Orwellian paranoia but of great expectations. The professor's discourses undoubtedly gave an exciting picture of the grand sweep of history and the elite circles of actors shaping it, as well as the possibility of access to this select few who did the molding. Quigley put particular emphasis on the Round Table Groups of the arch-imperialist Cecil Rhodes as one of these secret bodies shaping world affairs. In Quigley's book *The Anglo-American Establishment*, he presented the Rhodes Scholarship as "merely a facade to conceal the secret society, or more accurately, they were to be one of the instruments by which the members of the secret society could carry out his purpose." Put in such a seductive light, it's no wonder that Clinton went in for a Rhodes Scholarship. The same urge to be part of a select group undoubtedly attracted him to the Democratic Leadership Council, which, without a grassroots constituency, tasked itself with saving the Democratic Party from above. For all his Southern pol's outward show of gregarious warmth and charm, Clinton was no populist: in the year of populism and voter rage and "throw the bastards out," he was a dedicated elitist. One Georgetown teacher even suggested that he become a Jesuit and was disappointed to learn that Clinton was Southern Baptist. But if he was an elitist, he was an aspirational one, unlike Pappy Bush, with his Yale and Skull and Bones and CIA.

Quigley believed it was the role of places like Georgetown to help the less fortunate rise in social station: "The large number of Catholic men's colleges in the country, especially those operated by the Jesuits, had as their basic, if often unrecognized aim the desire to transform the sons of working class, and often immigrant, origins into middle class in professional occupations (chiefly law, medicine, business, and teaching)." But he was highly suspicious of people from a "petty bourgeois" background, like Clinton, whose stepfather was a car salesman. According to Quigley, they were "often very insecure, envious, filled with hatred, and are generally the chief recruits for any Radical Right, Fascist, or hate campaigns against any group that is different or which refuses to conform to middle-class values."

And when the petty bourgeois weren't filling out the ranks of Goldwaterites and worse, they were entering the meritocracies, powering a "surge" of "recruits over the faltering bodies of the disintegrating middle class." As they did so, they exhibited a pathological variant of the middle-class outlook Quigley otherwise celebrated, replete with "neurotic drives of personal ambition and competitiveness": "The petty bourgeoisie, as the last fanatical defenders of the middle-class outlook, had in excess degree, the qualities of self-discipline and future preference the middle class had established." Quigley held the accomplishments of petty bourgeois aspirants—like Clinton, who managed to excel in school and come out at the top of their classes—in low regard: "These new recruits were rigid, unimaginative, and narrow." He even had something to say about their eating habits: "The petty bourgeoisie . . . tend to overeat or to be neurotic snackers." (The media was about to discover—and take delight in—Clinton's penchant for fast food.) And although Quigley spoke of the centrality of "middle-class, Protestant, and northwestern European" principles to American civilization, he believed that they were being superseded by the '60s ethos and that their defenders were often reactionaries, who were worse: "In America today, those who wish to preserve them frequently show a tendency to embrace fanatical Right-wing political groups to implement that effort, and often speak among themselves of their efforts to preserve the values of the WASPS."

For Quigley, the future of American society and Western civilization itself relied on finding the middle ground. First there had to be some kind of cultural synthesis between the middle-class values of discipline—"we still need these qualities so that young people will be willing to undergo the years of hard work and training that will prepare them to work in our complex technological society"—and the empathy ethos of the flower children: "We must get away from the older crass materialism and egocentric individualism, and pick up some of the younger generation's concern for the community and their fellowmen." You needed someone who was a little bit of a hippie, but also a bit of an old-fashioned striver. In other words, a person a little like Bill Clinton. In politics, there was also to be moderation, comity, and stability: "The argument that the two parties should represent opposed ideals and policies, one, perhaps, of the Right and the other of the Left, is a foolish idea acceptable only to doctrinaire and academic thinkers. Instead, the two parties should be almost identical, so that the American people can 'throw the rascals out' at any election without leading to any profound or extensive shifts in policy." In other words, you needed a politician a little like Bill Clinton.

Quigley divided history into "Tragedy" and "Hope." The tragedy of the twentieth century was the fruit of the nineteenth century: "Two terrible wars sandwiching a world economic depression revealed man's real inability to control his life by the nineteenth century's techniques of laissez-faire, materialism, competition, selfishness, violence, and imperialism." But for Quigley, hope lay in a further past. Wars and depressions could be "avoided in the future by turning from the nineteenth-century characteristics just mentioned and going back to other characteristics that our Western society has always regarded as virtues: generosity, compassion, cooperation, rationality, and foresight, and finding an increased role in human life for love, spirituality, and self-discipline." But how much hope really was there? Even Quigley was not certain. He conceded that while the "tragedy of the period" was "obvious," "the hope may seem dubious to many." The masses certainly were not to be trusted; America's future required the cultivation of a virtuous elite who knew how to handle the issues of society via technocratic means: "We know fairly well how to control the increase in population, how to produce wealth and reduce poverty or disease, we may, in the near future, know how to postpone senility or death," and in the employment of these methods "we can avoid the horrors of 1914–1945." If that type of catastrophe could be avoided, then a moderate optimism was in order, a return to gradual civilized development.

As much as his campaign made gestures to the Puritans' Covenant and the austere New English origins of America, Clinton declined to pin a scarlet letter on Murphy Brown. He did mutedly offer that Murphy Brown was "not the best example for children." Hillary agreed, but at a Santa Clara University appearance she also remarked, "We shouldn't have some single ideological vision of what a traditional family is. I don't think anybody needs a lecture about what is and isn't a family." After all, Bill made an awkward Neo-Puritan. He particularly lacked the vaunted virtues of self-restraint and self-denial: despite his ambition, "future preference" was a problem for him—he had a tendency to seek out immediate gratification. Everyone still remembered the January press conference where Gennifer Flowers attested to a twelve-year affair with the Arkansas governor. (When one of the characters on *The Howard Stern Show*, "Stuttering John," crashed a press conference and blurted out the question "Did Governor Clinton use a condom?" Flowers rolled her eyes but then couldn't resist a knowing smirk and a subtle nod to the cameras. Perhaps Clinton exercised some Protestant self-restraint, after all.) As the campaign proceeded, Clinton handled the values question carefully. "I've worked on family issues harder and longer than anybody running for president this year, and I do believe that they are at the heart of our national discontent," he said at a speech at Cleveland's City Club. He gave some qualified praise for Quayle's Murphy Brown speech, saying it had "more substance" than an earlier "family values" speech by Bush: "Unfortunately, the vice president's speech is also, in my view, cynical election-year politics [in that] it ignores the relationship of our family problems to our national economic decline." According to Clinton, the "substance" of the speech that he liked came from "the empowerment agenda that is most closely identified with HUD Secretary Jack Kemp . . . more home ownership for poor people, urban enterprise zones, and welfare reform designed to encourage work and independence." In fact, Clinton echoed some of the same solutions. Quayle called for "dismantling" welfare. Since the beginning of the campaign, Clinton had adopted the slightly softer "end welfare as we know it" as a slogan, and in his Cleveland speech he declared, "I want to put an end to welfare as a permanent way of life."

But no amount of cautious difference-splitting or talk of new covenants could seem to get the Clinton campaign out of the mud. The primaries were effectively done, the lion's share of delegates had been won: he sealed the deal, but with his low standing in the polls against Bush and Perot, it was looking like a Pyrrhic victory. And each win just brought more doubt. Two-thirds of voters in New York said they wished they had a choice other than Clinton or Jerry Brown. After Clinton's April win in Pennsylvania, a two-way poll showed Bush beating the Democrat 50 to 34 nationally. Pennsylvania governor Bob Casey took a shot at Clinton's consistently low turnout: "We've got a tiny minority of Democrats voting for Bill Clinton, and he's winning every race without generating any sparks, any enthusiasm, any momentum." Casey even floated the idea of going with another man: "Maybe he can turn this around. I hope so. But if he can't, convention rules provide for the selection of an alternative candidate. Let's pick a winner." There were now whispers of a brokered convention, with the fighting liberal, Mario Cuomo, sweeping in to rescue the party. But it wasn't just the liberals: even colleagues in the Democratic Leadership Council were grumbling about their man. At his May 2 address to the group, Clinton raised the standard of welfare reform and law and order as solutions to the riots, but DLCers still weren't "bubbling with confidence and pride." Clinton wasn't the "the pure messenger they sought," and they worried about the accusations of marital infidelity and draft dodging, and felt he'd won a "hollow victory." Some polls showed him coming in third, behind Bush and Perot. *The New Republic* back in February had named Clinton "The Anointed"; by early May it splashed WHY CLINTON CAN'T WIN on the cover, dedicating an entire issue to his faults and problems.

With California came another tainted victory. CLINTON WINS A MAJORITY FOR NOMINATION, BUT PEROT'S APPEAL IS STRONG IN 2 PARTIES. The *New York Times* headline was an understatement: a plurality of Democratic voters said they wished they could've voted for Perot instead. Clinton slammed a fist on a table when he heard the news. The campaign and the candidate had hit an "emotional low point." "What should have been a grace period for the likely Democratic nominee, a time to polish his image and consolidate his support, has instead become a struggle to simply be heard over the roar of Perotism," the *Times* reported. "Frustration" became a word commonly affixed to the Clinton camp in the papers; "defensive," "confusion," "bewilderment," and "baffled" were some others.

The sobriquet "Slick Willie" had been stuck on Bill, but these days he looked anything but slick. He was often losing his temper, a fact he couldn't hide very well: the fair-skinned Clinton flushed red when he got mad. An AIDS activist from ACT UP heckled Clinton at a fundraiser in New York; Clinton returned the harangue with one of his own: "Let me tell you something else. You do not have the right to treat any human being, including me, with no respect because of what you're worried about. I did not cause it. I'm trying to do something about it . . . I feel your pain, I feel your pain, but if you want to attack me personally you're no better than Jerry Brown and all the rest of these people who say whatever sounds good at the moment." (That "I feel your pain" line instantly entered the public consciousness as an emblem of risible faux empathy.) At Harlem Hospital, what was planned to be a staid policy speech, Clinton's favored mode of campaigning to that point, "disintegrated into a raucous shouting match" between Clinton and the far-left New Alliance Party candidate Lenora Fulani, the

Times reported. "You just met black people on Super Tuesday when you needed them," she hollered from atop a chair. Clinton lost his shouting match with Fulani and the protesters shouting "Democracy now!"; he beat a retreat into another room and sulked, snapping at reporters when they brought up the question of his falling behind Perot, saying he wouldn't answer "foolish questions about polls." He bristled at what he called "process questions" about his strategy and complained that he wasn't asked about his policy. It didn't stop the reporters from asking. Gwen Ifill of *The New York Times* reported that at a Q&A session at Florida A&M, the candidate appeared "agitated and visibly frustrated" by questions about his character and that "at times his remarks began to resemble a tirade."

Clinton and his campaign couldn't escape a sense of being snake-bitten, or "betrayed by the process," as one aide put it.

The biggest problem continued to be Perot, who was totally dominating media coverage. And Perot hadn't even really articulated what policies he would enact as president. In fact, he refused to, saying his supporters didn't care about that and actually urged him not to. "It's a non-issue with them," Perot said on NBC's *Today*. "We're not interested in detailed positions. Everybody has detailed positions. Nobody implements them." Instead Perot called for movement. "These are great ideas that could fix most of the problems our country faces, and everybody sits around talking about them. Nobody does anything about them," he continued. "Taking action in Washington is apparently an unnatural event. But that's what people want. If they put me there, that's what we'll do. We'll have action." It was true that Perot's people didn't seem to mind the lack of specifics. Volunteers continued spreading out across the country to gather signatures to get their man on the ballot. In his movement they found meaning, even if the content was unclear. "I got to tell you this is the most rewarding thing I've ever done in my life," Dick Jordan, a North Carolina Perot volunteer and retired former manager for Ralston Purina told *New York* magazine's Joe Klein. "Parking our camper out at the mall, signing up people. It's amazing—all these young people who say they are fed up with the way things are. Hell, they're too damn young to be really fed up like we are. Tell me, Marty"—Dick turned to Marty Henderson, the North Carolina volunteer state chairman and an executive at an electronics supply company—"we are gonna get this guy on the ballot. If we don't, I might commit suicide."

Volunteers did sometimes get curious about Perot's positions. "Mr. Perot will have a platform if he decides to run," Henderson told his troop in North Carolina. Asked about abortion, Henderson, who had never done anything political before he heard about a Perot meeting on a local radio talk show, assured the volunteers, "Mr. Perot isn't pro-abortion. He's in favor of getting the federal government out of it." Perot then went on *Meet the Press* and said he'd favor federal funding for abortions through Medicaid. None of it seemed to matter. The petitions kept coming in. At the Vietnam Veterans Memorial, POW/MIA activists put up a banner that said AMERICA NEEDS PEROT, PRESIDENT IN '92. The group was also selling PEROT FOR PRESIDENT T-shirts. The National Park Service asked them to stop and take down the banner. The activists took it to be political harassment from the Bush administration.

The Clinton campaign decided to alter its strategy. TV was the way to go. They would contest the talk show circuit that contributed so much to Perot's success. The candidate did the *Today* show twice, *CBS This Morning*, and ABC's *Good Morning America*. He did *Larry King*. On June 3, the day after the California primary, he appeared on *The Arsenio Hall Show* in sunglasses, leading the band with a competent rendition of "Heartbreak Hotel" on the saxophone. "It's nice to see a Democrat blowing something other than the election," Arsenio quipped. Clinton's monologue was dedicated to jokes about Bush, Quayle, and Perot. But it wasn't all jokes. Arsenio let Clinton get into substantive issues and talk about his plans, uninterrupted. Here there was less talk about personal responsibility and middle-class values and ending welfare and more about a kind of Marshall Plan that would redirect the post–Cold War defense budget into investing in education and the economy. There was talk of racial reconciliation and understanding. For the second half of the interview, Hillary came out and sat with Bill. "It's hard to think, you're never like, 'Who is Gennifer? Who the hell is she?'" Arsenio pushed. "I know Gennifer, I know who she is," Hillary replied. Arsenio: "And you know what her problem is?" Hillary: "She's got lots of problems." Everyone was relaxed, having a good time. Still, *The New York Times* put the picture of Bill in shades playing the sax under the fold; Perot got the headlines at the top of the paper.

Clinton made sure to phone in to the National Association of Radio Talk Show Hosts convention in Washington, D.C. The second question asked was about POW/MIAs. "Apparently, the bureaucracy has hidden a great deal of information from the politicians. The Senate committee has been a whitewash. What will your administration do to bring home our boys once and for all?" Clinton replied that there "will never be normalization or improvement of relations [with Vietnam] until we're sure that we have all the evidence not only from that country or from any others, I would proceed on that basis. I have never been convinced that we know the whole truth about this. We may, but I'm not convinced we do, and I would like to see it through to the very end."

It was Bush's turn to get frustrated. Speaking to a group of Republican contributors in Detroit, the *Times* reported that he was "waving his arms in the air and nearly shouting"; the president said he was tired of not getting the credit for ending the Cold War, the Gulf War, and for arms control with Russia. "I have worked my heart out as President of the United States," Bush ranted to the party stalwarts. "I'm getting a little sick of being on the receiving line—receiving end—of criticism day in and day out." He complained about his opponents going on "weird talk shows," but then he scheduled his own TV appearances, albeit on the more respectable network Sunday shows. His attempts to appear presidential kept blowing up in his face. "We had Yeltsin standing here in the Rose Garden, and we entered into a deal to eliminate the biggest and the most threatening intercontinental ballistic missiles—the SS-18's of the Soviet Union—and it was almost, 'Ho-hum, what have you done for me recently?'" Bush complained to reporters. In fact, the new president of Russia upstaged and possibly traduced his American counterpart by stressing a political issue that Bush might've preferred to go away. One of the members of his delegation, General Dmitri Volkogonov, hand delivered a letter from the Russian president to Senator John Kerry, chairman of the POW/MIA committee, and Bob Smith, the ranking Republican. The letter referred to hundreds of downed American pilots who'd been interned by the Soviet Union. Most of these were members of World War II bomber crews who'd crash-landed in Soviet territory. There were also mentions of Korean War pilots who were interrogated by the Soviets but never detained on Soviet territory. Then there were nine military aircraft downed over the Soviet Union during the Cold War, with eight survivors confined in Soviet prison camps. The letter said it couldn't be ruled out that some might be alive. The only information about Vietnam was that some American defectors had been clandestinely moved to the USSR, but only for a short period of time. A typical headline: YELTSIN: SOVIETS HELD HUNDREDS OF U.S. AIRMEN. During a joint press conference at the White House, Yeltsin said, "Maybe some of them are still alive and are still in Russia." Bush said that determining the fate of the prisoners was "the highest national priority" but cautioned about the possibility of "false hope."

POW/MIA family members and activists immediately took the story as encouragement of their deepest hopes. "We've been told we're crazy, 'You people are nuts, there couldn't possibly be any Americans left anywhere in the world as POWs,'" Larry Stevens told the *Los Angeles Times*. His brother had been shot down over Laos and he'd been glued to news reports of Yeltsin's remarks. "I can't imagine [Yeltsin] saying these things and not being able to back them up." Yeltsin also inflamed the sense among activists that the administration hadn't done enough for the prisoners. "I'm personally deeply ashamed, down to the bone marrow, of President Bush and his utter lack of leadership in this matter," said Virginia Nasmyth Loy, the sister of a POW who'd been freed in 1973. "I think Bush ought to get on a plane, go over, and pick them up and bring them home," said Gary Parker, the head of Ventura County's Vietnam Veterans missing soldiers committee. "That's it. Real simple."

The hearings of the Senate Select Committee on POW/MIA Affairs were coming up on June 30. Perot was scheduled to testify, but he canceled. "These hearings, controlled by Democrats and Republicans and conducted just before the political conventions, with a witness who is being placed on the ballot as an independent, will tend to become a political circus," Perot wrote in a letter to the committee. The National League of Families, the "mainstream" POW/MIA group with close ties to the GOP, which had been struggling with the more militant activists championed by Perot, denounced his decision to renege. Probably the real reason Perot backed out was that he didn't want to answer questions about his attempts to do business with Hanoi.

But the Perot campaign was growing more erratic overall despite the appearance of going from success to success. The drip-drip-drip of media reports on his business practices was starting to have an effect, not least perhaps on the candidate's psyche. A telephone interview with NPR degenerated into angry accusations when it got to his business dealings in the early '70s. "I assume this is the sole reason for your taped interview . . . your classic setup. So now that you have—you know, whoever you're trying to do a favor for, you've done it, and I'm sure you had a smirk on your mouth as you got me into this . . . What is your show anyhow?" The host, Linda Wertheimer, replied, "*All Things Considered.*" Perot: "And this is a radio program? It's really a radio program? You're not just somebody calling in?" Dan Quayle brought up Perot's penchant for putting private investigators on his opponents, musing that Perot might use the CIA and FBI to do the same. "Hitler's propaganda chief would be proud of what we are about to see," Perot exploded when they played the clip on *Today*. He complained that he was the victim of a concerted "dirty tricks campaign." His contacts from the seedier side of the POW/MIA movement, former "intelligence operatives" and "special ops" guys, were feeding him a steady stream of stories about Republican plots and intrigues against him. He bristled at the suggestions of the political professionals—one Democrat and one Republican—who were brought in to transform the campaign from insurgency into viable run. He suspected their motives. In the polls, Perot's negatives were creeping up. And Clinton finally found a way to blow a hole in Perot's nonstop television coverage.

9

"WE'RE AT WAR"

What was to be done about Jesse Jackson and the Rainbow Coalition? Although the reverend chose not to run in '92, that was more a sign of the widespread belief among Democrats that it was a "bad year" than any real decline in his political career.

Jackson retained his position as the major broker for two key centers of Democratic power: Black voters and unreconstructed New Deal liberals. The candidates in the race did a complicated dance around Jackson, approaching and avoiding as their political needs required. An approach could be hazardous: Jerry Brown found that out in New York when—to Howard Stern's disgust—he floated Jackson as a vice presidential candidate. But there were risks in keeping one's distance as well.

Clinton had kept a degree of remove from Jackson, but when he was told—erroneously, in fact—that Jackson had endorsed Tom Harkin during a February TV interview, he had one of his tantrums. "It's an outrage. It's a dirty double-crossing, back-stabbing thing to do," Clinton exploded to his aides, thinking he was off the air. "There's only one person can be hurt by this . . . I mean, I want you to say, listen, I came to that guy's house at midnight. I have called him, I've done everything I could. For him to do this . . . For me to hear this on a television program is an act of absolute dishonor." But the most revealing comment perhaps was "That is not what we want. We want him not involved at all." Clinton was trying to arrange a non-endorsement from Jackson, with the understanding that he also would not endorse anyone else.

The press lapped up the gaffe. Columnists even celebrated the outburst. Bill Thompson of the *Fort Worth Star-Telegram* applauded Clinton's "spontaneity," "honest emotion," "impromptu anger." Thompson wrote that the affair really reflected more on Jackson than on Clinton: "If this was Clinton's immediate reaction to what he thought was a double-cross by Jackson, perhaps we could draw a conclusion: Perhaps Bill Clinton knows, or at least suspects, that Jesse Jackson is a double-crossing backstabber. Clinton seemed angry. He didn't seem surprised." There were gains to be had in attacking Jackson: an appreciative audience in the press. Inside the Democratic Party, especially in the South, other voices were urging Clinton to go after Jackson. A party activist and fundraiser told Clinton that he could benefit by "telling old Jesse where to stuff it."

From a certain perspective, the Democratic Leadership Council was a coalition of anti-Jackson Democrats. It was founded in 1985, right after Mondale's general election loss and Jackson's surprisingly strong primary campaign and keynote speech at the 1984 Democratic Convention. The New Democrats, as the DLC members came to be known, blamed Jackson and the liberals for the catastrophic losses by Mondale and then Dukakis. William Galston's postmortem identified the Democrats' "liberal fundamentalism" and catering to minority groups as their fatal flaw. Jackson quickly understood the nature of the group and returned the favor, calling them "Democrats for the Leisure Class." Still, the two wings of the party attempted reconciliation; Jackson was invited to speak at the 1990 DLC conference in New Orleans, but he took the opportunity to gently mock the group. He was not invited back in '91. But Clinton was clearly anxious about totally severing ties with Jackson. Now that he was running, he privately questioned the decision to not have Jackson speak at the '92 convocation, thinking it might threaten party unity.

Clinton developed a kind of two-step of defiance and courting. In January, the governor had left the primary campaign trail to return to Arkansas to oversee the execution of Ricky Ray Rector, a mentally disabled Black man. Jackson had led a campaign to try to get Clinton to grant clemency for Rector. The next day, Clinton spoke at a Rainbow Coalition conference, enduring a smattering of boos from the audience. (They also booed his defense of Arkansas as a "right to work" state.) He concluded with a rousing vow: "Let me just say this one last thing in closing: If you're worried about this race-baiting in this election, let me tell you, as a Southerner I was raised with this, I know all about the politics of racial division. George Bush is in trouble now, he said on national television he will do anything, anything, anything it takes to get re-elected . . . You want someone who can beat that? Vote for me, I've lived with this all my life. If they run this race-baiting on me, I will jam it to 'em and bring this country back together." He received polite, if not enthusiastic, applause. Then in March, Clinton caused a stir when he posed with Georgia senator Sam Nunn in front of a group of inmates standing at attention at Stone Mountain Correctional Institution—Stone Mountain, the site of a massive monument to Jefferson Davis and Robert E. Lee, being the "spiritual home" of the KKK. Jackson characterized the event as "a version of the Willie Horton situation," but mostly held his fire, as he did two weeks later when Clinton played golf at an all-white country club in Little Rock.

Clinton cultivated ties with Black politicians. Most of them were moderates, safely within the DLC brand, like Mississippi congressman Mike Espy and L.A. mayor Tom Bradley, but he also made inroads in the ranks of Jackson's own organization, winning over such members of the working-class left as South Central representative Maxine Waters, as well as getting the nod from such civil rights stalwarts as

Georgia's John Lewis. The endorsements paid off for Clinton, as no other Democratic candidate even bothered to make a systematic effort to court Black political leadership, but Black primary voters evinced the same enthusiasm gap as the rest of the public. Clinton sought to shore up the Black vote ahead of the decisive Southern primaries, but it was clear to many that his overall strategy for the election relied not on boosting Black turnout, but on bringing the white lower middle class back into the Democratic fold.

The young, college-going, and upwardly mobile Black constituencies were not particularly impressed with the down-home style of interracial solidarity he tried to hawk. "I grew up in the segregated South," Clinton told a half-full auditorium at Morehouse College in Atlanta. "I'm telling you, you look at our experience, every time we have permitted ourselves to be divided by race in this region, we have been kept dumb and poor." The students who attended weren't convinced. They pressed Clinton on his support for the death penalty and his constant references to "the forgotten middle class." "He's saying a lot of things that need to be said and he says them with a sense of conviction and credibility. But I'm not sure I believe any of them," Sean Barnave, a Morehouse sophomore told the Associated Press. "A lot of African Americans are certainly disenchanted with the whole system."

On college campuses in particular, middle-class Black youths were discovering more radical styles of political consciousness than that offered by Jesse Jackson and the civil rights–era establishment. A sense of alienation from and rebellion against the older institutions and leadership of mainstream Black civil and political society spread among the young, who chose solidarity with the victims of apartheid and the American ghetto over the promise of social mobility or conventional politics. The theories of Molefi Asante, a professor at Temple University and the author of *Afrocentricity*, which sought to recenter the birth of civilization from Greece to Egypt, imagined as a Black society, spilled out of academia and entered public consciousness as part of a national debate on "multiculturalism" and public school curricula.

While Asante's critics charged that his pedagogy was designed more with a mind to restoring the damaged self-esteem of Black Americans or creating a countermyth to white supremacy than to transmitting historical truth, Asante replied that, like the Boers in South Africa, they were using Eurocentrism to maintain the racial status quo: "The real division on the question of multiculturalism is between those who seek to maintain a Eurocentric hegemony over the curriculum and those who truly believe in cultural pluralism." Though in 1992 Asante claimed that "Afrocentricity does not seek to replace Eurocentricity in its arrogant disregard for other cultures," his book told a slightly different story: it repeatedly refers to the "decadence" of Western society and proposes Afrocentricity as an all-encompassing social and intellectual framework, a rival to other ideologies and religions.

The films of the upper-middle-class Black directors John Singleton and Spike Lee contained Black Nationalist themes. Ahead of the October release of Lee's *Malcolm X* biopic, hats emblazoned with *X* became a popular fashion statement. Rap groups like Public Enemy, Brand Nubian, A Tribe Called Quest, X-Clan, and Arrested Development all provided a combination of Black Nationalist, Pan-African, and Afrocentric motifs. Some of the Afrocentric aesthetic communicated positive, easygoing, hippieish messages of communal self-affirmation and growth, but other artists were confrontational, explicitly political, and angry, and were now competing with the raw fury of the more proletarian gangsta rap rising on the West Coast.

The Afrocentric movement—as a symptom of Balkanizing "multiculturalism," "political correctness," and an excessive focus on victimization and ethnic grievance—generated a good deal of consternation and polemic among the intelligentsia, both left and right, Black and white. In *Time* magazine, the critic Robert Hughes, a native of Australia, took a break from the art beat to inveigh against it, as part of a piece titled "The Fraying of America": "The word self-esteem has become one of the obstructive shibboleths of education. Why do black children need Afrocentrist education? Because, its promoters say, it will create self-esteem. The children live in a world of media and institutions whose images and values are created mainly by whites. The white tradition is to denigrate blacks. Hence blacks must have models that show them that they matter. Do you want your children to love themselves? Then change the curriculum. Feed them racist claptrap à la Leonard Jeffries, about how your intelligence is a function of the amount of melanin in your skin, and how Africans were sun people, open and cooperative, whereas Europeans were ice people, skulking pallidly in caves." Arthur M. Schlesinger, grand old man of American history and keeper of the sacred flame of postwar liberal consensus, took on Afrocentrism as part of his book-length meditation on multiculturalism and its discontents, *The Disuniting of America* (1991). "The best way to keep a people down is to deny them the means of improvement and cut them off from the opportunities of national life," Schlesinger warned. "If some Kleagle of the Ku Klux Klan wanted to devise an educational curriculum for the specific purpose of handicapping and disabling black Americans, he would not be likely to come up with anything more diabolically effective than Afrocentrism."

In a lecture for the Heritage Foundation, "The War over Culture in Education," the neoconservative and former Reagan education secretary William Bennett essentially cribbed Schlesinger, albeit with a harder, more imperial edge, a civilizing mission: "It has been said before, but it needs to be said again: if you were Grand Kleagle of the Ku Klux Klan, you could think of no better way to keep blacks out of the mainstream of American life than to give them a curriculum which is entirely divorced from the mainstream of American life. Many advocates of an Afrocentric curriculum may have the best intentions in the world, but this will be the effect of their effort. What these children need is an immersion in the culture of America and the West. They need an immersion not for our sake but for their sake, because we would like to see them have the same equal educational opportunity as everyone else."

Black scholars also had concerns about Afrocentrism's sweeping oversimplifications and—often explicit—chauvinism. Henry Louis Gates Jr., Harvard's chair of African American studies, wrote "Beware of the New Pharaohs" for *Newsweek*, pleading for a more nuanced and historical approach: "The truth is, too many people still regard African-American studies primarily as a way to rediscover a lost cultural identity—or invent one that never quite existed. And while we can understand these impulses, those in our field must remember that we are scholars first, not polemicists . . . African-American studies should be the home of free inquiry into the very complexity of being of African descent in the world, rather than a place where critical inquiry is drowned out by ethnic fundamentalism."

On the right fringe of the discourse, Samuel Francis had a more political—and perversely sympathetic—interpretation of the stakes of Afrocentrism. In his monthly *Chronicles* column he compared the ideas of the Afrocentrists to the political mythmaking he lauded in such "populist" figures as David Duke, trying to forge new "peoples" out of the deracinated "clusters" of the population: "Only leadership can accomplish that, which is why people like Mr. Duke and those who may soon start emulating him are important. They—if there is a 'they'—have the opportunity to build not just a coalition or a third party but a new people, as it were, by uniting these clusters and informing them with a new understanding of who they are and what destiny they should seek." And he added, "That, more or less, is what various black leaders are trying to do today through articulating a myth of 'Afrocentric' history and reformulating political and cultural issues in terms of that myth . . . It ought to be rather obvious that 'Afrocentrism,' whatever its other virtues, doesn't have much to say to non-black Americans, and the myths, history, and identity of white Americans are increasingly suppressed and delegitimized by the elite itself."

Whatever the ultimate political and cultural meaning of resurgent Afrocentrism and Black Nationalism, a generation gap was evident at the annual Malcolm X celebration in Anacostia Park in Washington, D.C., which took place three weeks after the Rodney King riots.

Older leaders and artists were politely greeted, but the young crowd responded enthusiastically to the keynote speaker, Sister Souljah, an exemplar of the new radical generation.

Born Lisa Williamson in the Bronx, the daughter of a truck driver who could no longer work because of epilepsy, Sister Souljah grew up in poverty and on welfare before her mother moved the family to Englewood, New Jersey. A star student, Williamson won a scholarship to Cornell University's advanced placement summer program, interned in the office of a Republican congressman, and then attended Rutgers University, where she pursued a double major in history and African studies. Not content with the path of upward social mobility, she chose to dedicate herself to activism, becoming involved in efforts to divest the college from its involvement with apartheid South Africa, and then, after leaving school, organizing a sleepaway camp in North Carolina for the children of homeless families. Touring as a lecturer, Williamson met Chuck D, the front man of Public Enemy, who was impressed with her rhetorical skills. In 1991 she guest appeared as Sister Souljah on Public Enemy's 1991 album *Apocalypse 911 . . . The Enemy Strikes Black*. Chuck D then asked her to replace Professor Griff as Public Enemy's "Minister of Information" after antisemitic remarks Griff had made came under scrutiny. An album deal with Epic Records followed quickly thereafter, and in March 1992 Sister Souljah's solo debut *360 Degrees of Power* dropped, featuring the singles "The Hate That Hate Produced" and "The Final Solution: Slavery's Back in Effect."

Deliberately blurring the line between art and activism, and employing a lyrical style closer to spoken word than to rapping, Sister Souljah's album created more of a sensation in the media than with the listening public. *360 Degrees of Power* barely broke into the top *Billboard* hip-hop charts and failed to go gold. But declarations like "I am African first, I am Black first / I want what's good for me and my people first / And if my survival means your total destruction / Then so be it!" proved irresistible bait for journalists. Souljah's statements to the press while promoting the album were no less provocative. "Despite what we've been lulled into believing, it is a race war—don't kid yourself," she told the *Los Angeles Times*. "Call it prejudice, I don't care," she said of her attack on whites. "When I see whites, I see people who for generations were oppressing my people. Knowing their history, how can I feel favorable toward any whites?"

At the Malcolm X Day festival in Washington, D.C., the young, politically conscious crowd swarmed Sister Souljah for autographs and photos, her modest record sales notwithstanding. "We're at war, and we must stop assisting the forces that are working against us," Souljah told the crowd, preaching the Black Nationalist gospel of economic self-reliance. "Instead, let us begin to focus on creating a network for Black business and other professionals." And she knocked the old leadership a bit for its hidebound ways. "Any movement that only has elders is bound to be retarded in some shape or form," she told *The Washington Times*. "There always needs to be new blood." One of the festival's organizers, Charles Stephenson, noted the burgeoning generation gap. "Young blacks in this country are very frustrated and they lack any kind of patience . . . There's a rift in the leadership, the Jesse Jacksons and the Sister Souljahs," he said. "I think it's about [young people] wanting more respect." For her part, Souljah indicated a willingness to enter into dialogue with the elder leaders—if they "see us as welcome."

It was not surprising then that Jackson invited Sister Souljah to participate at the "Youth Empowerment Summit" at the Rainbow Coalition conference in Washington. Organized by the reverend's son Yusef, the event would be a roundtable discussion, with forty participants, mixing people in their twenties and older figures intended to act as mentors. Reverend Jackson, dedicated to his pastoral vocation and an inveterate coalition builder, was trying to reintegrate the wayward youth into a unified movement, to refocus the discussion away from "racial and ethnic unity" and toward "unity, healing and coalition." It was not a particularly successful effort; the elder generation was taken aback by what they heard from the young people. "As an observer at the meeting and a veteran from the previous generation of social activists, I must frankly admit dismay at the state of affairs among the younger set," one participant later wrote to *The New York Times* in defense of the effort. "With a few exceptions, I saw little evidence that they have their eyes on the prize of a society characterized by racial and economic justice."

The commentariat registered discomfort with the degree of radicalism that Black college students were expressing. In *The Atlanta Journal-Constitution*, the columnist Dick Williams reacted to a full-page ad taken by Atlanta University Center students in the aftermath of unrest on campus. It spoke of "practices . . . designed for the eventual cultural, social and physical genocide and suicide of the African diaspora." Williams responded, "Hatred is the logical result for anyone who believes he or she is the target of genocide. But there is no intentional genocide. So we are confronted with fantasy turned to hate." Then he turned to rap music. "We know of the bitter racism recited by such as Ice Cube. We know of Sister Souljah, who legitimizes violence . . . It is a narrow ledge between Sister Souljah and the letter from AU Center students. Too narrow.

"In white America, the David Duke philosophy turned out to attract but 2 percent support. He is back in his dark cellar. But on the other side, self-help and the individual are being swept aside by the hatred, open bigotry and paranoid theory."

In the aftermath of the Rodney King riots, the press sought out Sister Souljah as the interpreter of young Black anger. "Describe, as you see it, the gap between those young people and the rest of society," Bill Moyers prompted her on his PBS show *Listening to America*. "The gap between young people and the rest of society is that young people don't have hope," Souljah replied immediately. "Jesse Jackson says, 'Keep Hope Alive,' but there is no hope, because they look at the leadership and they say, 'Okay, to get along in American society, you have to be a sell-out, you have to put on a suit, talk like a white man, ask for what white people want, say what people like, to be successful. Young black people don't see that as something to strive for; they want to be who they are, talk how we want to talk, walk how we want to walk, live how we want to live and be producers and providers for our children in the future. We want to be African."

The most infamous post–Rodney King media appearance for Sister Souljah was an interview for a feature story written by David Mills of *The Washington Post*, published on May 13, 1992: "During an interview in Washington last week, Souljah's empathy for the rioters reached a chilling extreme. Forget the statistics emerging on the racial variety of looters and people who died. Forget the economic motives of those who plundered stores. To Souljah, this was a black-on-white 'rebellion,' plain and simple and righteous." Then Souljah's quote—*the* quote: "I mean, if black people kill black people every day, why not have a week and kill white people? You understand what I'm saying? In other words, white people, this government and that mayor were well aware of the fact that black people were dying every day in Los Angeles under gang violence. So if you're a gang member and you would normally be killing somebody, why not kill a white person? Do you think that somebody thinks that white people are better, or above dying, when they would kill their own kind?"

Sister Souljah later protested that she was being asked to interpret and defend the actions of the rioters and was not herself calling for violence, that Mills had taken her remarks out of context. In response, the *Post* later reproduced a partial transcript to defend their coverage. (Mills had also included parts of his questions in the original piece.) Mills's full question was "But even the people who were perpetrating the violence, did they think it was wise? Was that wise, reasoned action?" He then followed it up with, "I'm just asking what's the wisdom in it? What's the sense in it?" Souljah: "It's rebellion, it's revenge. You ever heard of Hammurabi's Code? Eye for an eye, a tooth for a tooth?

It's revenge. I mean, that seems so simple. I don't even understand why anybody [would] ask me that question. You take something from me, I take something from you. You cut me, I cut you. You shoot me, I shoot you. You kill my mother, I kill your mother."

Mills presented Souljah's remarks as a "wake-up call" showing the importance of rap music. "The King verdict and its backlash have shown America the power of hip-hop music as a political medium. Television coverage of the crisis confirmed, as never before, the status of hard-edged rappers as spokesmen for the black lower class, delegates of America's angry youth. Opinion-makers. Leaders." Perhaps, but like the rest of the public, the rioters were unlikely to have even listened to Sister Souljah.

Some commentators pointed to angry rap music as a symptom of underlying issues, a weathervane of the larger crisis in the nation, and a harbinger of things to come. Speaking to *CBS This Morning*, James Bernard, senior editor at the hip-hop magazine *The Source*, said, "People who are surprised at what happened two weeks ago in LA haven't listened to Ice Cube. And if people had taken the time to listen, you would know—people would know the level of frustration in the young community there, and they would have understood it."

Leonard Pitts Jr., the *Miami Herald*'s pop music critic, made a similar point. "The L.A. Riot was not a surprise. The L.A. riot has been foreshadowed for years. In rap . . . if the music has elements of hatred, self-hatred, violence and inarticulate rage, remember that, in those elements, it is much like South Central Los Angeles. And if it is a hard music to listen to, remember that South Central, Bed-Stuy, Liberty City and on and on are hard places to live." Pitts also pointed out that the music's appeal was not limited to Black youth. "The feeling of disenfranchisement, of having nothing to lose, does not run solely along racial fault lines. Consider how many blond, blue-eyed kids show up at Public Enemy concerts. Consider the fact that when Ice-T played the Button South in Hallandale a few months ago, his audience was as much as 90 percent white. And consider, too, the plaintive plea from the white heavy metal band Poison a couple of years ago: 'Just give me something to believe in.'"

But rap music also provided a convenient scapegoat for more intractable problems. Buchanan's "Winning Back the Soul of America" speech asked, "Where did the mob come from?" One of the answers: "It came out of rock concerts where rap music celebrates raw lust and cop-killing." The head of the Los Angeles Fraternal Order of Police told *CBS Evening News*, "I believe that the rap music promotes, by its very language and by its very actions—promotes violence against authority and, consequently, violence against law enforcement." The music was "infecting young people with hate and bigotry," editor Philip Gailey wrote in *The St. Petersburg Times*. "No amount of government aid to the cities will be able to repair the damage the hate rappers are doing to race relations. They are as sick as any Klansman." At the Time Warner shareholders' meeting, Charlton Heston demanded that the company pull Ice T's "Cop Killer" from the market. "Let me suggest another thing. Homosexuals and Jews are targets of violence as well, sometimes murderous violence, although not as frequently as police officers," said Heston to Def Jam's David Harleston on *The MacNeil/Lehrer NewsHour.* "Let me ask you, sir, if the title of this song 'Cop Killer' in the album were 'Fag Killer' and the lyrics said, 'Die, die, die Kike, die,' would you be as comfortable about Time Warner distributing the record?"

The national discourse moved further and further away from the proximate cause of the riots—the acquittal of the four police officers in the Rodney King trial—and even underlying causes such as poverty and the pattern of police brutality. The media found it easier to discuss abstract terms like "hate" or "culture." The youth could not represent themselves, they had to be represented. Rappers were given or willingly took on the role of the only authentic voice.

In his *Washington Post* feature on Sister Souljah, David Mills wrote, "This is a new media age. Top 40 radio is dead, and '[expletive] tha Police' is in the American consciousness. Carson is history, and KRS-One is in America's bedrooms requesting 'amnesty,' for 13,000 (presumably black) prisoners in Los Angeles." Public Enemy's Chuck D called hip-hop "CNN for black people." Some gladly took the role on themselves, with the riots serving as a call to public service. "I'm like most every other young black male in New York or south-central," said Q-Tip from A Tribe Called Quest, organizing a march with Public Enemy's Chuck D. "I never cared about politics before . . . I'm going to show the 80,000 people who listen to my music that I'm serious about changing things. We need new leaders." Others, like N.W.A.'s Eazy-E, actually from Los Angeles, were more circumspect about their role, for either good or ill. "You don't make nobody go out and do this. I mean, if we wouldn't have did the record, it still would have happened." Eazy-E also happened to be one of the few people who still spoke of the actual precipitant of the riots. "Nobody wants to hear us lecture them. What they want is to see something done to those four officers . . . They want justice."

In the meantime, Bill Clinton had pissed people off again. He'd asked to appear at the convention of the National Newspaper Publishers Association, a group representing 205 Black-owned newspapers. Then he backed out forty-eight hours before the event. He didn't want to share the forum with Lenora Fulani of the New Alliance Party, who had heckled him back in April. The members and leadership of the newspaper association were not happy, and they held a press conference. "To me that is an affront that shows a disrespect and lack of consideration of a body of people who have traditionally voted very strongly Democratic," said Frances Draper, president of the Baltimore *Afro-American* newspaper. And the association president, Robert W. Bogle, said, "I can assure you, this is an issue which we will bring to the country, to the African-American community, and I don't give a damn about Bill Clinton if that's what he wants to say to my community."

Clinton would shortly have an opportunity to bring his message to the Black community, however. On June 13, Jesse Jackson's National

Rainbow Coalition would hold its leadership conference, "Rebuild America: 1992 and Beyond." Reporters were informed by the campaign beforehand that the governor was going to say something newsworthy. The callers into C-SPAN before the event aired were divided, largely along racial lines, about Clinton's decision to snub the National Newspaper Publishers Association. A caller from Martinsville, Virginia: "I don't think Bill Clinton should have shown up at that press conference. I saw what Ms. Fulani did to him when he was in New York in that hospital. It was an embarrassment, he wasn't allowed to speak, and I don't blame him. I'm not a racist." Silver Springs: "I think this is one of the reasons Bill Clinton is gonna develop a credibility problem in the African-American community. And it's gonna cause many of us Democrats to reexamine Perot and perhaps pursue that, because the Democratic Party takes Black votes for granted. And we're rather tired of it." Texarkana: "I'd like to apologize for our governor. I am a Democrat, I am black, and I am a nurse. I can identify with both sides because I see the poor and the rich and I see the difference in how they are treated across the nation. And it was an insult to me being an Arkansan, thinking that our governor would turn down an event of people who were trying to identify what his goals were for America." Yuma, Arizona: "I put this station on and I see 'black press of America.' There's so much being talked about racial discrimination, etcetera, but if there would be a 'white press of America' we would be lambasted that we're discriminating. I did not see one white person there."

In his introductory remarks for Clinton, Jesse Jackson brought up the anniversary of the killing of Medgar Evers, which was one day earlier. "For 29 years, the man whose fingerprints were on the gun that killed Medgar Evers roamed the street free, freed by an unjust jury. A persistent state's attorney, 29 years later, now has Mr. De La Beckwith back in the throes of the judicial process. In the same spirit . . . as I stood where Rodney King was beaten two weeks ago, I couldn't help but observe the window from which the film was shot that exposed the

Rodney King beating . . . George Holliday, a white gentleman . . . with his instincts filmed [the beating] and with his character and courage made it public . . . On this night we all honor George Holliday as a bridge-builder, as a samaritan, and an authentic point of light."

Jackson's encomium to racial unity continued. "And while the focus has been on the blacks that beat the truck driver once the police deserted their post of duty, there has not been much focus on the four blacks who saved his life when they did. And we brought them here today, because we shall honor them tonight as our four samaritans . . . won't you stand? They saved Mr. Denny's life, they are the good samaritans from Los Angeles, give them a hand. Give them another hand, they deserve it, they risked danger and saved a man's life." The audience and the panel rose to their feet to applaud. Then Jackson went on to describe the various initiatives and discussion groups of the conference, including the youth circle that Sister Souljah attended. "A generation of youth sat around a common table, and tried to take the pain of this generation and turn it into power, that they might use their strength and move our society from dope to hope and higher ground. What power our youth have, used constructively."

Clinton's speech began with a warm embrace of Jesse Jackson and the Rainbow Coalition, praising them for "not just pointing the finger of blame but taking up the burden of responsibility," followed by some of his good-natured bonhomie, emphasizing his modest origins in the Deep South. Then he turned to his vision for the post–Cold War country, pleading with the crowd to avoid distractions. "Don't let this election be about Willie Horton or Murphy Brown. Don't let this election be about the denial of the need for new directions by all people of both parties in Washington. Don't be prisoners of the past or the politically correct. Let us be bold and chart a new course." But Clinton's bold new course included a lot of references to the past: it was a somewhat contradictory mélange of invocations of big government initiatives like the G.I. Bill, the Marshall Plan, and the Peace Corps and praise for the ethic of the small producer; a simultaneous call for massive reinvestment and tax relief for manufacturing and fiscal responsibility, with his pledge to reduce the deficit.

Clinton praised Jack Kemp's "weed and seed" plan for inner cities, which would combine aggressive law enforcement with community investment. He said that the people he spoke to in riot-torn Los Angeles agreed. "Most people I talked to in Los Angeles didn't want more big government. They wanted more jobs, and they wanted small business. Most people said what they really wanted was a Washington that would support their efforts at work, and they knew that Washington had failed them but also that their banks had not met their responsibilities to reinvest in their communities." He reiterated his call to "end welfare as we know it" but "in a way that lifted all of our people instead of using welfare as a divisive issue." Then came the moment that the reporters had been told in advance to watch for.

"Finally, let's stand up for what has always been best about the Rainbow Coalition, which is people coming together across racial lines," Clinton began. "You had a rap singer here last night named Sister Souljah. I defend her right to express herself through music, but her comments before and after Los Angeles were filled with the kind of hatred that you do not honor today and tonight." He repeated her *Washington Post* remarks and an earlier comment. "Last year she said, 'You can't call me or any black person anywhere in the world a racist. We don't have the power to do to white people what white people have done to us. And even if we did, we don't have that low down and dirty nature. If there are any good white people I haven't met them. Where are they?' Right here in this room. That's where they are." A smattering of applause.

"I know she is a young person, but she has a big influence on a lot of people. And when people say that, if you took the words white and black and reversed them, you might think David Duke was giving that speech." Clinton then took "responsibility" for his own racial insensitivities. "Let me tell you, we all make mistakes, and sometimes we're not as sensitive as we ought to be. And we have an obligation, all of us, to call attention to prejudice wherever we see it. A few months ago I made a mistake. I joined a friend of mine, and I played golf in a country club that didn't have any African-American members. I was criticized for doing it. You know what, I was rightly criticized for doing it. I make a mistake. And I said I would never do that again." Of course, he could never mention the Ricky Ray Rector execution or even the Sam Nunn photo op; it could never be admitted that there was any racial subtext there. Instead, he got to confess to the venial sin of going to play golf—not so bad when compared with Sister Souljah's invective and incitement, right?

Clinton was employing the strategy his handlers called "counter-scheduling"—making statements that would displease the specific crowd he was in front of, but would get repeated in the national media and appeal to the broader public. Jackson understood that he and the Rainbow Coalition, not Sister Souljah, were the real target. He tried to look impassive and stoical, but tension and displeasure were evident in his face: he was insulted. Still, as the speech ended, he was cordial, even asking Clinton to return to play his saxophone.

Clinton and Jackson were due to speak in private at a hotel suite after the speech. According to Jackson, he confronted Clinton, saying, "You violated us. Why did you do this?" Clinton protested that it was a minor part of a longer speech, but Jackson pointed to the fact that Clinton had a copy of Sister Souljah's remarks in his pocket as a sign of premeditation. The idea that it was all a stunt for the cameras became clear to Jackson later on, when his advisers told him that the Clinton campaign had been whispering to reporters that something dramatic was going to take place. After the meeting, the Clinton campaign tried to suggest that Jackson was seeking the vice presidential nod and the governor had flat-out refused, angering Jackson.

At first Bush's arms summit with Yeltsin still dominated the headlines, but little by little the media turned to the Jackson-Clinton spat. It didn't hurt that Jackson decided to press the issue in public, returning to a tried-and-true tactic of twisting the arms of Democratic leaders that perhaps had lost its strategic viability. The reverend told *The New York Times* that Clinton had come to the Rainbow Coalition conference to "stage a very well-planned sneak attack, without the courage to confront but with a calculation to embarrass." He mentioned Clinton's having "exposed a character flaw," a sore spot for Clinton since Gennifer Flowers. Jackson said that Clinton's "Machiavellian maneuver" was meant to "purely appeal to conservative whites by containing Jackson and isolating Jackson." An astute reading, but what of Jackson's own maneuvering? He would not participate in any denunciation or even mild criticism of Sister Souljah, saying only that she had been "misquoted" or "misunderstood."

Why stick with Souljah, who had razzed him, made fun of "keep hope alive," even referred to older leaders like him as "retarded"? Pride? Solidarity? Principle? Jackson's politics certainly relied on the performance of those virtues; he had wrung political successes by cleaving to them in the past. But Jackson knew that he was losing the youth, and perhaps feared alienating them further. He saw his coalition at risk, thinking that if he could keep it together, he might be able to launch one more offensive. He even signaled taking his troops over to Perot. "There's a lot we don't know about him," Mr. Jackson told *The New York Times*, "but he's certainly in the realm of possibility and critical debate. When he questions going too fast on free trade with Mexico, when he talks about equal funding for all schools in public education and freedom of choice for women on abortion, we need to listen." But instead of finding a flexible position from where he could strike out in any direction, Jackson was being cornered.

Clinton continued to bind Jackson to the rock of Sister Souljah. "I bragged on the Rainbow Coalition and its programs," Clinton told reporters. "I criticized divisive language by Sister Souljah. If Jesse Jackson wants to align himself with that now and claim that's the way he felt, then that's his business." Jackson shot back: "The attempt to align me with her is an attempt to malign me with her." True enough, but he still wouldn't try to distance himself from Souljah or downplay their connection, or even put her participation in the Rainbow Coalition meeting in context. For her part, Sister Souljah protested that her words had been taken out of context, saying, "'Sister Souljah' was used as a vehicle, like Willie Horton and various other black victims of racism—a poor excuse for an agenda-less candidate."

Praise began to pour in for Clinton. Carl T. Rowan, a Black columnist for the *Chicago Sun-Times*, wrote in DENOUNCING HATRED BOOSTS CLINTON: "Clinton played it exactly right Saturday. He will win some white votes for speaking the truth about Sister Souljah, and he won't lose many black votes by standing up for racial sanity." The *New York Times* editorial desk averred that "Sister Souljah is no Willie Horton. She's a rap singer who has said things that were hateful when she said them—and still are." In a headline on her syndicated column, Mary McGrory, white, declared, BILL CLINTON IS STARTING TO LOOK LIKE A SAVVY POLITICIAN. "Clinton has already been rewarded for his boldness. After weeks of languishing in the classifieds, he has been catapulted back to page one. Jackson is calling editors and reporters to rail about the injustice of it all. But he can hardly tell his followers to vote for [Ross] Perot because Clinton dared question him." Clarence Page, a Black syndicated columnist, praised Clinton for breaking one of the "notsapostas," those political taboos Barney Frank had criticized.

There were dissents. From the left, Alexander Cockburn in the *Los Angeles Times* declared that Clinton's "double-cross" would backfire and cost him Black votes without gaining white ones. In the *Chicago Sun-Times*, Vernon Jarrett was even more acerbic, calling the whole thing a bit of a put-on by the press and by politicians. "Let the royal trumpets blare. Greet the new queen of black America. Hail Sister Souljah. Made in America. Made by the mass media with the help of a desperate candidate for the presidency of the United States," he wrote. "It was not Jackson but the editors of the Washington Post who chose to bypass other outspoken blacks and interview Sister Souljah for a lengthy feature story on America's racial crisis. There is nothing wrong with a newspaper seeking the views of a rap performer. But how often do the major media bother to heed or canvass the analytical thinking of black scholar-activists who dare tell the harsh truth?" Jarrett particularly resented the public elevation of the Black lumpenproletariat in the aftermath of Rodney King. "Is it mere coincidence that on Monday when I noticed the face of Sister Souljah on *Newsweek*, I saw on Page 1 of *The Wall Street Journal* an announcement that investment money was coming to make entrepreneurs of the Crips and the Bloods? The street gangs will be given business opportunities not previously available to other blacks, including those who never spent a day in jail and who never committed arson. The message to blacks is clear: If you want our (white) support, you must be a Clarence Thomas on one end of the spectrum or a violence-prone, hell-raiser on the other. If you're black, there's no genuine respect for those of us in between."

But perhaps more important than newspaper columnists, talk radio had also perked up. SISTER SOULJAH FLAP HELPS CLINTON, RADIO TALKERS SAY, *The Palm Beach Post* reported. "I'm getting more and more interested in Clinton," said Bob Stephens of the Independent Broadcasters Network in Clearwater, Florida, who voted for George Bush in 1988. Clinton had even begun to cut into Perot-mania. "All said Texas independent Ross Perot still is the hottest political topic on talk radio, popularly regarded as a telling barometer of voter moods in America. But they all said their listeners had responded favorably to the Arkansas governor's denouncement of racially inflammatory language *The Washington Post* attributed to Sister Souljah during the Los Angeles riots." Then there were the endless panels on CNN, discussing the moment ad nauseam.

Jackson even began to show signs of preparing for detente, offering praise for Clinton's economic plan, which now included tax hikes to pay for infrastructure expansion: "The Clinton plan points us in the right direction, down the right road. It deserves serious analysis and comprehensive debate. To paraphrase a gospel song, he has come a long way from where he started."

Under different circumstances, Sister Souljah might have found much to praise in Clinton's program as well, informed as she was by the Black Nationalist tradition of self-reliance. As she would later write in her memoir, *No Disrespect*, "Welfare is designed to keep you trapped. We must abandon the notion of welfare as a way of life, or even as a way to survive . . . Any program that offers genuine job training or helps you to develop employable skills is worth taking seriously. Any program that offers you an opportunity to return to school or to start your own business is worth pursuing." She might have applauded Clinton's family-centric focus as well, as she decried welfare's corrosive effects on forming family units as much as any neoconservative or New Democrat: "This policy perversely encourages single-mother households, as women are asked to choose between their man and the financial survival of their children. It destroys any impulse of self-improvement. It is a system designed to fail." If the colors had been switched, you might have thought Bill Clinton was giving that speech.

But what did it all amount to? Polls still showed broad discontent with both Bush and Clinton, and now the public was beginning to sour on Perot as well. Clinton was viewed favorably by only 16 percent of the public, Perot by 26 percent, while Bush was at 29 percent. But there was now the perception, fueled by the media desperate for a story, that something had changed, Clinton had *done something* and had turned a corner, accomplished something bold and new. If nothing else, it got attention: Clinton had desperately been trying to break Perot's hold on the media and now seemed to have accomplished it. But he also judged the national mood correctly. People wanted to be pissed off, but the specifics were too irritating and difficult: the details of urban policy didn't get people going, dwelling on the scenes of burned-out Los Angeles was too depressing and hopeless. Reality had to be left behind. People wanted to talk about something else while seeming as if they were still addressing the serious issues. As always, symbols—actors, rappers, songs, movies, culture—were needed to stand in for complex issues.

Quayle had tried it out on Murphy Brown, but the white lady was not threatening enough. Who could believe that Candice Bergen was responsible for America's ills? But Sister Souljah was Black, aggressive, young, putatively the representative of a culture and a people that white America feared. She had attempted to bring politics into the realm of culture, but in a way that reflected the logic of the market. It worked in a certain way: she achieved more political importance than cultural renown. But the political importance she took on was the opposite of the one she intended. She was not a wholly fictional character like Murphy Brown; she was a living person, albeit also a persona that represented—or was made to represent—a whole climate of public opinion.

She attempted to use her voice and assert herself, but in the end her name became a symbol, a signifier, a catchword. Her actual remarks are largely forgotten. Sister Souljah is now known for what Clinton said about her, not for anything she said herself.

10

"BUYING THE COUNTRY BACK"

Buchanan finally wrapped up his campaign in early June after the California primary, returning to Manchester, New Hampshire, where it all started. He addressed a crowd of a thousand jubilant supporters chanting "Pat '96!" at the Courtyard banquet hall. He had some fond remembrances of kicking off the campaign in the winter. "When I did get up to speak, some of the AIDS activists acted up, and two of my aides decided they would help me out . . . Just as my speech got to the point where I talked about compassion for the forgotten American, they were body-slamming an AIDS activist on the sidewalk." Buchanan guffawed; the crowd shrieked with delight. Buchanan wrote his campaign into the annals of history: "In the last analysis, Teddy Roosevelt tried to take the nomination away from a sitting Republican president and didn't do it, Ronald Reagan in 1976 tried to take the nomination from a sitting president and couldn't do it. And I guess in the last analysis, Pat Buchanan couldn't do it, but as W. B. Yeats wrote, 'All is changed utterly, a terrible beauty is born.' New Hampshire was the beginning, but Houston is not the end.

Houston is a truce line, is not a surrender." Pat had already started negotiating for speaking time at the convention.

From the syndicated column he had taken over from Buchanan for the duration of the campaign, Sam Francis offered his buddy's run a mixed review. "He started out fine, announcing a 'Middle American Revolution,' a 'new nationalism' and a 'new populism' based on the legitimate economic, cultural and political grievances of the middle-class core of American civilization," Francis wrote. "But somewhere along the line, the tone changed, and the other side of the brain seemed to take control. By the end of the campaign, Mr. Buchanan was running pretty much as a conservative torch-bearer, claiming his purpose was to push President Bush to the right, reweave the Reagan mantle and take the party back."

Buchanan's campaign wasn't quite the real deal Francis had in mind: "The truth is that, for all his radicalism proclaimed and attributed, Pat remained simply too bourgeois and too Beltway." Francis didn't think much of Perot's effort, either. "What Americans want and need to hear is how their leaders will exercise leadership to save them from the economic and cultural abyss that peers menacingly over the lips of their morning coffee cups. What Mr. Perot seems to offer is the illusion that he knows how to do that, and unlike Mr. Buchanan, he doesn't have the baggage that would weigh him down from doing it." But Perot's employment of political professionals boded ill: "The problem is there's no reason to think Mr. Perot or anyone else really does know how to do it, and it's unlikely his wrapping himself in Beltway insiders . . . will help him. For all the energy that stirs in him, Mr. Perot looks like an empty vessel."

Francis still had a role for Buchanan. "If Mr. Buchanan is smart, he'll fill that vessel—not by running for office again but by returning to what he does best, the wielding of jawbones against the cant and folly of the incumbent elites of culture and politics . . . By doing so, Mr. Buchanan can help rewrite the rulebooks of politics in an age when old rules have ceased to apply. He may not be The Terminator, but he can still be the godfather of a new political and cultural movement that can leave Mr. Bush's party where it lies and take back our country."

Buchanan's aides still felt that they needed to defend their boss's honor. In a letter to *The Washington Times*, Buchanan's research director used Koreatown's choice of Buchanan over Bush to defend Pat's Middle American street cred. "In Koreatown, ground zero for the Los Angeles riots, 52 percent of the Republican voters picked Pat Buchanan over George Bush in last week's California primary . . . This week, Samuel Francis wondered in print (Commentary, June 9) why Mr. Buchanan, whom he described as simply too bourgeois and too Beltway, would 'keep running as a Republican after the chance for victory was mathematically zilch.' If Mr. Francis would like to take a trip out to L.A., the folks in Koreatown would be happy to acquaint him with the middle-American answer to his question."

But Korean Americans in Los Angeles were not exactly who Francis had in mind as "middle Americans." In the June issue of *Chronicles*, dedicated to "restoring the republic," he offered his vision of a reconstituted United States in an essay titled "Nationalism, Old and New." Francis described the "old nationalism" not as a unifying force in American history, but as a corrosive one, tearing up the bonds of locality and kin in favor of ever greater agglomerations: "From the days of Alexander Hamilton, nationalism has meant unification of the country under a centralized government, the supremacy of the executive over the legislative branch, the reduction of states' rights and local and sectional parochialism, governmental regulation of the economy and engineering of social institutions, and an activist foreign policy—expansionist, imperialist, or globalist—that costs much money and requires at least occasional wars." According to Francis, "The national state the nationalists defended and constructed was born with the ratification of the U.S. Constitution, reached adolescence in the victory of the North in the Civil War, and grew to a corpulent adulthood in the 20th-century managerial state of Woodrow Wilson, Herbert Hoover, Franklin Roosevelt, and Lyndon Johnson."

The "old nationalism" was opposed by what Francis called "republicanism," embodied first by the anti-federalists who opposed the Constitution's centralizing thrust and then in "John Randolph, John C. Calhoun, the leaders of the Confederacy, the Populists of the late 19th century and the Southern Agrarians of the early 20th, and in the Old Right conservatism of the era between Charles Lindbergh and Jesse Helms." This republican tradition, based on the ideal of a virtuous, self-reliant citizenry, stood up for all the prerogatives of particularity against universalism: the patriarchal household, agricultural toil or the artisanal shop (in contrast to mass production), states' rights, regional and local traditions and customs.

According to Francis, "nationalism" conclusively defeated "republicanism" in the twentieth century: "The national state has long since triumphed, and with it, wedded to it like Siamese siblings, multinational corporations, giant labor unions, universities and foundations, and all the titanic labyrinth of modern bureaucratic organizations in both the 'public' and the increasingly illusory 'private' sectors have won as well." These "leviathan" institutions, which Francis called "mass organizations," were governed by a "managerial elite" who possessed a "degree of power unknown to the most imperious despots of the past" and who controlled "not only . . . the state but also the dominant organizations of the economy and culture, so that our incomes and our very thoughts, values, tastes, and emotions are conditioned and manipulated by them." The population was now so dependent on these mass organizations that they no longer possessed the self-reliant "virtue" necessary for a republican citizenry:

> Today, virtually everyone in the United States is habituated to a style of living that is wrapped up in dependency on mass organizations of one kind or another—supermarkets, hospitals, insurance companies, the bureaucratized police, local government, the mass media, the factories and office buildings where we work, the

> apartment complexes and suburban communities where we live, and the massive, remote, and mysterious national state that supervises almost every detail of our lives. Most Americans cannot even imagine life without such dependencies and would not want to live without them if they could imagine it. The classical republicans were right. Having become dependent on others for our livelihoods, our protection, our entertainment, and even our thoughts and tastes, we are corrupted. We neither want a republic nor could we keep it if we had one. We do not deserve to have one, and like the barbarians conquered and enslaved by the Greeks and Romans, we are suited only for servitude.

Even though "classical republicanism" was "defunct as a serious political alternative to the present regime," that did not mean that "Americans should either embrace the old, Hamiltonian nationalism or merely squat passively in their kennels waiting for the next whistle from their masters." Instead, Francis envisioned another political order based on the "large number of Americans, perhaps a majority, whose material interests and most deeply held cultural codes are endangered by the national (and increasingly supranational) managerial regime":

> These "Middle Americans," largely white and middle class, derive their income from their dependence on the mass structures of the managerial economy, and, because many of them have long since lost their habits of self-reliance, they also are dependent on the services of the government (at least indirectly) and the dominant culture. Yet despite their dependency, the regime does little for them and much to them. They find that their jobs are insecure, their savings stripped of value, their neighborhoods and schools and homes unsafe, their elected leaders indifferent and often crooked, their moral beliefs and religious professions and social codes under perpetual attack even from their own government, their children

> taught to despise what they believe, their very identity and heritage as a people threatened, and their future—political, economic, cultural, racial, national, and personal—uncertain.

Functioning like Marx's proletariat, these Middle Americans are despised and oppressed, but also integral to the maintenance of the system: "They are the Americans sneered at as the 'Bubba vote,' mocked as Archie Bunkers, and denounced as the racists, sexists, anti-Semites, xenophobes, homophobes, and hate criminals who haunt the dark corners of the land, the 'Dark Side' of America, even as their own energy, sacrifice, and commitment make possible the regime and the elite that despise them, exploit them, and dispossess them. They are at once the real victims of the regime and the core or nucleus of American civilization, the Real America, the American Nation."

What these middle Americans needed was "a political formula and a public myth that synthesize the attention to material-economic interests offered by the left with the defense of concrete cultural and national identity offered by the right." To accomplish this, Francis proposed a "new nationalism," which he thought was the only force sufficiently energetic and massive enough to resist the forces of "managerialism" and "globalism." It would be particularist enough to preserve the identity of middle Americans, while universal enough to "mobilize passions of mass solidarity and sacrifice." In effect, this nationalism would create a true American nation for the first time:

> The pseudo-nationalist ethic of the old nationalism that served only as a mask for the pursuit of special interests will be replaced by the social ethic of an authentic nationalism that can summon and harness the genius of a people certain of its identity and its destiny. The myth of the managerial regime that America is merely a philosophical proposition about the equality of all mankind (and therefore includes all mankind) must be replaced by a new myth of the nation as a historically and culturally unique order that

> commands loyalty, solidarity, and discipline and excludes those who do not or cannot assimilate to its norms and interests. This is the real meaning of "America First": America must be first not only among other nations but first also among the other (individual or class or sectional) interests of its people.

If "old nationalism" was the thesis, and "republicanism" the antithesis, then "new nationalism" was their synthesis, "a resolution of the conflict between the classical republicanism and the nationalism around which much American political history has swung." The accomplishment of this nationalist program would require not just electoral victories, but "cultural hegemony" achieved through a "long countermarch through the institutions of the dominant culture." But the hour was late, the nation was at risk of being swallowed up by the Leviathans, and the work of cultural struggle could not be delayed.

> The affirmation of national and cultural identity as the core of the new nationalist ethic acquires special importance at a time when massive immigration, a totalitarian and antiwhite multiculturalist fanaticism, concerted economic warfare by foreign competitors, and the forces of antinational political globalism combine to jeopardize the cultural identity, demographic existence, economic autonomy, and national independence and sovereignty of the American nation.

In July, Francis followed up with a friendlier assessment of his pal's primary run in "The Buchanan Revolution," which cast Pat as tribune of the Middle American revolution: "No one should imagine either that the revolution is over. Indeed, Mr. Buchanan's presidential campaign was only the opening shot, and whether he runs again or does or does not eventually win the White House, he has unleashed a force in American politics that cannot be bridled. Its main mission now is to embark on a long march that will popularize and legitimize its claims to be the vehicle of a reborn national consciousness, and that mission is only in part political in the narrow sense. As a great global democrat once said, a house divided against itself cannot stand, and the main message of the Middle American Revolution is that the real masters of the house are ready to repossess it and drive out the usurpers."

For the time being, that would have to wait. Immediately after suspending his campaign, Buchanan was hospitalized for heart surgery: he had to have his aortic valve replaced. And he still seemed determined to muscle his way back into the Republican fold rather than burn it all down, threats to put on his own counterconvention notwithstanding. The party seemed ready to oblige. His sister Bay was put in charge of negotiations with the RNC. She made it clear that his price for endorsing Bush would be a prime-time speaking spot at the Houston convention in August.

The Bush campaign was desperate to bring back the conservatives—to do anything of any political substance whatsoever. The president appeared to be bouncing from one mishap to another. While visiting Panama, Bush had to flee a rally that had been planned with the country's president. Demonstrators protesting his 1989 invasion had gotten too close, and Panamanian security forces fired warning shots at the crowd and deployed tear gas that wafted back over the dais, causing both Bush and the First Lady to be "mildly affected" by the gas. Heavily armed Secret Service agents had to shuttle them away. Shortly before Bush arrived in the country, gunmen had attacked a military convoy, killing a U.S. soldier and wounding another. The trip was supposed to bring attention to the administration's successful removal of Manuel Noriega. Marlin Fitzwater tried to spin it as a win: "In some sense, it is a symbol of democracy that there can be protesters . . . It's been a very good trip, with the exception of the tear gas."

Bush had another close call at the end of June. The Supreme Court was hearing a challenge to *Roe v. Wade—Planned Parenthood v. Casey*. The defendant was Bob Casey, the pro-life Democratic governor of Pennsylvania who was defending his state's Abortion Control Act of 1982. The law required a twenty-four-hour waiting period before an abortion, minors to get consent from their parents, and married women to inform their husband of their intent to get an abortion. This looked like the big one: William Brennan and Thurgood Marshall had been replaced by Bush's picks, David Souter and Clarence Thomas. Eight of the justices were Republican selections, and five had been chosen by Reagan or Bush. Officially, the Bush administration said it wanted the court to strike down *Roe*: the solicitor general, Ken Starr, filed an amicus brief to that effect. But behind closed doors, the White House fretted over the potential bombshell of reversing *Roe* in an election year.

Despite publicly taking a hard line on abortion, Bush may have also had mixed feelings. His father, Prescott Bush, was an early supporter of Planned Parenthood, then progressive reformer Margaret Sanger's "Birth Control League." As a Connecticut High WASP, there was undoubtedly a eugenic tinge to these beliefs: many with similar stands were concerned as much about the proliferation of poor Catholics as about women's reproductive freedom. His son took some valuable lessons from his father's experience with the issue of family planning. "My own first awareness of birth control as a public policy issue came with a jolt in 1950 when my father was running for the United States Senate in Connecticut," H. W. wrote in the foreword of a 1973 study on the "World Population Crisis" while he was U.S. representative to the United Nations. "Drew Pearson, on the Sunday before Election Day, 'revealed' that my father was involved with Planned Parenthood. My father lost that election by a few hundred out of close to a million votes. Many political observers felt a sufficient number of voters were swayed by his alleged contacts with the birth controllers to cost him the election." But that didn't stop Bush *fils* from being a key Republican backer of Title X, legislation that provided federal funding for family planning, including money to Planned Parenthood. His tireless dedication to the issue even earned him the nickname "Rubbers." In 1980 he told *Rolling Stone* that, while Reagan opposed *Roe*, "I happen to think it's right." But like his namesake, he was flexible, elastic: he backed the antiabortion platform as Reagan's vice presidential nominee and, when he became president, continued the previous administration's policy of denying the funding for the U.N. family planning fund that he had supported as ambassador to the U.N. But grassroots conservatives never fully forgot he was once "Rubbers," another reason why recapturing the backing of the earthy Catholic Buchanan to cover up his bloodless Episcopalianism felt so important. Still, campaign manager Bob Teeter reminded everyone that three out of four Americans opposed overturning *Roe*. Closer to home, some Republican women were dissatisfied with the party's full turn on abortion and planned to make an issue of it at the convention.

The Bush administration caught a break when the Supreme Court handed down a compromise on June 29. Ruling 5–4, the justices preserved key portions of the Pennsylvania law but also upheld *Roe*, striking down the portion of the Abortion Control Act that placed an "undue burden" on the mother's efforts to seek an abortion, which was just the spousal notification requirement. The court also overturned the trimester standard governing abortion restrictions in favor of the looser concept of "viability." Sandra Day O'Connor, writing the majority opinion, expressed a degree of exasperation with the Republican administration's continued efforts to attack *Roe*: "Liberty finds no refuge in a jurisprudence of doubt. Yet 19 years after our holding that the Constitution protects a woman's right to terminate her pregnancy in its early stages, *Roe v. Wade*, 410 U. S. 113 (1973), that definition of liberty is still questioned. Joining the respondents as amicus curiae, the United States, as it has done in five other cases in the last decade, again asks us to overrule *Roe*." Justice O'Connor's opinion also included a good deal of concern for the institutional damage that would happen if the court were politically whipsawed to overturn the settled precedent of *Roe*: "A decision to overrule *Roe*'s essential holding under the existing circumstances would address error, if error there was, at the cost of both profound and unnecessary damage to the Court's legitimacy, and to the nation's commitment to the rule of law. It is therefore imperative to adhere to the essence of *Roe*'s original decision, and we do so today." In his dissent, Chief Justice William Rehnquist complained that the court had rendered *Roe* a "facade" and replaced it with something "created largely out of whole cloth" and "not built to last." "*Roe v. Wade* stands as a sort of Potemkin village," Rehnquist wrote, "which may be pointed out to passers-by as a monument to the importance of adhering to precedent."

Abortion rights activists tended to agree. "George Bush's Court has left *Roe v. Wade* an empty shell that is one Justice Thomas away from being destroyed," said Kate Michelman, president of the National Abortion Rights Action League. A day after the decision, the House Judiciary Committee approved a bill, the Freedom of Choice Act, that would codify *Roe* into law. It would undoubtedly be vetoed by President Bush, but it would at least put him "on the record" about the abortion question and possibly trigger voter mobilization. Democratic leadership promised that the Senate and House would pass the act before the Republican convention. It moved quickly through committees. Then nothing happened. Democrats doubted they could get enough votes to get past a Senate filibuster: although the bill had Republican cosponsors, they were unwilling to move it forward as a means to beat up on the president. Members of Congress also felt little urgency to do anything after the court had explicitly upheld *Roe*. And so the Freedom of Choice Act languished.

Bush's luck wouldn't last long. On June 30 Aetna Life and Casualty announced that it was going to lay off 10 percent of its workforce. On July 1 Hughes Aircraft announced a cut of nine thousand jobs, primarily in Southern California. By July 2, the state of California had gone bankrupt and was paying government employees with IOUs for the first time since the Depression. On July 3 the Bureau of Labor Statistics reported that the unemployment rate in June had risen from 7.5 percent to 7.8 percent, with most of the drop in payrolls occurring in manufacturing and construction.

White-collar workers were affected, too: in the month of June, 117,000 of their jobs were lost. The Fed immediately moved to cut rates by half a percent, something the administration had been pushing for, even though the previous rate cuts didn't help much. Analysts raised fears of a "triple dip recession." Bush put the blame on Congress for not passing his economic package, which included cuts to the capital gains tax. The front page of the *New York Post* read TEN MILLION AMERICANS OUT OF WORK—GEORGE MAY BE NEXT.

The Bush campaign had decided it was time to turn most of their fire on Perot, even breaking with their original strategy of keeping the president out of negative campaigning until after the convention so he could remain "presidential." The media was also scrutinizing him more closely: articles appeared in *The Washington Post*, *Time*, and *The New Republic* dealing with his use of private investigators to snoop on competitors, perceived enemies, and even his own children. A focus group indicated that Perot's potential authoritarianism and use of investigators was a real concern for Republican voters. Dan Quayle had started to call him "Inspector Perot." When the *Post* reported that Perot had investigated Bush's children, Pappy told Perot, "Leave my kids alone," saying his sons were "all straight arrows, uninvolved in intrigue." (That was overstating it a bit: even son Neil Bush, who presided over an infamous savings and loan collapse, admitted to the House Banking Committee that some of his deals looked "a little fishy.") Father Bush, former director of the CIA, also said that it wasn't "particularly American" for Ross Perot to try to dig up dirt on him.

The Bush camp, from George and Barbara on down, unleashed a fusillade of comments to make Perot look nuts: "Temperamental tycoon," "beyond the pale," "sick," "frightening," bizarre," "erratic," secretive," "eccentric," "scary," "paranoid." Marlin Fitzwater continued to wonder aloud what Perot would do in charge of the FBI, CIA, and IRS. In order to refute all this, Perot hosted an angry press conference where he berated reporters and blamed all the negative coverage on the "Republican dirty tricks crowd": "My total experience in investigating people is like a grain of sand on a large beach compared to the ongoing investigations day after day after day after day from the Republican Dirty Tricks committee. And we have members of the Washington press corps here, you know who they report directly to." He refused to give the press any evidence of the dirty tricks allegation. He also continued to decline to give any specific information about his platform. When asked whether the pressures of the campaign were getting to him, Perot shot back, "You guys don't understand what tough is. This is Mickey Mouse tossed salad."

Despite the media storm and indications that Perot's image in the public eye was beginning to be tarnished, the thousands of volunteers who had mobilized on his behalf stayed enthusiastic. For his sixty-second birthday on June 27, volunteers from Dallas rolled out a giant birthday cake in the shape of the White House and put on a choreographed dance number. A chorus line of women in red shirts that said PEROT GIRLS sang Johnny Mercer's "Something's Gotta Give" with the lyrics as "Something's gotta give—Bush has gotta go—the people want Perot." In Oxnard, California, volunteers sculpted an eight-foot plaster of paris bust of Perot based on a photo in a newspaper. On July 3, Perot, before a backdrop of two hundred fluttering American flags, addressed a petition rally of close to six thousand at the state capitol in Olympia, Washington. ACT UP activists, angered by his statement that he would not appoint gay members to his administration, stormed the stage before Perot's speech. He didn't have them forcibly removed by staffers, as Buchanan had, partly because he couldn't: the rally was on public property and he hadn't secured a permit. He agreed to meet with the activists to address their concerns, and the rally was able to go on. Volunteers had to get two hundred signatures for Perot to appear on the ballot; they hosted hundreds of mini-conventions around the state in churches, homes, and community centers and got fifty-five thousand people to sign. One sign-in station at a rest stop attracted hundreds of bikers on their way from Seattle to Oregon.

Outside of the volunteer cadre, Perot looked like he was continuing to consolidate popular support. Despite his consistent anti-union behavior as an employer, and their organizations' formal support for Clinton, labor leaders reported the rank and file expressing friendly curiosity about Boss Ross. The head of the Texas AFL-CIO told NPR's *Morning Edition*, "Let me assure you, he is—he is very much—particularly in the interest of the workers, the things that impress workers. For an example . . . how many employers would risk public embarrassment, financial loss, etc. to venture in to get his employees out of Iran? That's very impressive for workers, any worker, union or otherwise." The United Auto Workers remembered Electronic Data Systems' union-busting moves when they were joined with General Motors. Pete Kelly, of UAW Local 160 in Warren, Michigan, glumly reflected on the appeal of hollow populist rhetoric: "A lot of working people, including people in the UAW, voted for Ronald Reagan, OK? And it's not until after, you know, eight years of Reagan and another four years of Bush that people understand as to—what the Reagan and Bush administration has done. Quite frankly, Perot is to the right of Bush, OK? I mean, he's more conservative and probably even more anti-union than Bush."

Tensions were developing between the volunteers and the "whiteshirts," the field operatives recruited from the ranks of Perot Systems, mostly young military veterans sporting crew cuts, rigorously observing the company dress code, and following a top-down chain of command that went all the way up to the boss. The volunteers had taken to heart Perot's vow that he was "buying the country back" for its "rightful owners," and they expected that the movement would be their own, but Perot's need for control overrode his populist rhetoric: the whiteshirts descended on regional offices and began to micromanage and even strong-arm longtime organizers and push them out of the movement. From the perspective of the operatives, they were creating the disciplined organization necessary to win, tamping down factional infighting that had broken out and purging unreliable and untrustworthy staff. The volunteers were mostly of middle age or older, and they did not like being bossed around by the younger staffers. Others had stronger words. After the whiteshirts pushed out Jack Gargan, one of the earliest people to encourage Perot to run, he told *Larry King Live* that there was widespread dissatisfaction with the field operatives among the volunteer cadre: "I've heard the word 'Gestapo,' 'The Dallas Mafia.' It's incredible." Volunteers complained of harassment and intimidation, some even claiming that they were being targeted by orchestrated smear campaigns in the press or that they received anonymous death threats through the phone. One former leader said that the whiteshirts used "tactics from Nazi Germany . . . they slandered, brow-beat, vilified and intimidated us." One former campaign staffer attributed their zeal to becoming a fiefdom of their own and their fealty to the chief: "They were very decent people, they just got way too caught up in allegiance to Caesar; they were very suspicious." For the most part, even volunteers shunted to the side still tended to admire and support Perot and believed he was unaware of the actions of the field operatives.

The biggest strains in the Perot campaign were emerging at the very top. In order to move the campaign toward a more permanent footing, Perot had decided to hire two political professionals, Jimmy Carter's former chief of staff Hamilton Jordan and Ed Rollins, the director of the 1984 Reagan-Bush campaign, but Perot never entirely trusted them and refused to delegate important tasks. Rollins was used to "directing" the former actor Reagan, but Perot would not cooperate. Perot was scheduled to address the NAACP in Nashville, and his press secretary Jim Squires, a veteran journalist, cautioned him not to tell his down-home stories of his friendly encounters with Black people as he was growing up in Texarkana.

The NAACP speech started out fine enough. "You have made tremendous progress in your work, but there's more to be done. There's more to be done. I hope before I turn out the lights that every single American is looked on as an absolute first-class full partner in our country without all the biases and prejudices." There were applause and cheers as Perot turned to the deficit and the wave of layoffs and unemployment. "And I say with that in the background, financially at least it's going to be a long, hot summer, right? And I don't have to tell you who gets hurt first when this sort of thing happens, do I? Y— You—Your people do. Your people do. I know that, you know that." An icy, cavernous silence fell on the ballroom; Perot looked visibly uncomfortable. A voice in the audience jeered. Perot: "I didn't understand you, sir." He pressed on to the stories. Tales of his parents' benevolent treatment of elderly Black employees and Black hobos in the Depression, of going to the Black church and loving the singing, failed to win the crowd back over. Evidently Perot was unaware of how badly it went until he found all the reporters hounding him outside. "I didn't realize I upset anybody . . . I apologize." Privately, he was furious, feeling it was another "setup." Jesse Jackson's brief flirtation with supporting Perot quickly fizzled.

But the most deranging preoccupation for Perot was becoming "Republican dirty tricks." The source of this notion was one Scott Barnes, a former soldier with a failed career in law enforcement who claimed to have connections to Special Forces and the intelligence community. Even among the "Rambo Set," the seediest fringes of the POW/MIA community, Barnes had a low reputation as a fake and a falsifier. In 1981, he had tagged along on one of Bo Gritz's expeditions to Thailand and claimed that they had found POWs in Laos but also that they had received a sinister order from the CIA to "liquidate the merchandise." When he returned to the states, *Soldier of Fortune* magazine did a feature on Barnes titled "My Favorite Flake." Gritz also disputes his account. In the mid-1980s, a reporter named David Taylor had connected Barnes and Perot. Perot began calling Barnes regularly and, according to Barnes, paying him. Barnes fed him stories about POW/MIA issues and other high-level government conspiracies. In 1986 Taylor videotaped Barnes—who'd been injected with sodium amytal, so-called "truth serum"—swearing up and down to his POW stories. Present at the taping was also an attorney who worked with

Perot on trying to acquire the purported "slave labor" tape of POWs. In 1987 Barnes published a book called *BOHICA: A True Account of One Man's Battle to Expose the Most Heinous Cover-up of the Vietnam Saga!* and became a favorite of POW conspiracists. ("BOHICA" stands for "Bend over, here it comes again.") The National League of Families of American Prisoners called the book "exploitation at its most obvious, and worst."

During the '92 campaign, Barnes started calling GOP operatives and telling them he had compromising information about Perot. They seemed to show no interest. At the same time, he was telling Perot that Republicans were conducting a clandestine operation against him. In particular, Barnes told Perot that Republicans had tapped his phone and also planned to ruin his daughter's August wedding by releasing doctored photos of her in a compromising lesbian tryst. The newspapers were talking about his attempts to gin up business in Hanoi. As mid-July rolled around, polls showed Perot's numbers tanking. The carefully constructed myth of Perot was fading fast, being replaced with something risible, a target of *Saturday Night Live*'s lampoons. Frustration, paranoia, and recrimination took over campaign headquarters. All the contradictions inherent in the notion of a "populist billionaire"—a folksy man of the people who also demanded drill and perfection, a democratic mass movement that hinged on the whims and fancies of a single eccentric, an anti-political political campaign, a selfless servant of the people whose entire life was devoted to self-promotion—were rapidly becoming manifest. To his staff, Perot grumbled about "pulling the plug on the whole thing."

In New York, Democrats were gearing up for their convention, a bit tensely. Clinton seemed to be holding things together. Voters appeared to like his safe pick of Tennessee senator Al Gore as a running mate. Jesse Jackson concluded his talk show by endorsing Clinton, albeit without much enthusiasm. Jerry Brown still had not endorsed Clinton. Pennsylvania's pro-choice governor Bob Casey, of *Planned Parenthood v. Casey*, wanted to address the convention and was complaining that he had been given the cold shoulder. New York City had fallen off its 1990 crime highs, but still averaged more than two thousand murders a year. The national perception of New York was as dark, dirty, and dangerous. It fell to Democratic mayor Dinkins to clean things up and keep the peace during the convention. Manhattan DA Robert Morgenthau and the mayor's director of Midtown Enforcement announced a crackdown on brothels a month ahead of the event; officials were hoping to avoid embarrassing headlines. A dozen hotels in Midtown were set on fire in the month before Democrats were due at Madison Square Garden; the NYPD arrested a homeless teen who they said was responsible for half of them. New York had avoided a conflagration in the wake of Rodney King, but the previous year's rioting in Crown Heights, which pitted Blacks against Orthodox Jews, still hung heavy.

The city issued dozens of permits for demonstrations ahead of the convention and police braced for rioting. The *Palm Beach Post* correspondent called it "Protest City," quipping, "You need a scorecard to keep track of all the discontent blossoming around the Democratic National Convention." Lenora Fulani and Al Sharpton led a thousand protesters with signs raging that JESSE CAN'T DELIVER OUR VOTE and JESSE IS A SELLOUT. Advocates for homeless people's rights doled out thousands of free meals for the hungry. A group of Vietnam vets demanded more investigations into live prisoners. Pro-life demonstrators picketed thirty-one clinics citywide and paraded around with a nineteen-week-old aborted fetus in a container. The next day, they tried to push the fetus on Clinton while he was leaving his hotel for his morning jog. "They tried to hand it to me, but I wouldn't take it," Clinton told reporters. WHAT IF IT HAD BEEN A GUN? the front page of *Newsday* breathlessly asked. But the biggest demonstration was a crowd of more than ten thousand AIDS activists who marched from Columbus Circle to Times Square.

Inside Madison Square Garden, only a group of disgruntled Jerry Brown delegates were standing in the way of the "love fest" for Clinton. Shouting matches broke out on the convention floor. One Brown delegate wrapped a torn bedsheet around her mouth to signify that she had been censored. Cries of "Let Jerry Speak" greeted each speaker. Hillary Clinton's address to the California delegation was drowned out by "Let Jerry Speak." Even when Brown finally addressed the hall, his supporters chanted "Let Jerry speak." Still, on the whole, things went smoothly, according to plan. The buzz on the convention floor turned from angry arguments between Brown and Clinton delegates to excitement over the news that Ed Rollins, Perot's campaign comanager, had resigned. Something was up. Mario Cuomo summoned all his powers of oratory to nominate "the Comeback Kid." Then, on Thursday morning, the news broke: Perot announced that he was dropping out. He even cited the "revitalized Democratic Party" as part of his decision. But not everyone in the Clinton camp shared in the jubilation. Hillary Clinton smelled a rat: she thought Perot was faking a withdrawal to stage a dramatic comeback in the fall.

In his acceptance speech, Clinton reached out to would-be Perot voters. "I am well aware that all those millions of people who rallied to Ross Perot's cause wanted to be in an army of patriots for change. Tonight I say to them, join us, and together we will revitalize America." The address was yet another of the candidate's "New Covenant" speeches, with an obligatory reference to his old professor Dr. Carroll Quigley, "who said to us that America was the greatest Nation in history because our people had always believed in two things—that tomorrow can be better than today and that every one of us has a personal moral responsibility to make it so." The New Covenant would change everything and also keep it all the same—"a new choice based on old values": "In the end, my fellow Americans, this New Covenant simply asks us all to be Americans again—old-fashioned Americans for a new time. Opportunity, responsibility, community."

The consensus among commentators was that the speech was adequate: not a "home run," but it got the job done. The moderate message got through. Cuomo's and even Al Gore's speeches got better marks.

And to some, the mention of Quigley vibrated at a frequency only they could hear. John Elvin wrote in his gossipy *Washington Times* column, "Poor Mr. Quigley—he didn't live to see a day when one candidate, George Bush, would staunchly advocate the New World Order, and the other, Mr. Clinton, would be a proud member of the Trilateral Commission and would sing Mr. Quigley's praises in his acceptance speech." In her syndicated column, Phyllis Schlafly, vanquisher of the Equal Rights Amendment, former John Birch Society member, and now one of the country's most famous conservative activists, also noted the reference. "The singling out of Mr. Quigley was curious," she wrote. "Mr. Quigley described the conflict between grassroots Americans and the big financial interests as 'the Midwest of Tom Sawyer against the cosmopolitan East.' Bill Clinton may look like just a poor guy from Hope, Ark., but he is no Tom Sawyer. He learned a lot from his mentor about how things happen in America. When he became a Rhodes Scholar, he tied in with the power centers and learned how to tap into the country's financial moguls. If Mr. Clinton is elected president, will the man from Hope, Ark., make the 'Hope' from Carroll Quigley's book our national goals and policies?" But the party had pulled together, the convention was a success. The momentum had swung in their favor. For once, Democrats were feeling good.

Feeling less good was Perot's suddenly demobilized army. AMERICAN DREAM ENDS IN DESPAIR ran the headline in the *Orlando Sentinel*. "People have been calling in crying," Ken Wood, a volunteer, told *The Seattle Times*. "I was answering the phones, but I was crying, too, so it didn't do any good." Disappointment and shock were turning into feelings of betrayal and anger. "The party is over," an L.A. county volunteer bitterly remarked. "Now the hero, the man in the white hat, turns out to be just another . . . rat." Another volunteer joked about taking barbiturates and drinking a bottle of Jack Daniel's. At the Ventura County headquarters, volunteers pulled down the eight-foot sculpture of Perot, placed a noose around its neck, and forklifted it into a dumpster. In Long Beach, a man who said he had spent more than $2,000 supporting Perot flew a massive twenty-by-forty-foot ELECT ROSS PEROT flag upside down. In Florida, volunteers refused to accept it: headquarters faxed the state's eleven subsidiary offices: "Florida demands that he run for President. We refuse to pull out."

If Perot's withdrawal was all theater, it was being performed in a convincing manner. At Dallas main headquarters, the whiteshirts were shutting everything down with their military precision: going from office to office with walkie-talkies, unhooking computers, and disconnecting phone lines. "What is this, Nazi Germany? They're boarding the buses for Buchenwald. They're taking us to Buchenwald!" a campaign staffer was yelling through a rolled-up tube of paper. "The train for Buchenwald leaves at five!"

Perot quickly started sending mixed signals out to his heartbroken volunteers. He was going to leave his name on the ballot. On Friday, he was back on *Larry King Live.* "In a sense, you're still sort of hanging that leaf out." "That's the magic, Larry." "If they don't satisfy your people, your people should protest vote for you?" "They have that option."

Volunteers were looking around for an alternative. Some turned to Bo Gritz, recently nominated as candidate for the Populist Party, the former vehicle for David Duke. Gritz's campaign manager claimed to receive pledges of support from Perot's former chiefs in New York, West Virginia, Ohio, and Georgia. The former Green Beret was traveling across the western states, a POW/MIA flag draped across his podium, encouraging audiences at his campaign stops to form citizen militias. Using an obscure part of the U.S. Code, he even claimed to be able to draft them into an "unorganized militia" through a show of hands.

The two remaining major candidates were scrambling after Perot's people. It wasn't going all that well for Bush. At a POW/MIA event in Crystal City, Virginia, the crowd put the president's speech on hold for five minutes as they chanted "No more lies!" and "Bush must go!" Secret Service agents inserted themselves in front of the dais to block the president, who stood away from the microphone, an awkward rictus painted on his face. When the crowd finally settled, Bush appeared to be conciliatory. "This is very emotional, understandably emotional," he said, setting his jaw. "The thing I would say to you, however, as a veteran, one who still wears my Navy wings from time to time, I hope you understand how I feel about patriotism, about service to my country, and I will put my record up against anybody here." This just provoked the crowd, which began to heckle and yell again. "Would you please be quiet and let me finish?" He started to raise his voice. "*Would you please shut up and sit down?*"

Getting the Buchanan Brigades back into the fold was becoming imperative. In late July, Bush's people surrendered to Bay Buchanan's demands: Pat would get his prime-time speech, on the first night, right before Ronald Reagan's. In his *Los Angeles Times* column, Murray Rothbard celebrated the detente with a lukewarm endorsement of the president: "At last, Bush has shown some smarts, and perhaps even a spark of a sense of justice. After a vicious and despicable smear campaign by Rich Bond, William Bennett, Dan Quayle et al., the Bush people—while of course not apologizing—are at least implicitly repudiating their own smears by rolling out the welcome mat for Buchanan." Rothbard then turned his guns on the Clintons, particularly on Hillary: "Sure, they cleaned up her act until November; they shut her up, bobbed and blonded her hair and took that damned headband off, and made her look like a sophisticated matron instead of an aging grad student. But if Clinton wins in November, Hillary will be back: in control, nasty, tough and very leftist." Particularly galling to Rothbard, whose form of libertarianism advocated total parental ownership of children, was Mrs. Clinton's advocacy for children's rights.

> Hillary is the prophet of the children's "rights" movement, a movement that encourages 11-year-olds to sue their parents for "malpractice," and you know who will really be doing the suing: leftist ACLU-type lawyers in the mold of Hillary . . . A vote for Bill Clinton is a vote to destroy the last vestige of parental control

> and responsibility in America. A victory for Bush will—at least partly—hold back the hordes for another four years. Of course, that is not exactly soul-satisfying. What would be soul-satisfying would be taking the offensive at long last, launching a counter-revolution in government, in the economy, in the culture, everywhere against malignant left-liberalism. When oh when do we get to start?

Maybe sooner rather than later. In Houston, the mood was gloomy and a bit anxious. Bush's loyalists on the platform committee had easily beat back an attempt by pro-choice delegates to soften the party's hard-line 100 percent no abortion plank, but it left a bitter tinge in the air. Delegates felt that the party needed a shot in the arm. "There's a real concern about Bush's message, which has to be different this time. There's a mood of 'throw out the incumbents' and clearly an element of voter dissatisfaction," a Virginia delegate told *The Washington Times.* Houston itself, overcast and muggy, seemed to be in a bad mood. The correspondent wrote, "Houston, which got up and dusted itself off after the '80s oil bust only to be knocked down again by the national recession, is rather cranky lately. Maybe it's just August, with the unbearable temperatures. But a recent Rice University poll shows the city's mood at its lowest in years. The famed can-do spirit seems a tad forced." PBS's Mark Shields found the crowd on the floor to be "pessimistic." CNN's William Schneider spoke of "a Republican coalition that is about to collapse."

Fearful of leaks, Buchanan jealously guarded his speech, but eventually he had to relent and show it to Bush's advisers. They approved and faxed it to the president, who wrote back, "Thumbs up!" CBS's Dan Rather, broadcasting from the convention, got a copy shortly before it was delivered: "A lot of applause here as our convention builds to the point—but first we're going to hear from Pat Buchanan, and the Pat Buchanan speech is out in printed form and it is what is known in politics as raw meat. This is not just red meat that Pat Buchanan's going to talk about tonight. It's already been called by some of the reporters here speech tartare. That's how rough and tough it is."

After quick congratulations to Bush and promising his support, Buchanan immediately started swinging in a harsh, steely voice. "My friends, like many of you last month, I watched that giant masquerade ball up at Madison Square Garden—where 20,000 liberals and radicals came dressed up as moderates and centrists—in the greatest single exhibition of cross-dressing in American political history." Buchanan went on to praise Reagan's legacy for several minutes before offering Bush as an adjunct figure. Then back to bashing the liberals. "When the Irish-Catholic governor of Pennsylvania, Robert Casey, asked to say a few words on behalf of the 25 million unborn children destroyed since *Roe v. Wade*, Bob Casey was told there was no place for him at the podium at Bill Clinton's convention, no room at the inn. Yet a militant leader of the homosexual rights movement could rise at that same convention and say: 'Bill Clinton and Al Gore represent the most pro-lesbian and pro-gay ticket in history.' And so they do." A furious roar from the crowd.

The country was in a grave spiritual crisis—a war: "My friends, this election is about more than who gets what. It is about who we are. It is about what we believe, and what we stand for as Americans. There is a religious war going on in this country. It is a cultural war, as critical to the kind of nation we shall be as was the Cold War itself, for this war is for the soul of America. And in that struggle for the soul of America, Clinton & Clinton are on the other side, and George Bush is on our side. And so, to the Buchanan Brigades out there, we have to come home and stand beside George Bush."

Buchanan turned to his memories of the campaign trail. "There were those workers at the James River Paper Mill, in Northern New Hampshire in a town called Groveton—tough, hearty men. None of them would say a word to me as I came down the line, shaking their hands one by one. They were under a threat of losing their jobs at Christmas. And as I moved down the line, one tough fellow about my age just looked up and said to me, 'Save our jobs.'" He reminded the Republicans that they could not rely solely on the country club set and spoke of a broader conservative constituency. "My friends, these people are our people. They don't read Adam Smith or Edmund Burke, but they come from the same schoolyards and the same playgrounds and towns as we come from. They share our beliefs and convictions, our hopes and our dreams. They are the conservatives of the heart. They are our people. And we need to reconnect with them. We need to let them know we know how bad they're hurting. They don't expect miracles of us, but they need to know we care."

The speech's furious coda referred to the riots in Los Angeles—"the worst riot in American history." Buchanan recalled speaking to the National Guardsmen who told him a story of defending an old-age home from looters. "The troopers came up the street, M-16s at the ready. And the mob threatened and cursed, but the mob retreated because it had met the one thing that could stop it: force, rooted in justice, and backed by moral courage . . . And as those boys took back the streets of Los Angeles, block by block, my friends, we must take back our cities, and take back our culture, and take back our country. God bless you, and God bless America." The story about the old folks' home in L.A. wasn't quite true: when the Eighteenth Cavalry arrived on May 1, there was no mob threatening the home; elderly residents had stood guard over their own retirement community.

Presenting the country as beset by tragic job losses and locked in apocalyptic conflict was perhaps not the best message for the incumbent's side. But Buchanan had, in fact, toned things down: there was no mention of "America First," no "nationalism," no "Middle American revolution." It was a hard-edged form of Reaganism. Too hard-edged, as it turned out, even for Reagan himself: he wasn't happy with the speech; it was too dark; it ran over and pushed his own out of prime time, and he didn't like the gay bashing. On the floor, the speech whipped the delegates into a frenzy, but the party leadership was uneasy. The president's son, George W. Bush, was overheard by a journalist, remarking, "This is disastrous." Governor Tom Kean, the head of the New Jersey delegation, told CBS's Connie Chung on the floor, "Well, Pat Buchanan represents the far right of the party. He turns a phrase very well. There were some wonderful phrases in that speech. But there are also some views that the rest of us don't subscribe to. But, you know, he represents the far right of the party. The majority of—the majority of the people here represent other points of view, but everybody's come together behind the president." Or, as Molly Ivins would later quip in *The Nation*, "Many people did not like Buchanan's speech; it probably sounded better in the original German."

For their part, TV anchors praised Buchanan for his use of rhetoric. ABC's David Brinkley said, "It was an astoundingly good speech." Ted Koppel: "They walked out of here tonight enthusiastic, they walked out of here with something the Republicans have not had for quite a few months, a sense of optimism."

It wouldn't last: delegates went home let down after Bush's acceptance speech. "There is no enthusiasm, no energy" . . . "It is certainly not the kind of electrifying experience I expected" . . . "It doesn't seem to have the fire" were some of the remarks from the delegates. The crowd seemed to get most jazzed up when Bush admitted that going back on the "no new taxes" pledge had been a mistake.

As for Buchanan, the delegates had loved the speech, but the RNC leadership hadn't. "The convention got out of hand," a convention planner would tell William Safire. "We had in mind stressing the good family values, positive stuff that nobody can complain about. But we gave Buchanan prime time at the start—what a mistake—and he let loose with all the vicious stuff. Then, when our innocuous family values came on, it was tainted—we seemed to be endorsing Pat's gay-bashing and the platform's 100 percent anti-abortion plank." In a *Times* op-ed Garry Wills declared George Bush the "Prisoner of the Crazies": "The crazies are in charge. The fringe has taken over." A year earlier, Wills recalled, the televangelist Pat Robertson had published *The New World Order*, "arguing that the President's gulf war, his proudest achievement, was part of a diabolic plot to destroy America. By submitting to the U.N. and calling the world to its banner, President Bush was proclaiming the New World Order of the Antichrist. Near the original site of Babylon, the United Nations was raising a new Tower of Babel to challenge God's supremacy." Now Robertson was speaking at the convention. And a month later, in *The New York Review of Books*, Wills put his finger on the center of Buchanan's speech: "While some are talking about postwar conversion problems in terms of phasing out the cold war military establishment, Buchanan thinks of conversion as a turning of energies from an outer enemy to an inner one."

11

THE HOWLING WILDERNESS

On August 21, 1992, the day after the Republican National Convention ended in Houston, the Associated Press newswire announced, MARSHAL SHOT AND KILLED NEAR CABIN OF FEDERAL FUGITIVE. The cabin, in the wilds of the Idaho Panhandle just forty miles south of the Canadian border, belonged to Randy Weaver, the "federal fugitive," and his wife, Vicki Weaver. The Weavers had moved nine years earlier from Iowa with their three children to a remote promontory in the Selkirk Mountains, called Ruby Ridge. There they built their shelter from scratch over the course of several years; it had no running water or electricity. They had another child. They lived the life of settlers, pioneers of a century or two earlier. Why did the Weavers make this errand into the wilderness? Much for the same reasons the Puritan settlers came to America: to escape a corrupted world and found a new one in conformity with God's teachings. There would be no "New Covenant" for them: they followed the laws of the Old Covenant, called God "Yahweh," and, like the Puritans in New England, thought themselves to be the Israelites of the Bible. And, also like those old Puritans, they believed the End was at hand; all the signs of the modern world pointed to the coming Apocalypse. But before the reign of Christ would come the Antichrist.

Shortly before they left Iowa in late 1982, the Weavers were interviewed in their living room in Cedar Falls by the Waterloo *Courier.* "The Bible teaches that somewhere near during the reign of the one world leader, God will remove the restraining hand from Satan, the destroyed, and let him wreak havoc on the inhabitants of the earth for a period of time known as the great tribulation," Randy told the paper. To prepare for this tribulation, the Weavers had acquired "several military assault rifles and shotguns as well as a variety of handguns and more than 4,000 rounds of ammunition." They had already put their home up for sale and revealed their plans to move out West, to the mountains of Idaho. Neighbors were concerned that they had formed a cult.

The Weavers once seemed to be the most mainstream and conventional of Americans, sturdy heartland folk, yet they had moved to the very edge of the country. When they were dating as kids back in Iowa, their friends joked that they were "the all-American couple." Vicki Jordison grew up on a farm. Her mother was a Congregationalist and her father a member of a branch of the Mormons, the Reorganized Church of the Latter Day Saints. Both churches had strong concepts of election: the Calvinist Congregationalists, originating in the earliest Puritan churches, believed in a predestined elect; the Mormons taught that they were God's chosen people, the Israelites of Scripture, and that America was a modern Zion. Randy Weaver's father was an agricultural supplies salesman, but the family lived on a working farm. He took his children on a tour of Protestant churches—Evangelical, Baptist, Presbyterian—but none of them were quite strict enough. Weaver recalled growing up in a typical 1950s idyll, listening to *The Lone Ranger* on the radio and watching *The Big Picture* on TV, a documentary series about the Korean War, which he remembered being about World War II. "Watching this and saying 'The Pledge of

Allegiance' every morning gave me a strong sense of patriotism," he would later write. But according to Weaver, the patriotism was tinged with distrust of government as well, brought on by the experience of losing the family farm during the Depression.

Out of a sense of patriotic duty, Randy Weaver enlisted in the army in 1968. He joined the Airborne Corps and trained with the Special Forces as a Green Beret. He wanted to ship out to Vietnam, but was instead stationed stateside at Fort Bragg. He later wrote that he was "disappointed" that he was never sent to Southeast Asia. Weaver witnessed disillusion with the war and corruption in the military. He thought both the anti-war protesters and the government itself were trying to lose the war. He told friends that he participated in a narcotics bust at the base, but he strongly suspected that the military police just pocketed the drugs for themselves.

Randy moved back to Iowa, started driving a Mustang, and grew his hair out; he proposed to Vicki. They got married in a Congregationalist church but an RLDS pastor shared responsibilities in the ceremony. After trying to sell Amway products to their hometown friends, the couple moved to Cedar Falls so Randy could go to college on the G.I. Bill. He still wanted to serve his country and become an FBI or Secret Service agent, and he quit college after a few semesters and instead went to work at the John Deere tractor plant in Waterloo, where wages were good. Vicki's sister Julie got married to a rock musician who opposed the Vietnam War, but Vicki and Randy were getting into another counterculture. Randy tried to convince friends to buy precious metals to avoid the Federal Reserve's currency devaluation. But the real moment of revelation for the Weavers came when Vicki read *The Late Great Planet Earth* by Hal Lindsey.

First published in 1970, *The Late Great Planet Earth* was the best-selling nonfiction book of that decade. It led to a prime-time TV special and a documentary narrated by Orson Welles. It was one of the primary texts of the so-called Jesus People, a charismatic movement that grew out of the wreckage of the hippie counterculture and proposed evangelical Christianity as the solution to the feeling of living in a heartless world and in a society that had lost its way. Written in the chatty argot of self-help, *The Late Great Planet Earth* did not augur the dawning of the Age of Aquarius: it was a book of biblical prophecy that foresaw the Apocalypse at hand. Drawing on the books of Ezekiel, Daniel, and Revelation, Lindsey gives particular centrality to Israel as a sign of the end-times: the foundation of the state in 1948 and the capture of Jerusalem in 1967 were to be imminently followed by the rebuilding of the Temple, a sure sign of the Second Coming of Jesus Christ. The book predicts the battle of Armageddon in the form of a war between Israel and the Soviet Union, identified as the forces of Gog from the Bible. The Jews are placed at the center of world history but given an ambivalent role. One the one hand, their return to the Promised Land is celebrated as a necessary prelude to the Messianic Age; on the other, the hostility of the Jews to Jesus is persuasive evidence: "If there is one thing that guarantees the historical accuracy of what the New Testament authors wrote it is the animosity of the Jewish people who crucified Jesus . . . If those who crucified Jesus could have disproved any of the historical realities of these events they would have done so and destroyed the whole movement from the beginning. But they didn't bring up any refutation of the facts of fulfilled prophecy; instead they put to death the persons who were proclaiming the facts."

The Baptist Church in Waterloo soon proved unsatisfactory to the Weavers. Other congregations also failed to grab their imagination. Faith and ideas came through the media: cable evangelism like the *PTL Club*, Pat Robertson's *The 700 Club*, and Jerry Falwell. There were such books as Ayn Rand's *Atlas Shrugged*, however atheistic; Ralph Woodrow's *Babylon Mystery Religion*, which proposed a connection between ancient Babylonian paganism and the Roman Catholic Church; and *None Dare Call It Conspiracy*, by Gary Allen, which used Carroll Quigley's work as evidence of a vast cabal comprising the financiers of the Eastern Establishment and international communism. Then there were endless newsletters, pamphlets, comics, and tapes. Randy Weaver would go down to a local diner and gab with like-minded folks or preach to the unconvinced. Vicki Weaver wanted to homeschool the kids, but that wasn't permitted in Iowa. The couple brought prominent conspiracists to town to give lectures.

This was not all just the lonely crusade of an isolated family. Apprehension, fear, and unease blanketed the Great Plains in the late 1970s and early '80s. High commodity prices driven by inflation and global demand for American crops had brought prosperity to the region's farmers. They were encouraged by Nixon's secretary of agriculture Earl Butz to "go big or go home" and "plant fencerow to fencerow." Low interest rates meant they could borrow to acquire more land, bigger combine harvesters and tractors, modern fertilizers, genetically modified seeds, pesticides, and herbicides. So long as the prices of crops went up, so did the value of land. Lenders drove up and down country roads practically begging farmers to take more loans.

While farmers integrated with the global economy, the new high-productivity farming was lonelier, if less tedious and difficult, work. At the beginning of the century, farmers made up about a quarter of the population, now they made up around 2 percent. You needed far fewer people to work a farm that was outfitted with tractors and combines. Attracted to the efficiency and the ideal of being self-reliant, the farmers found the new machinery irresistible. But that got rid of the communal spirit of threshing and harvesting season. "I would never want to go back to the past, plowing four acres a day with a team of horses. I'm just saying the sense of fellowship is gone, replaced by machinery," one veteran farmer reflected. With each farm supposedly a self-reliant unit but actually more dependent than ever on the market, neighbors became competitors. "The farmers who survive—often wealthy, aggressive men—consolidate, picking up the place next door, the piece of land down the road. The enemy of the family farmer is, as much as the corporation, the family farmer next door," wrote William Serrin for *The New York Times* in 1979. Family farms looked less and less like the Jeffersonian ideal of independent yeomen and more like a factory, and the family itself more like a corporation: the lines between agribusiness and family farming blurred, with even some of the biggest producers being "family owned" while operating on an industrial scale. The subsidies developed during the New Deal to save family farms were more likely to pad the profits of a sprawling concern than to save a smallholder from going under in a bad year.

All the growth in productivity and capacity proved to be as much a curse as a blessing when agricultural prices started to fall. By 1977 there was a surplus; production costs were higher than prices. Adjusted for inflation, total farm incomes were at their lowest point since the Great Depression. Then there was a drought: Dust Bowl conditions returned. In response to their plight, some farmers in the Plains mobilized, forming the American Agriculture Movement. The AAM proposed a farm strike that would stop production, draw attention to their plight, and seek to gain national support for "parity," that is to say, subsidies that would permit farmers to maintain their purchasing power amidst fluctuations in the market for their products. Few farmers actually ended up participating in the strike, a sign of the difficulty of coordinating action among such a far-flung and atomized population, with each one looking after their own concerns.

The AAM tried another tactic: "tractorcades." In January 1978, thousands of farmers drove their tractors into Washington, D.C., to demonstrate. The tractorcades made the farmers visible to the urban population. Maybe too visible. While city dwellers publicly sympathized with the Jeffersonian rhetoric the AAM employed about the family farm being the basis of a wholesome and democratic society, the appearance of the tractors seemed to contradict the mythos: this massive and often very expensive machinery, replete with stereos and air-conditioning, did not suggest a struggling peasantry, even if it was all bought largely on credit. The farmers also made themselves a nuisance, causing heavy traffic and paralyzing commutes.

When the tractorcade returned in February 1979, the tone turned uglier: the farmers burned a tractor in front of the Capitol and tipped a combine onto the White House lawn. Urbanites gave them the cold shoulder, disdaining the sight of these epitomes of American rugged individualism and self-reliance essentially asking for government welfare. They looked more like any other businessmen than like Jefferson's yeomen. The farmers returned to their fields, even more sullen and angry, open to more radical views.

Then everything really went to hell. The Federal Reserve chairman Paul Volcker's drastic interest rate hikes, designed to fight rampant inflation, devastated commodity prices and made the debts of farmers onerous. The new strength of the dollar made American crops look unattractive to the foreign markets that had once gobbled them up. The expansion in capacity that once enriched farmers had actually sowed the seeds of disaster: there was a glut, overproduction. The loans the farmers had taken out were backed by the land, and when they could not pay them, they lost the farms.

Iowa was the worst-hit state. As farms went under, rural communities collapsed. Farm implements sales plummeted, local retail outlets like grocery stores and gas stations disappeared, the state's population dipped as birth rates fell and people left to look for work elsewhere. The local banks that lent to the farmers started to fail. Then manufacturing, especially if it built farm equipment, went: the sector lost a quarter of its jobs between 1979 and the mid-1980s. The Farm Crisis of that decade, an economist at the University of Iowa would write in 1988, represented "a pattern of economic and social disintegration unparalleled since the Great Depression." Suicides and "family annihilations" were on the rise. One in six Iowans fell under the poverty line. All the ills associated with inner-city life started to show up in Iowa: drugs, crime, rampant unemployment, and, most perversely among conditions of agricultural overproduction, hunger.

The John Deere plant in Waterloo where Randy Weaver worked started to lay off workers: 300 in 1980, 1,300 more in 1982, and then 400 more that same year. In 1984, when Reagan campaigned in Waterloo, UAW Local 838 set up a soup kitchen across the street from the rally to drive the point home. By that time, the president of the local claimed that five thousand union members in Waterloo had lost their jobs. Still, John Deere remained profitable, largely because they were employing new technology and automating their plants. Computers now controlled production at the Waterloo tractor works: workers would plug codes into a terminal and robots would cast and machine the parts. Machinists like Weaver were no longer much in demand. It's probably not surprising then that the Weavers' paranoid fantasies started to center on computers: to them, the Beast of Revelation signified computers and the number "666," serial and credit card numbers. "The beast, Randy said, was a metaphor for computers. Soon, everything would be catalogued on computer: births, schooling, purchases, homes. And every credit card, connected as they are by computers, would mark people with the number of the beast, Vicki said. Of course, once the currency was devalued and finally changed, no man could buy or sell without a credit card, without 666," wrote Jess Walter in his book on the Weavers.

There was the paradox of plenty among the poverty. Iowa farmhouses looked run-down, with peeling paint and cracked walls, but inside, the houses were often stocked with brand-new consumer electronics. In the driveway of a farm that looked forsaken there might be a brand-new tractor, bought on credit of course. As long as Randy could stay employed at John Deere, the money was pretty good. He could afford to treat himself to a Corvette, motorcycles, snowmobiles, fishing gear. He could get a ranch house for his family in Cedar Falls. But this material plenty could not fill the sense that something was missing for the Weavers, and their most greedy acquisitiveness went toward collecting explanations in the form of conspiracy literature.

On the shop floor of the Waterloo plant, Weaver apparently encountered an Aryan Nations member who was spreading the message of a neo-Nazi group based in Idaho. The extreme right pumped the Plains states full of propaganda, sensing an opportunity in the farm crisis. Lyndon LaRouche, a former New Left activist who had started a cultlike movement and become a perennial presidential candidate, infiltrated the American Agriculture Movement, swaying some members of its leadership and propounding his kaleidoscopic conspiracy theories about the Trilateral Commission, "British-Maltese-Zionist" bankers, the queen of England, the Rockefellers, and the Federal Reserve. While running for president in 1980, LaRouche got sympathetic coverage in Iowa's press: the Waterloo *Courier* presented him as simply a "conservative Democrat" who decried the lack of "moral leadership" in D.C. Willis Carto, the founder of Liberty Lobby and the Populist Party, pushed his *Spotlight* tabloid in the Midwest, where it became favored reading by farmers hit by the crisis, reaching a circulation of around a quarter million. The paper's regular charge was that "Zionist" bankers were responsible for the plight of the family farm. It also included advertisements for other organizations, such as Richard Butler's Aryan Nations in Idaho. "Concerned about today's problems? Then grab your gun, your wife, and your kids, and head for Hayden Lake, Idaho!" read one ad. Civil society organizations sprang up with benign-sounding names like "Iowa Society for Educated Citizens," meeting in the basements of churches and family restaurants, where they brought in speakers and put out spreads of conspiracy and antisemitic pamphlets. The campaign bore fruit: a 1986 Harris Poll of residents of Iowa and Nebraska found that 27 percent of respondents agreed with the statement "Farmers have always been exploited by international Jewish bankers, who are behind those who overcharge them for farm equipment and jack up the interest on their loans." Nearly half of respondents agreed that Jews should stop complaining about what happened to them in Nazi Germany.

Along with the efforts of Carto and LaRouche, there were other tendrils of extremist infiltration in the Great Plains during the Farm Crisis, including an ideology that called itself "Christian Identity" and a related movement that called itself "Posse Comitatus." Both programs sought to graft themselves onto the roots of American culture. Christian Identity, nominally a religion, can be traced back to an idea called

"Anglo-Israelism" or "British-Israelism"—the belief that the Anglo-Saxons and other "Teutonic" peoples are descended from the lost tribes of Israel. This notion was the brainchild of an Irish autodidact named John Wilson, the son of a radical weaver who toured Britain lecturing on his "findings," which combined biblical exegesis, pseudo-philology that connected ancient Hebrew to Indo-European language through made-up etymologies, racial science, and phrenology. The analogy between the Israelites of the Bible and the community of believers was an old theme of Protestantism, with the Puritans being particularly attached to the notion that they inherited the Israelites' Covenant with God. But Wilson stipulated that the British were not just "a spiritual, or surrogate Israel" but the "literal Israel," descended by blood. Wilson's teachings would be published in 1840 as *Lectures on Our Israelitish Origin*, which also demoted actual Jews to a lower status, saying that their often swarthy complexion could be explained by their regrettable interbreeding with the children of Ham.

It might be expected that Wilson's doctrine would remain on the crackpot fringe of society from where it came, but it gained an audience in the respectable middle class. After Wilson's death, British-Israelism's primary evangelist was a bank clerk named Edward Hine, who turned the idea into a social movement with formal organizations and wrote books and pamphlets that gained a readership of millions. Anglo-Israelism attracted the attention of the astronomer Charles Piazzi Smith, who lent to it his belief that the Great Pyramid in Egypt was built by Israelites and, if interpreted with the proper mathematical formulas, could yield the precise date of the Second Coming. British-Israelism also attracted growing numbers of members of the aristocracy and military. The movement itself became a pillar of pro-imperialist sentiment in civil society.

In the late nineteenth century, British-Israelism got its first foothold in the United States through the efforts of Joseph Wild, the preacher of the Union Congregational Church in Brooklyn, who lectured and wrote and brought Hine to visit the country. It makes sense that a Congregational church, heir to the Puritan tradition of identifying America with a New Jerusalem, should have served as the gateway for Anglo-Israelism in the New World. From Brooklyn, it spread across the country and wove itself into American life as a minor strand in the quilt of the country's voluntary associations. Its adherents moved in and out of other groups that mushroomed up in the American Protestant *Urwald*—groups as different as Christian Science and the Ku Klux Klan. And like all things that came from across the sea, it gradually crept its way westward, obeying the law of Manifest Destiny.

One major stop on British-Israelism's voyage west was Detroit, where William J. Cameron, head of public relations at Ford Motor Company, the editor of Henry Ford's *The Dearborn Independent*, and principal author of that newspaper's series on "The International Jew," cofounded the Anglo-Saxon Federation of America with a New Englander named Howard Rand, described as "bland," a "faceless functionary" who delivered his lectures in a "dull monotone." While British-Israelism could lead its adherents to broadly philosemitic or Christian Zionist conclusions, Cameron, who had republished *The Protocols of the Elders of Zion*, wielded it as a justification for explicit antisemitism. The Great Depression proved to be particularly fertile years for the apocalyptic themes contained in Anglo-Israelism, and branches of the federation sprung up across the nation. In the 1930s, Cameron made an effort to link Anglo-Israelite ideology with right-wing politics, engaging in outreach through the American Coalition of Patriotic Societies, an umbrella organization of more than a hundred conservative civic groups, including the Sons of the American Revolution and the Daughters of the American Revolution.

But it was upon its arrival at the extreme edge of the nation that British-Israelism definitively morphed into Christian Identity. In the middle of the twentieth century, as Los Angeles grew into a major metropolis, the city experienced a desert bloom of cults and sects. In this environment, Anglo-Israelite beliefs combined with migrant fundamentalist preachers from the South and former members of William

Dudley Pelley's Silver Shirts—a failed attempt to create an American fascist organization—to give birth to Christian Identity. The various small congregations were united under the banner of the Huey Long lieutenant Gerald L. K. Smith, who moved operations of his Christian Nationalist Crusade to the West Coast. And it was in L.A. that the definitive theological doctrine of Identity was developed by the preacher Wesley Swift: that the Jews were not some subsidiary or impure tribe of Israel, but rather they were Satan's seed, the direct blood descendants of the devil.

Swift, who had at one point tried to revive the Klan in Los Angeles, also experimented with creating new organizations. He formed the "Great Pyramid Club," which used Israelite pyramidology as a front to bring in potential recruits. He also founded the California Rangers and the Christian Defense League. These were attempts to form armed militias backed by Christian Identity thought, but with rhetorical appeals that could reach a broader right-wing audience. These groups were active enough to draw the attention of the California attorney general by the mid-1960s.

After Swift's death, his principal protégés and followers, jockeying to inherit his mantle, split up into their own groups. These tribes wandered the country and came to settle in different places: Richard Butler moved to the Idaho Panhandle and established the Aryan Nations compound; James K. Warner ended up in Louisiana, where he linked up with David Duke; and William Potter Gale, a retired army colonel and former member of General Douglas MacArthur's staff, brought the Identity gospel to distressed farmers in the Midwest and, following the organizational entrepreneurialism of his mentor, founded Posse Comitatus. In a 1971 issue of his newsletter *Identity*, Gale published a "Guide for Volunteer Christian Posses," which claimed that "By Authority of the Constitution of the United States" the "county has always been—and remains to this day—the TRUE seat of government for the citizens who are inhabitants thereof. The County Sheriff is the only legal law enforcement officer in these United States of America." The sheriff could mobilize a posse of all men between the ages of eighteen and forty-five, but also anybody could form the posse if they so desired: "Since the Sheriff is the servant of the citizens who are inhabitants of the County, it is not his choice as to whether or not the Posse is organized and brought into being." The sheriff's posse had the responsibility to "protect citizens who are being subjected to unlawful acts by officials of government, whether these be Judges of Courts or Federal or State Agents of any kind whatsoever." These "unlawful acts" included federal intervention in schools, the income tax, the Federal Reserve System, and "unconstitutional" rulings of the judiciary. There were directions on how to form "citizen's grand juries," essentially lynch mobs, with spurious constitutional law behind them.

Copycat groups appeared, and Gale's appeals were reproduced in the literature of tax protesters and gun rights activists, along with the robust merchandising of fake sheriffs' badges, as well as a variety of bogus legal documents and warrants. Posse Comitatus chapters began popping up and spreading back eastward, over the Rockies and into the Midwest. Identity groups formed rural enclaves where they stockpiled arms. Their ranks included a group—called The Covenant, the Sword and Arm of the Lord—which operated a compound called "the Farm" in Arkansas and Elohim City, Oklahoma. Posses took part in confrontations with officials, attempting "arrests" and assaulting officials. In 1975 a Posse was called up by tomato farmers in Stockton, California, to prevent United Farm Workers union organizers from recruiting in the fields. The Posse ended up in a shootout with the actual sheriff's deputies.

With the onset of the Farm Crisis and the rise of the AAM tractorcades, Posse activists quickly saw an opportunity. James Wickstrom, an Identity believer, circulated pamphlets blaming farm foreclosures on a Jewish plot to nationalize agriculture. Failing to accomplish its goals, the AAM fell prey to the conspiratorial explanations offered by Posse Comitatus. Beset by banks and debts, the movement found tempting arguments that taxes were illegal and the Federal Reserve's currency wasn't real, and the fake legal solutions provided an apparent easy way out. By the early 1980s, taped sermons from William Gale and James Wickstrom could be regularly heard on a Dodge City, Kansas, radio station. "You're damn right I'm teaching violence," one of Gale's broadcasts declaimed. "You better start making dossiers, names, addresses, phone numbers, car license numbers, on every damn Jew rabbi in this land, and every Anti-Defamation League leader or JDL leader in this land, and you better start doing it now . . . You get these roadblock locations, where you can set up ambushes, and get it all working now." Wickstrom and Gale started giving paramilitary training to AAM farmers.

In 1983 U.S. marshals in North Dakota attempted to arrest Gordon Kahl, a farmer and Posse Comitatus member, for violating the parole of his sentence for federal income tax evasion. Kahl and his son opened fire on the marshals, killing two, then escaped and led authorities on a three-month manhunt that ended with Kahl cornered in Arkansas, dying under a hail of bullets in a burning barn. Later that same year, Robert Matthews, a regular visitor to Richard Butler's Aryan Nations, formed The Order, the group whose terror spree against what they called "Zionist Occupied Government" (ZOG) culminated in the assassination of the Denver talk radio host Alan Berg. (Matthews and his group were one of the examples of the violent, "post-bourgeois" right that Samuel Francis would later identify in his *Chronicles* column as fighting back against "dispossession.") In early 1984 James Wickstrom appeared on *Donahue* as "National Director of Posse Comitatus." In October of that year, Arthur Kirk, a deeply indebted farmer from Cairo, Nebraska, who became convinced by fake legal doctrines that his loans were illegal and could be obviated, got into a standoff with sheriff's deputies who came to take possession of crops and equipment he'd posted as collateral. Kirk told reporters that the "Jews," and the Mossad in particular, were responsible for his situation and then attempted to attack the SWAT team surrounding his farm with an AR-15. Kirk was shot and killed. In December, Robert Matthews would be gunned down after being surrounded by federal agents on an island off the coast of Washington State.

In 1983, amidst the lengthening shadows of the Farm Crisis and the onset of violent confrontations with the government, the Weavers sold their house, packed up their belongings, and headed west. The sight of their loaded truck reminded Vicki's sister Julie "of the Okies moving west, of *The Grapes of Wrath*." In Boundary County, Idaho, they found a twenty-acre mountaintop plot of land they could afford and began to build their cabin. The Weavers were not totally isolated: they began to integrate into the surrounding community, making friends with neighbors, many of whom shared their radical anti-government beliefs. The family took in a troubled local teenager named Kevin Harris. Randy ran for sheriff of Boundary County on a Posse Comitatus–inspired platform. And he brought his family down to the Aryan Nations compound in Hayden Lake, about an hour's drive away, for the group's yearly gathering. It was there, in 1986, that he met a confidential informant for the Bureau of Alcohol, Tobacco, and Firearms, posing as an outlaw biker gun dealer.

In the aftermath of The Order's terror campaign, the federal government had flooded Idaho with agents attempting to infiltrate Aryan Nations and flush out successor groups to Matthews's organization. There'd already been a wave of bombings in Coeur d'Alene. According to the government informant, in 1989 Weaver declared his intention to form a group to carry on the struggle against ZOG and also expressed interest in selling sawed-off shotguns to earn money to support his family. The government instructed the informant to follow through with the plan, which would involve Weaver in a felony. (Weaver and his attorney, Gerry Spence, would later claim that he was entrapped.) Weaver sold two illegal shotguns to the informant and then was contacted by federal agents who told him he was going to be indicted on illegal weapons charges and asked for his cooperation. He refused. Vicki Weaver wrote a letter addressed to "Aryan Nations and all our brethren in the Anglo-Saxon Race":

> We have decided to stay on this mountain, you could not drag our children away from us with chains. They are hard core and love the truth. Randy's first thought was to let them arrest him to protect his children—but he is well aware that once they have him the Feds will send agents to search and destroy our home, looking for "evidence." He knows his children—they won't let that happen to their mother.
>
> Let Yah-Yashua's perfect will be done. If it is our time, we'll go home. If it is not, we will praise his Separated Name! Halleluyah!

In 1991 ATF agents posing as stranded motorists managed to arrest Weaver. He was arraigned and released, but failed to show up for his court dates. A warrant was issued for his arrest, and the U.S. marshals took over the case. Letters from Vicki flowed into the U.S. Attorney's Office addressed "To the Servant Queen of Babylon," with lines like "Whether we live or whether we die, we will not bow to your evil commandments." Quotes from Robert Matthews particularly concerned the prosecutors. The marshals erred on the side of caution, believing it likely that the well-armed Weavers, who had just had another baby, would resist. They learned from neighbors that Weaver talked about shooting federal agents, and they also erroneously believed that he had booby-trapped the property and had a much more extensive criminal past. They tried to negotiate Weaver's surrender, but were rebuffed.

Then the media caught wind of the Weavers' holdout. A reporter from the Spokane *Spokesman-Review* broke the story in March 1992: FEDS HAVE FUGITIVE "UNDER OUR NOSE." It was quickly picked up by major newspapers and the wire services. FEDS WARY OF FLUSHING WELL-ARMED FUGITIVE, the Associated Press reported. The *Sun* tabloid buzzed the cabin with a chopper. Geraldo wanted to do an interview with the family. When the Weavers refused to speak to "Jewraldo," his crew also rented a helicopter to fly over Ruby Ridge and then claimed that Randy had fired at them while they hovered overhead the cabin. Later, the crew admitted they had probably not been fired upon.

Now the Justice Department had a public embarrassment on its hands. The U.S. attorney and the trial judge in Idaho were also particularly adamant about a quick arrest as the only acceptable outcome. The marshals had preferred to use neighbors as intermediaries to get Weaver to surrender voluntarily but now decided to insert a U.S. Marshals Special Operations Group, or SOG, team, a tactical unit that would surveil Ruby Ridge and develop a plan to seize Weaver when he was isolated. They flew surveillance aircraft over the cabin and infiltrated camouflaged commandos onto the property, armed with submachine guns and equipped with night-vision goggles. A full-fledged military operation was now being directed at one man who'd been charged with a rather minor crime. (A memo penned during the siege by Deputy FBI Director Danny Coulson called the charges "bullshit.") And it confirmed the paranoid worldview of the Weaver family that the government was bearing down with all its powers on them in particular.

On the morning of August 21, a three-man SOG recon team was creeping around the Weaver property in camouflage when their scent was picked up by the Weavers' dog. Behind the dog was Randy Weaver; Weaver's fourteen-year-old son, Sammy; and their friend Kevin Harris, all armed with rifles. The marshals emerged from cover and attempted to identify themselves. A shoot-out ensued, with both sides claiming that the other fired first. In the ensuing firefight, a U.S. marshal deputy and Sammy Weaver were shot and killed, as well as the Weavers' dog. Though the marshals hadn't planned for a confrontation, Randy Weaver took the events to be a ZOG ambush.

Within hours, hundreds of federal agents, including the FBI's elite Hostage Rescue Team outfitted with choppers and armored personnel carriers, surrounded Ruby Ridge. Their plan was purely tactical: it involved no provision for negotiations. The FBI issued "shoot-on-sight" rules of engagement permitting agents to fire on any armed person they saw. These orders were later deemed unconstitutional. Snipers took up positions overlooking the cabin. On August 22, one of those snipers, Lon Horiuchi, shot and wounded Randy Weaver as he was investigating the sound of a helicopter as it flew over the property. As Kevin Harris ran for cover in the Weavers' doorway, Horiuchi shot at him. The bullet entered the doorframe he was diving for, wounding him and also hitting Vicki Weaver—who was carrying the infant Elisheba—in the head. She was killed instantly.

At this point, unaware that Vicki Weaver had been killed, the FBI chose to attempt negotiations. Weaver believed that the FBI was taunting him and would finish off the rest of the family if they emerged from the cabin. News vans started to show up at the roadblock set up at the edge of the Weavers' driveway. There was also now a swelling crowd of sympathizers: survivalists, Christian Identity believers, neo-Nazi skinheads, but also incensed locals, camped out by the side of the road, holding vigils and signs. Weaver was becoming a folk hero even beyond the confines of the white supremacist subculture. A group of armed skinheads were caught trying to sneak onto the Weaver property, apparently in a rescue attempt or to provide reinforcements. Into this scene strode Bo Gritz, the Populist Party candidate, grandstanding in front of the cameras and the gathered crowd. "It takes Special Forces to understand Special Forces. We're not like other people," the former lieutenant colonel told reporters. He demanded to speak to the agent in charge. Refused in this, he attempted to serve a citizen's arrest on the FBI officials at the scene. Out of options, the FBI eventually relented and agreed to Gritz's offer to serve as intermediary with Weaver.

Gritz was successful. After a few days, he coaxed Kevin Harris and then Randy Weaver and the remaining children off the mountain, to be arrested by the FBI. Gritz was aided in this effort by a letter he drafted and urged the neo-Nazi skinheads to sign. When only two would agree to sign it, he forged the signatures of a few more. After coming down from the mountain to address the protesters and reporters, Gritz said, "By the way, Randy told me to give you guys a salute." Gritz raised his right arm in a Heil Hitler salute. "He said you'd know what that meant." The skinheads returned it. Gritz's campaign later claimed that it was just a wave, that he was "just trying to appeal to the masses."

The next year, Harris and Weaver would be acquitted of all charges, except for Weaver missing his court date and violating his bail. The trial turned into a total humiliation for the Department of Justice. The judge found the FBI in contempt of court for delaying and obstructing the course of the trial. The special agent in charge of the operation was censured and suspended.

Directly after the end of the siege, members of the extreme right seized on Ruby Ridge as a cause célèbre, forming Citizens United for Justice as an organization dedicated to the Weaver case. In October 1992 a Christian Identity minister named Pete Peters called for an emergency meeting at a YMCA youth camp in Estes Park, Colorado, to respond to Ruby Ridge. In attendance were Richard Butler of Aryan Nations, Klansman Louis Beam, and Militia of Montana leader John Trochmann, who had helped deliver supplies to Weaver while he was a fugitive on Ruby Ridge. But also there were members from the broader right, such as Steve Graber of the Christian right Rutherford Institute and Larry Pratt of the Gun Owners of America. Beam advocated for a strategy he called "leaderless resistance," lone-wolf attacks that could not be traced to any central organization. A fellow member of Citizens United for Justice, Identity believer, and Bo Gritz campaign volunteer named Chris Temple advocated for a united front strategy behind Weaver—a strategy that could bring in members of the Christian Right who were not explicit racists and antisemites. Weaver would be portrayed as just a Christian gun owner who above all wanted to be left alone. "All of us in our groups," Temple said in his speech, "could not have done in the next twenty years what the federal government did for our cause in eleven days in Naples, Idaho . . . What we need to do is to not let this die and go away." Larry Pratt, who had written a book called *Armed People Victorious* on anti-communist death squads in the Philippines and Guatemala, advocated for the creation of militias. Pete Peters distributed audiocassettes of speeches from the conference as well as a "Special Report on the Meeting of Christian Men Held in Estes Park, Colorado."

Earlier martyrdoms, such as the deaths of Gordon Kahl and Robert Matthews, had not elicited much sympathy beyond the subcultural world of the extreme right. In fact, Kahl's demise had brought scrutiny and had hurt the public reputation of the "Posse Comitatus" idea. Matthews and The Order had revealed the frightening truth about the far right and brought the power of the federal government to bear on it. But as successful as the state was in crushing the initial group, it could not follow up. A 1988 sedition trial of fourteen prominent members of the white supremacist movement, including Richard Butler and Louis Beam, resulted in an acquittal. The incompetent effort to turn Weaver into an informant was an extension of the investigation of The Order's support networks and possible successor groups. As the movement understood quickly, the killings of Vicki and Sammy Weaver had an entirely different appeal from earlier deaths. Here was a man who was just trying to keep his family safe from the New World Order, and when he could not escape its clutches, they went and killed his family. The story of a vast, tyrannical state intent on crushing white Christian Americans now looked plausible. Weaver's ties to the farthest fringe of politics would be played down. He was just an eccentric minding his own business. The "tragedy of Ruby Ridge," as it would become known, was a massive propaganda victory for the extreme right, leading to a hearing of their ideas in a broader segment of American society.

The Weavers made what was an apparently lonely *voortrek* from the very center of American life to its margins, from the most conventional heartland existence to an eccentric life of crankery. Randy Weaver, the former Special Forces soldier who wanted to be a G-man, ended up the sworn enemy of his own country's government. But perhaps the road into the wilderness was not as long as it appeared. In a way, the Weavers were just doing what earlier generations of Americans had done in the face of shrinking opportunities and the spiritual destitution or corruption of the settled areas: they headed west. Notions about divine election and imminent apocalypse were close to home as well, familiar from their upbringing in America's various offshoots of Calvinism. They feared social collapse, a Great Tribulation, but in a sense they were both its products and its agents. Mainstream American society had stopped providing them with a plausible story: army service was demoralizing, the churches had nothing to say to them, materialism could not fill the gap, and all around them were signs of decay. The oldest material basis of American life, the family farm, the homestead, appeared to no longer be viable. The family itself was in danger, surrounded by a seductive world of vice and corruption. The world they grew up in and took for granted no longer existed. Surely these were the signs of coming Armageddon and the doings of a malign, Satanic force.

Neo-Nazi propaganda successfully tapped into the mythic core of American society and lured the Weavers into the West and to their doom. They left behind reality and entered a phantom world of battles between tribes and races. They tuned in to an endless stream of propaganda, and with the unwitting assistance of the FBI, they themselves became propaganda, material for the furtherance of the movement they were often only partially conscious of being part of. Randy and Vicki believed they had broken away from an incipient totalitarian society and made themselves independent and self-reliant, but in fact they served the agenda of a totalitarian movement, one that came to dominate their entire existence. The alternate world the Weavers entered was not built to be the harmless fantasy of a few eccentrics out in the wilderness; its intent was the wholesale destruction and replacement of America with another America.

12

THE MOSAIC

I curse people. Everybody does it. We're human. We're bums. We're bums in the street.

—JOHN GOTTI

Could I have ended up being a wise guy? Maybe.

—RUDY GIULIANI

I never prayed to God / I prayed to Gotti.

—JAY-Z

After John Gotti had dodged conviction three times, the feds finally got him. On June 23, 1992, the boss of the Gambino family was being sentenced. "First of all, I would like to say emphatically that I am innocent," Frank LoCascio read from a statement he had handwritten in a spiral notebook. "I am guilty though. I am guilty of being a good friend of John Gotti. And if there were more men like John Gotti, we would have a better country." LoCascio and his good friend and boss John Gotti had just received life sentences without parole for murder and racketeering. Gotti declined to give a statement, but his lawyer told the newspapers that he turned to LoCascio and said, "We have just begun to fight," channeling the Revolutionary War hero John Paul Jones.

Outside the U.S. District Court Building in Brooklyn, the other good friends of John Gotti began to fight. Close to a thousand demonstrators had gathered in Columbus Park for the sentencing, some arriving on chartered buses from Ozone Park in Queens and Little Italy in Manhattan. They waved American flags and held placards reading FREE JOHN GOTTI, NO MAN OR GOVERNMENT ABOVE THE LAW, and ANOTHER GOVERNMENT CONSPIRACY. A woman wearing a THANKS JOHN T-shirt held up a sign that read EQUANIMITY [*sic*] UNDER THE LAW. Someone played the theme from the Francis Ford Coppola film *The Godfather* on a boom box. Equanimity was the last thing on their minds. "No justice for the Italians!" yelled one Gotti supporter who identified herself to the *New York Post* as "Roseanne from Mulberry Street." "There is something dangerous going on in America," Michael Strippoli, a retired jewelry salesman from Queens, told a *Times* reporter. "Look at what they got away with in the Rodney King thing. We Italians are a minority too, and we have to stand up and say this is wrong."

When news of the sentence spread outside, the crowd broke through the police lines and surged toward the courthouse. "Down with the government," cried Richie Gotti, John's elder brother, throwing his first in the air and rushing forward. Scuffles with the cops broke out. The mob smashed the windows of the U.S. marshals' cars parked in front of the court, overturning one of them. They reached the glass doors of the courthouse, trapping the people inside for close to an hour. "A gangster version of Bastille Day in Brooklyn," Mike McAlary dubbed it in his next day's *New York Post* column, adding, "Only the street mob *is* the mob." Some even managed to get into the Federal Building, leading to a turbulent scene at the door of the room that hosted the naturalization ceremonies for new American citizens. "Your government is the enemy," a woman holding an American flag screamed at the people inside. McAlary recorded that this harangue was answered by one newly minted American, a Guyana-born transit worker named Maurice Nusa, who stood in the doorway with his own small American flag and shouted "I love my country" back at the demonstrators.

At a press conference, Andrew Maloney, U.S. attorney for the Eastern District of New York, scolded the media. "You made him somewhat of a folk hero," Maloney told the gathered reporters. "You made him somewhat of a Robin Hood, and I told you on the day he was indicted he's not any of those things—he's a murderer and we proved that." The New York FBI chief James Fox said that the incident at the courthouse was "orchestrated and planned," not a spontaneous outpouring of public outrage. But even if the buses may have been paid for, plenty of people were more than willing to come along for the ride. When Gotti was convicted, his daughter told the papers, "My father is the last of the Mohicans." Many people agreed. During the trial, the *New York Post* used a 900 number to ask readers if Salvatore "Sammy the Bull" Gravano, Gotti's former underboss who testified against him, was telling the truth or if Gotti was. More than half sided with Gotti. Outside the Bergin Hunt and Fish Club, the boss's hangout in Ozone Park, Queens, neighborhood denizens lined up to pay solemn respects to John's brother Peter. Just to the south, in the slightly more genteel Howard Beach, residents put up yellow ribbons like the ones people had put up for the troops during the Gulf War. And it wasn't just the lower-middle-class borgatas in the outer boroughs or "an assemblage of $10-an-hour idiots," as the *Post*'s McAlary described "the rabble" outside the federal court. The trial was one of the hottest tickets in town, with celebrities lining the aisles. "The spectators' gallery looked like Spago, the ritzy Manhattan restaurant. Gotti guests included actors [Mickey] Rourke, [Anthony] Quinn, John Amos and 'Grandpa' Al Lewis, singer Jay Black and lawyer F. Lee Bailey. Each got a wave or wink from the defendant," the Associated Press reported. A *Time* magazine cover story on the mob featured a painting of Gotti by Andy Warhol. *Newsday* "learned that two prestigious law school deans have contacted Gotti, offering their services and those of their entire third-year classes to work on the Gotti appeal." *Newsday* also employed a fashion designer to sketch the colorful attendees' outfits, printing the standouts in a column called "Gotti Garb" four times a week. One "Gotti Garb" was dedicated to "Feds Threads," providing commentary alongside the drawings that highlighted the "WASPishness" of the U.S. attorney's outfits in contrast to the "the swaggering double-breasted outfits worn by Gotti and most of his backers." The civil rights lawyer William Kunstler marched at an earlier rally at the courthouse and took up Gotti's cause pro bono after house counsel Bruce Cutler was disqualified by the judge.

The unsophisticated nature of Gotti's crimes attracted scorn from the feds, who read Gotti's ascent as a sign of mob decline, or at least their own success at prosecution. "The quality of leadership keeps declining," Rudolph Giuliani, the former U.S. attorney for the Southern District, told *Newsweek* after Gotti's conviction. "You go from a Carlo Gambino to a Paul Castellano to a John Gotti, a basic brute-level guy. This is just a mass murderer, another form of Jeffrey Dahmer, a person who enjoys killing." "The taped conversations reveal that he is just a cheap thug, and not a particularly bright one," remarked Ronald Goldstock, head of New York State's Organized Crime Task Force. Of course, the feds wanted it both ways: Gotti was the Godfather, *capo di tutti capi*, in charge of a vast empire of crime and vice but also a character from Scorsese's *Goodfellas*, a street punk, a nobody, a wannabe.

Although Gotti rose to be in charge of the crime family that served as the inspiration for the Corleones in *The Godfather*, he certainly was from humble origins: "I wasn't born with four fuckin' cents." Although journalists had spun a myth about Gotti's parents as hardworking immigrants, they'd crossed the Hudson—not the Atlantic in steerage class. "These fucking bums that write books, they're worse than us. My fuckin' father was born in New Jersey. He aint never been in Italy his whole fuckin' life. My mother neither." Gotti's grandparents were from Naples; the surname comes from *i goti*, the Goths, who invaded and ruled Italy in the Dark Ages. The "hardworking" part wasn't quite right either, at least according to Gotti. "This guy never worked a fuckin' day in his life. He was a rolling stone; he never provided for the family. He never did nothin'. He never earned nothin'. And he never had nothin'." Gotti's father did work, but irregularly and at menial jobs like construction or garbage collecting. Like his son, he loved to gamble, which made providing for the thirteen Gotti siblings more difficult than it might have been. Back in Naples, he might've been called part of the *lazzaroni*: the urban mob of partially employed and unemployed lumpenproletariat. Gotti Sr. did manage to scratch enough money together to move the Gotti brood from East Harlem down to Sheepshead Bay in Brooklyn, following the migration toward ever more suburban forms of dwelling. That didn't last, though: the family had to move to the more working-class quarter of East New York, then crawling with the remnants of Albert Anastasia's Murder, Inc., now dubbed "the Gambino family" after its new boss.

Gotti started out in a local street gang and soon wandered into many of East New York's mob-run "social clubs." It wasn't long before Gotti and his first captain, Carmine Fatico, left East New York, along with many other Jews and Italians. The crew moved to nearby Ozone Park, opening up a new club called the Bergin Hunt and Fish Club, after Bergen Street, their old Brooklyn haunt—the name was a throwback, a nostalgic nod to a slightly earlier time of white working-class New York. Of course, the white flight had been helped along by the mob's own "blockbusting" scam. To launder heroin money, the mafia put cash into real estate fronts that gobbled up cheap houses by telling their owners that "the niggers are coming; you better sell now while you can." They also told prospective low-income Black buyers that they could afford their own homes and gave them cooked Federal Housing Administration applications. If they defaulted, the government picked up the bill and the fronts rebought the house in foreclosure and started all over again.

Even as a teen, Gotti made a powerful impression on the older mobsters, or so they told the press. "He reminded me of a Caesar or a Napoleon," Henry Hill, the real-life model for the main character in

Scorsese's *Goodfellas*, would later recall. East New York and Ozone Park were in close proximity to John F. Kennedy Airport, where Gotti made a living hijacking truckloads of cargo coming from the airport. He "made his bones"—or was initiated into the mafia as a "made man"—after helping out in the 1972 slaying of James McBratney, "Jimmy from Queens," who had been kidnapping local mobsters for ransom. Gotti was arrested and charged with murder, but the Gambino house counsel Roy Cohn got the charge down to attempted manslaughter in the second degree, a remarkable achievement, as the man had actually been killed.

The promotion of Gotti's patron, Aniello "Neil" Dellacroce, to Gambino underboss took Gotti to the Ravenite Social Club in Manhattan's Little Italy, the more fashionable address from which he started to make inroads into high society. He entered the public eye after he masterminded the assassination of the Gambino boss Paul Castellano in front of Sparks Steakhouse in Midtown, a hit with "panache" that "seemed almost an homage to the classic New York rub-outs: Albert Anastasia in the Park-Sheraton barber shop, Kid Twist out a window in the Half Moon Hotel, Carmine Galante's last supper," *The Village Voice* wrote. According to Gotti's own telling, Big Paul Castellano's slide into gentility cost him his life. "He was a fuckin' fish in the desert. He was a fish outta water. He didn't know this life." Gotti's loyalty was always to Dellacroce—a "man's man," whom he felt Big Paul did not appreciate—who died of cancer not long before the hit on Castellano. But, as with many things in La Cosa Nostra, the decision to assassinate Castellano was more pragmatic than an affair of honor. Gotti decided to whack Big Paul after a member of Gotti's crew and close friend, Angelo Ruggiero, was caught on FBI tapes talking about the crew's drug dealing; Ruggiero had been given the nickname "Quack Quack" because he could never shut up, and now the tapes were about to go public at trial. Because of the famed—but irregularly enforced—Gambino family ban on drug dealing, this would've given Big Paul a pretext to wipe out the whole Gotti crew. A blue-collar crew like Gotti's needed the drug money. So they got him before he could get them.

After the Castellano murder, Gotti dared to venture from the red sauce coast of southern Brooklyn and Queens to such trendy, yuppified spots on the east side of Manhattan as P.J. Clarke's on Third Avenue. "He no sooner walked in the side door than everyone knew he was there," said one regular at P.J.'s. "It was as though Marlon Brando walked in," another regular told the *Times.* At Da Noi on the east side, owned by a close personal friend, he sipped champagne with Anthony Quinn, and the two reminisced about growing up in tough neighborhoods. Taking up residence at the Ravenite or Rusty Staub's steak house on the Upper East Side, Gotti had made what Norman Podhoretz called "the longest journey in the world" from the outer boroughs into Manhattan. "He has made the crossing from Queens to Manhattan that is the dream of every child of talent who stands on what he thinks is the wrong side of the water from the topless towers across the way," wrote the journalist Murray Kempton. Still, for all the glamour and the reputed $600 million yearly haul of the Gambinos, Gotti stayed conspicuously middle class. His favorite restaurant remained a "generic Neapolitan dump in Queens" where the waiters "greeted him and other patrons at the door with the challenging question, 'Hey you hungry, or what?'" Unlike Big Paul Castellano, who lived on a palatial estate on Staten Island, Gotti remained at his modest two-story brick and vinyl-siding house in Howard Beach. Every Fourth of July he threw a block party for Ozone Park's residents, replete with fireworks he set off in defiance of city codes.

The FBI surveillance tapes presented at his trial revealed not an urban stoic—"the last of the Mohicans"—but a man who directed a constant stream of anxiety at his underlings: from worries over the bills, worries over not making enough money, and complaints over petty slights and his soldiers' lack of earning to things as prosaic as house and car payments and insurance. Gotti: "I got nothing! Peter, me and my wife, we pay for that Blue Cross, and ah, and the fire insurance on the house. Nothing, believe me!" LoCascio: "Blue Cross? You covered under Blue Cross? Extended coverage or something?" Gotti: "Yeah special kind of coverage, you know. God forbid . . . But ah, then fire insurance on the house, stupid things. Ehh, forget about it! Couple thousand a month, Frank." (Gotti found these revelations of his interior life, with its pedestrian worries and complaints, particularly unmanning and shameful, telling underboss Gravano, "You feel like you're being raped with these tapes!" Nor did it help that now his lieutenants could see him complaining about and criticizing them.)

He did treat himself to a cigarette boat after one his acquittals, though, christened with the fitting name *Not Guilty*. He was not much of a capitalist: unlike the model for the Godfather himself, Carlo Gambino, he did not use his ill-gotten accumulation to bequeath his children "legitimate" businesses so they wouldn't have to be in the mob anymore. He was caught on tape insisting on his fealty to the old ways. "And this is gonna be Cosa Nostra til I die. Be it an hour from now or be it tonight or a hundred years from now when I'm in jail, it's gonna be a Cosa Nostra." It may have been less about trying to stay down to earth or the desire to keep a low profile that kept Gotti in Queens than about his gambling habit. He was a perpetual loser at every kind of gambling he tried his hand at: cards, sports, and especially the horses.

He did have enough cash on hand to live up to one of his tabloid honorifics, "The Dapper Don": the $1,800 (he made sure to correct the newspaper when they misreported the cost at $1,000) double-breasted suits, the monogrammed Gucci socks, the silk painted ties, the smirk, the springy shock of professionally coifed silver hair that one British newspaperman said was "like Stalin's." At one trial, his flamboyant house counsel Bruce Cutler declaimed to jurors that the suits were a sign of Gotti's substance: "So when he sits there resplendent in his suit, it's not out of being bold! It is out of pride! That's what made this country great!" The don also always had an insouciant quip for the grateful press. He showed up for one trial in Gucci loafers, but then in front of the gathered press he changed into Reeboks, more appropriate for the jailhouse, and declared he was "Ready for Freddy!"

In public, Gotti liked to play the part of a gent. Holding doors, generously tipping, reprimanding his men for breaches of etiquette. The media delighted in the way he held the door for his prosecutor, U.S. attorney Diane Giacalone. But the trial strategy he cooked up with his attorney Cutler was somewhat less gentlemanly. Cutler got one government witness to call Giacalone a "slut" and a "blowjob." A defense witness testified that Giacalone, to entice him to testify against Gotti, "gave me her panties out of her bottom drawer and told me to facilitate myself." They managed to paint her as both an uptight bureaucrat who resented Gotti's lifestyle because he enjoyed himself and sexually promiscuous, a pervert. The trial ended in an acquittal for Gotti.

Gotti liked to make grand gestures of largesse in front of TV cameras: he once gave a homeless man a $50 bill, and then, when asked if he usually gave fifties to the homeless, he asked "Was that a fifty?" took back the $50 and replaced it with a crisp C-note. At one trial he instructed lackeys to go and give cash to the homeless living in cardboard boxes on the street. After his 1990 acquittal he practically reenacted a Roman triumph. "He left the courthouse through the judge's entrance, smiling and dapper like a triumphant politician, and the press and the crowd of admirers were waiting, as always, to pay homage to this man with the aura of invincibility," *The New York Times* reported. "He raised his fist in a salute to the faithful, and they surged behind the police barricades on White Street outside State Supreme Court and cheered his name and his victory."

Even a venerable highbrow like Murray Kempton could not fully resist the charisma and even dignity of John Gotti. "The television cameras were fixedly staring at John Gotti; and his mien offered every satisfaction to those who inclined to detect a growth toward statesmanly proportions," Kempton wrote archly in his *Newsday* column. "He had . . . the look that announces the full recognition of the responsibilities just placed upon him by his fellow citizens and the entire readiness to bear their burden." At his 1990 acquittal, a maroon Cadillac was waiting for the don to take him a few short blocks uptown to his Little Italy headquarters on Mulberry Street. "Another crowd roared as he stepped from the sedan, and several women ran up and kissed him as he strode to the door of the Ravenite Social Club, where his closest friends were waiting to offer tribute and congratulations." In the evening Gotti stepped back out onto the street to witness the fireworks set off in his honor. "He's like the Mayor, I guess you'd say," a man named Joseph outside the Ravenite told the *Times*. "He treats the people very respectably. He's friendly and he always talks to the elderly people. He's very popular in the neighborhood because he pets the dogs and kisses the babies." Edith, outside the Ravenite to show her support, thought the authorities were targeting Italian Americans. "They always pick on us," she said. "We're not bad people. We have priests, lawyers, doctors. We never killed our mothers. Why don't they go after the rapists, the murderers, the real criminals?" Gotti was on the cusp of being something more than a gangster: he was wooing and apparently winning public opinion. He seemed to be becoming a *political* phenomenon.

Gotti's rise as a celebrity coincided with a period in which New York City seemed to be going over the precipice into total chaos. Newspaper editorials spoke of "decline," "moral anarchy," and "despair." In 1991 New Yorkers lost a record-breaking 213,000 jobs. During the entire recession, 400,000 jobs would be eradicated, or 12 percent of all employment in the city. Death stalked the avenues. By the beginning of the 1990s, AIDS became the number one killer of men in New York age twenty-five to forty-four. In 1989 there were 1,905 murders in the city. In 1990 murders peaked at 2,245. In 1991 there were 2,225. Nor were the killings limited to the internecine feuds of drug dealers. The public recoiled at stories of seemingly random vicious attacks, such as the 1990 murder of Brian Watkins, a twenty-two-year-old tourist from Utah, stabbed to death while protecting his family from a gang attempting to rob them on a Midtown subway platform. Then there was the Happy Land Social Club fire, a 1990 arson at a Bronx bar that claimed the lives of eighty-seven people. In 1989 there was the infamous Central Park Jogger case, when a young white woman was raped and nearly beaten to death. Five youths who were allegedly on a "wilding spree," attacking and harassing pedestrians in the park, were arrested and charged with the crime. Donald Trump put a full-page ad in the *Daily News* screaming, "*BRING BACK THE DEATH PENALTY! BRING BACK THE POLICE!*... What has happened to the respect for authority, the fear of retribution by the courts, society, and the police for those who break the law? What has happened is the complete breakdown of life as we know it." Trump wasn't the only one to decry the case. David Dinkins, the Harlem pol running to be the city's first Black mayor, called the suspects "urban terrorists" and declared he'd be "the toughest mayor on crime this city ever had." In 1992 the lead detective on the case was discovered to be involved in a sprawling corruption scandal. The so-called Central Park Five would be exonerated a decade later.

While the reign of crime took hold, the city pined for earlier days and more familiar forms of banditry. The hottest ticket on Broadway was a revival of *Guys and Dolls*, a musical based on Damon Runyon's stories of Prohibition-era rascals. Crowds lined up for Scorsese's *Goodfellas* and the third installment of Coppola's *Godfather* saga. Readers hungrily consumed books on the mob, many of them memoirs written by former gangsters themselves. "England has their Queen. The Italian mob is like the royalty in this country," one author-convict told the *Times* while on the phone from federal prison in Colorado. The city even had a certain affectionate curiosity about the newly infamous Westies, the wild Irish Hell's Kitchen gang that did contract hits for Gotti and the Gambinos: the neighborhood might be gentrifying, but here was still a hint of the old days. Of course, by the early 1990s the Westies were becoming multicultural. They were led by Boško "the

Yugo" Radonjić, a Serb nationalist who had once been imprisoned for a bombing at the Yugoslav consulate in New York. After the Westies and a stint in prison, Radonjić returned to politics, going back to Serbia, where he became a close confidant of the war criminal Radovan Karadžić.

The city fractured along racial lines. In August 1989, four Black teenagers, including sixteen-year-old Yusuf Hawkins, had gone to Bensonhurst, Brooklyn, in hopes of buying a used car. They were ambushed and beaten by a mob of Italians who were trying to waylay a Black teen who was reputedly dating a local girl, and they were apparently prepared to attack any Black youths entering the neighborhood. One member of the gang, armed with a handgun, shot Hawkins twice in the chest, killing him. It was the third killing of a Black man by white mobs in the city in the past decade. The Reverend Al Sharpton, preparing to lead a march through Bensonhurst, was stabbed by a local and seriously wounded. The mob that killed Hawkins was organized, as it were: a soldier in the Gambino family had given orders to prepare the ambush, and the shooter was a Gambino "associate." This was not the only involvement of the Gotti clan in racial violence: shortly after John's sentencing, his seventeen-year-old son, Peter Gotti, was a primary suspect in a gang of teens who attacked another Black teenager with a pellet gun. (Also present in the car was the son of the vice president of the International Brotherhood of Locomotive Engineers.) And there was a long-standing neighborhood rumor that Gotti's oldest son, "John Jr.," was present at the 1986 Howard Beach house party that sparked the mob that attacked and killed a young Black man named Michael Griffiths.

The experience of moral anarchy was not restricted to slums and working-class districts, it penetrated the upper reaches of society. The decade of Wall Street and "Greed Is Good" came to a halt with the 1987 crash. Shortly before the music stopped, there was the revelation that the "masters of the universe" were just masters of the scam. Ivan Boesky's magic formula for massive profits turned out to be insider trading. Boesky informed on the junk bond king Michael Milken of Drexel Burnham Lambert, who was sentenced to ten years in prison and fined $600 million in 1990. The U.S. attorney for the Southern District, Rudolph "Rudy" Giuliani, used the same racketeering laws to ensnare Wall Street felons that he used against the heads of the "Commission"—the legendary council of the five principal mafia families. Tabloid covers were constantly splashed with the greed and squalor of New York's upper crust, such as the hotelier Leona Helmsley, the "Queen of Mean," who terrorized her employees and evaded taxes. Giuliani also took Helmsley down.

Then there was Donald Trump, another arriviste who emerged from the outer boroughs' squat, humble dwellings for the lower-middle class into the adamantine canyons of Manhattan. Less predator than scavenger or parasite, Trump took advantage of the openhanded giveaways to developers in the wake of the city's fiscal crisis and feasted on the decaying hulk of the city. Trump Tower was built with the helpful assistance of S&A Concrete, a joint venture of the Genovese boss "Fat Tony" Salerno and Paul Castellano. The three men shared a lawyer in Roy Cohn, who generously provided his town house living room for a meeting between Trump and Salerno to work out the details of the contract. Trump quickly grew tired of building and engaged in an orgy of acquisitions beyond his means. By 1992, his empire had collapsed under the weight of unserviceable debt, a victim as much of his own prodigality as the recession in the real estate market. Appropriately, he ran aground in Atlantic City, a casino town past its prime. Meant as a bid for legitimacy and belonging in the city patriciate, Trump Tower became a favorite place of residence for organized crime figures. By the early '90s Trump and his second wife, Marla Maples, had become the butt of jokes and tabloid fodder, apparently with their own encouragement. Negative attention was better than no attention. While Trump raged against the accused rapists in 1989, in 1992 he was giving press conferences offering a scheme in which convicted rapist Mike Tyson would avoid prison by paying off his accuser.

In this atmosphere, one could understand the weary shrug or even the knowing wink the city gave to John Gotti. At the very least, he did not seem like a terribly big villain. "Tapes have revealed Gotti as an exceedingly poor businessman and one of the nation's worst horse players. If he or the Gambino family enjoyed half the influence they are supposed to have, then all their kids would be at Choate-Rosemary Hall. The guys would have wormed their way on the board of at least two or three clearinghouse banks by now and be regulars at Mortimer's. They'd own the New York Stock Exchange and Mike Milken would be wearing cement for muscling in on mob territory," *Newsday* opined.

Corruption, vice, and chaos extended all the way from the streets to city hall. The Yusuf Hawkins killing and the ensuing sense that the city was coming apart occurred just as the 1989 mayoral election was heating up—with Mayor Ed Koch about to face his challenger Dinkins in the Democratic primary. Born in the Bronx, Koch started his political career in Greenwich Village as an upwardly mobile Manhattanite liberal reformer and opponent of the Tammany Hall boss Carmine DeSapio. But over the years his style had gradually moved back toward the white ethnic *Heimatland* in the outer boroughs. Now the brash style of labeling people "putzes" and "schmucks," the irreverent Yiddishkeit that had once endeared him to New Yorkers, didn't fit the moment. Neither did Koch's frequent poking and baiting of Black leadership with comments like "blacks are anti-semites" seem particularly constructive.

It wasn't just the changing times and demographics, or simply that the city was fed up with Koch's antics. The mayor's cultivation of pals in the outer boroughs meant that he was now also tainted by corruption. Shortly after his third inauguration, in 1986, the Queens borough president Donald Manes was found in his car alongside the Grand Central Parkway near Shea Stadium. He'd been swerving through traffic before coming to a stop on the side of the road, where he slit his wrists. He made up a story about an attempted kidnapping.

Ed Koch, an old friend, visited Manes at his hospital bed, giving him a kiss on the forehead. Manes eventually confessed that his wounds were self-inflicted, but he didn't want to discuss what had driven him to attempt suicide. Jimmy Breslin of the New York *Daily News* knew why: a "business associate" of Manes's, a shrink of dubious credentials, Geoffrey Lindenauer, was explaining to Rudy Giuliani's office how they turned the Parking Violations Bureau into a personal trough in a scheme that involved much of the city's Democratic leadership. "Even as in the grand old days of Boss Tweed's Forty Thieves, this gang of brigands now quite merrily began helping itself to pretty much anything that didn't appear to be nailed down," Breslin cracked wise. A few weeks later Manes made another, successful suicide attempt. Then the indictments started to rain down. A cascade of federal and local investigations followed, revealing an intertwined mob and machine: $22 million in city contracts had been rewarded to John Gotti's plumbing company. The Bronx Democratic leader Stanley Friedman, an associate at Roy Cohn's law firm; Bronx congressman and former NYPD officer Mario Biaggi; Bronx borough president Stanley Simon; and Brooklyn boss Meade Esposito from Canarsie's Thomas Jefferson Democratic Club, who also happened to be Fred and Donald Trump's political patron back in their Brooklyn days, all ended up being convicted for filching from the city in various ways. Koch was not directly involved, but he had been friends with several of the men and had duly put their people in city offices. He had come into office as a reform candidate who pledged to clean up corruption, but he would never have become mayor without relationships with the borough bosses. Even though he declared himself "betrayed" by his buddies, he looked like a hypocrite now, part of the same old machine. That machine might not give out turkeys on Christmas anymore, but it could still steal for its members.

The shattering of New York's Democratic machine and the weakening of Ed Koch appeared to be a Machiavellian masterstroke by Giuliani, who, not long after completing his demolition job on the old order, resigned from the U.S. Attorney's Office and announced that he'd be running for mayor in 1989 on the Republican ticket. He had made himself a public figure and media darling as the man who went after corruption and the mob, and he'd just given a series of sharp blows to the party organization that would oppose him, but his path still wasn't free of obstacles. First he had to face an unexpectedly bitter primary challenge from the businessman Ronald Lauder, heir to the Estée Lauder fortune, who was sicced on him by Senator Alphonse D'Amato, the preeminent figure in New York's GOP. D'Amato essentially wanted to take Giuliani down a peg to ensure his own power base and patronage, but there were also clouds of corruption around the senator. Lauder spent millions of his own money on a campaign that had no real focus, paying a small fortune to a series of expensive GOP political consultants who also happened to have close connections with D'Amato. But he did manage to ding up Giuliani before the former prosecutor could prevail over him in the primary.

But the prospective electorate was as wary of Giuliani as his own party was. His image as G-man and "Mr. Clean" didn't particularly endear him to white ethnics, particularly fellow Italian Americans. The legendary adman and Coney Island native Jerry Della Femina gave his appraisal in a *Newsday* column:

> Rudy, I don't know how to break it to you, you're not the most popular Italian in this town. That's right, baby. John Gotti runs rings around you. Great dresser, great voice, great charisma. How long before some smart-aleck reporter on "A Current Affair" decides to do an all-Italian Mayoralty Survey? Can you just see Maury Povich giving the camera his most sincere fish-eyed stare and saying, "Tune in tomorrow for the shocking results of our Italian Mayoralty Survey, titled Robin Hood vs. the Lisping Sheriff of Nottingham"? And you know what the result of that survey is, Rudy? You lose, and you lose big. Sure, crime was a big issue, but

> Rudy's was the wrong type of crime fighting, not "real" crime: Crime, crime, crime, that's all you know—and it's not even the right kind of crime. It's white-collar crime.

At the Bergin Hunt and Fish Club, they hung up a Dinkins poster—probably an endorsement he could do without. Campaigning in the Italian enclave of Arthur Avenue in the Bronx, Rudy had to dodge tomatoes thrown from the rooftops. Giuliani had taken a shot at the Board of Elections member Vincent Velella, calling him a "mob lawyer" and bringing up his friendship with the Genovese family boss "Fat Tony" Salerno. His son, Guy Velella, who was the Republican chairman for the Bronx, wrote a letter to his constituents calling Giuliani a "fair-weather Italian." One of Giuliani's detectives on the Knapp Commission, tasked with uncovering corruption in the NYPD, remarked to *Newsday*, "I remember the first time I met Rudy, thinking, 'Here's one of those Italians that wants to be a WASP.' There was no emotion." The former president of the Sons of Italy, Joseph Say, wrote a letter to voters, stating, "Rudy Giuliani has not shown he is responsive to the needs and desires of the Italian-American community." "Tell that to my mother and father," Giuliani shot back to reporters when asked about it. But he might not have wanted them to take too close a look at his origins.

Giuliani was indeed trying to escape from certain aspects of the Italian American experience. His father, Harold Giuliani, born in Italian Harlem, was arrested in 1934 for robbing a milkman at gunpoint in an east side tenement. He was sentenced to two to five years in Sing Sing. After being paroled, he married his sweetheart, Helen D'Avanzo, and the couple moved to East Flatbush in Brooklyn, where Rudy was born in 1944. Unable to find work, Harold Giuliani tended bar at Vincent's, the restaurant owned by his brother-in-law Leo. The restaurant was named after Leo's brother, a cop in the Sixty-seventh Precinct, but it was the center of Leo's loan-sharking and gambling operations. Harold wasn't just the bartender, he was Leo's enforcer, menacing anyone late with their payments with the baseball bat he kept behind the bar—and sometimes more than menacing. In the '50s, to get away from Vincent's and East Flatbush, Helen and Harold moved their family to the Long Island suburb of Garden City. Harold started working as a groundskeeper at a nearby public school. To fit in in the lily-white suburb, the couple changed their party registration from Democratic to Republican. Rudy commuted on the LIRR to Brooklyn's Bishop Loughlin Memorial High School, where he was educated under the stern and watchful eye of Father O'Leary. He attended Manhattan College in the Bronx, another school run by the Christian Brothers order.

Rudy's heroes, as was the case with many integrating Catholics, were Jack and Bobby Kennedy. When Bobby Kennedy ran for New York's U.S. Senate seat in 1964, Rudy defended him in the college newspaper from the charge that he was a carpetbagger: "Let us hope that cosmopolitan New Yorkers can rise above the ridiculous, time-worn provincial attitudes that has so disunited our nation. A Kennedy victory will bring about the assertion of the most valuable precedent; that a representative from a particular state must be able to think and vote in the light of national leads and not only to local and sectional pressures." In another op-ed, he denounced the John Birch Society as the "disgusting, neurotic fantasy of a mind warped by fear and bigotry." Rudy was leaving behind his own provincialism, his own "local and sectional pressures": East Flatbush, the bat behind the bar at Vincent's, the cousins who were either capos or cops—he didn't like to talk too much even about the cops, probably because the line between the wise guys and the cops was pretty blurry. He chose the liberalism of the age: rational, competent, orderly, and universalistic, with a law-and-order edge, like Bobby the AG, Bobby the Inquisitor going after the mob. Instead of the patronage, the payoffs, the rackets, the numbers, all the hugs, kisses, and slaps on the backs, the smoke-filled rooms where ex-prizefighters became politicians and politicians doled out beatings as well as jobs, the Brooklyn way, that was behind Rudy, that was all in the past now. Even the church was not universal enough: after considering the priesthood, he turned instead to the law, enrolling in NYU School of Law. Even in his love life, he showed a yen for the American mainstream: college buddies described Rudy's penchant for "WASPy blondes." He married Regina Peruggi, whom he'd known since childhood, but filed for divorce after going gaga over the blond WPIX anchorwoman Donna Hanover. Rudy even got an annulment through the Church, because he "discovered" that he and Peruggi were actually second cousins. He would be an upholder of the public good, a prosecutor, a fed, a G-man, and, then, one day, the first Italian American president of the United States.

Even as he ran for mayor in 1989 as a Republican, he viewed himself in the mold of "Fusion"—liberal, reform, good government Republicans like Mayor Fiorello La Guardia, who defeated the Tammany Hall machine, and Thomas Dewey, the prosecutor who took on Lucky Luciano and Dutch Schultz in the 1930s. To cement those credentials, Giuliani even wrangled the ballot line of New York's Liberal Party, which had once carried the liberal Republican John Lindsay to the mayoralty. But that didn't mean what it once did. Tracing the course of the city in miniature, the "LP" was once the center of New York's Jewish labor left idealists, the party of David Dubinsky of the International Ladies' Garment Workers' Union and Alex Rose of the United Hatters of North America, but also the Protestant theologian Reinhold Niebuhr. Over the years, however, the party had lost its ideological bearings and degenerated into just another racket. What remained of the ILGWU was a Gambino fiefdom, and the Liberal Party was a patronage machine for its leader, Raymond B. Harding (born Branko Hochwald), and his cronies, including Harding's family members. The joke went that the Liberal Party was neither liberal nor a party. The endorsement was easy to obtain; there were no policy concessions or ideological vetting: Giuliani just had to promise Harding's men jobs in his administration. But first Rudy would have to get through David Dinkins.

If Rudy Giuliani portrayed himself as the "reform" candidate, David Norman Dinkins was the machine "regular." He was a protégé of J. Raymond Jones, nicknamed "the Fox," the leader of Harlem's George Washington Carver Democratic Club and the last Grand Sachem of Tammany Hall. The son of a barber, Dinkins was born in Trenton, New Jersey, and raised in Harlem. He joined the Marine Corps during the Second World War. The war ended before he could see combat, but he got a bitter taste of Jim Crow while stationed in the South. He attended Howard University on the G.I. Bill, majored in mathematics, and intended to pursue a grad degree in that subject before switching to law. Back in Harlem, he married Joyce Burrows, the daughter of Daniel Burrows, the founder of the United Mutual Life Insurance Company and one of the few Black state assembly members and Tammany district leaders. Dinkins decided to enter politics as well, at first as a way to build his legal career as much as to dedicate himself to public service.

Just as the Tammany system started to fall apart, Blacks and Puerto Ricans started to arrive in large numbers in the city. The Tammany system, as it had done in the past, tried to accommodate the growing number of new voters, reserving the Manhattan borough presidency as "the black seat" on the powerful Board of Estimate, which set the city budget. J. Raymond Jones leveraged the independent power center around the spectacularly popular Harlem congressman Adam Clayton Powell Jr. to gain control over Tammany. The succession appeared complete: first the Irish, then the Jews and Italians, now the Blacks. But by the time Jones became Grand Sachem of Tammany Hall in 1961, the system he presided over was but a shadow of its former self and the spoils he could divvy up were drying up. Companies that offered manufacturing jobs, the basis of working-class life, left the city in search of cheaper labor. The port wasn't deep enough for modern freight, and the lack of a direct rail hookup to the rest of the country meant that shipping started to flow into New Jersey instead of the city. New York's industrial base was not like the vast steel mills of Pennsylvania or the car plants of the Midwest: it was not dominated by one industry or type of manufacture. Instead, there was a panoply of hundreds of firms dedicated to small-scale and often custom production. The city produced everything from ships for the navy to ladies' garments to chewing gum, and it printed books and newspapers in great quantities. This variety added to the city's sense of vibrant, kaleidoscopic pluralism, but in lean times its dark sides were more visible: the sprawling factory floors of the Midwest bred alienation but also mass solidarity, while small shops honeycombed the city with jealously held fiefdoms, reinforcing ethnic parochialism as one immigrant group or another dominated a trade and saw it as their birthright. The city's craft-type unions were based on doling out jobs via seniority and patronage, making them easy prey for mafia takeovers. Local leaders had built up a generous system of social welfare during the boom years. Now the erosion of the tax base and its simultaneous swelling of the welfare rolls to deal with the growing poor caused bitter struggles, with racial and ethnic overtones. Then, in the mid-'70s, came the fiscal crisis: the city went broke, and control over the budget fell into the hands of the Emergency Financial Control Board—a new body made up of four elected officials (only one from the city itself) and three corporate chiefs appointed by the governor—which pursued painful cuts in services. Even after "Emergency" was dropped from the title and the FCB no longer had direct control over the city budget, it would monitor and could reassert control of spending if it got too high. Then came the Reagan administration's cuts of federal funding for cities: hundreds of millions slashed from job training, day care, housing, child welfare, food stamps, Medicaid, transit, and infrastructure maintenance and development.

Under these straitened circumstances, Dinkins rose slowly and steadily—from registering voters as a member of Jones's George Washington Carver Democratic Club to district leader and the captaincy of the local machine, to county clerk, to Manhattan borough president. Everything Dinkins did was methodical, steady, and deliberate; he attributed this to his background in mathematics. An almost punctilious formalism extended to his wardrobe and manners: he was immaculately dressed in custom-made double-breasted suits (of a much less gaudy cut than Gotti's, of course) and silk pocket squares, and he cut an elegant figure in a tux at the city's many black-tie galas. He was unfailingly polite, his diction even a bit courtly and antiquated, and it was rumored that he so valued cleanliness that he showered several times a day. His favorite pastime was tennis, which brought him into contact with New York's elite. In particular, he became a trusted contact of the city's increasingly powerful real estate developers, who judged him "a reasonable man."

Giuliani's plan had been to face a weakened Koch, present himself as a liberal reformer, and peel away Black and Latino Democrats who had no feelings for the mayor. He had been knocking Koch for his racial insensitivity, accusing the mayor of using "code words" to divide "one religious group from a racial group or an ethnic group from another ethnic group." He kicked off his campaign with a compassionate note about the city's homelessness crisis, and he had discovered, through remarkable and complex theological casuistry, that a pro-choice position could coexist with a Catholic conscience. Giuliani even had planned to bid for the support of Jesse Jackson. He moved so far to the left that *The Wall Street Journal* was even calling him a "John Lindsay Republican" and predicting he'd defect from the GOP if he was elected. The Machiavellian plan in the months before the Democrats selected their candidate had been to wound Koch, not to kill him, but when Koch succumbed to his wounds, Giuliani was left without a strategy.

The jump from prosecutor to pol was not easy: he garnered comparisons to Savonarola, the puritanical Dominican friar who denounced corruption but established a tyrannical rule over Florence; he was called "stiff," "awkward," and "uncomfortable" on the trail, rarely taking his jacket off or mingling with crowds. “Can we live with a mayor who detests all sins, including the Seven Deadly Ones with which we comfortably had lived with so long and so contentedly?” asked Murray Kempton coyly. Joe Klein, at the time *New York* magazine’s maven of local politics, called it “the single most incompetent campaign I’ve seen in 20 years—single, state, or local.” Rudy brought on Republican boogeymen Roger Ailes and Roger Stone to provide some nasty edges, but nothing seemed to work. Giuliani wasn’t comfortable with race-baiting, the obvious move for a Republican white ethnic against a Black candidate. Surrogates tried for him, but it backfired. Jackie Mason, the honorary campaign chair and quintessential Borscht Belt comic, attempting to give the Giuliani campaign a *heimish* touch, called Dinkins a “fancy shvartze with mustache” and said that “some Jews vote for black candidates out of guilt.” The next day, Mason was asked to resign from the campaign. Dinkins had always been sensitive to Jewish issues: he’d denounced Farrakhan, supported Israel, and even knocked his ally Jesse Jackson when he called New York “Hymietown.” And Giuliani couldn’t even rally a united Italian American front. Ozone Park remained iffy on this paisan. “Put this down: Giuliani’s no damn good,” a sanitation worker told a reporter shortly before the election. “He’s no good because he thinks all Italians are mafia.” One of Giuliani’s supporters, while admiring his “toughness” and “guts” for trying to “put the big guy away,” thought the big guy might even make a better candidate: “Come to think of it, maybe Gotti should be mayor.”

The New York Times endorsed Dinkins as a “conciliator” whose “decency can help the city confront its biggest foreseeable problems: a sagging economy and tension between the races. The two together. Because tax revenues are down, the city already faces a deficit of half a billion or more. The next mayor will have to ask for, and sell, sacrifice to all New Yorkers, most notably the poor citizens hurt by reductions in city services. Mr. Dinkins seems better qualified to persuade all New Yorkers to share the burdens ahead.” Still, the endorsement was tepid.

Dinkins was the conservative choice, the force of tradition: "David Dinkins, warts and all, is a known quantity. He's a practical Democrat who has come up through the ranks and who knows what he stands for. He understands New York's government, neighborhoods and people. He is not the ideal candidate but he is a good man likely to make a decent mayor." But even if he embodied the spirit of unity, the path to victory was mechanical: he also had the endorsement of the powerful public sector unions that had replaced the old party machine's patronage hierarchy. And if he won, he would have to reward them, not least to persuade them to share sacrifices.

Win he did. Giuliani's furious last-minute offensive—trying to connect Dinkins with financial improprieties and tar him as a corrupt Democratic regular—cut into Dinkins's polling lead, but it couldn't put Giuliani over the top. In the end, the election was closer than the polling suggested: Dinkins won 50.4 percent to 47.8. Staten Island and Queens had gone to Giuliani. He won a majority of the white Catholic and Jewish vote, but Dinkins maintained a healthy 40 percent of the Jews.

On January 1, 1990, Dinkins gave an inauguration speech that was soaring, triumphant, connecting the election of New York's first Black mayor to the ending of the Cold War and the beginning of the end of apartheid. Democracy was on the march again. The mayor invoked the spirit of the New Deal and the Good War. "We are all foot soldiers on the march to freedom, here and everywhere." The advance of democracy, freedom, and the rights of man was inevitable. "Human rights is the most powerful idea in human history. And now we know—and yes, we don't just hope, we know—that some day soon the bells of freedom will also ring in Tiananmen Square and in Soweto." Dinkins returned to his favorite metaphor, the city as a "gorgeous mosaic of race and religious faith, of national origin and sexual orientation, of individuals whose families arrived yesterday and generations ago, coming through Ellis Island or Kennedy Airport or on buses bound for the Port Authority." The government was to be both plural and popular: "And the government we inaugurate here will belong to you, not to any elite or any narrow interest. Ours will be a civic forum, an open democracy that hears diverse views and voices before it decides, a democracy that holds out hope for the hopeless and assuages the fears of the fearful, a democracy that appeals to what is best in us and strives to bring us together."

But the pluralism of the city looked less like a mosaic than shards of shattered glass, some with very sharp edges. Immediately Dinkins fell afoul of each group of interests he sought to serve. He promised raises for his supporters in the municipal unions, but the budget shortfall made it impossible; he had to turn around and roll the raises back, or even propose layoffs. Labor leaders he called his friends called him a liar; he promised more cops to get tough on crime, but then couldn't deliver them. He befriended the business community, but now they were concerned about his spending, raised the specter of another fiscal crisis, and wondered aloud to reporters if Dinkins was up to the job; businesses threatened to leave, further imperiling tax revenues. Governor Cuomo, although also a Democrat, didn't benefit much from helping the city, but he did from talking tough about urban prodigality; he mooted the possibility of another Financial Control Board takeover. Felix G. Rohatyn, the famed investment banker who had engineered New York City's bailout in the 1970s, declared in *The New York Review of Books*, "New York City is facing a social, political, and economic crisis far more serious than the fiscal crisis of the 1970s." His program: more austerity. But then some of the cuts proposed in city services looked too bloody even for Rohatyn, and he floated the idea of letting the city have a period of deficit financing. To Rohatyn, the glue that helped hold the city was gone: "New York City, during the 1975 fiscal crisis, could still be described as a 'gorgeous mosaic.' Mosaics are held together by some bonding material that keeps them from falling apart. During the 1970s there were, I believe, widely shared hopes that the city could provide opportunity for its citizens. Today, New York has become a city full of anger and violence in which ethnic groups are turned against other ethnic groups, races against other races, classes against other classes."

On Monday, August 19, 1991, the front-page headline of the Brooklyn edition of *New York Newsday* read BLACKS AND JEWS: WHAT WENT WRONG? The columnist Sheryl McCarthy outlined growing tension between the city's two communities, most recently inflamed by public comments from CUNY professor Dr. Leonard Jeffries, a leading proponent of Afrocentrism. In a speech broadcast on public access TV, Jeffries blamed Jews for the slave trade and claimed that "there was a conspiracy, planned and plotted and programmed out of Hollywood by people called Greenberg and Weisberg and Trigliani . . . Russian Jewry had a particular control over the movies, and their financial partners, the Mafia, put together a financial system of destruction of black people." The outrage prompted calls for Jeffries's dismissal as chairman of Black studies at CUNY's City College. Callers and hosts came to his defense on WLIB, a Black-owned talk station. Jeffries was a frequent guest on the station's Gary Byrd show. Another guest was Sonny Carson, the leader of a Korean deli boycott that had begun in January 1990 when a shopkeeper allegedly assaulted a Haitian customer. Carson remarked on the air, "The Jews, when they left, they made sure that they turned those stores over to people who would continue the trickery."

That Monday night in Crown Heights, a car bringing up the rear in the convoy of the Lubavitcher rebbe Menachem Mendel Schneerson ran a red light to keep up with the rest of the cars. The driver, a Hasidic man named Yosef Lifsch, was sideswiped in the intersection and his station wagon careened onto the sidewalk, striking and killing a seven-year-old boy named Gavin Cato and seriously injuring the boy's cousin Angela. An angry crowd surrounded the vehicle and started to chant "Jews! Jews! Jews!" The police instructed one of the Lubavitchers' Hatzoloh volunteer ambulances to take Lifsch away for his own safety, leading to the rumor that the Jews tended to their own before helping the children. Four days of rioting followed. A gang of youths stabbed an Orthodox man named Yankel Rosenbaum, a visiting student from Australia, who would succumb to his wounds in the hospital. An elderly Holocaust survivor committed suicide. The famed columnist Jimmy Breslin, covering the riots, was pulled from his cab, beaten, and robbed. He was rescued by a passerby brandishing a large knife. Altogether, 152 police officers and 38 civilians were injured, and 27 police vehicles were destroyed. The press called it America's first pogrom, with the implication that Dinkins had tolerated or even encouraged the upheaval. When Dinkins arrived on the scene and tried to calm the rioters by talking to them on a bullhorn, they threw bottles and bricks at him, chanting, "The mayor is not safe!" The initial police response was scattershot and disorganized. The cops perpetuated the rumor that they had been deliberately restrained by the Dinkins administration. The head of the Patrolmen's Benevolent Association, Phil Caruso, circulated a statement to precinct houses: "In Crown Heights, mob rule now prevails. Over the last three nights, New York's Finest have been transformed into New York's lamest." He declared that the cops "need not cower in fear . . . If police officers are placed under life-threatening attack, they should use their nightsticks or firearms."

Immediately there was a bevy of explanations and recriminations and counter-recriminations: permissive liberalism, Black antisemitism, racism, the insularity of Hasidic Jews, the unfair privileging of the Lubavitcher community above their Black neighbors, apartheid, and the Israeli-Palestinian conflict were all cited as causes. But just about everyone could agree on one thing: David Dinkins was partly to blame. Somehow, he both tolerated and encouraged Black nationalists and was a weak and pliable Uncle Tom, doing the bidding of the white establishment. Just a few days after the Crown Heights riots subsided, the city itself provided a not-too-subtle metaphor: a number 4 express train jumped the tracks at the Fourteenth Street–Union Square station, killing five straphangers. Things were going off the rails.

As 1992 began, the new year didn't portend better times. On New Year's Eve, a twenty-two-year-old Black man was beaten to death in

Ozone Park by a group of whites; the police, after labeling it a "bias attack," tried to downplay the racial component. The Bronx witnessed a wave of escalating racial attacks, this time among teenagers. The city seemed to be Balkanizing, almost literally: the police were on the hunt for a teen gang called the Albanian Bad Boys for starting tit-for-tat violence with their attacks on Black kids. Governor Cuomo met with Dinkins to discuss the racial violence. "I don't remember a lot of times as troublesome as this moment in terms of anger, in terms of violence, in terms of this particular insidious kind of violence," Cuomo told the press. In the first quarter of the year, there were 149 reported bias incidents.

When the Rodney King verdict came down in L.A. at the end of April, New York braced for the worst. Panic and rumors of violence spread. Shops closed. Wall Street quietly emptied. News stations were inundated with reports of a department store being looted, rioting at a train station in Queens, a cop being shot in the head. They actually checked the stories before airing them. Very little of it was actually happening. There were a few isolated incidents, but the city was more or less peaceful. Dinkins was calling the newsrooms and asking them to be careful with their coverage. In fact, Dinkins was furiously at work to prevent a riot: going on TV to denounce the verdict but also to call for calm, meeting with community leaders to ask them to use their influence, and walking the streets of Harlem to meet constituents and shake hands. The storm never came. The conciliator had conciliated. And for once, David Dinkins got some credit. DAVE, TAKE A BOW blared the front page of the *Post*. Visiting Queens, the mayor was a little surprised to find himself thronged by adoring crowds. There was more good news: the city had turned out to have a half-billion-dollar budget surplus for 1992. The crime numbers for 1991 even revealed a modest but real decline. *New York* magazine called him "Air Dinkins." *The New York Times* declared, DINKINS IS MASTERING THE ART OF MAYOR. His poll numbers were up across the board.

Dinkins also suddenly got the opportunity to outmaneuver one of his most entrenched political opponents: the New York Police Department. No matter what painful cuts happened elsewhere in the city budget, no matter how many city workers were laid off, the police had the magical power to grow. Who would dare make cuts to the cops when there was so much crime? The Patrolmen's Benevolent Association jealously guarded the prerogatives and powers of the police, resisting the most modest measures of accountability. In response to anti-corruption measures after cops were caught stealing drugs, the PBA staged an illegal work slowdown, calling in sick, jamming radios, and declining to make arrests. After an officer was indicted for shooting an elderly woman during an eviction, PBA president Phil Caruso led a protest rally of eight thousand off-duty officers—a third of the force—outside the State Supreme Court Building. After Wajid Abdul-Salaam, an MTA employee, died after being hog-tied by police, the police commissioner banned the hog-tying of prisoners. Phil Caruso appealed the rule in court, saying that it was "callously insensitive to the operational needs of police officers and totally ignores their safety, as well as the safety of innocent citizens." After an inquiry was opened into the police beating of a school board chairwoman and her adult children, Caruso led a rally of five hundred off-duty officers outside a precinct house in Brooklyn, chanting, "No justice, no police!" and "Dinkins must go." The PBA, representing a department of twenty-seven thousand officers that was still 75 percent white, defied Dinkins from the beginning. Early in his administration, when he went to address a PBA dinner regarding what he wanted to do about crime, the gathered cops kept talking loudly throughout his speech so he couldn't be heard. He tried to get their attention with jokes and flattery, and then played it off—"They paid enough attention at the right times. It's a festive occasion. I think the reception was excellent." The message the cops were sending was clear.

But in early May '92 the police were not in a position for arrogant displays of heedlessness. Suffolk County detectives arrested five New York City officers for running a coke ring and offering protection services for Dominican gangs. One gang member told investigators that Officer Michael Dowd, the apparent leader on the cops' side, had kidnapped a competitor in Washington Heights and turned him over to the gang to be murdered. The cops were making up to $200,000 a week dealing drugs, so much that they sometimes didn't bother to pick up their NYPD paychecks. Internal Affairs had eyed Dowd in particular for years, but senior officers had prevented a serious investigation. Then *New York Newsday* reported that the Southern District of New York was investigating ten city precincts for corruption. "If they are looking for more Dowds, they came to the right place," an anonymous cop at the Thirty-fourth Precinct in Washington Heights told a *New York Times* reporter. Brooklyn DA Charles Hynes was said to have his eyes on three precincts in the borough, but reports emerged that some years earlier Hynes's office had neglected to go after Dowd when alerted about his activities by another officer. Police commissioner Lee Brown insisted that police corruption was "not systemic." But the presumption that larger systemic corruption did exist was an alibi for dirty cops. "Cops perceive this corrupt system at the top," a police source told the *Newsday* columnist Sydney Schanberg, "and it has a corrosive effect. It's one of the big reasons why cops go sour. They say to themselves, 'Why should I sacrifice myself for a corrupt society.'"

Dinkins swiftly made strong moves, announcing a five-member special commission to be led by former deputy mayor Milton Mollen. Phil Caruso insisted that there was "nothing behind the claim that we have widespread, systemic corruption that's endemic to the whole force," calling the special investigation "a knee-jerk political reaction" that would create "public distrust and [shatter] public confidence in the ability of the police." Dinkins simultaneously released a proposal for an independent Civilian Complaint Review Board to review claims of police misconduct. The CCRB was a long-standing bright red line for the thin blue line of NYPD and the PBA. With the political wind at Dinkins's back and the corruption revelations, it looked like its moment had come again. But just as everything seemed to be coming up Dinkins, the city exploded again.

On July 3, 1992, Michael O'Keefe, a plainclothes officer of the same Thirty-fourth Precinct that housed Michael Dowd, shot and killed a twenty-three-year-old Dominican man named Jose "Kiko" Garcia in the lobby of a Washington Heights apartment building. Police recovered a .38 pistol from the scene, and O'Keefe claimed that he was scuffling with Garcia and feared for his life when he shot him at point-blank range. Witnesses on the scene claimed that O'Keefe had callously executed Garcia—whom the police called "a small-time drug dealer"—while he begged for his life. Locals claimed O'Keefe was a member of a rogue gang of cops who ripped off drug dealers. O'Keefe had in fact been the subject of an Internal Affairs investigation after a woman reported that an officer had let a drug dealer go in exchange for money or drugs, but the charge was never substantiated.

Reports of "disturbances"—trash cans being overturned and garbage being burned—filtered out of Washington Heights. David Dinkins rushed to the neighborhood, attempting to defuse tensions, meeting with Garcia's family. Robert Morgenthau announced that he was investigating the shooting. A vigil and march led by local leaders began peacefully but encountered a line of riot cops as it approached the Thirty-fourth Precinct. Earlier that day, the *New York Post* featured a comment made by a cop over his radio: "NAPALM THE 'HOOD." Scuffles broke out between cops and demonstrators, and the crowd began to throw rocks and bottles at the police. Crowds "rampaged" through the streets, as the newspapers put it, with hundreds of cars burned or overturned, windows broken, and stores looted. Gunfire forced a police helicopter to retreat. Groups of youths threw objects onto traffic on the George Washington Bridge. A man fell from a rooftop while being chased by the cops. Residents said he was thrown off by a police lieutenant. When police reported the arrival of Al Sharpton in the neighborhood, one officer cracked over his walkie-talkie, "Shoot him."

Dinkins returned to Washington Heights with Cardinal O'Connor. Together they met again with Kiko Garcia's family, who joined them in a call for calm. Dinkins paid for Garcia's funeral and arranged for his body to be flown to the Dominican Republic. The PBA, reeling from the wave of corruption allegations, saw an opportunity to hit back hard. Phil Caruso took out a full-page ad in the *Post*, charging that the "mayor has tossed gasoline on what has become an anti-police conflagration." Decrying "mob rule," Caruso also complained about the Civilian Review Board proposal and the police corruption probe, as well as Dinkins's reluctance to adopt a proposal to replace officers' revolvers with 9mm automatic pistols. "In obsequiously giving celebrity status to the family of a convicted drug dealer, the mayor callously ignored the traumatic plight of the police officer involved and managed to transform a drug villain into a martyr," Caruso harangued. "This served to exacerbate the rioting, looting and burning, as misguided individuals and street punks rallied around a convoluted cause." In bold capital letters, Caruso concluded, "WAKE UP NEW YORK, WAKE UP BEFORE IT'S TOO LATE."

Giuliani, itching to resurrect his flagging race against Dinkins, also saw a chance. He penned a letter to *The New York Times*, slamming the mayor's response to the Washington Heights incident. It was basically a higher-brow "amen" to Phil Caruso's *Post* letter. "David Dinkins helped make Mr. Garcia a martyr, in part to promote his crusade for an all-civilian police review board—an idea unpopular with the Police Department leadership, including Mr. Brown." Giuliani also made sure to praise Phil Caruso and his purported decision to leak Garcia's criminal history. "Four violent days passed—in which dozens of stores were looted, cars were overturned and one man was killed—before the public learned of Mr. Garcia's history . . . The president of the Patrolmen's Benevolent Association, Phil Caruso, finally opened the books: Mr. Garcia was a member of Los Cibanos, a Dominican drug gang, and had been convicted of selling drugs and was wanted for violating probation. Mr. Dinkins said he first learned of Mr. Garcia's record in a newspaper." This was not really true. It had been Dinkins's own deputy mayor, Fritz Alexander, who spoke to the press on the record about Garcia's criminal past before the unrest.

Giuliani was cementing his ties with Phil Caruso and the PBA as the cops' candidate. That required him to temper his old zeal as untouchable anti-graft fighter a bit. Mario Biaggi, the former Bronx congressman and onetime cop who'd been convicted by Giuliani's office for extortion, who was now fresh out of federal pokey, announced that he was running in his old district. He was endorsed by the Patrolmen's Benevolent Association. As a prosecutor, Giuliani had called him "blatantly corrupt" and "a thug in a congressman's suit." Now, eyeing another run for mayor, he was spotted shaking hands with Biaggi at a yacht party. "Perhaps a fusion ticket—ex-con/ex-prosecutor—in the works," the *Post* quipped. In the meantime, Giuliani had also mended fences with Senator Alphonse D'Amato.

With open letter after open letter assailing Dinkins in the *Post*, Caruso was rallying his troops and getting them in a high, frothy rage. Dinkins pointed out that the PBA was entering into negotiations with the city at the time: "What they can't get at the bargaining table, they're trying to get by beating on me," the mayor opined. Phil Caruso, Staten Island borough president Guy Molinari, and Giuliani, along with Officer O'Keefe, were to address a protest by the police at City Hall.

On the morning of September 16, ten thousand off-duty police—nearly two-thirds of the force—descended on Lower Manhattan. They carried signs that said MAYOR, HAVE YOU HUGGED YOUR DEALER TODAY; HEY DINKINS, WE'LL PAY FOR YOUR FUNERAL; and DINKINS, WE KNOW YOUR TRUE COLOR—YELLOW BELLIED. One placard featured a silhouette of a face with an exaggerated Afro and giant lips that read DINKINS SUCKS; another read DUMP THE WASHROOM ATTENDANT, taking radio shock jock Bob Grant's favorite epithet for Dinkins. They chanted "Dinkins must go," "No justice, no police," and "The mayor's on crack." Many were drunk, openly swilling from beer cans.

The throng circled city hall two times, as if on some hostile hajj to the Civic Center. "Let's take another turn," Caruso was reported to have said. The situation deteriorated rapidly from there. A group got past the barriers on Broadway and blocked traffic, surrounding a yellow taxi, rocking it back and forth, jumping on its hood and chanting "Dinkins must go." More cries of "Take the hall!" rose up from the crowd. Three thousand officers broke through the barricades surrounding the hall and rushed up the stairs. The three hundred uniformed police assigned to the protest were unable or unwilling to control the crowd. The guards inside city hall had to barricade the doors as the crowd climbed onto the windowsills and banged against the windows. They jumped on top of the official vehicles parked in front. "Someone ought to call a cop," said a Brooklyn city councilman who was trapped inside. The joke got a nervous laugh. Dinkins was not inside: he was uptown attending a funeral.

City council member Una Clarke tried to cross Broadway to get to city hall, identifying herself as an official to a group of officers in PBA T-shirts who were blocking her way. "This nigger says she's a City Council person," one said. "Here let me grab your ass," one cop said to a female TV reporter. "Just let me a get a handful." After recognizing the columnist Jimmy Breslin, officers taunted him: "How did you like the niggers beating you up in Crown Heights? Now you got a nigger right inside City Hall. How do you like that? A nigger mayor."

The crowd split up. Guy Molinari and Rudy Giuliani led a group down Murray Street to the site of the official rally. The bars along the street were packed with cops, reportedly drinking on an open PBA tab since early in the morning. Cops, with their guns on their waists, swaggered down the lane, carrying beers and shoving a Black deliveryman into the street. *The New York Times* painted the scene: "Beer cans and broken beer bottles littered the streets as Mr. Giuliani led the crowd in chants." From the podium, Giuliani declaimed, "The reason the morale of the police department of the City of New York is so low is one reason and one reason alone: David Dinkins!" The crowd cheered.

Giuliani conceded that there was a real need to investigate corruption in the department. The crowd didn't like that much. Then, his voice rising to a high shriek, he charged that the Mollen Commission, which had been set up by the mayor to investigate corruption, was "Bullshit" and that "Dinkins is trying to protect his political ass!" The cops started to chant, "Rudy! Rudy! Rudy!" Caruso's operatics followed Giuliani: "The forces of evil are all around," he said. "They are trying to surround us. They are trying to defeat us."

Meanwhile, a group of several thousand cops had moved east from City Hall Park to block the Brooklyn Bridge. There they knocked over and punched a *New York Times* photographer and kicked the *Times* bureau chief in the stomach. They jumped on the trapped cars and taunted the drivers. *Newsday* described it as a "scene from a fraternity keg party gone amok." One cop in a mock-whine screamed at the motorists, "Are we inconveniencing you?" A woman got out of her car to shout at the Hessians that her baby was suffering from the heat, and the police jeered at her: "Hey, why don't you call a cop." Eventually, after an hour, superiors managed to get the cops to quit the bridge.

MUTINY! the front page of the *Post* declared the next day. Apparently even Phil Caruso thought things had gotten out of hand: slightly embarrassed, he telephoned acting commissioner Ray Kelly to privately apologize. Publicly, he was less contrite. When Dinkins blamed him for actions "bordering on hooliganism," Caruso shot back that Dinkins "was responsible for convening that emotional response." Dinkins also took a crack at Giuliani: "He's clearly an opportunist, he's seizing upon fragile circumstances in our city for his own political gain." Giuliani called Dinkins's remarks "desperate and offensive." Yet not all the cops were in lockstep behind Caruso's leadership. "It's easy for him to fan the flames of racism here and then go home to his peaceful suburban home on the island," said Eric Adams, head of the Grand Council of Guardians, the NYPD fraternal organization of Black officers.

The consensus was that Giuliani had wounded himself, maybe even fatally. Mike McAlary called him "the human scream machine" in the *Post*: "This is still all Giuliani offers New York—screeching racial paranoia." Breslin: "And, elegantly, calmly, but firmly, David Dinkins will turn yesterday into the greatest political break seen around here in a long time. It is something these poor fools from the suburbs don't understand: They gave their enemy a ton of votes in the next New York City election." Kempton: "This may well have been the first riot stimulated although not quite incited by a former United States attorney. The text of Rudolph Giuliani's speech to these demonstrators is unavailable and would perhaps be unprintable since its published shards pulsed with obscenities that in the old and finer times could have earned Giuliani 30 days for disturbing the peace. We have no evidence from lips other than his that Giuliani made any effort to slow the progress from discourse to riot. When the friends of John Gotti showed up to protest his sentence, Bruce Cutler, a mob lawyer, did what he could to contain them. Cutler failed; but the most conspicuous prosecutor of hoodlums in recent history doesn't seem to have even tried."

On WLIB radio, a host talking to Deputy Mayor Bill Lynch compared Giuliani's actions to the Willie Horton gambit. Lynch answered, "It's more like a David Duke for me than a Willie Horton, in that you try to inflame racial tensions rather than try to bring people together." Giuliani shot back: "To compare me to David Duke is sick, and suggests what you're interested in is not racial peace, but racial polarization . . . The mayor plays the racial card when he thinks it is to his advantage, and then he condemns others when they play it. It's phony." Even Dinkins seemed a little bit taken aback at his deputy's bluntness. "I think Bill would probably rethink that," he said. Now Jimmy Breslin opined that Dinkins's attacks were rescuing the drowning Giuliani: "He has no right being on land and on his feet but here he is, shouting at Dinkins and almost beginning to look like an equal. He is perfectly comfortable with a thing like this, a long series of charges and cute arguments and rebuttals, because he always has done this for a living. And Dinkins, who spent so many years only in politics, and thus not holding a real job, is turning amateur. The guy is supposed to be dead and he is trying to give him a whole new life." Dinkins disagreed. "He's not winning on this," Dinkins said on *Weekend Sunday Edition*. "He's losing badly."

Giuliani's advisers tended to agree. The "vulnerability study" he had commissioned for his campaign advised him to back away from the rally and soften his image on race, to return to his liberal Republican "Fusion" strategy, and to reemphasize his time fighting corruption in the police. The study warned him against being seen as the "Human Scream Machine," as the *Post*'s McAlary dubbed him after the cop riot. He didn't take the advice. The supposed political amateur saw something the professionals missed. The path to victory lay not in being Rudolph W. Giuliani, U.S. attorney for the Southern District of New York, but in being "Rudy! Rudy! Rudy!" as the cops on Murray Street chanted. He'd have to foam at the mouth, rant and rave, go a little berserk: he'd have to become the human scream machine.

Giuliani, who had spent his life trying to get rid of the mob, was discovering in practice what the paleos had identified in theory: the mob was inescapable. For the paleos, the mobster, especially as portrayed in *The Godfather*, was a governing American myth on the level of the cowboy. After all, Samuel Francis had encouraged Buchanan to become "the godfather" of a new political movement. In a 1990 review of Martin Scorsese's *Goodfellas*, Rothbard proposed that the mafia movie had provided a mythic American cinema to replace the Western, which itself had been destroyed by left-wing political correctness. Now *Goodfellas*, with its less idealized portrayal of the mafia, risked destroying the mafia film as well. While *The Godfather* films depicted "an epic world, a world of drama and struggle . . . beautifully and broodingly photographed, in which greed struggled with the great virtues of loyalty to the famiglia," *Goodfellas* portrayed the mafia as merely sordid. The violence in *The Godfather* is governed by "the codes of honor and loyalty without which the whole enterprise would simply be random and pointless violence." In contrast, Rothbard complained, "Instead of good versus bad entrepreneurs, all working and planning coherently and on a grand scale, *GoodFellas* [*sic*] is peopled exclusively by psychotic punks, scarcely different from ordinary, unorganized street criminals."

Rothbard looked at the world of *The Godfather* as a utopian vision of the society he wanted to create: "Just as governments in the Lockean paradigm are supposed to be enforcers of commonly-agreed-on rules and property rights, so 'organized crime,' when working properly does that same . . . Organized crime is essentially anarcho-capitalist, a productive industry struggling to govern itself." The key moment signifying the "moral code" of the gangsters in *The Godfather* is the rejection of drug dealing: "In *Godfather*, one Mafia leader of the old school clearly and eloquently rejects traffic in drugs as immoral, in contrast to other venerable goods and services, such as liquor, gambling, and 'loan sharking.' 'Leave drugs to the animals—the niggers—they have no souls,' he admonished. (All right, I never said that the Mafiosi were racially enlightened.) Here is a powerful and dramatic theme of keeping the old Mafia moral code as against the temptation of making a great deal of money in a technologically innovative field." Rothbard misremembers the scene: the Don in question is not rejecting dealing drugs as such, he's saying they should just deal them to Black people, and he does not use the n-word.

While *The Godfather* was essentially a right-wing utopia, Rothbard believed the assault on property and persons in *Goodfellas* reflected the actually existing liberal dystopia of street violence: "Alas, the corrupt nihilist value-system of avant-garde left-liberalism related happily to the value system of the deranged *GoodFellas*. 'This,' say these critics contentedly of the world of the *GoodFellas*, 'is what life is all about. *Godfather* romanticizes life (and is therefore wrong).'" *The Godfather* was capitalist society as it should be: private interest ordered by firm but benign patriarchal rule; *Goodfellas* was capitalist society as perverted by "our leftist culture," which "hates and reviles the Mafia and organized crime, while it excuses and apologizes for chaotic and random street punks." *Goodfellas* lacked real authority figures. It ruined the fantasy. Of course, Rothbard just ignores the tragic fall of the Corleone family. And the fact that *Goodfellas* was based on a true story, while *The Godfather* was not.

Samuel Francis was more sensitive to the tragic side of *The Godfather*, but his reading was similar to Rothbard's. In October '92, Francis published an extended essay in *Chronicles* titled "The Godfather as Political Metaphor." To him, *The Godfather* begins "with not merely an analogy between the warfare and power struggles among criminals on the one hand, and the more normal civil relationships of legitimate society on the other, but also with an actual genealogy that traces the latter to their origins in force and fraud." Marlon Brando's Don Corleone represented the ultimate authority figure, a Prince in the Machiavellian sense: "The Prince is not only above the law but the source of law and all social and political order, so in the Corleone universe, the Don is 'responsible' for his family, a responsibility that authorizes him to do virtually anything except violate the obligations of the family bond."

Like Rothbard, Francis thought the *famiglia* in *The Godfather* stood for an earlier, more wholesome and integrated social form fighting to keep itself intact in an American culture that threatened to dissolve it. The unsatisfactory nature of the broader American society is on display at the beginning of the movie, when the Italian undertaker, having been let down by the American system of justice, comes to Don Corleone for vengeance. "America, as the Don describes it and as Bonasera has experienced it, does not behave like the Corleone family after all, and the differences between the two societies do not favor America. The differences between the two are precisely those between two kinds of social organization that sociologists describe as *Gemeinschaft* and *Gesellschaft* respectively. *Gemeinschaft* refers to a kind of culture characteristic of primitive, agrarian, tribal societies, in which bonds of kinship, blood relationship, feudal ties, social hierarchy, deference, honor, and friendship are the norm." *Gesellschaft*, on the other hand, represented modernity: rationality, calculation, "an essence expressed in such modern organizations as corporations (for which *Gesellschaft* is the German word) and the formal, impersonal, legalistic, bureaucratic organization of the modern state." The Corleones are pitted against modernity: "It is a principal thesis of *The Godfather* that American society is a *Gesellschaft* at war with the *Gemeinschaft* inherent in the extended families of organized crime, and it is the claim of the novel and even more intensely of the films that the truly natural, legitimate, normal, and healthy type of society is that of the gangs." But not all the gangs. For Francis, the Jewish mobsters Moe Greene and Hyman Roth are particularly representative of *Gesellschaft*: they are "motivated mainly by avarice, and the cash bond is the only one they understand."

For Francis, the tragedy of *The Godfather* is that Michael Corleone cannot preserve the *Gemeinschaft* of the family in the midst of the American *Gesellschaft*: his attempts to wield power to protect the family are self-undermining, and he destroys his family: "That was his tragedy, as it is the tragedy of human society. Power is not only necessary to the functioning of society, as Machiavelli taught; it also possesses a relentless logic that eventually eats up itself as it irresistibly converts *Gemeinschaft* into *Gesellschaft* and turns the consensual and deferential social bonds of the former into the coercive commands and cash relationships of modernity." But the exercise of power is unavoidable and necessary, even if it is self-destructive, and Francis celebrates *The Godfather*'s "slap in the face" of "the favorite American myth that through assimilation into the institutional environment offered by the democratic capitalism of the American *Gesellschaft*, human beings can be perfected and force and fraud as enduring and omnipresent elements of social existence can be escaped." The regime of force and fraud had to be accepted, embraced even, albeit without the hypocrisy of liberalism: "Evil, as Machiavelli taught, is a necessary part of social and political organization, though it is to be recognized as such and not disguised through the illusory cant of modernist ideology."

When Gotti went on trial in March, *Newsday* asked several public figures, "Why are we so intrigued by Gotti?" Giuliani supplied one answer: "[The mob] exists because we have great trouble, both philosophically and emotionally, dealing with the place authority should play in our lives. Because America was born as a kind of revolt against authority, we elevate notions of individual liberty very high—and should, right? But then we have a hard time dealing with how we're going to relate to authority. We're not mature about the balance between authority and individual rights . . . We haven't figured out how internalizing the rule of law doesn't oppress you—it makes you free." He might have learned something from the author Robert Lacey's take, just below his own: "Gotti's a satanic sort of authority figure." When New York turned its lonely eyes to John Gotti, it was longing for another kind of authority than the type Giuliani had represented up to that point. It didn't really want the law, universalism, meritocracy, rationality, bureaucracy, good government, reform, blind justice, and all that bullshit. The institutions had failed, the welfare state had failed, the markets had failed, there was no justice, just rackets and mobs: the crowd didn't want the G-man dutifully following the rules, and it didn't want to be part of the "gorgeous mosaic"; it wanted protection, a godfather, a boss, just like the undertaker at the beginning of *The Godfather*. Gotti was not really a figure of revolt and anarchy at all, he was a symbol of order, the old order that many longed for still, an order more real and deeper than the law, upheld by brute power. The papers made much of Giuliani's use of "obscenity" in his speech. Giuliani understood that the voice of real authority was obscene. Maybe all the city's fractious parts came together to make a mosaic, but it was in the form of an icon of John Gotti, a negative spirit of the city as a warren of rackets, mobs, and grasping, fighting individuals. And if Giuliani wanted to be mayor, he'd have to light a candle at the altar.

13

". . . THE ECONOMY, STUPID"

The presidency of George H. W. Bush was going down in history: he had some of the worst approval ratings since late-stage Richard Nixon and Harry Truman. *The Orange County Register*, publishing out of the heartland of Reagan country, had another analogy in mind: "Mr. Bush has failed every bit as much as that last notable failure, Jimmy Carter." The editorial board was calling for him to pull out of the race. So was the conservative activist Richard Viguerie on *Sunday Newsmakers*: "I think the president should follow the example of Harry Truman, Lyndon Johnson, and Richard Nixon and step aside—preserve his place in history, he'd do his party and his country a great service." Bush had a different Harry Truman in mind: not the 1952, step-aside Truman, but the 1948, give-'em-hell Harry, come-from-behind-to-win Truman. He had been reading David McCullough's new mammoth biography of the thirty-third president. Or rather, he had skipped to the end, the parts where Truman triumphed as an apparent underdog, and he'd taken notes. "I cut to about Page 650 or way back in the book, read the chapter or chapters on the whole '48 campaign," Bush told the *Washington Times* editor Wesley Pruden in an Oval Office interview. "It was different then. There was no television to speak of. Truman took his case by train to the American people, and at every stop assailed the Congress that he had called back into session and, once again, had done nothing." Bush said he would also go after a "do-nothing Congress." White House aides talked about him "being in Harry Truman mode." But Harry Truman mode evidently couldn't end his verbal awkwardness: "I'm going to do what Harry Truman did. No, it's not give 'em hell; they're going to think it's hell when I get through with them." He kept invoking Truman's name, intoning it really, repeating it as a mantra or a chant: every line of a stump speech in Waukesha, Wisconsin, began with "Harry Truman."

In one sense, Harry Truman was a natural analogy to reach for. If Reagan was Roosevelt, the president who led a grand realignment and reshaped the nation, then Bush was Truman, the understudy who dutifully continued his work. Maybe they were also fixated on a comment about Perot that was made in a focus group of 1988 Bush voters: "He's no nonsense, he's like Harry Truman." But the comparison between Bush, the country club prep, a Thomas Dewey man back in '48, and the Missouri haberdasher was more than a little strained. "The president 'redefined' himself as Harry Truman because he could not define himself as George Bush," cracked William Safire in *The New York Times*. Margaret Truman, Harry's daughter, sent an op-ed into *The Washington Post* saying that her father would have "not been flattered" and would have been "flabbergasted to learn that he has become the mascot of the Republican Party." She went on to call the president a "political plagiarist" behind an "Ivy League facade," concluding, "To paraphrase Sen. Lloyd Bentsen when in 1988 he rebuked Dan Quayle for comparing himself to John F. Kennedy, I would say to George Bush, 'You are no Harry Truman.'"

Bill Clinton decided it was *he* who was actually Harry Truman. He traveled to Independence, Missouri, Truman's hometown, and gave a speech in front of his statue: "If you give me a chance at the end of the Cold War, I will do what Harry Truman did at the end of

World War II—more opportunity, more responsibility, an America strong at home as well as abroad." But if anybody thought a little about the analogy between 1948 and 1992, they'd have to reflect that the country was almost in the opposite place as it was back then. In 1948 the country was starting to reap the bounty of postwar prosperity and was gearing up to face the Soviet threat; in '92, the country was in a recession, hoping for a "peace dividend" but apparently falling apart amidst the absence of its old rival. This didn't stop Bush from keeping up the Truman show: even going on a whistle-stop tour on the back of a train. Along the way, a couple and their three children dropped their pants and mooned Bush's train as it rolled by. Still, anything that could remind people of glories past; maybe in the haze of nostalgia they'd forget who was a Republican and who was a Democrat. Bush was even paraphrasing lines from FDR. In Longview, Texas, Bush appeared in front of a plane like the one he piloted during the war. "That's the kind of torpedo bomber I flew. I'm proud that I served my nation in combat," he said, making a not-so-subtle jab about Clinton dodging the draft during Vietnam. In the Bush ancestral home of Connecticut, Pratt and Whitney, the company that had once built the engines for World War II planes and that state's biggest private employer, announced that it was laying off 3,600 more workers.

"The economy, stupid." The Clinton campaign had picked its lane of attack: James Carville hung a sign like this in campaign headquarters, and they insistently hammered away on it. "Harry Truman's legacy is the great American middle class," Clinton reminded the crowd in Independence. "George Bush's legacy is the destruction of that very middle class." There was more than a little to it: the bad economic news was relentless. Front page of *The New York Times*, September 3: 63 DAYS AFTER ITS CASH RAN OUT, CALIFORNIA PASSES AUSTERE BUDGET. September 4: RANKS OF U.S. POOR REACH 35.7 MILLION, THE MOST SINCE '64. September 5: 167,000 JOBS LOST IN U.S. BUSINESSES; FED CUTS INTEREST. September 7: INCOME DATA SHOW YEARS OF EROSION FOR U.S. WORKERS.

Nothing Bush could throw at Clinton seemed to stick. The campaign abandoned "family values" when they found it unpopular with voters for being too sanctimonious. Even the constant assault on Hillary Clinton was backfiring: she was becoming a sympathetic figure. Still, as the Bush camp softened its shriller tones, the hard right wanted to continue the *Kulturkampf* launched in Houston. Back at his syndicated column, Pat Buchanan defended his speech against Mario Cuomo's remarks on *Face the Nation*—"What do you mean by 'culture'? That's a word they used in Nazi Germany." Films, education, art, music, history—all were fronts for Buchanan in the cultural war. "While we were off aiding the contras, a Fifth Column in our own country was capturing the culture," he thundered. "Today, the standards are gone. Does it make a difference? Only if you believe books and plays and films and art make a difference in men's lives. Only if you believe Ideas have Consequences." To the litany of cultural degradations Buchanan added the Lost Cause. "Demands are heard throughout the South that replicas of the Battle Flag of the Confederacy be removed from state flags and public buildings. The old iron Confederate soldier who stood for decades in the town square must be removed; after all, he fought in an ignoble cause . . . Slavery vs. freedom, that's all it was about, they tell us . . . They were fighting for the things for which men have always fought: family, faith, friends and country." This last statement brought a rebuke in the form of a letter to the editor from one of the right's intellectual giants, Harry V. Jaffa: "Of course, as much might be said, and said truly, of the German soldiers who fought and died in the Wehrmacht in World War II. The fact is, however, that the armies of the Confederacy served the cause of slavery quite as much as the armies of the Third Reich served the cause of Adolf Hitler."

Murray Rothbard connected the Woody Allen–Soon-Yi Previn–Mia Farrow imbroglio—which was then splashed all over the tabloids—to the culture war. "Woody and Mia's living arrangements constituted a veritable metaphor of what left-liberal 'alternative lifestyles' are all about: out-of-wedlock, separate apartments, Mia's adopting a veritable zoo of multicultural kids, one after the other—all very mod, very trendy, very politically correct. And then, whamo! Woody goes over just about the last line, or, if you want it put that way, the 'last frontier'—incest," the self-proclaimed anarchist wrote. "And here we are. It's Woody Allen, 'If It Moves, Fondle It,' alternative 'families' as any-two-or-more-beings coupling, versus the Traditional, two-parent family, moral principles and restraints, and yes, *Ozzie and Harriet*, the Cleavers and the Waltons. The corrupt, rotten New Culture, versus the glorious life-affirming Old. There is our Cultural War, and it has come none too soon, and just in time."

Introducing Bush at a campaign appearance, Newt Gingrich made a similar attack, ignoring the warnings and objections of Bush's aides: "Woody Allen is not having incest with his non-daughter for whom he has been a non-father because they have a non-family. It's a weird situation and it fits the Democrat Party platform perfectly." Bush's aides had to distance the campaign from these remarks: "The president is not going to make Woody Allen an issue . . . The important thing is that surrogates back the president . . . We do not stand foursquare behind every single statement each of them make."

If not a war zone exactly, American culture near the election did seem full of strange dreams and troubled cries. David Mamet's *Glengarry Glenn Ross* opened in theaters, hailed as *Death of a Salesman* for the modern age. But if *Death of a Salesman*, on the verge of the 1950s, portrayed the American Dream and middle-class life as shallow and materialistic, *Glengarry Glenn Ross* showed them as totally out of reach, an impossible goal for sad and struggling men. "The shabby Chicago real estate office, huddled under the L tracks, could be any white-collar organization in which middle-aged men find themselves faced with sudden and possibly permanent unemployment," Roger Ebert wrote in the *Chicago Sun-Times*. The opening of Spike Lee's *Malcolm X* showed the footage of the Rodney King beating, backed with Malcolm's 1964 "The Ballot or the Bullet" speech, concluding with the lines "I don't see any American dream; I see an American nightmare."

The former Harvard Law professor Derrick Bell, a pioneer of the legal doctrine called "critical race theory," published *Faces at the Bottom of the Well: The Permanence of Racism*, which climbed the *New York Times* bestseller chart. "The racism that made slavery feasible is far from dead in the last decade of twentieth century America," Professor Bell wrote in the introduction. "Despite undeniable progress for many, no African Americans are insulated from incidents of racial discrimination. Even the most successful of us are haunted by the plight of our less fortunate brethren who struggle for existence in what some social scientists call the 'underclass.' Burdened with life-long poverty and soul-devastating despair, they live beyond the pale of the American Dream. What we designate as 'racial progress' is not a solution to that problem. It is a regeneration of the problem in a particularly perverse form." The book took the form of allegorical tales told by the fictional "lawyer-prophet" Geneva Crenshaw. In the final story, the sci-fi tale "The Space Traders," advanced aliens arrive on Earth and offer the United States government gold, technology that could clean up pollution, and a clean source of nuclear energy in exchange for all its Black people. After some fretting and fitful resistance to the idea, America takes the ETs up on their offer: the end of the story shows millions of Black Americans, enchained, being loaded into the Space Traders' ships.

Around the same time, another strange tale of science fiction hit bookstores with a deus ex machina to America's racial nightmare, this time an alternate history rather than vision of the near future. In Harry Turtledove's *The Guns of the South*, time-traveling members of the Afrikaner Weerstandsbeweging, a South African neo-Nazi group, hoping to prevent the end of apartheid, supply Robert E. Lee's Army of Northern Virginia, then on the verge of defeat, with AK-47s. The automatic rifles help the Confederacy win the war, but then the plan falls apart. The kindly General Lee is elected president of an independent South—defeating the KKK founder Nathan Bedford Forrest in the election (who chivalrously concedes)—but Lee has reservations about racism and introduces measures to gradually emancipate the slaves. The time travelers turn on him, and they battle it out with the Confederate army and lose. Lee survives, and slavery is abolished by the Confederate States of America. The near polar opposite of *Faces at the Bottom of the Well*, *The Guns of the South* supplied a fantasy of incorruptible white-national virtue and redemption: even the enslavers could easily turn into emancipators. Not only was racism not permanent, it had barely existed in the first place. The real problem was *extremism*: at one point, Lee, realizing the perfidious nature of his time trekkers, compares their racial fanaticism to that of John Brown. One could thereby preserve the Lost Cause mythos of Southern gallantry and honor and rest assured that racism and slavery were merely a historical accident to be quickly corrected. The unavoidable suggestion was that things may have been actually *better* if the South had won, which made apartheid and time-traveling Nazis historically necessary: hard-core white supremacy was just a useful stage to be eventually overcome and cast aside.

Right at the top of the bestseller list was another dream of America redeemed: Ross Perot's *United We Stand: How We Can Take Back Our Country*. Released after Perot dropped out of the race, it was to have been his platform and plan for national reorganization. The central focus was the deficit and the national debt—"the crazy aunt that we keep in the basement. All the neighbors know she's there, but nobody wants to talk about her"—which Perot connected to the downturn: "We add $1 billion in debt every 24 hours. Does anyone think the present recession just fell out of the sky?" Perot's prescription for "An America in Danger" was a combination of populist political reform to sweep away corrupt lobbyists, politicians, and bureaucrats; industrial policy and protectionism to reinforce national competitiveness with Europe and Asia; and austerity: cuts to entitlements like Medicare, Medicaid, and Social Security. The book envisioned America as a nation of industrious small-business owners, working hard and saving, and, above all, willing to make "sacrifices," to tighten the belt. The government was a business, the people were its owners, and if the business didn't perform, there would be downsizing. It was the Protestant ethic as political theory: frugality, thrift, hard work, and sacrifice. The idea was apparently popular, but who would bear all the sacrifice was a little hazy: polling showed that Perot's supporters were no more willing to face cuts in their Social Security than anybody else. Still, the exhortation was stirring; the book concluded with a call to action: "Only the people can remake our country. Time is short. History is merciless. The whole world awaits your decision." Perot's economic plan was particularly popular among conservative economists. Although they admitted that its combination of tax increases and spending cuts would make the recession worse, they believed that "in the long term" it would eventually put the country in a healthier place.

As Perot exhorted the people, he hoped they would exhort him in turn. He was putting out feelers about getting back into the race. He said he wanted to return so he could buy television ads to publicize his economic plans. "They won't sell it to me unless I declare as a candidate. So I may be the first guy in history that had to declare he was a candidate so he could buy TV time," he told NBC's *Today.* His volunteers had kept up the diligent work of petitioning, and despite "dropping out," he was almost on the ballot in all fifty states. In fact, his organization remained largely intact, but purged of activists he considered troublemakers and firmly under the control of the whiteshirts. He signaled to the volunteer coordinators that they were not enthusiastic enough about pushing him to reenter, but then he would bristle, refuse their entreaties, and push out volunteers who were too forceful with him in the meetings. On *Larry King Live*, Perot announced a new 800 number where supporters could have their say if he should reenter the race; once you called in, there were no options given, just a recording that said "Thank you again for your valued support." In its first three hours, 1.5 million people called into this telephonic plebiscite. As volunteers secured the fiftieth state ballot for Perot, he summoned the other campaign staffs to an audience where they would have an opportunity to put their case to him regarding why he should not reenter. It was pure theatrics, but neither campaign felt they could afford to anger Perot voters.

On October 1, at a press conference in Dallas, Perot announced that he was officially reentering the race. "I know I hurt many of the volunteers who worked so hard through the spring and summer when I stepped aside in July," he declared. "I thought it was the right thing to do. I thought that both political parties would address the problems that face the nation. We gave them a chance. They didn't do it." Perot would have to do a lot more to regain voters' trust: once polling in the mid-30s, he had fallen to a measly 7 percent. He now had a 66 percent unfavorable rating. And the Perot campaign acknowledged the truth of a CBS News story that it had hired private investigators to look into its own volunteers and had credit checks done on them. "The American people are concerned about a government in gridlock," he said. "We know that we cannot constantly pass on a $4 trillion debt to our children. The people want . . . our financial house back in order. The people are concerned that our government is still organized to fight the Cold War. They want it reorganized to rebuild America as the highest priority . . . The people want a new political climate where the system does not attract ego-driven, power-hungry people."

Some last chilly drafts of the Cold War were still blowing through the Bush White House. A new memo released from the office of the former secretary of defense Caspar Weinberger contradicted the president's contention that he had been "out of the loop" during the Iran-Contra affair, portraying Bush instead as directly arguing in favor of the scheme. Now, on top of Iran-Contra, there was what was being called "Iraqgate." A man named Christopher Drogoul, former manager of the Atlanta branch of Italy's Banca Nazionale del Lavoro, pleaded guilty to making billions in fraudulent loans to Iraq that had contributed to Saddam Hussein's military buildup prior to the Persian Gulf War. But at his sentencing hearing he requested to withdraw his guilty plea, stating that his superiors in Rome knew of the scheme, as did high-ranking members of the American national security establishment. Moreover, he said that the U.S. government had guaranteed the loans to the credit-risky nation. Around the time the loans were made, Bush had issued a secret national security directive encouraging financial support to Saddam's regime in order to "moderate" it. This directive came despite congressional pressure to sanction Iraq for the 1988 Halabja gas massacre of Kurds as well as intelligence community warnings that Saddam was pursuing a nuclear weapons program.

Drogoul alleged that he'd been essentially a patsy and was offered the plea deal in exchange for his silence. After first refusing the request to withdraw his plea, federal judge Marvin Shoob granted it and noted in his order, "It is apparent that decisions were made at the top levels of the United States Justice Department, State Department, Agriculture Department and within the intelligence community to shape this case and that information may have been withheld from federal prosecutors seeking to investigate the case or used to steer the prosecutions." It turned out that the White House counsel was calling the U.S. attorney in Atlanta for updates on the case. Attorney General William P. Barr, whom columnist William Safire had started to dub Bush's "Cover-Up General," still refused congressional requests to appoint an independent counsel.

Totally bereft of ideas, direction, or meaning, the Bush campaign itself had started to function like a Cold War intelligence operation. The campaign began to go "100 percent negative" and to rely on the dossiers of the "Oppo" department. There was one red line, though: no sex scandals. This was probably less about a sense of decency than a fear of mutually assured destruction: *Spy* magazine had already published a tantalizing look at Bush's alleged pattern of womanizing. Very little else was off the table. Campaign chief Jim Baker had political appointees at the State Department pull passport records after hours. They were looking for information on a 1969 Christmas-break trip Bill Clinton had taken to Moscow. For good measure, they also looked into Clinton's mother, Virginia Kelley. The little caper blew up in Bush's face: Clinton got a lot of mileage in speeches accusing Bush's people of messing with his "mama." Kelley herself went on *Good Morning America* and angrily denounced the probe into her files: "I'm insulted, I'm indignant, you know I'm at the age that I lived through Hitler and his Gestapo, I lived through the police state, I do not want this to happen to my country."

In keeping with his campaign's throwbacks to the 1940s and '50s, Bush tried a little casual McCarthyism, too. The Orange County representative and Bush campaign California cochairman Robert Dornan started making late-night speeches on the House floor that aired on C-SPAN, alleging that Bill Clinton had traveled to Moscow as a guest of the KGB, which took him around in a limousine and persuaded him to take part in demonstrations against the Vietnam War. Dornan had no evidence of this, and he admitted that he was just "surmising." He headed to the White House, leading a delegation of Republican congressmen who were concerned about the issue, and they left a letter that the Bush-Quayle campaign put out in a press release. It contained a series of questions, including "Did any member of the Communist Party or the Soviet government contact you prior to the trip?" and "Who sponsored your trip and how did you get your visa?" When asked about the Moscow trip on *Larry King Live*, Bush said, "I don't want to tell what I *really think*," then implied that there was a connection between Clinton's visit to the Soviet capital and his decision as a Rhodes Scholar at Oxford to demonstrate "against his own country" while "on foreign soil." Maybe Perot's "dirty tricks" allegations weren't so crazy after all.

At least one candidate was on a mission to Moscow. The nationalist Russian newspaper *Dyen* published an interview with David Duke in an issue calling for a "National Salvation Front," a red-brown alliance of extreme left and extreme right to oppose Boris Yeltsin and replace him with a strongman. "I want Russia to be a strong power, a stronghold between East and West," Duke told the reporter Vladimir Bondarenko. "In my opinion, the destruction of white Russia would be a great explosion for all of Europe. It would be the end of the European blood heritage. If Russia is destroyed, all of us—including Americans—will be destroyed." Asked if he supported the paper's proposal to replace Yeltsin's "treacherous" government with a "white general," Duke replied, "Undoubtedly I will support a man or a party in Russia who will help Russians become strong. I don't care if they follow certain articles of the constitution or not. I think Russia needs a strong personality in order to overcome all the difficulties." NPR interviewed the editor of *Dyen* alongside an aide who was wearing a David Duke button: "The Soviet Union will be restored. It will be called maybe something else. It won't be socialist Soviet Union. It won't be the Russian empire, but a great state and this territory will inevitably rise. I want to turn the will of history back. I want to see Russia, that great mighty nation that I saw in my youth." Shortly after the issue came out, Yeltsin declared the National Salvation Front unconstitutional and banned it. In February, a Constitutional Court ruling reversed Yeltsin's ban. Seven months later, the National Salvation Front were central players in a coup attempt to overthrow Yeltsin.

But back home, interest in the former Wizard had waned. He manned a lonely booth at the "Fall Home Fest," selling DUKE FOR PRESIDENT T-shirts, National Association for the Advancement of White People literature, and a service called Discount Long Distance. "He looked sort of pitiful," observed a Tulane librarian at the convention. "No one was paying attention to him." He was still appearing on talk radio, warning of national riots that would break out when *Malcolm X* hit the theaters. "I think the sentiment of the country will swing my way in the next couple of years," Duke said. "People will look for people like me."

In Seattle, the Populist Party candidate Bo Gritz announced that he would be moving to Washington to start a youth camp to train young people in survival techniques—"but no paramilitary training." The announcement was somewhat overshadowed by news that Gritz had allegedly attacked a documentary filmmaker covering the Preparedness Expo where Gritz was to speak. After being asked a series of "provocative questions," Gritz reportedly lunged at him. The filmmaker said that Gritz then tried to beat him with the camera and Gritz's campaign manager and security guard grabbed him.

Perot's plan for rehabilitating his image with the American people was an all-out TV blitz. No more rallies, no more mobilizing volunteers across the country: just get his face up there, for as long as possible. He bought a series of thirty-minute blocks on the networks in the middle of prime time to put on infomercials. They were to have no special effects, no file footage, no graphics: just Ross, sitting at his desk, holding up charts and a pointer, and talking to the camera. Perot's media advisers warned him that people would immediately change the channel. "Now, I can't compete with some of these other entertainment shows. But please, stay with me on this program tonight because we're going to go down in the trenches and talk about your jobs and talk about why our country is in decline," Perot earnestly entreated the viewers. Then followed half an hour of folksy doom and gloom. The biggest issue was the debt, but he also dealt with the failure of supply-side economics—"Well, I'll tell you one of the reasons we've fallen off the edge of the cliff, we got into trickle-down economics, and it didn't trickle"—and U.S. defense commitments to its allies: "We are draining our treasury to defend the world. The other countries who are rich, the other countries who have what used to be our money, are not bearing their fair share of the defense burden. We've got to change that. They need to do their share." People loved it: the first infomercial, airing on CBS and costing approximately $400,000, garnered more than sixteen million viewers, or 20 percent of all TV sets on at the time.

Perot followed up with slick thirty-second spots that featured scrolling text and an ominous voice-over, with patriotic horns and drums: "While the Cold War is ending, another war is now upon us. In this new war, the enemy is not the red flag of communism, but the red ink of our national debt, the red tape of our government bureaucracy. The casualties of this war are counted in lost jobs and lost dreams. As in all wars, the critical issue to winning is leadership. In this election you can vote for a candidate who has proven his leadership by making the free enterprise system work . . . The candidate is Ross Perot." These spots didn't come cheap. Perot was spending an absolute fortune on ads: $24 million in the first two weeks of October. At an annualized rate, he was spending more than the advertising budget of Chrysler or Nabisco.

The Bush and Clinton campaigns both decided that they could not exclude Perot from the debates except at their peril. He would appear in all three presidential debates, and Admiral James Stockdale would appear in the one vice presidential debate. In the first debate Bill Clinton offered himself as a departure from both "trickle-down economics" and "tax and spend economics." Bush tried to present himself as the voice of "experience," opening up an easy attack for Perot, who countered, "I don't have any experience in running up a $4 trillion debt. I don't have any experience in gridlock government, where nobody takes responsibility for anything and everybody blames everybody else. I don't have any experience in creating the worst public school system in the industrialized world, the most violent crime-ridden society in the industrialized world."

Bush's message was essentially that things weren't so bad: "[Governor Clinton] thinks, I think he said that the country is coming apart at the seams. Now, I know the only way he can win is to make everybody believe the economy is worse than it is. But this country's not coming apart at the seams, for heaven's sakes. We're the United States of America. We—in spite of the economic problems we are the most respected economy around the world. Many would trade for it." When asked a question from a seventy-five-year-old retired saleswoman about his plan to convert the defense industry to peaceful purposes, Bush misunderstood and thought she had been laid off from a job. He repeated his refrain: "Her best hope for the short term is job retraining if she was thrown out of work at a defense plant, but tell her it's not all that gloomy. We're the United States. We got—we've faced tough problems before."

Perot seemed quick, funny, interesting, direct. Clinton seemed prepared, sincere, reasonable—and Bush? He was a little waspish and defensive. A tone of pleading, even whining, entered into his responses. After the three debates, Perot had recovered some support, climbing to around 20 percent in the polls. Perot was many people's pick to have done the best in the debates, even if they didn't support him. Fifty percent said they were more likely to vote for him. Not even a majority of Bush supporters thought Bush did the best job. Perot's good marks held up even after his running mate's disastrous effort. "Who am I? Why am I here?" James B. Stockdale began with a rhetorical question that appeared less rhetorical as the debate went on: he looked dazed by the studio lights, he could not keep up, seemed to have only a vague understanding of his ticket's own platform, and frequently sounded "addled," as the *Times* put it, and even bizarre. Speaking about the urban crisis, Stockdale changed the subject to his time in a Vietnamese prison camp. "I ran a civilization for several years, a civilization of 3 to 4 hundred wonderful men. We had our own laws. We had our own, practically our own constitution," the admiral explained. "I was the sovereign for a good bit of that." *Saturday Night Live* ran a skit with Dana Carvey as Ross Perot and Phil Hartman as a confused and senile Stockdale. The two are driving in the country together; Perot tricks Stockdale into getting out of the car and then drives away.

The focus of the campaign may have turned to the economy, but voters had trouble differentiating between the candidates' economic plans. They were all variations on a few themes: tax cuts, deficit reduction, retraining, belt-tightening, but also a focused industrial policy—although Bush could not call it that—to help America recover international competitiveness. Perot successfully turned the deficit and debt into a proxy for the general economic state of the nation. The public liked the sound of tackling these things but usually balked when asked about specific cuts that could do it. Clinton had to walk a tightrope: appear to be serious about the deficit but also willing to use "activist government" to stimulate the economy. "There may be some way to increase investment without increasing the deficit," he told a crowd in Richmond. "We have to keep these things in very careful balance." Clinton not only feared the voters—he was also worried that merely proposing a stimulus that could add to the deficit might spook the bond traders and hurt the economy even more. "You have to be very respectful of the need to reduce the deficit over the medium- and long-term and you have to be very respectful of the financial markets' sensitivities," opined Roger Altman, economic adviser to Clinton and a former partner at Lehman Brothers.

One constituency seemed to appreciate the difference between Bush and Clinton: Silicon Valley bosses. Clinton won the endorsement of twenty industry executives, the majority of them Republicans, such as John Sculley of Apple, Inc., and Hewlett-Packard's John Young. They were fed up with the Bush administration's lack of interest in investing in technology and bothered by the fact that trade negotiations with Japan favored the interests of the auto industry rather than themselves and by the remark of the White House economic adviser Michael Boskin that $100 worth of potato chips was no different from $100 of computer chips. "Clinton's policies read like a grab bag of goodies for Silicon Valley," one California paper put it. He offered anti-dumping policies for foreign-made semiconductors, a more level trade playing field for electronics producers, more protections for intellectual property rights, financing for fiber-optic networks, and tax credits for new manufacturing equipment and research and development. The discovery of a new friend in Clinton was somewhat less than serendipitous: the Clinton plan had been pretty much written by the executives themselves, and the campaign's policy statement quoted their remarks extensively. The executives presented their interests as the national interest, their issues as the country's—they were the key to the future and the only way to survive. "We are no longer a post-industrial economy. We are on a path to becoming a de-industrial economy," said one Silicon Valley venture capitalist, a former executive at Intel and Hewlett-Packard. "We will be a nation of knowledge workers or a colony of post-industrial serfs."

For the rest of the country, the present state of the economy seemed to stand for a deeper sense of national disintegration. Jon Margolis, a *Chicago Tribune* columnist, disputed that "the economy" was really the issue at all: "This campaign is taking place amidst economic doldrums, but in neither recession nor high inflation. That is why the real problem now is not that 'the economy' is in bad shape. It's worse than that. Were it only 'the economy,' an incumbent president who'd won a war and who was not suspected of stealing the White House silver would not be in such straits. George Bush is in such straits not because 'the economy' alone is in bad shape, but because the country is in bad shape. The United States' economy, to begin with, yes, but also its culture, its confidence, its sense of what it is. And the country is in bad shape because it broke the deal." According to Margolis, the deal had been that the citizens would do something productive and in return would get a comfortable standard of living, rising prospects for their children, and protection "from most calamities." At some point the "country opted out and the citizens know it. That's why more than just the economy is troubled; the whole society is. A sense of security that blanketed most of it for decades has been snatched away." This was obscured by the economic growth of the Reagan years, but when that growth stopped, that security went with it: "The reality was exposed. There is no deal. Without it, the United States is a different country, and an unhappier one." The prospects of postindustrial life, of a nation of "knowledge workers," seemed grim: "Making big, thick, heavy things can provide the average person with a pretty good wage. Sending electronic impulses rarely does."

Ross Perot seemed to be steadily recapturing that sense of broad discontent. He was going to start up with rallies and public appearances again, delighting the faithful. Perot's southwestern Pennsylvania coordinator, a dentist, told the *Times* that he had to "hit myself in the chest to prove this was really happening." The manager of a Perot campaign office in New Jersey was transported to even further regions: "It's going to be like seeing a Virgin Mary or an apparition or something." Someone covered the first five letters of the Hollywood sign in Los Angeles so that it read PEROTWOOD. But the invocation of an "apparition" was perhaps too apposite. Just as Perot's shape reappeared and consolidated, seemed solid and real again, it started to fade. Appearing on *60 Minutes*, he went public with his beliefs about the Republican dirty tricks campaign against his daughter, saying that it was the real reason he dropped out in July. Perot told Lesley Stahl, "I received multiple reports that there was a plan to embarrass her before her wedding and to actually have people in the church at the wedding to disrupt her wedding. I finally concluded that I, as a father who adores his children, could not take that risk. And since the wedding was on a finite date, I made the decision that I would step aside, which I did." He alleged that the Bush-Quayle campaign had doctored a photo of his daughter. He would not give the names of his two sources, denying that Scott Barnes, a former soldier with a failed career in law enforcement who claimed to have connections to Special Forces and the intelligence community, was the primary one. On the program, Barnes alleged that the Bush campaign had contacted him with a scheme to wiretap Perot's office. The FBI had investigated Barnes's and Perot's claims and even attempted a sting operation on Bush's Texas campaign chief, and they'd come to the conclusion that the entire thing had been concocted by Barnes. Perot hoped his *60 Minutes* interview would help expose the Bush campaign's skullduggery, but it just made him look a little nuts again, an impression not helped by a news story that a number of former volunteers had asked the feds to investigate the Perot campaign for its credit checks on them. Perot's momentum stalled out—the public had grown weary.

But now it was Clinton's turn to falter. His formidable lead appeared to evaporate. Polling during the final stretch showed Bush surging, with the election practically in a dead heat. Perhaps the relentless attacks on Clinton's "character" and truthfulness were working? A sense of panic descended on Clinton's vaunted war room. Would it all slip away at the last minute? Bush turned frenzied, even approaching stream of consciousness, in his assaults on Clinton and Gore. He started calling Gore "Ozone Man": "You know why I call him Ozone man? This guy is so far off in the environmental extreme, we'll be up to our neck in owls and out of work for every American. This guy's crazy. He is way out, far out. Far out, man!" In Ohio, he pressed the "message" home: "Governor Clinton and Ozone all they do is talk about change. My dog Millie [a springer spaniel] knows more about foreign affairs than these two bozos." The crowds seemed to enjoy it, but Bush's aides were discomfited.

Then the final nail. Just as Bush was preparing to appear on *Larry King Live*, a federal grand jury handed down an indictment of former secretary of defense Caspar Weinberger. Weinberger had lied to the House Iran-Contra committee that he had made no notes about meetings relating to the scheme. He had in fact recorded them meticulously. The evidence that accompanied the indictment included a note that recorded Bush's support for a plan to sell anti-tank missiles to Iran in exchange for releasing five hostages. The notion that Bush was "out of the loop" during Iran-Contra was an utter falsehood. The Clinton adviser George Stephanopoulos even called in to *Larry King* to berate the president about it. The issue of "truthfulness" had been turned around conclusively on Bush. Internally, his campaign all but conceded defeat.

On Election Day, Tuesday, November 3, 58 percent of the American public turned out, a major reversal from years of declining participation. In sheer numbers, more Americans than ever before voted. The results were quick and clear: Clinton secured an Electoral College blowout: 370 to 168. He got 43 percent of the popular vote to Bush's 37.5; Perot got 18.9 percent, the best result for a third-party candidate since Teddy Roosevelt's 1912 run. Clinton largely brought back the so-called Reagan Democrats who had defected to the GOP. Although Black voter turnout decreased, he stayed solid with that core Democratic constituency, with 83 percent. He also received votes from upper-middle-class suburban voters, a demographic that the Democrats had struggled to crack beforehand. But despite a commanding win in the Electoral College, it was difficult to claim a powerful mandate with a mere plurality of the popular vote. And a majority of voters still described themselves as "concerned," "scared," or "apprehensive" at the prospect of a Clinton presidency.

In *The Washington Times*, Sam Francis faulted the Bush campaign for giving up on the cultural front. "Let's get one thing straight right now: Bill Clinton did not win the election by winning the Reagan Democrats. President Bush lost the election by losing the Reagan Democrats," he propounded. "Moreover, Mr. Perot—as well as Mr. Clinton—were able to run off with a good many Reagan Democrats by their vague but distinct affirmations of the economic interests of the middle-class and the nation, without exhibiting any hostility to middle-class culture and national identity. Mr. Bush and the conservatives have generally beat the drum for one version or another of globalism—free trade, unlimited immigration and global political intervention—that has no appeal outside their Beltway egghead allies." According to Francis, the Republicans should've hammered home the stark message of culture war: "It wasn't enough just to slap the Hollywood-Manhattan 'cultural elite' axis. The point was to connect Mr. Clinton and his campaign with that elite, to make voters believe that Mr. Clinton's running mate was Woody Allen and his campaign manager Ice-T. Then Reagan Democrats might have stayed put."

In his monthly *Chronicles* column, titled "An Electorate of Sheep," Francis was more openly apoplectic and wrathful, slamming the American voters' willingness to be manipulated and managed:

> It is all very well to blame the politicians, managers, media wizards, and incumbents who profit from this system, but the truth is that it is the citizens themselves who permit it to flourish and endure. It is a universal characteristic of modern mass organizations that they encourage dependency and passivity, that most of the individuals who are members of these organizations cannot possibly understand or acquire the highly technical skills that enable the organizations to exist and function, and that the role of most of their members is entirely passive and subordinate while power and responsibility are centered in an elite that does understand and perform their technical operations. Lacking any real power

or responsibility, the members merely do their jobs and behave as they are told to behave.

According to Francis, "even Populist revolts like that of the Perot movement . . . cannot survive apart from manipulation and managed leadership." Perot's followers, he suggested, were crybabies who should've taken matters into their own hands after he "betrayed" them. Then Francis turned to the lack of revolt on the part of the public:

> What is really amazing about American society today is not that there is so much violence and resistance to authority but that there is so little, that there is not or has not long since been a full-scale violent revolution in the country against the domination and exploitation of the mass of the population by its rulers. A people that once shot government officials because they taxed tea and stamps now receives the intrusions of the Internal Revenue Service politely; a society that once declared its independence on the grounds of states' rights now passively tolerates federal judges and civil servants who redraw the lines of electoral districts, decide where small children will go to school, let hardened criminals out of jail without punishment, and overturn local laws that are popularly passed and have long been enforced.

Invoking *The Magnificent Seven*, Francis concluded that Americans would soon have to relearn to fight: "If there remain today any Americans who are not sheep, they'll stop trying to hire phony populist gunfighters to save them from the wolfish bandits who run the country, and in the next four years they'll start learning how to shoot for themselves."

The new Clinton administration, after a hopeful inauguration, was running into frustrating problems. Plans to open the military to gays and lesbians leaked to the news, making it appear that this, not the economy, was the new president's top priority. The military made it clear that they would fight him on it. Advisers explained to him that financial market conditions made many of his economic plans impossible. A modest stimulus program was blocked by a Republican filibuster in the Senate. Concerned about higher interest rates, Clinton decided to favor the approach of the deficit hawks in his circle, proposing $253 billion in spending cuts.

At the postelection Republican retreat in New Jersey, everyone crowded around Frank Luntz, a former pollster for Buchanan and Perot. He gave a presentation called "The Perot Vote and the GOP's Future" and breakfasted with House minority whip Newt Gingrich, who had barely fended off a primary challenge over his twenty-two bad checks. "If they don't go after the Perot voter like Clinton is, they'll be in the wilderness for a long time," Luntz warned the Republicans. Luntz's research found that Perot's vote had become steadily more male, more conservative, less educated, and less well-off as Election Day approached. He counseled the Republicans to pursue "economic or political reform issues; speak to the forgotten middle class; speak in plain, non-political English; avoid ideological labels; cast doubt on Clinton's honesty."

Around noon on February 26, 1993, a bomb detonated in the parking garage under the North Tower of the World Trade Center in New York City. Six people died, and more than a thousand were injured. The plan, concocted by Islamist radicals who'd trained at a camp in Afghanistan run by a group known as Al-Qaeda, was to send one tower crashing into the other, bringing down both skyscrapers in the process. It seemed an outlandish and impossible goal: the bomb had barely damaged the building. Two days later, federal agents got into a shootout while attempting to serve a search warrant on the compound of a heavily armed "doomsday cult" led by a charismatic preacher named David Koresh outside of Waco, Texas. Four ATF agents were killed and fourteen injured. The FBI initiated a siege, which attracted a camp of anti-government demonstrators, seeing in it a repeat of Ruby Ridge. Among them was a Gulf War veteran named Timothy McVeigh. Fifty-one days later, the FBI attempted to break the stalemate with a tear gas attack on the compound. A fire engulfed the buildings, where seventy-six people—including twenty-five children—were killed.

In April, Ross Perot was hitting the shows again. On *Meet the Press*, he campaigned against the North American Free Trade Agreement, or NAFTA, brandishing a handful of print advertisements intended to entice American manufacturers to relocate their plants down to Mexico. He had another book out—*Not for Sale at Any Price: How We Can Save America for Our Children*. Its chapter dedicated to NAFTA was called "A Giant Sucking Sound," a phrase Perot had used to great effect in his debate with Clinton and Bush: "If this agreement is signed as it is currently drafted, the next thing you will hear will be a giant sucking sound as the remainder of our manufacturing jobs—what's left after the two million that went to Asia in the 1980s—get pulled across our southern border." After months of debate, Clinton would get NAFTA passed, but only with Republican help; in the House, the majority of his own party voted against it, 156 to 102.

In May, Sam Francis gave a presentation at a conference on "Winning the Culture," which had been organized by Pat Buchanan's new American Cause foundation. "The first thing we have to learn about fighting and winning a cultural war is that we are not fighting to conserve something; we are fighting to overthrow something," Francis began. To effect this overthrow, he told his audience, they had to look to the left, since the conservative tradition was focused "on the defense of existing authority." The figure the right should refer to was "the Italian communist Antonio Gramsci, whose idea of 'cultural hegemony' has facilitated the cultural revolution that the enemies of American civilization have pulled off in the last half century." According to Francis, Gramsci's idea "recognizes that political power is ultimately dependent on cultural power—that human beings obey because they share, perhaps unconsciously, many of the assumptions, values, and goals of those who are giving them orders—and, second, that in order to challenge the dominance of any established authority, it is necessary to construct a countervailing cultural establishment, a 'counter-hegemony' (or, as the New Left called it, a 'counterculture') that is independent of the dominant cultural apparatus and is able to generate its own system of beliefs." This insight had been shared by others as well: "It is interesting to note that Adolf Hitler seems to have conceived much the same idea in the aftermath of his failed 1923 Beer Hall Putsch . . . In the years between Hitler's failed putsch and his coming to power in 1933, he and the Nazis built up an entire series of party institutions that paralleled and duplicated those of the existing state, including groups for women, youth, workers, students, artists, and intellectuals, as well as the party's propaganda organs and its paramilitary forces, so that by the time Hitler became chancellor in 1933, the national socialist state had already been 'prefigured' (to use a term of Gramsci) in the party organization, and the actual seizure of state power merely enabled the party to substitute its own apparatus for that of the old state." The American right should emulate this approach: "While Gramsci and Hitler sought to develop their cultural strategy for totalitarian ends, communist in the case of Gramsci and national socialist in the case of Hitler, the same strategy can be used for conservative purposes, and probably even more successfully in the United States since beneath the encrustation of the dominant cultural apparatus of the left in this country there still persists an enduring cultural core of traditional beliefs and institutions." This could not be accomplished by "movement conservatism," dominated by corrupt "neoconservatives" and "globalists" content to hold petty sinecures within the regime. Instead, grassroots efforts, "independent of both the federal state and its cultural tentacles . . . with their own vision of culture," should grow their numbers, use issues like "abortion . . . homosexuality, school curricula and gun control" to "raise consciousness" and "inform previously inactive citizens and groups of how they are all the victims of an alien domination and of what they can do to resist it." Then these local movements should consolidate into a national movement and form "the effective base for a national political campaign or a presidential administration." Francis concluded: "The strategy by which this new American revolution can take place may well come from what was cooked up in the brain of a dying communist theoretician in a Fascist jail cell 60 years ago, but we can make use of it not to build the lies of socialism and the enslavement of communism but to conserve the freedom and dignity that American civilization has always represented and can represent again, if only we have the strength and the will and the common purpose to take back our country and our culture."

A diehard anticommunist was invoking a communist revolutionary as his prophet. The dialectic was turning: history, if not ending, was oddly twisting inside out. The main enemy was at home now. But Francis couldn't have known that the "new American revolution" when it came might look more like something led by one of those "phony populist gunfighters" than a tightly organized national mass movement. And that a guardian of the "dignity that American civilization has always represented" might look more like something out of *Goodfellas* than *The Godfather*.

The week after Election Day, *New York* magazine put Donald Trump on the cover in a prizefighter's stance: FIGHTING BACK: TRUMP SCRAMBLES OFF THE CANVAS. Trump was working on *The Art of the Comeback*, a follow-up to *The Art of the Deal*, and in the new book he was linking his own misfortunes to the economic downturn—"I was the cover boy, I was the leader of the depression," he recited into a mini tape player. Still technically without assets because of his bankruptcies, Trump was trying to get the world-famous architect Philip Johnson, pioneer of modernism and postmodernism, now age eighty-six, to redesign the facade of the Trump Taj Mahal in Atlantic City.

As a young man, under the influence of the American fascist Lawrence Dennis, Johnson had quit his job at the Museum of Modern Art and taken a road trip with a fellow Harvard grad down to Huey Long's Louisiana. He told friends he was "leaving to be Huey Long's minister of fine arts." The *New York Herald Tribune*'s Joseph Alsop covered it with a bit of a smirk: "Two Quit Modern Art Museum for Sur-Realist Political Venture." "All you need is faith, courage, and loyalty. If you have them, you'll get things done," the young Johnson told Alsop. "That's the terrible thing today, why the Dillinger and Capone gangs are the only groups that have got courage. Beyond that nothing is needed, not even consistency. The only necessary consistency is consistency of feeling."

Almost sixty years later, Johnson listened to Trump rant and rave in the limo drive on the way to Atlantic City. "You'd make a good mafioso," Johnson said. "One of the greatest," Donald replied.

NOTES

Introduction: The End

3 *"negative solidarity"*: The concept originates in Arendt, Hannah. *The Origins of Totalitarianism.* 1st ed. Harcourt, Brace, Jovanovich, 1973, 601.

4 *politics of national despair*: This is a variation on Fritz Stern's "the politics of cultural despair" from Stern, Fritz. *The Politics of Cultural Despair: A Study in the Rise of the Germanic Ideology.* University of California Press, 1974.

5 *"toward home"*: Reagan, Ronald. "Transcript of Reagan's Farewell Address to American People." *The New York Times*, January 12, 1989.

5 *two Manhattans*: Lohr, Steve. "Banking's Real Estate Miseries." *The New York Times*, January 13, 1991, sec. 3.

5 *five hundred banks*: "What Are Bank Runs and Bank Failures—and How Common Are They?" Accessed July 27, 2023. https://usafacts.org/articles/what-are-bank-runs-and-bank-failuresand-how-common-are-they/.

6 *income from rents*: Phillips, Kevin. *The Politics of Rich and Poor: Wealth and the American Electorate in the Reagan Aftermath.* 1st ed. Random House, 1990, 11.

6 *shrank by 20 percent*: Morin, Richard. "America's Middle-Class Meltdown." *The Washington Post*, December 1, 1991.

6 *"job polarization"*: Jaimovich, Nir, and Henry E. Siu. "Job Polarization and Jobless Recoveries." Working Paper. NBER Working Papers Series. National Bureau of Economic Research, August 2012.

7 *"diminished expectations"*: Krugman, Paul R. *The Age of Diminished Expectations: U.S. Economic Policy in the 1990s.* 5th printing, 1st paperback ed. MIT Press, 1992.

7 *"If Marx"*: Will, George F. "What Dukakis Should Be Saying." *The Washington Post*, September 15, 1988.

7 *"individualism grown cancerous"*: Bellah, Robert Neelly. *Habits of the Heart: Middle America Observed.* Hutchinson, 1988, 13.

7 *"Darwinian"*: Phillips, *The Politics of Rich and Poor*, 67.

7 *business failure*: "Economic Report of the President," February 1992, 404.

7 *states struggled*: Grant, Don Sherman. "The Political Economy of Business Failures Across the American States, 1970–1985: The Impact of Reagan's New Federalism." *American Sociological Review* 60, no. 6 (1995): 851–73.

8 *"fratricidal competition"*: Crotty, James R. "Rethinking Marxian Investment Theory: Keynes-Minsky Instability, Competitive Regime Shifts and Coerced Investment." *Review of Radical Political Economics* 25, no. 1 (1993): 1–26.

8 *About half*: Goldstein, Dan. "Uncertainty, Competition, and Speculative Finance in the Eighties." *Journal of Economic Issues* 29, no. 3 (September 1995): 719–46.
8 *"Today's corporate executives"*: Reich, Robert B. "Leveraged Buyouts: America Pays the Price." *The New York Times*, January 29, 1989, sec. 6.
9 *hitting an all-time record*: Phillips, Kevin. *Boiling Point: Republicans, Democrats, and the Decline of Middle-Class Prosperity*. 1st ed. Random House, 1993, 178.
9 *rang hollow*: Duffy, Michael, and Dan Goodgame. *Marching in Place: The Status Quo Presidency of George Bush*. Simon and Schuster, 1992, 31.
10 *"it's jobs"*: Germond, Jack W., and Jules Witcover. *Mad as Hell: Revolt at the Ballot Box, 1992*. Warner Books, 1993, 47.
11 *"worse than Hitler"*: Hurst, Steven. "The Rhetorical Strategy of George H. W. Bush During the Persian Gulf Crisis 1990–91: How to Help Lose a War You Won." *Political Studies* 52, no. 2 (June 2004): 376–92.
12 *Jewish bankers*: Robertson, Pat. *The New World Order*. Word Publishing, 1991, 81.
12 *"mirage in the desert"*: Germond and Witcover, *Mad as Hell*, 39.
12 *recession that took hold*: Walsh, Carl E. "What Caused the 1990–1991 Recession?" *Economic Review: Federal Reserve Bank of San Francisco* 2 (1993): 33–48.
12 *"animal spirits"*: Blanchard, Olivier. "Consumption and the Recession of 1990–1991." Working Paper. Department of Economics, Massachusetts Institute of Technology and National Bureau for Economic Research, January 1993.
12 *"jobless recoveries"*: Jaimovich and Siu, "Job Polarization and Jobless Recoveries."
12 *white-collar*: Phillips, *Boiling Point*, 175.
12 *"wrong track"*: Phillips, *Boiling Point*, 58.
12 *"a behemoth system"*: Harwood, Richard C. "Citizens & Politics: A View from Main Street America." Kettering Foundation, 1991, 19.
13 *"a corrosive cynicism"*: Barta, Carolyn. *Perot and His People: Disrupting the Balance of Political Power*. Summit Group, 1997, 64.
13 *worst off*: Phillips, *The Politics of Rich and Poor*, 25.
13 *"guillotine"*: Barta, *Perot and His People*, 66.
13 *"term limits"*: Francis, Samuel. "Term Limits—Tip of a Tidal Wave?" *The Washington Times*, November 12, 1991, final edition.
14 America: What Went Wrong?: Barlett, Donald L., and James B. Steele. *America: What Went Wrong?* Andrews and McMeel, 1992.
14 *"At the highest levels"*: Greider, William. *Who Will Tell the People: The Betrayal of American Democracy*. Simon and Schuster, 1992.
14 *"faction"*: Goodwin, Richard N. *Promises to Keep: A Call for a New American Revolution*. 1st ed. Times Books, 1992.
14 Culture Wars: Hunter, James Davison. *Culture Wars: The Struggle to Control the Family, Art, Education, Law, and Politics in America*. Basic Books, 1992.
14 *wave of immigration*: Arocha, Zita. "1980s Expected to Set Mark as Top Immigration Decade." *The Washington Post*, July 23, 1988.
15 *"deliberate Balkanization"*: Krauthammer, Charles. "'Melting Pot' Hardens into Warring Factions." *St. Louis Post-Dispatch*, September 4, 1990, Three Star edition, sec. Editorial.
15 *"decomposition of America"*: Schlesinger, Arthur M. *The Disuniting of America: Reflections on a Multicultural Society*. Norton ed., 1st paperback ed., 118.
16 *"promised land"*: West, Cornel. *Race Matters*. Beacon Press, 1993, 25.
17 *"very sad time"*: Fukuyama, Francis. "The End of History?" *The National Interest*, Summer 1989, 18.
17 *"belated discovery"*: Lasch, Christopher. "Liberalism and Civic Virtue." *Telos*, no. 88 (June 20, 1991): 57–68.
18 *"other evils"*: Lasch, Christopher. *The True and Only Heaven: Progress and Its Critics*. Norton, 1991, 17.
18 *"increasingly defensive"*: Lasch, *The True and Only Heaven*, 531.
18 *"real enthusiasm"*: Lasch, "Liberalism and Civic Virtue," 67.

18 *"old political ideologies"*: Lasch, *The True and Only Heaven*, 21.
18 *"the great masses"*: Gramsci, Antonio. *Selections from the Prison Notebooks of Antonio Gramsci*. International Publishers, 1971, 276.
18 *"representatives and represented"*: Gramsci, *Selections from the Prison Notebooks of Antonio Gramsci*, 210.
19 *"has lost its consensus"*: Gramsci, *Selections from the Prison Notebooks of Antonio Gramsci*, 275.
19 *"ruling class has failed"*: Gramsci, *Selections from the Prison Notebooks of Antonio Gramsci*, 210.
19 *"morbid symptoms"*: Gramsci, *Selections from the Prison Notebooks of Antonio Gramsci*, 276.
19 *"violent solutions"*: Gramsci, *Selections from the Prison Notebooks of Antonio Gramsci*, 305.

1. Swamp Creature

25 *"chicanery"*: Du Bois, William E. B. *Black Reconstruction in America: 1860–1880*. 1st ed. The Free Press, 1998, 478.
25 *"Lebanon"*: Brinkley, Alan. *Voices of Protest: Huey Long, Father Coughlin, and the Great Depression*. 1st ed. Knopf, 1982, 16.
26 *demagoguery*: Jeansonne, Glen. "Huey Long and Racism." *Louisiana History: The Journal of the Louisiana Historical Association* 33, no. 3 (1992): 265–82.
26 *old-age pensions*: Jeansonne, "Huey Long and Racism," 272.
26 *"nickel"*: Cummins, Light Townsend, Judith Kelleher Schafer, Edward F. Haas, Michael L. Kurtz, Bennett H. Wall, and John C. Rodrigue. *Louisiana: A History*. 6th ed. Wiley Blackwell, 2014, 340.
27 *Jesus*: Brinkley, *Voices of Protest*, 29.
27 *Pelley*: Schlesinger, Arthur Meier. *The Age of Roosevelt: The Politics of Upheaval*. Houghton Mifflin, 1960, 64.
27 *"totalitarian"*: Schlesinger, *The Age of Roosevelt*, 60.
28 *"middle class today?"*: Schlesinger, *The Age of Roosevelt*, 62.
28 *"corruption"*: Jeansonne, Glen. "Huey P. Long: A Political Contradiction." *Louisiana History: The Journal of the Louisiana Historical Association* 31, no. 4 (1990): 373–85.
29 *feux follets*: Houck, Olivia A. "The Reckoning: Oil and Gas Development in the Louisiana Coastal Zone." *Tulane Environmental Law Journal* 28, no. 2 (Summer 2015): 185–296.
29 *"Puke Duke"*: Bridges, Tyler. *The Rise of David Duke*. University Press of Mississippi, 1994.
30 *"Buchenwald"*: Jeansonne, Glen. "Huey P. Long, Gerald L. K. Smith and Leander H. Perez as Charismatic Leaders." *Louisiana History: The Journal of the Louisiana Historical Association* 35, no. 1 (1994): 5–21.
30 *particular book*: Bridges, *The Rise of David Duke*, 3.
30 *"equalitarian"*: For a detailed treatment of Putnam, see Jackson, John P., Jr., *Science for Segregation: Race, Law, and the Case Against* Brown v. Board of Education. NYU Press, 2005.
30 *curriculum*: John P. Jackson Jr., *Science for Segregation*, 120.
32 *shirtless*: Bridges, *The Rise of David Duke*, 76.
32 *"Jonathan Swift"*: Rider, Andrea. "Conduct Unbecoming a Racist." *Spy*, September 1991, 41.
32 *"fellatio"*: Bridges, *The Rise of David Duke*, 78.
33 *"no qualms"*: Rider, "Conduct Unbecoming a Racist," 40.
33 *"seducing"*: Rider, "Conduct Unbecoming a Racist," 40.
34 *piano*: Bridges, *The Rise of David Duke*, 106.
34 *chemical peels*: Bridges, *The Rise of David Duke*, 104.
34 *craps*: Bridges, *The Rise of David Duke*, 103.
34 *"basic alien nature"*: Bridges, *The Rise of David Duke*, 39.
35 *wages*: Powell, Laurence N., "Slouching Towards Baton Rouge." In *The Emergence of David Duke and the Politics of Race*. Edited by Douglas D. Rose. University of North Carolina Press, 1992, 29.
35 *jobs*: Powell, "Slouching Towards Baton Rouge," 28.
35 *"a microcosm of white America"*: Maraniss, David. "Winning Support with a White-Power Image; Voters Warm to Ex-Klan Leader as Louisiana Establishment Worries." *The Washington Post*, February 14, 1989.

37 *"I'm in the closet about it"*: Bridges, *The Rise of David Duke*, 141.
37 *"totalitarianism"*: Duke, David. "David Duke Answers James Gill." *The Times-Picayune*, January 10, 1989, A-8.
37 *"illegitimate"*: Bridges, *The Rise of David Duke*, 141.
38 *"interest at heart"*: Rose, *The Emergence of David Duke and the Politics of Race*, 28.
38 *"sleepy"*: O'Byrne, James. "Duke: Anatomy of an Upset." *The Times-Picayune*, March 5, 1989, A-13.
38 *"Providence"*: O'Byrne, "Duke: Anatomy of an Upset," A-14.
38 *"colored"*: Maraniss, "Winning Support with a White-Power Image; Voters Warm to Ex-Klan Leader as Louisiana Establishment Worries."
39 *"establishment"*: Theim, Rebecca. "Bush, Reagan Endorse Treen in Race." *The Times-Picayune*, February 16, 1989.
39 *"Goliaths"*: Rose, *The Emergence of David Duke and the Politics of Race*, 27.
39 *HOW TO VOTE!*: Rose, *The Emergence of David Duke and the Politics of Race*, 27.
39 *"president"*: O'Byrne, "Duke: Anatomy of an Upset."
39 *"gas chambers"*: Maginnis, John. *Cross to Bear.* Pelican Publishing, 2011, 29.
39 *"rednecks"*: King, Wayne. "Bad Times on the Bayou." *The New York Times*, June 11, 1989.
40 *"our people"*: Bridges, *The Rise of David Duke*, 155.
40 *"They've accepted me:"* Rose, *The Emergence of David Duke and the Politics of Race*, 119.
41 *"Who Owns America?"*: Do the White Thing; Who Owns America?; About Carly." News Broadcast. *ABC News Primetime Live*. ABC, November 2, 1989.
41 *"pendulum"*: Haygood, Will. "David Duke and the Politics of Fear." *The Boston Globe*, March 28, 1991, 69.
41 *"Huey in reverse"*: Maginnis, *Cross to Bear*, 91.
42 *"Two out of ten women"*: Maginnis, *Cross to Bear*, 7.
44 *"essentials"*: Maginnis, *Cross to Bear*, 48.
44 *"coalition"*: Rose, *The Emergence of David Duke and the Politics of Race*, 31.
44 *"serious times"*: The Hotline. "Louisiana Governor: Edwards Runs 'Cause 'It Turns Me On.'" February 12, 1991.
44 *"Adolf Hitler"*: Maginnis, *Cross to Bear*, 12.
45 *"Edwards knew"*: Bridges, *The Rise of David Duke*, 201.
45 *"Hitler is coming to power"*: Bridges, *The Rise of David Duke*, 205.
45 *"welfare underclass"*: Maginnis, *Cross to Bear*, 127.
45 *"babies"*: Johnson, Dirk. "The Louisiana Election; Duke's Loss Brings Joy Even as It Fans Anger." *The New York Times*, November 18, 1991, B-7.
46 *sorority*: Kurtz, Michael L. *Louisiana Since the Longs: 1960 to Century's End.* Center for Louisiana Studies, University of Southwestern Louisiana, 1998, 137.
46 *"pay taxes"*: Bridges, *The Rise of David Duke*, 211.
47 *"Yeltsin"*: "Duke Set for Louisiana Runoff, Calls Himself America's Yeltsin." *Orlando Sentinel* (Florida), October 21, 1991, A4.
47 *"welfare mother"*: Bridges, *The Rise of David Duke*, 222–23.
48 *Duke's past*: Becker, Joseph. "Duke Past Fine with Supporters." *The Times-Picayune*, November 15, 1991, B-9.
48 *"Broadcast"*: Applebome, Peter. "On the Past and Future of a Politician: Was Duke Made for TV, or Made by It?" *The New York Times*, November 20, 1991, A-18.
48 *"medium"*: "Who Is the Real David Duke?" *ABC News Nightline*. ABC, November 15, 1991.
49 *"lies"*: Applebome, "On the Past and Future of a Politician: Was Duke Made for TV, or Made by It?"
49 *"antiwhite"*: Black, Chris. "Bay State Contributors to Duke Cite Frustration with Status Quo." *The Boston Globe*, November 19, 1991.
49 *"I'm blind"*: Worthington, Rogers. "Diverse Group Backs Duke's Narrow Pitch." *Chicago Tribune*, December 29, 1991.
49 *"thinking"*: Worthington, "Diverse Group Backs Duke's Narrow Pitch."
49 *"jobs"*: "Louisiana Gubernatorial Debate." November 6, 1991, C-SPAN.org.

51 *"Prophecy"*: "Louisiana Gubernatorial Runoff Election." Broadcast. New Orleans: C-SPAN 1, November 16, 1991.
54 *"proverbial banana republic"*: Schott, Matthew, J. "Death of Class Struggle: End of Louisiana History?" *Louisiana History: The Journal of the Louisiana Historical Association* 31, no. 4 (1990): 349–71.
54 *"waking up"*: Maginnis, *Cross to Bear*, 295.
55 *"deterioration"*: Zatarain, Michael. *David Duke, Evolution of a Klansman*. Pelican, 1990, 297.

2. Winter of Discontent

56 *"repudiated"*: "Senators Press Bush to Endorse Civil Rights Bill." *The Miami Herald*, October 17, 1990, A10.
56 *"quotas"*: Devroy, Ann. "Bush Vetoes Civil Rights Bill." *The Washington Post*, October 23, 1990.
57 *"repugnant"*: Jennings Moss, J. "Civil Rights Override 1 Short." *The Washington Times*, October 25, 1990, A1.
57 *"overriden"*: Hallow, Ralph Z. "Duke Claims Partial Credit for Veto of Civil Rights Bill." *The Washington Times*, October 25, 1990, A4.
58 *"rhetoric"*: "David Duke's Revolution." *The Washington Times*, October 10, 1990.
58 *"'respectable'"*: Francis, Samuel. "'Respectable Racism'?" *The Washington Times*, November 6, 1990, G2.
59 *"clandestine"*: Helms, Jesse. "Remarks of Senator Jesse Helms." *Congressional Quarterly* 129, no. 130 (October 3, 1983).
60 *Confederacy*: Dougherty, Michael Brendan. "The Castaway." *America's Future* (blog), January 14, 2007. https://americasfuture.org/the-castaway/.
60 *surveillance*: Heatherly, Charles L., and Heritage Foundation, eds. *Mandate for Leadership: Policy Management in a Conservative Administration*. Washington, D.C.: Heritage Foundation, 1981, 903.
61 *"manipulation"*: "Terrorism: Origins, Direction, and Support." Hearing Before the Senate Subcommittee on Security and Terrorism, April 24, 1981, Office of Justice Programs.
61 *tapes*: Hochschild, Adam. "Opinion | Dis-(Mis-?)Information." *The New York Times*, October 14, 1981, sec. Opinion, A31.
61 *"toad"*: Stanley, Timothy. "Buchanan's Revolution." *American Conservative*, February 1, 2012, 31.
61 *"well fed"*: "Sobran's Washington Watch—Samuel Francis RIP." Accessed July 31, 2023. http://www.sobran.com/wanderer/w2005/w050224.shtml.
61 *intimacy*: Gottfried, Paul. Author interview, December 23, 2020.
61 *joviality:* March, Louis T. "Remembering Sam Francis." *The Occidental Quarterly* 5, no. 2 (March 2005).
61 *"affably"*: Cloud, John. "Angry White Male." *Washington City Paper*, January 19, 1996.
62 *"stomp"*: "Church Group Says Senator's Aide Insulted Them." Associated Press, October 17, 1985.
63 *intellectual vision*: Gottfried, Paul. *The Conservative Movement*. Twayne Publishers, 1993, 113.
63 *"expression"*: Whitaker, Robert W. *The New Right Papers*. St. Martin's Press, 1982, 66.
63 *"temperament"*: Whitaker, *The New Right Papers*, 66.
63 *"exploitation"*: Whitaker, *The New Right Papers*, 67.
64 *"dominant"*: Whitaker, *The New Right Papers*, 68.
64 *"hypocritical"*: Whitaker, *The New Right Papers*, 71.
64 *"exploited"*: Whitaker, *The New Right Papers*, 71.
64 *"corrupt"*: Whitaker, *The New Right Papers*, 73.
66 *"struggle"*: Francis, Samuel T. *Power and History: The Political Thought of James Burnham*. University Press of America, 1984, 32.
66 *"dominate"*: Francis, *Power and History*, 32.

67 *"counter-revolutionary"*: Francis, Samuel T. "James Burnham: 1905–1987." *National Review*, September 11, 1987, 38.
67 *"sociobiologists"*: Francis, Samuel T. *Beautiful Losers: Essays on the Failure of American Conservatism*. University of Missouri Press, 1994, 132.
68 *"victory"*: Francis, *Beautiful Losers: Essays on the Failure of American Conservatism*.
68 *"tumors"*: Whitaker, *The New Right Papers*, 76.
68 *"militants"*: Francis, Samuel T. "Revolution on the Right: The End of Bourgeois Conservatism?" *Chronicles*, June 1985, 28.
68 *"national myth"*: Francis, "Revolution on the Right: The End of Bourgeois Conservatism?," 27.
69 *With a chuckle*: Lind, Michael. "The Importance of James Burnham." September 1, 2021, https://www.tabletmag.com/sections/news/articles/burnham-michael-lind.
69 *"Reagan"*: van den Haag, Ernest. "The Coming Conservative Crack-Up." *The American Spectator*, September 1987.
71 *"'proposition'"* Bradford, Melvin Eustace. *A Better Guide Than Reason: Studies in the American Revolution*. S. Sugden, 1979.
71 *Feulner*: Gottfried, *The Conservative Movement*, 75.
71 *reenactment*: Foner, Eric. "Lincoln, Bradford, and the Conservatives." *The New York Times*, February 13, 1982.
73 *Dr. Gottfried:* Gottfried, *The Conservative Movement*, 118–41.
74 *"refugees"*: Judis, John B. "The Conservative Wars: Paleocons versus Neocons." *The New Republic*, August 11, 1986.
74 *"bourgeois"*: Francis, *Beautiful Losers: Essays on the Failure of American Conservatism*, 93.
75 *"Tel Aviv"*: Judis, John B. "Slurs Fly in Right's Uncivil War." *In These Times*, October 18, 1989, 3.
75 *"anti-Semitism"*: Judis, "The Conservative Wars: Paleocons versus Neocons."
75 "Holocaust Update": Judis, "The Conservative Wars: Paleocons versus Neocons."
76 *"Hobbesian conflict"*: Sobran, Joseph. "North Adams Transcript 30 May 1986," 4.
76 *"white racial pride"*: Judis, "The Conservative Wars: Paleocons versus Neocons."
76 *"controversy"*: Judis, "The Conservative Wars: Paleocons versus Neocons."
76 *"tendentiousness"*: Buckley (Jr.), William F. *In Search of Anti-Semitism*. Continuum, 1992, 11–12.
76 *"deracinated"*: Bernstein, Richard. "Magazine Dispute Reflects Rift on U.S. Right." *The New York Times*, May 16, 1989.
76 *"disease"*: Judis, John B. "The Conservative Crackup." *American Prospect*, Fall 1990.
78 *oil*: "NSD 54: Responding to Iraqi Aggression in the Gulf." Accessed July 31, 2023. https://irp.fas.org/offdocs/nsd/nsd_54.htm.
78 *"blood libel"*: Rosenthal, A. M. "Forgive Them Not." *The New York Times*, September 14, 1990, A-33.
78 *at it for years*: Farrell, John Aloysius. "Buchanan's Views on Jews Are in Question." *The Boston Globe*, February 7, 1992.
78 *"Jewry"*: Weisberg, Jacob. "The Heresies of Pat Buchanan." *The New Republic*, October 22, 1990.
79 *"genocidal offense"*: Buckley (Jr.), William F. "Two Good Fellows & Anti-Semitism." New York *Daily News*, September 19, 1990, 32.
79 *intervention*: Francis, Samuel. "Street-Fighting Men." *The Washington Times*, September 24, 1990, G2.
79 Richard III: Stanley, Timothy. *The Crusader: The Life and Tumultuous Times of Pat Buchanan*. Macmillan, 2012, 143.
79 *"Golden Calf"*: Buchanan, Patrick. "The Next Golden Calf." *Commentary, The Washington Times*, September 1, 1991.
79 *"democracy"*: Sobran, Joseph. "Beyond Delegated Powers." *The Washington Times*, October 2, 1991, F4.
79 *"conservative policies"*: Francis, Samuel. "But Why Were the Cannons Muffled?" *The Washington Times*, March 3, 1991, G3.

3. Chaos and Old Night

81 *"Prices"*: FDIC Division of Research and Statistics. *History of the Eighties: Lessons for the Future. Volume 1: An Examination of the Banking Crises of the 1980s and Early 1990s*. Federal Deposit Insurance Corporation, December 1997, 58.
82 *"criminogenic"*: Pontell, Henry N., and Kitty Calavita. "The Savings and Loan Industry." *Crime and Justice* 18 (1993): 203–46.
82 *criminal activity*: Pontell and Calavita, "The Savings and Loan Industry," 204.
83 *"worse"*: Mayer, Martin. *The Greatest-Ever Bank Robbery: The Collapse of the Savings and Loan Industry*. Collier Books, 1992.
83 *"depression"*: "Credit Availability and Economic Recovery." Washington, D.C.: C-SPAN, November 21, 1991. https://www.c-span.org/video/?22846–1/credit-availability-economic-recovery.
83 *Employment*: Klein, Matthew C. "Yes, the Early 1990s Really Were Bad." *Financial Times*, October 6, 2016, sec. Alphaville.
83 *Evangeline*: Germond and Witcover, *Mad as Hell.*
84 *"portfolio"*: Buchanan, Patrick. "Buchanan, Duke's Challenge to the Right." *The Washington Times*, October 23, 1991.
84 *"Big Government"*: Buchanan, Patrick. "Pre-Emptive Surrender?" *The Washington Times*, October 30, 1991.
84 *"obsessed"*: Stanley, *The Crusader*, 148.
84 *"It's a go"*: Hallow, Ralph Z. "On the Right, a Challenge." *The Washington Times*, November 14, 1991, A1.
84 *Fitzwater*: Pruden, Wesley. "Nervous Laughter at the Big House." *The Washington Times*, November 15, 1991, A5.
85 *"astonishing"*: Clayton Jr., William E. "Buchanan Rips 'Mites' Linking Him to Duke." *The Houston Chronicle*, November 21, 1991.
85 *Before Buchanan could officially*: Nichols, Bill. "Duke Is Back, This Time Aiming at Presidency." *USA Today*, December 5, 1991, 4A.
85 *"Big Picture"*: Nyhan, David. "For Candidates, a Surly N.H." *The Boston Globe*, December 13, 1991, 31.
85 *bankruptcies*: Skidmore, Dave. "Institute Predicts Record Number of Bankruptcies." Associated Press, September 4, 1991. Shaner, J. Richard. "Bankruptcies Setting Records in Atlantic Seaboard States." *National Petroleum News*, November 1, 1991.
86 *banks*: FDIC Division of Research and Statistics. *History of the Eighties: Lessons for the Future. Volume 1: An Examination of the Banking Crises of the 1980s and Early 1990s*, 398.
86 *20,000 jobs*: Hohler, Bob. "N.H. Victims of Crunch Strive to Keep Their Homes, Dignity." *The Boston Globe*, October 23, 1991, Metro, 1.
86 *"service jobs"*: Nyhan, "For Candidates, a Surly N.H."
86 *In the mid-1980s*: Kiernan, Laura A. "A Family's Life After Bankruptcy." *New Hampshire Weekly*, May 5, 1991.
87 *"defunct"*: Francis, Samuel. "From Household to Nation." *Chronicles*, March 1996, 16.
87 *"fighting faith"*: Buchanan, Patrick J. (Patrick Joseph). *Right from the Beginning*. Washington, D.C.: Regnery Gateway, 1990, 218.
88 *As a young man*: Buchanan, *Right from the Beginning*, 188.
88 *"They didn't like the Jews"*: Stanley, *The Crusader*, 17.
88 *"the least ideological statesman"*: Stanley, *The Crusader*, 35.
89 *"the lost opportunity"*: Blumenthal, Sidney. "Pat Buchanan the Great Right Hope." *The Washington Post*, January 8, 1987.
89 *"political counterrevolution"*: Blumenthal, "Pat Buchanan the Great Right Hope."
89 *"The greatest vacuum"*: Blumenthal, "Pat Buchanan the Great Right Hope."
91 *"Tell your friends"*: Pertman, Adam. "Gay Activist Dragged from Buchanan Event." *The Boston Globe*, December 11, 1991.
91 *"temperament"*: Buckley (Jr.), "In Search of Anti-Semitism." *National Review*, December 30, 1991, 40.

91 Crossfire: Dionne, E. J., Jr. "Is Buchanan Courting Bias?" *The Washington Post*, February 29, 1992, A1.
91 *"theft"*: Chiacu, Doina. "Buchanan Takes Ideology to the Streets." Associated Press, December 11, 1991.
92 *"gyrating"*: Elvin, John. "Rockin' with Duke." *The Washington Times*, January 1, 1992.
92 *"giggles"*: Cheakalos, Christina. "Candidate Seems Distracted." *The Atlanta Journal and Constitution*, February 22, 1992.
92 *baggage*: Zeskind, Leonard. *Blood and Politics: The History of the White Nationalist Movement from the Margins to the Mainstream.* 1st ed. Farrar, Straus and Giroux, 2009, 450.
92 *syndicate Buchanan's column*: Weisberg, Jacob. "The Heresies of Pat Buchanan." *The New Republic*, October 22, 1990. https://newrepublic.com/article/69035/the-heresies-pat-buchanan.
92 *Populist Party's executive committee*: Bridges, *The Rise of David Duke*, 245.
93 *contributor base*: Zeskind, *Blood and Politics*, 452.
93 *"gone native"*: Dowd, Maureen. "The 1992 Campaign: Republicans; Buchanan's Alternative: Not Kinder or Gentler." *The New York Times*, January 15, 1992, A1.
93 *"nature's retribution"*: Dowd, "The 1992 Campaign."
93 *Moynihan*: Dowd, "The 1992 Campaign."
93 *checkout scanner*: Rosenthal, Andrew. "Bush Encounters the Supermarket, Amazed." *The New York Times*, February 5, 1992, sec. U.S. A1.
94 *"putting nothing back"*: Dowd, "The 1992 Campaign."
94 *"suffering"*: 1992 Pat Buchanan for President TV Ad 1 New Hampshire Republican Primary—"Can't Trust Bush," 1992. https://www.youtube.com/watch?v=a6S7-AUvnv0.
95 *"articulateness"*: Warren, Donald I. *The Radical Center: Middle Americans and the Politics of Alienation.* University of Notre Dame Press, 1976, 6.
95 *"Message: I care"*: Dowd, Maureen. "The 1992 Campaign: Republicans; Immersing Himself in Nitty-Gritty, Bush Barnstorms New Hampshire." *The New York Times*, January 15, 1992, A1.
96 *At one meeting*: Author interview with Paul Gottfried, December 21, 2020.
96 *swimmingly*: Gottfried, *The Conservative Movement*, 147.
97 *"handout"*: Raimondo, Justin. *An Enemy of the State: The Life of Murray N. Rothbard.* Prometheus Books, 2000, 26.
97 *"cultural assimilation"*: Raimondo, *An Enemy of the State*, 26.
97 *"What's wrong with Franco anyway?"*: Raimondo, *An Enemy of the State*, 24.
97 *America Firsters*: Rothbard, Murray N. "Life in the Old Right." *Chronicles*, August 1, 1994. https://chroniclesmagazine.org/web/life-in-the-old-right.
97 *"I soon became established"*: Rothbard, "Life in the Old Right."
98 *"In Defense of Demagogues"*: Murray N. Rothbard. *Strictly Confidential: The Private Volker Fund Memos of Murray N. Rothbard*, 2010, 33.
98 *His Upper West Side*: Radosh, Ron. Author interview, December 19, 2019.
98 *"ontological"*: Murray N. Rothbard. *Egalitarianism as a Revolt Against Nature and Other Essays.* Libertarian Review Press, 1974, 11.
99 *tax consumers*: Rothbard, Murray N. *The Ethics of Liberty.* New York University Press, 2002, 176.
99 *"Toward a Strategy"*: "Rothbard, 'Toward a Strategy for Libertarian Social Change' (April 1977)." http://www.davidmhart.com/liberty/AmericanLibertarians/Rothbard/Strategy/1977TowardStrategyLibertarianSocialChange.html.
99 *"wilderness"*: Rothbard, Murray N. "Right-Wing Populism: A Strategy for the Paleo Movement." *The Rothbard-Rockwell Report*, January 1992.
101 *"Some even had tears"*: Elvin, John. "A Rebirth." *The Washington Times*, January 21, 1992.
102 *"redeem the time"*: Kirk, Russell. "May the Rising Generation Redeem the Time?" The Heritage Foundation. https://www.heritage.org/political-process/report/may-the-rising-generation-redeem-the-time.
102 *"Old Night"*: Kirk, Russell. *The Politics of Prudence.* Open Road Media, 2014, 16.

104 *"Reagan conservatism"*: Francis, Samuel. "Principalities & Powers." *Chronicles*, February 1992.
105 *"one of us to step forward"*: Duin, Steve. "America First Attracts Those on Last Legs." *The Oregonian*, January 16, 1992, B-7.
106 *"conservative element to this campaign"*: Meacham, Jon. *Destiny and Power: The American Odyssey of George Herbert Walker Bush*. Random House, 2016, 498.
106 *"looking at is 1996"*: "Rush Limbaugh Discusses His Radio Talk Show." *CBS This Morning*. CBS, January 6, 1992.
106 *"united in the pursuit"*: Conservative Political Victory Fund Dinner, C-SPAN.org. Accessed August 1, 2023. https://www.c-span.org/video/?24281–1/conservative-political-victory-fund-dinner.
106 *"Pat Buchanan's White House"*: Boyer, Peter J. "Bull Rush." *Vanity Fair*, May 1992.

4. The Voice of America

107 *Rush's grandfather, Rush Senior*: Boman, Dennis K. *The Original Rush Limbaugh: Lawyer, Legislator, and Civil Libertarian*. University of Missouri Press, 2012.
108 *"wise elders of Missouri"*: Colford, Paul D. *The Rush Limbaugh Story: Talent on Loan from God: An Unauthorized Biography*. St. Martin's Paperbacks, 1994.
108 *social capital into personal popularity*: Arkush, Michael. *Rush!* Avon Books, 1993, 23.
108 *"I played to be popular"*: Chafets, Ze'ev. *Rush Limbaugh: An Army of One*. Penguin, 2011, 20.
108 *"learn how to do it himself"*: Colford, *The Rush Limbaugh Story*, 5.
108 *"wound he would nurse forever after"*: Colford, *The Rush Limbaugh Story*, 6.
109 *"blue jeans"*: Colford, *The Rush Limbaugh Story*, 89.
109 *"stuck-up snob"*: Boyer, "Bull Rush."
111 *"irresponsible behavior"*: Chapman, Stephen. "Can We Recover from the Divorce Revolution?" *Chicago Tribune*, April 30, 1992.
112 *"scrap a civilization"*: "The Domestic Revolution, 1989." *National Review*, May 19, 1989, 59.
112 *"inequalities"*: Cook, James A. "The Divorce Revolution: The Unexpected Social and Economic Consequences for Women and Children in America by Lenore J. Weitzman." *Los Angeles Times*, November 17, 1985.
112 *similar critiques*: Fineman, Martha. *The Illusion of Equality: The Rhetoric and Reality of Divorce Reform*. University of Chicago Press, 1994.
113 *"accompanying loneliness"*: Sperling, Godfrey, Jr. "The Loneliness Issue." *The Christian Science Monitor*, December 10, 1985.
114 *"value people"*: "Loneliness as an American Epidemic." *U.S. News and World Report*, July 21, 1986.
115 *fear of abandonment*: Imrie, Robert. "Fear of Loneliness Key to Explaining Dahmer Killings, Investigator Says." Associated Press, August 3, 1991.
115 *"people yearn to connect"*: Hoyt, Mike. "Talk Radio: Turning Up the Volume." *Columbia Journalism Review*, December 1992, 46.
115 *"sights and scenes"*: Wallace, David Foster. "E Unibus Pluram: Television and U.S. Fiction." *The Review of Contemporary Fiction*, 13, no. 2 (Summer, 1993), 151.
115 *"something to say"*: Laufer, Peter. *Inside Talk Radio: America's Voice or Just Hot Air?* Carol Publishing Group, 1995, 15.
115 *"a lot of chatter"*: "Those Were the Days; Political Wrap; Closing Thoughts." *The MacNeil/Lehrer NewsHour*. PBS, December 31, 1993.
117 *"the excesses of genocide"*: Rosenberg, Howard. "The New Odd Couple: Metzger, Innis Take Their Feud on Road." *Los Angeles Times*, November 28, 1988.
118 *"parasocial relationship"*: Munson, Wayne. *All Talk: The Talkshow in Media Culture*. Temple University Press, 1993, 16.
118 *"'It probably saved my life'"*: Zoglin, Richard. "Shock Jock." *Time*, November 30, 1992. https://content.time.com/time/subscriber/article/0,33009,977117–3,00.html.
118 *"hate mail I get"*: Lacayo, Richard. "Show Business: Audiences Love to Hate Them." *Time*, July 9, 1984. https://content.time.com/time/subscriber/article/0,33009,950118,00.html.

119 *Berg mellowed*: Singular, Stephen. *Talked to Death: The Murder of Alan Berg and the Rise of the Neo-Nazis*. Berkley ed. Berkley, 1989.
119 *Don Imus*: Singular, *Talked to Death*, 19.
120 *"playing a part works so well"*: Bogosian, Eric. "What Radio Is Saying . . ." *The New York Times*, July 26, 1987.
121 *regulation had grown "ossified"*: Matzko, Paul. "Jimmy Carter vs. the Fairness Doctrine." *Matzko Minute* (blog), Substack, March 13, 2023. https://matzko.substack.com/p/jimmy-carter-vs-the-fairness-doctrine. Smith, Reed W. "Charles Ferris: Jimmy Carter's FCC Innovator." *Journal of Radio and Audio Media* 21, no. 1 (January 2, 2014): 149–62. https://doi.org/10.1080/19376529.2014.891212.
123 *"sexual or excretory"*: Justia Law. "*FCC v. Pacifica Foundation*, 438 U.S. 726 (1978)." Accessed August 11, 2023. https://supreme.justia.com/cases/federal/us/438/726.
123 *"racial slurs"*: McDougal, Dennis. "FCC versus Howard Stern: Agency's 'Indecency' Ruling Hasn't Stopped N.Y. Deejay." *Los Angeles Times*, August 19, 1987, 6–1.
123 *"porking"*: Kasindorf, Jeanie. "Bad Mouth." *New York*, November 23, 1992, 44.
124 *"anybody get AIDS"*: Kasindorf, "Bad Mouth," 44.
124 *"Being Jewish"*: Kasindorf, "Bad Mouth," 42.
125 *"I became a total introvert"*: Colford, Paul D. *Howard Stern: King of All Media: The Unauthorized Biography*. St. Martin's Paperbacks, 1997, 17.
125 *"a personality-less character"*: Colford, *Howard Stern*, 18.
125 *"master of the universe"*: Colford, *Howard Stern*, 27.
126 *"the utmost sincerity and responsibility"*: Limbaugh, Rush H. *The Way Things Ought to Be*. Pocket Books, 1992, 22.
126 *an outlet for "proletarian despair"*: Levin, Murray Burton. *Talk Radio and the American Dream*. Lexington Books, 1987, xiii.
127 *higher income than the general population*: Douglas, Susan J. *Listening In: Radio and the American Imagination*. 1st ed. University of Minnesota Press, 2004.
127 *likely to be rich*: "Rush Limbaugh: The 1991 60 Minutes Interview." *60 Minutes*, n.d. https://www.youtube.com/watch?v=017VvbOOQLo&ab_channel=60Minutes.yeah.
127 *tea bags*: Munson, *All Talk*, 93.
127 *"conspiracy"*: Munson, *All Talk*, 95.
128 *"let him go screw himself"*: *Howard Stern Archive [1992]*, 1992. http://archive.org/details/howard_stern_1992.
129 *"palimony suit against her"*: Hoyt, Mike. "Talk Radio: Turning Up the Volume." *Columbia Journalism Review*, December 1992.
129 *"attacking this man's character"*: Douglas, Jehl. "Clinton Takes a Grilling in N.Y. and Gains an Audience: Media: Donahue Pelts Arkansas Governor with Hostile Questions on Character Issue. But Many Angry Studio Members Side with the Candidate." *Los Angeles Times*, April 2, 1992.
130 *Gargan got a call*: Germond and Witcover, *Mad as Hell*, 215.
130 *Like Julius Caesar*: Ceaser, James W. *Upside Down and Inside Out: The 1992 Elections and American Politics*. Rowman and Littlefield, 1993, 89.
130 *"I don't want to"*: "CNN Transcript-Sunday Morning News: CNN 20: Ross Perot on 'Larry King Live,' February 20, 1992–February 20, 2000." Accessed August 11, 2023. http://edition.cnn.com/TRANSCRIPTS/0002/20/sm.12.html.

5. Little Caesar

133 *"loved his country"*: "Throw the Hypocritical Rascals Out." Forum. St. Petersburg, FL: C-SPAN 2, November 5, 1991.
133 *"folk-hero"*: *U.S. News and World Report*, 1988, 26.
133 *"the Rev. Horatio Alger"*: Porterfield, Bill. "Ross Perot: A Hero for Our Time." *Texas Monthly*, April 1, 1974. https://www.texasmonthly.com/news-politics/ross-perot-a-hero-for-our-time.

133 *"one of the last real Texans"*: Remnick, David. "Our Nation Turns Its Lonely Eyes to H. Ross Perot." *The Washington Post*, April 12, 1987.
133 *"I'm just a myth"*: Gross, Ken. *Ross Perot: The Man Behind the Myth*. Random House, 2012, 179.
133 *"P. T. Barnum without the elephants"*: Fineman, Howard. "The Man and the Myth." *Newsweek*, June 14, 1992.
134 *"finest parents any could have"*: Posner, Gerald L. *Citizen Perot: His Life and Times*. 1st ed. Random House, 1996, 8.
134 *"Rockwell painted what I strived to be"*: Remnick, "Our Nation Turns Its Lonely Eyes to H. Ross Perot."
134 *"Dad's paper route"*: Remnick, "Our Nation Turns Its Lonely Eyes to H. Ross Perot."
135 *doubt on the horseback deliveries*: Posner, *Citizen Perot*, 11.
135 *"a leader, very mature"*: Posner, *Citizen Perot*, 14.
136 *"Well, he's clean"*: Posner, *Citizen Perot*, 17.
136 *"I thought I was Billy Graham"*: Posner, *Citizen Perot*, 17.
136 *"stand on the quarterdeck"*: Posner, *Citizen Perot*, 20.
137 *"maladjusted for a regular Navy career"*: Posner, *Citizen Perot*, 22.
137 *Electronic Data Systems*: Dubie, Denise. "NW200 Miscellany." *NetworkWorld*, April 29, 2002.
138 *"on the SWAT team"*: Posner, *Citizen Perot*, 50.
138 *"Eagles don't flock"*: Gross, *Ross Perot: The Man Behind the Myth*.
138 *"'Every worker is a brother'"*: Remnick, "Our Nation Turns Its Lonely Eyes to H. Ross Perot."
140 *SSA told Texas Blue Shield*: Posner, *Citizen Perot*, 36.
140 *lost most of its corporate clients*: Posner, *Citizen Perot*, 38–46.
141 *"most complex business enterprise"*: Perot, Ross. *United We Stand: How We Can Take Back Our Country*. Hyperion, 1992, 11.
141 *some complained, like "storm troopers"*: Posner, *Citizen Perot*, 43.
142 *"We were considered undesirable"*: Posner, *Citizen Perot*, 44.
142 *to be personally racist*: "Taking Apart the Billionaire Who Would Be President: One Texan Insists, 'There Are Two Ross Perots—One Good and One Bad.' Here's a Look at His Personal and Corporate Style." *Newsday*, May 17, 1992.
142 *brought Wall Street calling*: Posner, *Citizen Perot*, 47.
144 *displayed at the Capitol*: Posner, *Citizen Perot*, 69–70.
144 *campaign ads never turned up*: Posner, *Citizen Perot*, 68.
144 *despite being on the board*: Blumenthal, Sidney. "The Mission: Ross Perot's Vietnam Syndrome." *The New Republic*, July 6, 1992.
145 *Dupont dissolved for good*: Posner, *Citizen Perot*, 72–83.
145 *Weinberger would later recall*: Posner, *Citizen Perot*, 87.
145 *Sơn Tây prison camp*: Posner, *Citizen Perot*, 89.
146 *Senator J. W. Fulbright*: "Fulbright Questions Reasons for Raid on Reported P. O. W. Camp." *The New York Times*, December 9, 1970.
146 *"a complete success"*: Cronkite, Walter. *Eye on the World*. Cowles Book Company, 1971, 95.
146 *Spotlights*: Blumenthal, Sidney. "The Mission: Ross Perot's Vietnam Syndrome."
147 *$90 million*: Posner, *Citizen Perot*, 101.
148 *Turkish border*: Posner, *Citizen Perot*, 114.
148 *"looks like a faggot"*: Posner, *Citizen Perot*, 115.
149 *"King"*: Posner, *Citizen Perot*, 122.
149 *"preoccupation with the Iranian hostage crisis"*: "What Newspapers Are Saying." United Press International, February 27, 1981.
149 *"the MIA (Missing in Action)"*: Wiggins, Wallace S. "Missing in Action." *Los Angeles Times*, February 13, 1980, 42.
150 *"I don't care about bones"*: Patterson, Charles J., and G. L. Tippin. *The Heroes Who Fell from Grace: The True Story of Operation Lazarus, the Attempt to Free American POW's from Laos in 1982*. Dell, 1987, 45.

151 *Gritz counted among his other backers*: Gallagher, Patrick. *Traumatic Defeat: POWs, MIAs, and National Mythmaking*. University Press of Kansas, 2018, 132–33.
151 *"the highest national priority"*: "President: MIA Accounting Is 'Highest National Priority.'" *The Miami Herald*, January 29, 1983, A2.
151 *"helpful to the Reagan administration's effort"*: Wilson, George C., and Art Harris. "Mercenaries Sent to Laos Seeking MIAs." *The Washington Post*, May 21, 1981.
152 *anti-communist guerrillas in Laos*: "Report Says Reagan Aide Sent POW Funds to Rebels." *The Washington Post*, January 14, 1993.
152 *National Security Council staffer*: Royce, Knut. "Perot's Hostage Deals. He's Funded Several Rescues, Ransoms—and Bent Rules." *Newsday*, May 20, 1992.
152 *The same secret DOD group—ISA*: Emerson, Steven. *Secret Warriors: Inside the Covert Military Operations of the Reagan Era*. Putnam, 1988, 79.
152 *had explicitly forbidden*: Albright, Joseph. "Perot Knew of Contra Fund-Raising Early; Maybe Before Reagan, North's Diaries Show." *The Palm Beach Post* (Florida), May 15, 1992.
152 *"Iran-Contra is all Perot's fault"*: "Oliver North Says Iran-Contra Can Be Blamed on Ross Perot." *Greensboro News and Record*, June 1, 1992. https://greensboro.com/oliver-north-says-iran-contra-can-be-blamed-on-ross-perot/article_20cd6a8e-45a8-53e8-adf5-6026f09d0ca9.html.
153 *at least one conversation*: Hamilton, Lee H., and Daniel K. Inouye. *Report of the Congressional Committees Investigating the Iran/Contra Affair*. Diane Publishing, 1995, 644.
153 *encouraging North to "tell the truth"*: Hersh, Seymour M. "Perspective on Ross Perot: A Loose Cannon from Dallas; A Reagan White House Memo Shows Him Acting as Middleman During the Iran-Contra Investigations." *Los Angeles Times*, October 30, 1992.
153 *"one mission in life"*: Blumenthal, "The Mission: Ross Perot's Vietnam Syndrome."
153 *chants of "Rambo! Rambo!"*: "Families of MIAs Warned Not to Have False Hopes." *Los Angeles Times*, July 19, 1985. https://www.latimes.com/archives/la-xpm-1985-07-19-mn-6514-story.html.
153 60 Minutes: "Dead or Alive?," *60 Minutes*, CBS, December 15, 1985.
153 *"convince you that God exists"*: Geyelin, Philip. "Bo Gritz Is Not the Issue." *The Washington Post*, March 31, 1983. https://www.washingtonpost.com/archive/politics/1983/03/31/bo-gritz-is-not-the-issue/7152db65-80c6-4bbd-8f91-f9ef88808640.
154 *hunger strike in a bamboo cage*: Gorman, Steve. "Reagan Phone Call Halts Hunger Strike." United Press International, December 6, 1985.
155 *"didn't want this man mad"*: Posner, *Citizen Perot*, 211.
156 *"improperly favored" over lower bidders*: Solomon, John. "Perot Contract Canceled in 1986; Procurement Improprieties Cited." Associated Press, June 18, 1992.
156 *"Viet Nam will appoint"*: Tyler, Patrick E. "The 1992 Campaign: Candidate's Record; Perot and Hanoi Discussed Business." *The New York Times*, June 4, 1992, sec. U.S.
157 *"business conversations with the Vietnamese"*: *United States Congress Senate Select Committee on POW/MIA. U.S. Government's Post-War POW/MIA Efforts: Hearings Before the Select Committee on POW/MIA Affairs, United States Senate, One Hundred Second Congress, Second Session . . . August 11 and 12, 1992*. U.S. Government Printing Office, 1993, 50.
157 *"Hail to the Chief"*: Remnick, "Our Nation Turns Its Lonely Eyes to H. Ross Perot."
157 *Perot Systems' first customer*: Pear, Robert. "The 1992 Campaign; Audits of Federal Contracts Indicate Major Failures by Perot Companies." *The New York Times*, June 24, 1992.
157 *"triumph of the system"*: Mason, Todd. *Perot: An Unauthorized Biography*. Business One Irwin, 1990, 16.
157 *appearance on the* Donahue *show*: Barta, *Perot and His People: Disrupting the Balance of Political Power*, 40.
158 *"privatizing by contracting out government"*: Rothbard, Murray N. "Column Right / Murray N. Rothbard; Little Texan Connects Big with Masses; Perot Is a Populist in the Content of His Views and in the Manner of His Candidacy." *Los Angeles Times*, June 1, 1992.
158 *"replaced by the* Geraldo *system"*: Blumenthal, Sidney. "Perotnoia." *The New Republic*, June 15, 1992, 23.

158 *"try to regain the country"*: Lacitis, Erik. "Jumping On the Bandwagon—They May Not Know Where He Stands on the Issues, but a Lot of Folks Just Feel Good About H. Ross Perot." *The Seattle Times*, April 3, 1992.
159 *"nuts for three days"*: Muller, H. "Working Folks Say . . . 'We're Not Interested in Your Damn Positions, Perot, We're Interested in Your Principles.'" *Time*, May 25, 1992.
159 *"the silent majority coming out in force"*: Barta, *Perot and His People: Disrupting the Balance of Political Power*, 137.
160 *"that it's too fragmented"*: Louv, Richard. "Perot Supporter Has Put Electronic Democracy On-Line." *The San Diego Union-Tribune*, May 27, 1992.
160 *"preparing for a NASA launch"*: Barta, *Perot and His People: Disrupting the Balance of Political Power*, 95.
161 *"reasonable degree of dignity"*: Balz, Dan. "Bush Ties Social Ills to Ailing Families." *The Washington Post*, May 18, 1992.
161 *Rush Limbaugh was invited*: Yorke, Jeffrey. "Limbaugh, Bush's House Guest." *The Washington Post*, June 9, 1992.

6. Rage

162 *"monster in a cave"*: McGrory, Mary. "Sizing Up the Monster of Voter Rage." *St. Petersburg Times* (Florida), April 15, 1992, City edition.
162 *"Americans are angry"*: Diebel, Linda. "U.S. Voters' Rage Throws Race Open." *Toronto Star*, March 26, 1992.
162 *"revolution in this country"*: Schmalz, Jeffrey. "The 1992 Campaign: Voters; Hurt and Angry Car Workers Say Brown Speaks for Them." *The New York Times*, March 13, 1992, A1.
162 *"to Europe in 1848"*: Diebel, "U.S. Voters' Rage Throws Race Open."
163 *"1 percent of American families"*: Nasar, Sylvia. "The 1980's: A Very Good Time for the Very Rich." *The New York Times*, March 5, 1992, sec. Business. https://www.nytimes.com/1992/03/05/business/the-1980-s-a-very-good-time-for-the-very-rich.html.
163 *Sheraton Hotel in Chicago*: Wilkerson, Isabel. "Refugees from Recession Fill Hotel's Payroll." *The New York Times*, March 1, 1992, A1.
163 *"New Deal only drove"*: Nasar, "The 1980's: A Very Good Time for the Very Rich."
164 *"systemic, institutional corruption, not personality"*: Krauss, Clifford. "The House Bank; Gingrich Takes No Prisoners in the House's Sea of Gentility." *The New York Times*, March 17, 1992, A18.
164 *"lions in the jungle night"*: Francis, Samuel. Review of *Principalities & Powers, Part Two: The Middle-Class Moment. Chronicles*, March 1992, 12.
165 *"contained no happy talk"*: Tsongas, Paul. *A Call to Economic Arms: Forging a New American Mandate.* Tsongas Committee, 1991, 9.
165 *"only one speaking for us"*: Schmalz. "The 1992 Campaign: Voters; Hurt and Angry Car Workers Say Brown Speaks for Them."
166 *"institutions in the Congress more efficient"*: Wines, Michael. "Bush Campaigning Against Congress." *The New York Times*, April 4, 1992, A7.
166 *"If Yelstin fails, the prospects"*: Schorr, Daniel. "How to Lose the Cold War." *The New York Times*, March 10, 1992.
167 *"Yankees up in Washington"*: Chapman, Stephen. "Pat Buchanan, in Hot Pursuit of the Segregationist Vote." *Chicago Tribune*, March 8, 1992, 3.
168 *"foundation for something big"*: Applebome, Peter. "The 1992 Campaign: Far Right; Duke's Followers Lean to Buchanan." *The New York Times*, March 8, 1992.
168 *a fit of giggling*: Cheakalos, "Candidate Seems Distracted."
168 *"certain amount of hypocrisy"*: Applebome, Peter. "The 1992 Campaign: The South; Duke Plays to Empty Houses as Spotlight Trails Buchanan." *The New York Times*, March 6, 1992.
168 *"denouement of the fascist idea"*: Krauthammer, Charles. "Buchanan Goes Past Racism to Fascism." *St. Louis Post-Dispatch*, March 1, 1992.
169 *D'Alessio*: Zeskind, *Blood and Politics*, 283.

169 *Cathey, Buchanan's North Carolina chairman*: Zeskind, *Blood and Politics*, 282.
169 *"The Civil War comparison"*: Williams, Dick. "'Tongues' Isn't Art, but a Skirmish in the Culture Wars Paid for by Tax Dollars," *The Atlanta Journal-Constitution*, July 20, 1991, 19.
170 *"pornographic and blasphemous art"*: User Clip: Pat Buchanan Ad Featuring Tongues Untied, 1992. https://www.c-span.org/video/?c4679699/user-clip-pat-buchanan-ad-featuring-tongues-untied.
170 *"George Bush stands for nothing"*: McDaniel, Ann. "Is Buchanan Running the Country?" *Newsweek*, March 16, 1992, 29.
170 *"in a coat and tie"*: Editorial. "Mr. Buchanan and Mr. Bond." *The Washington Times*, March 14, 1992.
171 *"Ms." rather than "Mrs."*: Holmes, Steven A. "The 1992 Campaign: Republicans; Buchanan's Wife Stays in Step with a Smile but Seldom a Word." *The New York Times*, March 15, 1992, A24.
171 *"pretty harmless"*: Reed, John Shelton. "Letter from the Lower Right." *Chronicles*, July 1992.
171 *"subsidiary of Japan Inc."*: Holmes, Steven A. "The 1992 Campaign: The Challenger; Buchanan Sees Foreign Influence in Bush's Camp." *The New York Times*, March 14, 1992.
172 *"cheering their heads off"*: Locin, Mitchell. "Buchanan Strikes Ethnic Chord." *Chicago Tribune*, March 15, 1992, 15.
172 *"what we call a photo op"*: Elvin, John. "Buchanan's Candor." *The Washington Times*, March 18, 1992.
172 *"The Cold War is over—Japan won"*: Federal News Service. "Address by Democratic Presidential Candidate Former Senator Paul Tsongas of Massachusetts to the United Auto Workers Convention Sheraton Washington Hotel." February 3, 1992.
172 *U.S. workers were "lazy"*: Ivanovich, David. "Anti-Japanese Feelings Erupt into Fury of Americanism." *Houston Chronicle*, January 24, 1992, A1.
173 *"draw a mushroom cloud"*: "Hollings-Japan-Bashing." *The Canadian Press,* March 3, 1992.
173 *Riegle echoed the sentiment*: Ivanovich, "Anti-Japanese Feelings Erupt into Fury of Americanism."
173 *wrote one "M. F. Swango"*: Swango, M. F. "Anti-Japanese Feelings Coming Much Too Late." *Houston Chronicle*, February 10, 1992.
174 *hate crimes against Asian Americans*: "Civil Rights Issues Facing Asian Americans in the 1990s." U.S. Commission on Civil Rights, February 1992.
175 *Japanese businessman in Ventura*: Mydans, Seth. "Killing Alarms Japanese-Americans." *The New York Times*, February 26, 1992.
175 *group of Japanese American Girl Scouts*: Mydans, Seth. "Japanese-Americans Face New Fears." *The New York Times*, March 4, 1992.
175 *"Made in the USA.'"*: Hernon, Peter. "Asian-Americans Are Suffering Backlash . . . 'Japan-Bashing' a Worry to Area; Groups." *St. Louis Post-Dispatch*, February 16, 1992.
175 *"current reactionary political climate"*: Kajihiro, Kyle. "Could 1942 Happen Again? Just Look Around in My Opinion." *The Oregonian*, February 20, 1992.
176 *violence against "innocent Asian-Americans"*: Pasco, Jean O. "Quayle Assails Anti-Asian Bigotry, Tells Crowd That US 'Is Your Home.'" *The Orange County Register* (California), March 19, 1992.
176 *encroachment in the Asian American vote*: Iritani, Evelyn. "Wooing Asian Voters; Growing Ethnic Group Seen as a Key Element in Presidential Race." *Seattle Post-Intelligencer*, April 20, 1992.
176 *"geisha for the economic Empire of the Rising Sun"*: Cregan, John P. *America Asleep: The Free Trade Syndrome and the Global Economic Challenge: A Conservative Foreign Economic Policy for America*. United States Industrial Council Educational Foundation, 1991, x.
177 *"No way, I told Mr. Milliken"*: "Requiem for a Patriot—Patrick J. Buchanan—Official Website." Accessed August 2, 2023. https://buchanan.org/blog/requiem-for-a-patriot-4589?doing_wp_cron=1637008312.0663468837738037109375.
177 *"strategy to bloody President Bush"*: Hallow, Ralph Z. "Buchanan Readies One-Two for Bush: Taxes and Deficit." *The Washington Times*, A6.

177 *for Caterpillar by two economists*: Krippner, Greta R. *Capitalizing on Crisis: The Political Origins of the Rise of Finance.* 1st paperback ed. Harvard University Press, 2012, 214–15.

178 *"occupying our Capitol Building"*: Reagan, Ronald. "Address Before the Japanese Diet in Tokyo." Speech, November 11, 1983. https://www.reaganlibrary.gov/archives/speech/address-japanese-diet-tokyo.

178 *$62 billion*: Bates, James. "Japan's U.S. Real Estate Buying Plunges." *Los Angeles Times*, February 21, 1992.

179 *Komatsu excavator*: Ivanovich, David. "Anti-Japanese Feelings Erupt into Fury of Americanism." *The Houston Chronicle*, January 24, 1992.

179 *on a single income*: Uchitelle, Louis. "Trapped in the Impoverished Middle Class." *The New York Times*, November 17, 1991.

179 *shuttered:* "Talks Snagged, Caterpillar Closes 2 Plants." *The New York Times*, November 8, 1991.

179 *Caterpillar stayed competitive not through international financial wizardry*: Franklin, Stephen. "At Caterpillar, a Classic Conflict: Big Labor vs. Big Business, and Only the Strong Survive." *Chicago Tribune*, September 6, 1992.

179 *"that of the Mexicans"*: Uchitelle, "Trapped in the Impoverished Middle Class."

181 *"middle range of the wage distribution"*: Research Group on the Los Angeles Economy. "The Widening Divide: Income Inequality and Poverty in Los Angeles."

181 *bed of the Los Angeles River*: Davis, Mike. "In L.A. Burning All Illusions." *The Nation*, June 1, 1992.

181 *"any chance for Christmas food"*: Chavez, Stephanie. "Thousands of Needy Gather for Giveaway on Skid Row." *Los Angeles Times*, December 22, 1991.

181 *charities found that their supply*: Willman, Martha L. "Recession Puts Charities in Twin Bind of Need, Funds : Donations: Groups Are Faced with More to Help and Fewer Resources," *Los Angeles Times*, December 22, 1991. https://www.latimes.com/archives/la-xpm-1991-12-22-me-1463-story.html.

181 *"toward some impossible Armageddon"*: Davis, Mike, and Robert Morrow. *City of Quartz: Excavating the Future in Los Angeles.* 1st ed. Vintage Books, a division of Random House, 1992, 316.

7. The Thin Blue Line

182 *"L.A. police chief Daryl Gates"*: "Public Papers—George Bush Library and Museum." Accessed August 3, 2023. https://bush41library.tamu.edu/archives/public-papers/2764.

183 *was not even in the room*: Gates, Daryl F., and Diane K. Shah. *Chief: My Life in the L.A.P.D.* Bantam Books, 1992, 1.

183 *"11 skull fractures"*: Timnick, Lois. "King's Damage Claim Is Rejected: Beating Case: Action by City Clears Way for Lawsuit. Altadena Man and His Wife Sought $83 Million." *Los Angeles Times*, June 27, 1991. https://www.latimes.com/archives/la-xpm-1991–06–27-me-1883-story.html.

184 *Gates disowned him*: Reinhold, Robert. "Fate of Police Chief in Los Angeles Is Vigorously Debated After Beating." *The New York Times*, March 14, 1991.

185 *he was "surprisingly cooperative"*: Katz, Jesse. "Gates Battles to Restore His and the LAPD's Image: Law Enforcement: Chief Goes on Offensive to Defuse Beating Furor and Its Impact on the Entire Department." *Los Angeles Times*, March 17, 1991.

185 *"submit to the lynch-mob mentality"*: Rojas, Aurelio. "L.A. Police Rally in Support of Chief Gates." United Press International, March 13, 1991.

186 *"blame them for hating you"*: Stolberg, Sheryl. "Officers Offer Support for Gates Amid More Attacks." *Los Angeles Times*, March 14, 1991.

186 *"I could be a* great *guy"*: Katz, "Gates Battles to Restore His and the LAPD's Image."

186 *"He was aggressive and abrasive"*: Shapiro, Daniel M. "Perspective on Police: This Is No Time to Play the Mob: Over the Years, Chief Gates Did What He Had to to Earn the Respect of His Officers." *Los Angeles Times*, April 9, 1991.

187 *"I'm talking about morale"*: Haddad, Annette. "L.A. Council Grills Police Chief—Gets Scolding." United Press International, March 20, 1991.

188 *"a weird balkanization had taken place"*: Domanick, Joe. *To Protect and to Serve: The LAPD's Century of War in the City of Dreams.* Pocket Books, 1994.

189 *"a little chat with him"*: Gates and Shah, *Chief*, 35.

189 *"mercenary army unofficially empowered"*: Kramer, Alisa Sarah. "William H. Parker and the Thin Blue Line: Politics, Public Relations and Policing in Postwar Los Angeles." Dissertation, American University, 2007, 250.

189 *emblem of apartheid South Africa*: "LAPD Probing South Africa Emblem Incident." *Los Angeles Sentinel*, August 17, 1989.

189 *"differ greatly from private industry"*: Parker, William H., and O. W. Wilson. *Parker on Police.* Charles C. Thomas, 1957, 139.

190 *The Public Information Division*: Domanick, *To Protect and to Serve*, 131.

190 *"BARBARIANISM within rotted the moral supporting timbers"*: Parker and Wilson, *Parker on Police*, 49.

190 *"Los Diabolos, the city of the devils"*: Parker and Wilson, *Parker on Police*, 32.

190 *"sympathy for the 'under-dog'"*: Parker and Wilson, *Parker on Police*, 6.

191 *"police must help them understand"*: Parker and Wilson, *Parker on Police*, 17.

191 *"premise of some eminent theologians"*: Parker, William H. "Can We Attain Total Prevention." *The Police Chief*, December 1956, 5.

191 *"Control, not correction, is the key"*: Parker, W. H. "The Police Role in Community Relations." *The Journal of Criminal Law, Criminology, and Police Science* 47, no. 3 (1956): 368–79. https://doi.org/10.2307/1140335.

191 *In Parker's opinion, including racial profiling*: For a useful discussion of Parker's philosophy, see Schrader, Stuart. *Badges Without Borders: How Global Counterinsurgency Transformed American Policing.* University of California Press, 2019, 217.

192 *"discrimination against the Anglo-Saxon commander"*: Parker, "The Police Role in Community Relations," 367.

193 *"come 1970, God help you"*: Shaw, Jaby David. "Chief Parker Molded LAPD Image—Then Came the '60s: Police: Press Treated Officers as Heroes Until Social Upheaval Prompted Skepticism and Confrontation." *Los Angeles Times*, May 25, 1992, A1.

193 *"downtrodden, oppressed, dislocated"*: Kramer, "William H. Parker and the Thin Blue Line: Politics, Public Relations and Policing in Postwar Los Angeles," 305.

193 *"endanger the effectiveness"*: California Governor's Commission on the Los Angeles Riots. *McCone Commission Report! Complete and Unabridged Report by the Governor's Commission on the Los Angeles Riot; Plus One Hundred Four Shocking Photos of the Most Terrifying Riot in History.* Kimtex, 1965, 14.

193 *"displease"*: Domanick, *To Protect and to Serve*, 115.

193 *"absolute traitor"*: Gates and Shah, *Chief*, 66.

194 *"a sort of government-in-exile"*: Sonenshein, Raphael. *Politics in Black and White: Race and Power in Los Angeles.* Princeton University Press, 1993, 156.

194 *"byzantine" organization with a "monolithic resistance"*: Domanick, *To Protect and to Serve*, 251.

194 *"Look at him!"*: Domanick, *To Protect and to Serve*, 247.

195 *"totally smitten" with the older man*: Gates and Shah, *Chief*, 32.

195 *"tremendous respect for him"*: Domanick, *To Protect and to Serve*, 247.

195 *"called 'Old Chubby Cheeks'"*: Gates and Shah, *Chief*, 33.

195 *"a paternal image"*: Gates and Shah, *Chief*, 39.

195 *"He was a police bureaucrat"*: Domanick, *To Protect and to Serve*, 253.

196 *"officers look like flower children"*: Gates and Shah, *Chief*, 113.

196 *"were his true constituency"*: Domanick, *To Protect and to Serve*, 281.

196 *killed the greatest number of civilians*: Domanick, *To Protect and to Serve*, 276.

197 *"hold hands"*: "Is the Battle Over?" *Los Angeles Sentinel*, May 4, 1989, A6.

198 *"'hard ball'"*: Robertson, Stanley G. "L.A. Confidential: As Thousands Cheer and Scream!" *Los Angeles Sentinel*, October 4, 1990, A6.

199 *"action of the board defames me"*: Serrano, Richard A. "Gates Voiced Concern, Anger to Commission; Confrontation: Transcript Shows the Chief Sparring with Police Board Members in the Meeting at Which They Placed Him on Leave." *Los Angeles Times*, April 9, 1991.

199 *"it's an isolated incident"*: Gollner, Philipp, and Michael Connelly. "Action Taken Against Gates Stuns Police, Critics Alike; Furlough: The Department's Top Valley Administrator Begins Visits to the Stations to Reassure Demoralized Officers." *Los Angeles Times*, April 5, 1991.

200 *business sector was "rallying around Gates"*: Bunting, Glenn F., Rich Connell, and Jane Fritsch. "Bradley Aides Regroup to Assess Gates' Future: Police: Options to Block Chief's Return Are Studied. Mayor Seeks to Distance Himself from the Dispute." *Los Angeles Times*, April 7, 1991.

200 *"If it wasn't for the helicopter"*: Wilson, Jeff. "Police Chief Daryl Gates Jokes About Videotaped Beating." Associated Press, April 5, 1991.

204 *"only files I have are in my head"*: Mitchell, Marsha. "Chief Denies Secret File Allegation, Angers Council." *Los Angeles Sentinel*, July 25, 1991, A1. Connell, Rich, and Sheryl Stolberg, "Rumors of Police Blackmail Surface; King Case: Chief Gates Flatly Denies Allegations That Secret Files Have Been Kept on Council Members to Coerce Them into Supporting Him." *Los Angeles Times*, May 22, 1991, B1.

204 *"Real power and authority"*: Warren, Christopher. *Report of the Independent Commission on the Los Angeles Police Department*. Diane Publishing, 1991, xxi.

204 *"13 years as Chief of Police"*: Warren, *Report of the Independent Commission on the Los Angeles Police Department*, 227.

205 *computer messages*: Warren, *Report of the Independent Commission on the Los Angeles Police Department*, xii.

205 *"a timetable for retirement"*: Bunting, Glenn F. "Bradley-Gates Struggle Has Old, New Twists." *Los Angeles Times*, July 11, 1991.

205 *"urge me to stay"*: Muir, Frederick M., and Sheryl Stolberg. "Gates Resumes Dance on Date of Retirement; Police: The Chief Says He Is Rethinking Intention to Leave in April. His Indecision Sparks Chorus of Criticism." *Los Angeles Times*, September 12, 1991.

206 *"respect for an adult"*: Stern, Patricia. "Parenting; Who Taught Values to Latasha?" *The Orange County Register* (California), November 22, 1991.

207 *"the chief's a wimp"*: Gates and Shah, *Chief*, 356.

207 *"the likes of Rodney King"*: Cannon, Lou. *Official Negligence: How Rodney King and the Riots Changed Los Angeles and the LAPD*. Times Books, 1997, 467.

207 *"This unpleasant incident is what we have police for"*: Mydans, Seth. "The Police Verdict; Los Angeles Policemen Acquitted in Taped Beating." *The New York Times*, April 30, 1992, A1.

208 *"first incidents of arson"*: Webster, William H., and Hubert Williams. *The City in Crisis: A Report by the Special Advisor to the Board of Police Commissioners on the Civil Disorder in Los Angeles*. National Policing Institute, 1992, 19.

209 *"confined to part of the 77th Street"*: Webster and Williams, *The City in Crisis*, 20.

209 *"two-hour helicopter ride"*: Webster and Williams, *The City in Crisis*, 109.

209 *"was roundly chewed out"*: Webster and Williams, *The City in Crisis*, 182.

209 *"less experienced subordinates"*: Webster and Williams, *The City in Crisis*, 25.

210 *"cynically enjoying"*: Davis, Mike. Author interview, October 8, 2021.

210 *"seven most active police Areas"*: Webster and Williams, *The City in Crisis*, 25.

211 *"take nightstick in hand"*: Francis, Samuel. "Street Justice . . . in a Power Void." *The Washington Times*, n.d.

211 *"they're going to be second-guessed"*: Staff of the *Los Angeles Times*. *Understanding the Riots: Los Angeles Before and After the Rodney King Case*. Edited by Shelby Coffey. Los Angeles Times, 1992.

213 *"Vengeance is taking place"*: Serrano, Richard A., and James Rainey. "Gates Says He Bluffed Staying, Lashes Critics; Police: The Chief Says 'Crummy Little Politicians' Endanger the Department. Sheinbaum Likens Him to a Lame-Duck Despot, and Calls Him 'Mean-Spirited.'" *Los Angeles Times*, June 9, 1992, A1.

213 *"He's a nice guy'"*: Puig, Claudia. "From Top Cop to Talk Jock; How Serious Is Daryl Gates About His New Job? Some Say Too Serious. He Shrugs Off the Critics—as Usual." *Los Angeles Times*, November 1, 1992.

8. Keeping America American

214 *"hooligans, criminals, and thugs"*: "Reaction to Los Angeles Police Trial." C-SPAN, May 5, 1992. https://www.c-span.org/video/?25999–1/reaction-los-angeles-police-trial.
215 *orders to "shoot to kill"*: Marelius, John. "Buchanan Shadowed at Border; Metzger Seizes Chance for Media Exposure." *The San Diego Union Tribune*, May 13, 1992.
215 *"knew what he meant"*: Brimelow, Peter. "Time to Rethink Immigration?" *National Review*, June 22, 1992.
216 *"fence in July and August"*: Rotella, Sebastian. "Buchanan Decries Illegal Immigration; Politics: The GOP Candidate Calls the Influx an Invasion and Says It Causes Social, Economic and Drug Problems." *Los Angeles Times*, May 13, 1992.
216 *"take back our cities"*: Dart, John. "Buchanan Calls Riots Part of War for Soul of U.S." *Los Angeles Times*, May 8, 1992.
216 *"The Buchanan people are going to Perot"*: "Buchanan's Bumpy Bandwagon." *The Orange County Register* (California), May 29, 1992.
217 *"a moment of critical mass"*: Deparle, Jason. "Kemp's Proposals on Poverty Given Sympathy, Not Action." *The New York Times*, July 1, 1991. https://www.nytimes.com/1991/07/01/us/kemp-s-proposals-on-poverty-given-sympathy-not-action.html.
217 *Kemp's chosen programs to deal with the urban crisis*: Deparle, Jason. "After the Riots; As Los Angeles Smoke Lifts, Bush Can See Kemp Clearly." *The New York Times*, May 7, 1992.
217 *"a pantyhose crotch closer"*: *Congressional Record*, May 12, 1992.
219 *"just another 'lifestyle choice'"*: Rosenthal, Andrew. "After the Riots; Quayle Says Riots Sprang from Lack of Family Values." *The New York Times*, May 20, 1992, A20.
219 *"without attacking big business"*: Lasch, *The True and Only Heaven*, 512.
219 *"MOTHER OF L.A. RIOTS"*: "Dan Quayle Blasts 'Murphy Brown' as Mother of L.A. Riots." *The Palm Beach Post*, May 20, 1992.
219 *vignette of Murphy Brown*: Wines, Michael. "Views on Single Motherhood Are Multiple at White House." *The New York Times*, May 21, 1992, A1.
219 *"ramifications of their programming"*: Wines, "Views on Single Motherhood Are Multiple at White House."
220 *"thought it was goofy"*: Wolfe, Charles. "Perot Files Ballot Petitions, Calls Murphy Brown Uproar 'Goofy.'" Associated Press, May 21, 1992.
220 *Galston told the papers*: "Bush Gives Murphy Brown Affair Low Rating." *Toronto Star*, May 23, 1992.
221 *"you owe something to the community"*: Voboril, Mary. "Have We Lost Sense of 'Us' in Favor of 'I'?" *The Miami Herald*, June 29, 1992.
221 *"professor named Carroll Quigley"*: "Remarks of Arkansas Governor Bill Clinton Democratic Presidential Candidate Georgetown University Washington, DC." Federal News Service, October 3, 1991.
221 *"future preference and self-discipline"*: Quigley, Carroll. *Tragedy and Hope: A History of the World in Our Time*. Macmillan, 1966, 1184.
221 *positive power of evil*: Quigley, *Tragedy and Hope*, 1239.
222 *"Africanization of American society"*: Quigley, *Tragedy and Hope*, 1264.
222 *"noisy, bigoted, and they drink"*: "1974 Carroll Quigley Interview. Interview Transcript Preceding Part 1." Accessed August 3, 2023. http://www.carrollquigley.net/Interviews/Carroll-Quigley-1974-Interview-Transcript-Preceding-Part1.htm.
225 *"Catholic men's colleges in the country"*: Quigley, *Tragedy and Hope*, 1249.
225 *"Radical Right, Fascist, or hate campaigns"*: Quigley, *Tragedy and Hope*, 1243.
225 *"preserve the values of the WASPS"*: Quigley, *Tragedy and Hope*.
227 *"some single ideological vision"*: Myers, Laura. "Rack One Up for Murphy Brown; Single Mother Joins Assault on Quayle." Associated Press, May 21, 1992.

227 *"worked on family issues"*: Battenfeld, Joe. "Clinton Calls President's Family Talk 'Lip Service.'" *Boston Herald*, May 21, 1992.
228 *Casey took a shot*: Tisdall, Simon. "Democrat Anxieties Resurface After Poll Setback for Clinton." *The Guardian*, April 25, 1992.
229 *won a "hollow victory"*: "Clinton and DLC: Impending Nomination a 'Hollow Victory'?" *The Hotline*, May 4, 1992.
229 *an "emotional low point"*: Germond and Witcover, *Mad as Hell*, 286.
229 *"the roar of Perotism"*: Toner, Robin. "The 1992 Campaign; Clinton Is Knocked Off Course by Tide for Perot." *The New York Times*, May 28, 1992, A21.
229 *"I feel your pain"*: "The 1992 Campaign: Verbatim; Heckler Stirs Clinton Anger: Excerpts from the Exchange." *The New York Times*, March 28, 1992.
229 *"a raucous shouting match"*: Ifill, Gwen. "The 1992 Campaign: New York; New Alliance Party Leader Attacks Arkansas Governor." *The New York Times*, March 29, 1992.
230 *"agitated and visibly frustrated"*: Ifill, Gwen. "The 1992 Campaign: Front-Runner; Questioned About Trust, Clinton Turns Angry." *The New York Times*, April 24, 1992.
230 *"It's a non-issue with them"*: Bayer, Amy. "Perot Says Voters Fed Up with Ideas, Want Action." *The San Diego Union Tribune*, May 19, 1992.
231 *"I might commit suicide"*: Klein, Joe. "Rescue Fantasy?" *New York*, May 18, 1992, 24.
231 *AMERICA NEEDS PEROT, PRESIDENT IN '92*: "Veterans and Perot." *USA Today*, May 15, 1992.
232 *"the bureaucracy has hidden"*: "Remarks by Governor Bill Clinton (D-Ar) to the National Association of Radio Talk Show Hosts Fourth Annual Convention (Via Radio from Little Rock) Mayflower Hotel, Washington, DC, Friday, June 19, 1992." Federal News Service, June 19, 1992.
232 *"waving his arms in the air and nearly shouting"*: Rosenthal, Andrew. "The 1992 Campaign: Political Memo; Taking Heat at Every Turn, Bush Shows a Boiling Point." *The New York Times*, July 1, 1992.
233 *YELTSIN: SOVIETS HELD HUNDREDS OF U.S. AIRMEN*: Raum, Tom. "Yeltsin Says It's 'Possible' Missing GIs May Still Be Alive." Associated Press, June 16, 1992, PM Cycle edition.
233 *possibility of "false hope"*: Bush, George H. W., and Boris Yeltsin. "The President's News Conference with President Boris Yeltsin of Russia." News Conference, June 17, 1992. https://www.presidency.ucsb.edu/documents/the-presidents-news-conference-with-president-boris-yeltsin-russia.
233 *"'You people are nuts'"*: Rother, Caitlin. "Yeltsin Raises POW Hopes in County; Vietnam War: His Remarks That Servicemen Were Moved to Russia Encourage Activists, Some of Whom Are Critical of Bush." *Los Angeles Times*, June 17, 1992.
234 *Wertheimer, replied:* "All Things Considered": "Perot: Who Paid for This Microphone?" *The Hotline*, May 15, 1992.
234 *"Hitler's propaganda chief would be proud"*: "Perot Likens Bush Attack to Hitler; Candidate Denies Ordering Probes." *Houston Chronicle*, June 24, 1992.

9. "We're at War"

236 *"double-crossing, back-stabbing thing to do"*: Germond and Witcover, *Mad as Hell*, 257.
237 *"spontaneity," "honest emotion," "impromptu anger"*: Thompson, Bill. "Clinton Gets Mad—and Looks Good." *The Miami Herald*, March 4, 1992.
237 *"telling old Jesse where to stuff it"*: Germond and Witcover, *Mad as Hell*, 293.
238 *"race-baiting in this election"*: "Clinton Campaign Speech, January 25, 1992, C-SPAN.org." Accessed August 3, 2023. https://www.c-span.org/video/?25085–1/clinton-campaign-speech.
239 *"disenchanted with the whole system"*: King, John. "Clinton Has Endorsements, Ties to Blacks; Enthusiasm Seen Lacking." Associated Press, March 1, 1992.
240 *"believe in cultural pluralism"*: Berman, Paul. *Debating P.C.: The Controversy over Political Correctness on College Campuses*. Random House Publishing Group, 1992, 309.
240 *"The Fraying of America"*: Hughes, Robert. "The Fraying of America." *Time*, February 3, 1992.

241 *"blacks out of the mainstream"*: Bennett, William J. "The War Over Culture in Education." The Heritage Foundation. Accessed August 3, 2023. https://www.heritage.org/education/report/the-war-over-culture-education.

242 *"critical inquiry is drowned out"*: Gates, Henry Louis, Jr. "Beware of the New Pharaohs." *Newsweek*, September 23, 1991.

242 *"myth of 'Afrocentric' history"*: Francis, Samuel. "Principalities & Powers." *Chronicles*, January 1991.

244 *"favorable toward any whites"*: Hunt, Dennis. "Pop Beat: Sister Souljah Gives Voice to Black Anger." *Los Angeles Times*, March 7, 1992.

244 *Malcolm X Day festival*: Lynette Figueroa, Darryl. "Malcolm X Day Yields to the Young." *The Washington Times*, May 18, 1992.

245 *"eyes on the prize"*: "Jackson Provided Forum for Many Voices." *The New York Times*, July 7, 1992.

245 *"hatred, open bigotry and paranoid theory"*: Williams, Dick. "Atlanta Students' Screed Serves Up Hatred." *The Atlanta Journal-Constitution*, May 9, 1992.

245 *"but there is no hope"*: "Sista Souljah Speaks on False Black Stereotypes." *Let's Unite Now!*, n.d. https://www.youtube.com/watch?v=tU2F0V65TVI&ab_channel=Let%27sUniteNow%21.

246 *"and kill white people"*: Mills, David. "Sister Souljah's Call to Arms." *The Washington Post*, May 13, 1992.

247 *"level of frustration"*: "Rap Musicians Say Warnings of Riots Were There All Along." *CBS This Morning*. CBS, May 18, 1992.

248 *"'something to believe in'"*: Pitts, Leonard, Jr. "L.A. Riots a Surprise? Listen to Rap Lyrics." *The Miami Herald*, May 10, 1992.

248 *"raw lust and cop-killing"*: "LA Police Union Blames Rappers for Provoking Violence." *CBS Evening News*. CBS, May 23, 1992.

248 *"sick as any Klansman"*: Gailey, Philip. "Rappers of Hate Spew the Poison of Bigotry." *The St. Petersburg Times* (Florida), May 17, 1992.

248 *"this song 'Cop Killer'"*: "Music or Mayhem? Conversation—Can We All Get Along?; Path of Destruction." *The MacNeil/Lehrer NewsHour*. PBS, July 23, 1992.

248 *Rappers were given or willingly took on the role*: "Riots Reflect Rage in Rap Music." *Orlando Sentinel* (Florida), May 3, 1992.

249 *convention of the National Newspaper Publishers Association*: "Black Publishers Group Denounces Clinton for Canceling Appearance." Associated Press, June 11, 1992.

250 *governor was going to say something newsworthy*: Germond and Witcover, *Mad as Hell*, 297.

250 *The callers into C-SPAN*: "Open Phones: Rainbow Coalition." *Call-In*. C-SPAN 1, June 13, 1992.

251 *"authentic point of light"*: "Clinton Campaign Speech." C-SPAN 1, June 13, 1992.

251 *"What power our youth have"*: "Clinton Campaign Speech." C-SPAN 1, June 13, 1992.

253 *"I made a mistake"*: "Clinton Campaign Speech." C-SPAN 1, June 13, 1992.

253 *angering Jackson*: Germond and Witcover, *Mad as Hell*, 299.

254 *Clinton's "Machiavellian maneuver" was meant to "purely appeal"*: Apple, R. W., Jr. "The 1992 Campaign: Democrats; Jackson Sees a 'Character Flaw' in Clinton's Remarks on Racism." *The New York Times*, June 19, 1992.

254 *"realm of possibility and critical debate"*: Apple, "The 1992 Campaign: Democrats; Jackson Sees a 'Character Flaw' in Clinton's Remarks on Racism."

254 *"divisive language by Sister Souljah"*: Ifill, Gwen. "The 1992 Campaign: Democrats; Clinton Won't Back Down in Tiff with Jackson over a Rap Singer." *The New York Times*, June 20, 1992.

254 *"malign me with her"*: Ifill, "The 1992 Campaign: Democrats; Clinton Won't Back Down in Tiff with Jackson over a Rap Singer."

255 *"standing up for racial sanity"*: Rowan, Carl T. "Denouncing Hatred Boosts Clinton . . ." *Chicago Sun-Times*, June 17, 1992.

255 *"Sister Souljah is no Willie Horton"*: "Sister Souljah Is No Willie Horton." *The New York Times*, June 17, 1992.
255 *"Like a Savvy Politician"*: McGrory, Mary. "Bill Clinton Is Starting to Look Like a Savvy Policitian." *Seattle Post-Intelligencer*, June 17, 1992.
255 *Clinton's "double-cross" would backfire*: Cockburn, Alexander. "Column Left / Alexander Cockburn; The Stupidity of Believing in Nothing; Clinton's Utterly Calculated Slap at Jesse Jackson Cost Him Many Votes and Gained None." *Los Angeles Times*, June 22, 1992.
255 *"Hail Sister Souljah"*: Vernon, Jarrett. "Whites Withhold Real Respect." *Chicago Sun-Times*, June 25, 1992.
256 *RADIO TALKERS SAY*: Shepard, Scott. "Sister Souljah Flap Helps Clinton, Radio Talkers Say." *The Palm Beach Post* (Florida), June 20, 1992.
256 *"To paraphrase a gospel song"*: Welch, William M. "Jackson Offers Praise for Clinton Economic Plan." Associated Press, June 23, 1992.
257 *"Welfare is designed to keep you trapped"*: Souljah, Sister. *No Disrespect.* 1st ed. Times Books, 1994, 352.
257 *"any impulse of self-improvement"*: Souljah, *No Disrespect*, 14.

10. "Buying the Country Back"

259 *"body-slamming an AIDS activist"*: "Buchanan Campaign Speech." Manchester, NH: C-SPAN 1, June 2, 1992.
260 *"He started out fine"*: Francis, Samuel. "Now to Prepare a New Foundation." *The Washington Times*, June 9, 1992.
261 *"folks in Koreatown"*: "Ask Why Koreatown Voted for Buchanan." *The Washington Times*, June 12, 1992.
264 *this nationalism would create a true American nation*: Francis, Samuel. "Nationalism, Old and New." *Chronicles*, June 1992.
266 *"real masters of the house"*: Francis, Samuel. "The Buchanan Revolution." *Chronicles*, July 1992.
266 *"exception of the tear gas"*: Wines, Michael. "Bush Made to Flee a Rally in Panama as Protest Erupts." *The New York Times*, June 12, 1992.
267 *"birth control as a public policy"*: Piotrow, Phyllis Tilson. *World Population Crisis: The United States Response.* Praeger, 1973.
268 *"to think it's right"*: Lauter, David. "President Seeks to Downplay Abortion Issue." *Los Angeles Times*, November 8, 1989.
271 *"Mickey Mouse tossed salad"*: "Republican Party Goes on the Offensive." *CBS Morning News.* CBS, June 25, 1992.
271 *eight-foot plaster of paris bust of Perot*: "Ventura County News Roundup: Oxnard; Sculptor Completes 8-Foot Bust of Perot." *Los Angeles Times*, July 10, 1992.
271 *got fifty-five thousand people to sign*: "Washington State Citizens Will Deliver Perot Petitions to Olympia Tomorrow." *PR Newswire*, July 1, 1992.
272 *"things that impress workers"*: "Perot's Unlikely Support Working Class." *Morning Edition.* NPR, June 16, 1992.
273 *"'Gestapo,' 'The Dallas Mafia'"*: Garrett, Major. "Volunteers Feel Shouldered Aside by Perot's Pros." *The Washington Times*, July 8, 1992.
273 *"tactics from Nazi Germany"*: Bragg, Roy. "Perot's Staff Harassed Them, Volunteers Report." *Houston Chronicle*, July 18, 1992.
273 *"allegiance to Caesar"*: Barta, *Perot and His People: Disrupting the Balance of Political Power*, 220.
274 *"I didn't realize I upset anybody"*: Broder, John. "NAACP Offers Chilly Response to Perot Speech—Correction Appended." *Los Angeles Times*, July 12, 1992.
275 *"exploitation at its most obvious"*: Posner, *Citizen Perot*, 302–303.
276 *"Protest City"*: Cerabino, Frank. "Convention a Lightning Rod for Discontented." *The Palm Beach Post* (Florida), July 13, 1992.
278 *"proud member of the Trilateral Commission"*: Elvin, John. "Clinton a Bircher?" *The Washington Times*, July 22, 1992.

278 *"national goals and policies"*: Schlafly, Phyllis. "Clinton's 'New Covenant.'" *The Washington Times*, July 30, 1992.

278 *"People have been calling in crying"*: Schaefer, David. "Gloom, Disbelief Pervade Perot's Local Headquarters." *The Seattle Times*, July 16, 1992.

278 *"the hero, the man in the white hat"*: Curtiss, Aaron. "Volunteers Are Stunned, Angry; Campaigns: At Ross Perot's Sherman Oaks Headquarters, Supporters React Emotionally to His Decision Not to Run for President." *Los Angeles Times*, July 17, 1992.

279 *"the buses for Buchenwald"*: Posner, *Citizen Perot*, 284.

279 *"That's the magic, Larry"*: "Perot Keeps Door Open to Candidacy." *CNN News*. CNN, July 18, 1992.

279 *Gritz, recently nominated as candidate*: Moore, Kimberly C. "Perot Supporters May Back Controversial Vietnam Vet." States News Service, July 17, 1992.

279 *At a POW/MIA event*: ""POW/MIA Affairs." C-SPAN 1, July 24, 1992.

280 *Rothbard celebrated the detente*: "Column Right/Murray N. Rothbard; Hold Back the Hordes for 4 More Years; Any Sensible American Has One Real Choice—George Bush." *Los Angeles Times*, July 30, 1992.

281 *"element of voter dissatisfaction"*: Hickey, Elisabeth. "Houston Does Its Best to Give a Warm Howdy." *The Washington Times*, August 17, 1992.

282 *"speech tartare"*: "John McKernan Discusses the Abortion Debate." CBS News Transcripts Campaign '92: The Republican National Convention. CBS, August 17, 1992.

283 *"these people are our people"*: "Buchanan, 'Culture War Speech,' Speech Text." Voices of Democracy. Accessed August 11, 2023. https://voicesofdemocracy.umd.edu/buchanan-culture-war-speech-speech-text/.

284 *"Buchanan represents the far right"*: "Thomas Kean Discusses Buchanan Speech." CBS News Transcripts Campaign '92: The Republican National Convention. CBS, August 17, 1992.

284 *"astoundingly good speech"*: Buchanan, Patrick J. "The Houston Syndrome." Accessed September 17, 2023. https://buchanan.org/blog/the-houston-syndrome-157.

284 *"a sense of optimism"*: "One Day in Houston." *ABC News Nightline*. ABC, August 17, 1992.

284 *"no enthusiasm, no energy"*: Black, Chris. "Letdown Amid the Cheering; Many from Region Saw Lifeless Party; Campaign '92 / Republican Convention." *The Boston Globe*, August 21, 1992.

284 *"convention got out of hand"*: Safire, William. "Bush's Gamble." *The New York Times*, October 18, 1992.

285 *"to challenge God's supremacy"*: Wills, Garry. "Opinion | George Bush, Prisoner of the Crazies." *The New York Times*, August 16, 1992. https://www.nytimes.com/1992/08/16/opinion/george-bush-prisoner-of-the-crazies.html.

285 *"a turning of energies"*: Wills, Garry. "The Born-Again Republicans." *The New York Review of Books*, September 24, 1992.

11. The Howling Wilderness

286 *MARSHAL SHOT AND KILLED*: "Marshal Shot and Killed Near Cabin of Federal Fugitive." Associated Press, August 21, 1992.

287 *"known as the great tribulation"*: "Survivalists Make Plans for Time of 'Great Tribulation.'" *The Courier* (Waterloo, Iowa), January 9, 1983.

287 *The Weavers once seemed*: Walter, Jess. *Ruby Ridge: The Truth and Tragedy of the Randy Weaver Family*. 1st trade paperback ed. Regan Books, 2002.

288 *"a strong sense of patriotism"*: Weaver, Randy. *The Federal Siege at Ruby Ridge: In Our Own Words*. Ruby Ridge, Inc., 1998, 12.

289 *"the facts of fulfilled prophecy"*: Lindsey, Hal. *The Late Great Planet Earth*. Bantam Books, 1973, 130.

289 *Faith and ideas*: Walter, *Ruby Ridge*, 13.

290 *"the sense of fellowship"*: Long, Robert Emmet, ed. *The Farm Crisis*. The Reference Shelf, vol. 59, no. 6. H. W. Wilson, 1987.

290 *"enemy of the family farmer"*: Serrin, William. "Plowing Farmers Under." *The New York Times*, May 23, 1979.

292 *rugged invidualism and self-reliance*: Stockwell, Ryan J. "Growing a Modern Agrarian Myth: The American Agriculture, Identity, and the Call to Save the Family Farm." Master's thesis, Miami University, 2003, 62.

292 *"unparalleled since the Great Depression"*: Davidson, Osha Gray. *Broken Heartland: The Rise of America's Rural Ghetto*. 1st ed. Anchor Books, 1991, 58.

293 *"no man could buy or sell without a credit card"*: Walter, *Ruby Ridge*, 41.

294 *"moral leadership"*: Gaertnier, Meta. "Presidential Hopeful Vows Moral Leadership." *The Courier* (Waterloo, Iowa), July 30, 1980.

294 *Aryan Nations in Idaho*: Aho, James A. *The Politics of Righteousness: Idaho Christian Patriotism*. University of Washington Press, 2014, 60.

294 *"Iowa Society for Educated Citizens"*: Davidson, *Broken Heartland*, 102.

295 *British-Israelism also attracted growing numbers*: Cottrell-Boyce, Aidan. *Israelism in Modern Britain*. Routledge/Taylor Francis Group, 2021.

296 *Anglo-Israelite ideology*: For an exhaustive treatment of Christian Identity's origins, see Barkun, Michael. *Religion and the Racist Right*. University of North Carolina Press, 1997.

297 *Gale published a "Guide for Volunteer Christian Posses"*: Levitas, Daniel. *The Terrorist Next Door: The Militia Movement and the Radical Right*. 1st ed. Thomas Dunne Books/St. Martin's Press, 2002, 108–10.

299 *"damn right I'm teaching violence"*: *The "Identity Churches": A Theology of Hate*. Anti-Defamation League of B'nai B'rith, Civil Rights Division, 1983, 7.

299 *Mossad in particular, were responsible*: Stock, Catherine McNicol. *Rural Radicals: Righteous Rage in the American Grain*. Cornell University Press, 2017, 172.

300 "The Grapes of Wrath": Walter, *Ruby Ridge*, 48.

303 *"Special Forces to understand Special Forces"*: Ashton, Linda. "Bo Gritz, Ex-Green Beret, Negotiated an End to Standoff." Associated Press, September 2, 1992.

305 *"in Estes Park, Colorado"*: Schlatter, Evelyn A. *Aryan Cowboys: White Supremacists and the Search for a New Frontier, 1970–2000*. 1st ed. University of Texas Press, 2006, 140–41.

12. The Mosaic

307 *"I am innocent"*: Lubasch, Arnold H. "Gotti Sentenced to Life in Prison Without the Possibility of Parole." *The New York Times*, June 24, 1992.

308 *"Italians are a minority"*: Fisher, Ian. "For Gotti's Supporters, Disbelief and Anger." *The New York Times*, June 24, 1992.

309 *"I love my country"*: Mike McAlary. "He's America's Own Citizen Bane." *New York Post*, June 24, 1992, 14.

309 *"somewhat of a folk hero"*: Fisher, "For Gotti's Supporters, Disbelief and Anger."

309 *"last of the Mohicans"*: Collins, Tom. "'We Love the Man.'" *Newsday* (New York), April 3, 1992.

309 *"wave or wink"*: Hampson, Rick. "Reputed Mob Boss John Gotti a Hometown Hero?" Associated Press, March 28, 1992.

309 *"prestigious law school deans"*: Stasi, Linda. "Rushing Gotti; Ivy League Joins Gotti Team." *Newsday* (New York), April 29, 1992.

310 *"WASPishness"*: Vlahou, Toula. "Going Ga-Ga over Gotti." *American Journalism Review*, May 1992.

310 *"not a particularly bright one"*: Nordland, Rod. "The 'Velcro Don': Wiseguys Finish Last." *Newsweek*, April 12, 1992.

310 *"I wasn't born with four fuckin' cents"*: Gotti, John, and Salvatore Gravano. *The Gotti Tapes: Including the Testimony of Salvatore "Sammy the Bull" Gravano*. Times Books, 1992.

311 *"blockbusting"*: Cummings, John, and Ernest Volkman. *Goombata: The Improbable Rise and Fall of John Gotti and His Gang*. 1st ed. Little, Brown, 1990, 86.

312 *"panache"*: Bastone, William. "The Mob Is Dead! Long Live the Mob!" *The Village Voice*, September 21, 1993.

313 *"Marlon Brando walked in"*: "New York Day by Day; Visiting Fashionable Bars." *The New York Times*, January 23, 1986.
313 *"crossing from Queens to Manhattan"*: Kempton, Murray. "John Gotti Touched by Glamor." *Newsday* (New York), February 8, 1990.
313 *"Neapolitan dump"*: Cummings and Volkman, *Goombata*, 226.
314 *"like Stalin's"*: Nadelson, Reggie. "The Godfather, He Is Invincible; John Gotti Was Freed Last Week and New York Loves It." *The Independent* (London), February 15, 1990.
315 *"slut" and a "blowjob"*: Targett, Jocelyn. "Boss of the USA: In New York, the Mafia Makes $600 Billion a Year. Most of It Ends Up with John Gotti, the Boisterous Godfather of the Gambino Family." *The Guardian*, August 10, 1990.
315 *"like a triumphant politician"*: McFadden, Robert D. "Elegantly Triumphant, Gotti Greets Admirers." *The New York Times*, February 10, 1990.
315 *"growth toward statesmanly proportions"*: Kempton, Murray. "Visiting the Victor, with Respect." *Newsday* (New York), February 10, 1990.
316 *"tribute and congratulations"*: McFadden, "Elegantly Triumphant, Gotti Greets Admirers."
316 *"the rapists, the murderers, the real criminals"*: McFadden, "Elegantly Triumphant, Gotti Greets Admirers."
317 *"like the royalty in this country"*: Hevesi, Dennis. "Literary Mobsters Find Enthusiastic Readers." *The New York Times*, March 15, 1992.
320 *"muscling in on mob territory"*: "Much Ado over the One That Got Away." *Newsday* (New York), December 13, 1990.
321 *"Boss Tweed's Forty Thieves"*: Breslin, Jimmy. "Corruption Scandal: Donny Manes and the Public Trough." New York *Daily News*. Accessed August 4, 2023. https://www.nydailynews.com/new-york/corruption-scandal-donny-manes-public-trough-article-1.816349.
322 *"Rudy, I don't know how"*: Della Femina, Jerry. "About Politics; The Selling of the Mayor; The Better Part of Valor." *Newsday* (New York), April 7, 1989.
323 *"I remember the first time"*: "RWG Vulnerability Study Part 2: Racism Charges." Accessed October 24, 2023, 26, https://www.documentcloud.org/documents/6591491-RWG-Vulnerability-Study-Racism-Charges.
324 *"Let us hope"*: Barrett, Wayne. *Rudy! An Investigative Biography of Rudolph Giuliani*. Basic Books, 2000, 51
324 *"disgusting, neurotic fantasy"*: Barrett, *Rudy!*, 51.
327 *The city's craft-type unions*: Freeman, Joshua Benjamin. *Working-Class New York: Life and Labor Since World War II*. New Press: Distributed by W. W. Norton, 2000.
329 *"the Seven Deadly Ones"*: Kempton, Murray. "A Vexing View of Giuliani." *Newsday*, April 27, 1989.
329 *"single most incompetent campaign"*: Cawley, Janet. "Political Misfire: Giuliani and the Case of the Bungled Campaign." *Chicago Tribune*, October 17, 1989.
329 *"fancy shvartze with mustache"*: Rich, Wilbur C. *David Dinkins and New York City Politics: Race, Images, and the Media*. State University of New York Press, 2007, 46.
329 *"Gotti should be mayor"*: Rist, Curtis. "Ozone Park, Queens; Up in the Air." *Newsday* (New York), October 18, 1989.
330 *"Dinkins, warts and all"*: "Opinion | For Mayor: David Dinkins." *The New York Times*, October 29, 1989, sec. Opinion.
331 *"strives to bring us together"*: Purdum, Todd S. "Mayor Dinkins; Dinkins Sworn In; Stresses Aid to Youth." *The New York Times*, January 2, 1990.
332 *"races against other races"*: Rohatyn, Felix G. "The Fall and Rise of New York." *The New York Review of Books*, November 8, 1990.
332 *"Greenberg and Weisberg and Trigliani"*: Stanley, Alessandra. "City College Professor Assailed for Remarks on Jews." *The New York Times*, August 7, 1991.
332 *"The Jews, when they left"*: Schwartz, Alan M., and David Evanier. "The Anti-Semitism of Black Demagogues and Extremists." ADL Research Report. New York: American Defense League, 1992.

334 *"insidious kind of violence"*: Purdum, Todd S. "To Counter Bias Attacks, Dinkins Is Spreading Message of Tolerance." *The New York Times*, January 17, 1992, sec. New York.
335 *"It's a festive occasion"*: Murphy, William. "Dinkins Loses War of Decibels." *Newsday* (New York), September 7, 1990.
336 *"came to the right place"*: Wolff, Craig. "U.S. Is Investigating Reports of Corrupt New York Police." *The New York Times*, June 19, 1992.
336 *"'for a corrupt society'"*: Schanberg, Sydney H. "Corrupt Cops: Scapegoats of Higher Ups." *Newsday* (New York), July 3, 1992.
336 *"widespread, systemic corruption"*: Gambardello, Joseph A. "Caruso 'Knees' Mayor; Calls Probe Just a Reflex." *Newsday* (New York), June 24, 1992.
337 *Internal Affairs investigation*: O'Shaughnessy, Patrice. "Dedicated Officer or Nabe Bully?" *Daily News*, July 8, 1992.
338 *"WAKE UP NEW YORK"*: Caruso, Phil. "An Open Letter to the Citizens of the City of New York." *New York Post*, July 13, 1992.
338 *"Mr. Garcia's history"*: Giuliani, Rudolph W. "Rumor and Justice in Washington Heights." *The New York Times*, August 7, 1992.
340 *"How do you like that?"*: Breslin, Jimmy. "Cops Show True Colors." *Newsday* (New York), September 17, 1992.
341 *"a fraternity keg party"*: Bunch, William. "The Cop Protest; What Went Down." *Newsday* (New York), September 25, 1992.
341 *"bordering on hooliganism"*: McKinley, James C., Jr. "Officers Rally and Dinkins Is Their Target." *The New York Times*, September 17, 1992.
341 *"fan the flames of racism"*: Liff, Bob. "PBA's Caruso Slams Dinkins." *Newsday* (New York), September 23, 1993.
342 *"screeching racial paranoia"*: McAlary, Mike. "Dave: Sack Those Hooligan Cops." *New York Post*, September 22, 1992.
342 *"elegantly, calmly, but firmly"*: Breslin, "Cops Show True Colors."
342 *"the first riot stimulated"*: Kempton, Murray. "The Creatures of Chaos." *Newsday* (New York), September 18, 1992.
342 *"more like a David Duke"*: Finder, Alan. "Bitter Dinkins-Giuliani Battle Veers from Politics to Race." *The New York Times*, September 23, 1992.
343 *"He's losing badly"*: Schwartzman, Paul. "Dave: Rudy's Behavior Will Haunt His Future." *New York Post*, September 1992.
344 *"hates and reviles the Mafia and organized crime"*: Rothbard, Murray N. "Mafia Movies." *The Rothbard-Rockwell Report*, November 1990.
346 *"the illusory cant of modernist ideology"*: Francis, Samuel. "Crime Story." *Chronicles*, October 1992.
347 *"satanic sort of authority figure"*: "Why Are We So Intrigued by Gotti? Does Our Fascination with the Mafia Don Say Something Awful About Us?" *Newsday* (New York), March 13, 1992.

13. ". . . The Economy, Stupid"

348 *"a great service"*: "Bush Adopts a Get Tough Campaign Posture." *CNN News*. CNN, August 1, 1992.
349 *"It was different then"*: Pruden, Wesley. "Bush: 'Who Do You Trust?'; President Frames Campaign." *The Washington Times*, August 13, 1992.
349 *"The president 'redefined' himself"*: Safire, "Bush's Gamble."
349 *"'You are no Harry Truman'"*: Truman, Margaret. "Mr. President, I Knew Harry Truman . . ." *The Washington Post*, August 27, 1992.
350 *"torpedo bomber I flew"*: Kelly, Michael. "The 1992 Campaign: The Republicans; Encircling Arkansas, Bush Opens Harsh Attack on Clinton's Record." *The New York Times*, September 23, 1992.
350 *"great American middle class"*: Seelye, Katharine, and Reed Karaim. "Both Bush, Clinton, Claim Truman's Mantle." *The Miami Herald*, September 8, 1992, A9.

351 *"a Fifth Column"*: Buchanan, Patrick J. "Yes, Mario, There Is a Cultural War." *Chicago Tribune*, September 14, 1992.

351 *"served the cause of slavery"*: Jaffa, Harry V. "What Confederate Troops Were Fighting For." *The Washington Times*, September 19, 1992.

352 *"There is our Cultural War"*: Rothbard, Murray N. "Kulturkampf!" *The Rothbard-Rockwell Report*, October 1992.

353 Faces at the Bottom of the Well: Bell, Derrick. *Faces at the Bottom of the Well: The Permanence of Racism*. Basic Books, 1992.

355 *popular among conservative economists*: Garrett, Major. "Texan's Plan Makes Sense to Economists; Billionaire's Long-Term Numbers Add Up." *The Washington Times*, October 3, 1992.

355 *"buy TV time"*: Berke, Richard L. "The 1992 Campaign: Ross Perot; Perot Says He May Rejoin Race to Publicize His Economic Plan." *The New York Times*, September 19, 1992.

359 *"Russia needs a strong personality"*: Montaigne, Fen. "David Duke Says He Backs a Powerful 'White Russia.'" *The Philadelphia Inquirer*, October 15, 1992.

359 *"that great mighty nation"*: *All Things Considered*. NPR, October 27, 1992.

359 *"sort of pitiful"*: Bridges, Tyler. "David Duke Slipping into Obscurity Again; Trade Show Visitors Ignore Blond Salesman." *The Plain Dealer* (Cleveland), November 16, 1992.

360 *lunged at him*: Bock, Paula. "'Bo' Gritz Moving to State, Will Operate Youth Camp." *The Seattle Times*, October 5, 1992.

363 *"in very careful balance"*: Greenhouse, Steven. "The 1992 Campaign: The Democrats; Budget Deficit Is the Thorn in Clinton's Economic Plan." *The New York Times*, October 17, 1992.

363 *"colony of post-industrial serfs"*: Enders, John. "Plight of Silicon Valley Representative of U.S. Problems, Meeting Told." Associated Press, October 14, 1992.

364 *"it broke the deal"*: Margolis, Jon. "Voters' Anger Goes Far Deeper Than Current Problems with the Economy; Sense of Betrayal Fuels U.S. Anger." *The Hamilton Spectator*, October 22, 1992.

367 *"losing the Reagan Democrats"*: Francis, Samuel. "When the Last Vote Is Cast . . ." *The Washington Times*, November 3, 1992.

367 *"It is all very well"*: Francis, Samuel. "Principalities & Powers: An Electorate of Sheep." *Chronicles*, November 1992.

369 *"The Perot Vote"*: Merida, Kevin, and Thomas B. Edsall. "Perot's Ex-Pollster in the Limelight at GOP Retreat." *The Washington Post*, March 1, 1993.

370 Meet the Press: Garrett, Major. "Perot Uses Airwaves to Spread Message Opposing Trade Pact." *The Washington Times*, April 26, 1993.

370 *"giant sucking sound"*: Perot, H. Ross. *Not for Sale at Any Price: How We Can Save America for Our Children*. Hyperion, 1993, 133.

370 *"the first thing"*: Francis, Samuel. "Principalities & Powers: Winning the Culture War." *Chronicles*, December 1993.

372 *"I was the cover boy"*: Baumgold, Julie. "Fighting Back: Trump Scrambles Off the Canvas." *New York*, November 9, 1992.

372 *"Huey Long's minister of fine arts"*: Schulze, Franz. *Philip Johnson: Life and Work*. Chicago: University of Chicago Press, 1996, 115.

372 *"All you need is faith"*: Schulze, *Philip Johnson*, 114.

372 *"You'd make a good mafioso"*: Baumgold, "Fighting Back: Trump Scrambles Off the Canvas."

ACKNOWLEDGMENTS

First of all, I would like to thank my wonderful family for all their love and support: my mom, Beth, and my dad, Bob; my sisters, Theresa and Sarah; my brothers-in-law, Aneece and Gary; and my niece and nephews, Sophia, William, Sammy, and Wally. Nothing is possible without all of you.

Thank you to my editor, Alex Star, who believed in this book when basically no one else did; to his great assistant, Ian Van Wye, who kept it very cool when things got a little choppy there at the end; and to everyone at Farrar, Straus and Giroux who brought it all together. And thanks to my agent, William Callahan, for first thinking I had a book in me.

Many friends, colleagues, and mentors helped me to get here. First, Chris Lehmann, who commissioned the piece upon which this book is based for *The Baffler* and, as its editor, gave it its first shape and direction. Thanks to Matthew Sitman and Sam Adler-Bell for helping me to better understand all of this stuff. I'm especially indebted to Jeet Heer, without whose timely intervention this book would not have happened and whose extensive erudition I called upon frequently. Rich Yeselson, for all your helpful comments and strong belief in this project. Rick Perlstein, whose wisdom guided me through some panicked moments. And thanks to Jamelle Bouie: our ongoing conversation about politics and history has come to inform all my writing. Thank you to the entire PPES chat, but most especially to Nina Eichacker for trying her best to teach me economics. A special thanks to Christopher Arp for reading the manuscript, listening to me rant and rave, and then gently explaining to me why none of it made sense. Then there's Will Rahn, who encouraged me to start writing and taught me how to think about politics: in many ways, this does not happen without you, dear friend. My deepest gratitude goes to my friends who have kept me going during all these years: Sonia Stagg, Natasha Stagg, Allie Van Zoeren, Sarah O'Brien, David Levine, Steven Klein, Josh Lee, Alex Press, Audrey Gelman, Megan Nolan, and Stacey Streshinsky—я уважаю тебя.

INDEX

A Note About the Author

John Ganz writes the widely acclaimed *Unpopular Front* newsletter for Substack. His work has appeared in *The New York Times*, *The Washington Post*, *The New Republic*, the *New Statesman*, and other publications.